THE PSYCHOLOGY OF AGEING

The Psychology of Ageing

From Mind to Society

Gary Christopher

Senior Lecturer, University of the West of England, Bristol

First published 2014 by
PALGRAVE MACMILLAN

Palgrave Macmillan in the UK is an imprint of Macmillan Publishers Limited, registered in England, company number 785998, of Houndmills, Basingstoke, Hampshire RG21 6XS.

Palgrave Macmillan in the US is a division of St Martin's Press LLC, 175 Fifth Avenue, New York, NY 10010.

Palgrave Macmillan is the global academic imprint of the above companies and has companies and representatives throughout the world.

Palgrave® and Macmillan® are registered trademarks in the United States, the United Kingdom, Europe and other countries.

ISBN 978–0–230–33721–3

This book is printed on paper suitable for recycling and made from fully managed and sustained forest sources. Logging, pulping and manufacturing processes are expected to conform to the environmental regulations of the country of origin.

A catalogue record for this book is available from the British Library.

A catalog record for this book is available from the Library of Congress.

Typeset by MPS Limited, Chennai, India.

For my wife, my parents and my late grandparents

Contents

Preface   viii

Acknowledgments   x

1   Introduction   1

2   Biological Changes   17

3   Basic Cognitive Processes   44

4   Short-Term Memory   58

5   Long-Term Memory   70

6   Metacognition   81

7   Everyday Functioning   96

8   Assessment of Cognitive Function   110

9   Personality, Intelligence, and Individual Differences   125

10 Adjusting to Change   144

11 Health and Ageing   160

12 Mental Health and Neurodegenerative Disorders   178

13 Neurodevelopmental Disorders   213

14 Looking Forward   227

References   242

Author Index   306

Subject Index   315

Preface

The idea for this book came about following a discussion with the commissioning editor of Palgrave Macmillan whilst attending the annual conference of the British Psychological Society. My research had started to change direction such that the focus was more towards everyday functioning of older adults. I was also in the process of developing a new module and jumped at the chance to write a textbook that would then form the basis for this course.

Having spent some time looking at the various texts on the psychology of ageing, I was struck by how little space was given to cognitive functioning. Taking my own bias to one side – I am a cognitive psychologist, after all – I felt that there was need for a text that more fully explored the impact of age on cognition. Rather than there being a solitary chapter on memory, I wanted to produce a book that explored all aspects of memory functioning in more detail. I also wanted to explore in greater depth some of the more basic cognitive processes that undergo change across the lifespan, with a strong emphasis on the biological architecture underpinning all such activity.

Given my own interest in everyday functioning, it was important to explore the role played by higher order functions such as metacognition in daily life. As assessment of cognitive function is such a fundamental topic, I decided also to include a chapter that provided a brief overview of some of the key measures as well as examining some of the main issues associated with structuring such assessment. Having said that, I did want to ensure that topics generally included in such texts were not left out.

When researching this book it was clear that another major gap that needed filling was the inclusion of a chapter on neurodevelopmental disorders. Difficulties faced by someone with a specific learning difficulty, for example, do not go away once adulthood is reached, or indeed older adulthood. Originally proposed as a book consisting of thirteen chapters I managed to persuade the commissioning editor that an additional chapter was needed to explore this topic in more detail. The added bonus was that there would now be fourteen chapters not thirteen, not that I am superstitious in any way (touch wood), even though this is my first book.

With the final chapter, I wished to indulge in a little speculation and in doing so provide a more positive selection of material. A full synopsis of each chapter is provided at the end of Chapter 1, and so I shall not spend any more time talking about the content at this stage. My aim here has been to identify the unique aspects to this book.

The fact that, on the whole, people are living longer presents many challenges, from the macro level of society and the economy to the micro level of the individual. The process of ageing is both unrelenting and fascinating. It is my hope this book provides a useful starting point at which to begin your exploration.

Acknowledgments

To begin with, I feel I should acknowledge the authors of all the material I have presented in this book. It would have been rather a short book without them. They have provided the intellectual impetus to complete this text.

My eternal thanks go to both of my PhD supervisors, Professor John MacDonald and Professor Tony Gale. I would also like to thank Professor Andy Smith for his support over the years.

As this has been a large undertaking, I really must take this opportunity to apologise to friends and family alike for being a ghost for the last couple of years and a grumpy one at that (okay, even more grumpy). The only hint of my existence has been the occasional loud blast of music peppering the otherwise subdued soundtrack of clicking keyboard and muttered oaths. My wife has been a constant source of support throughout all of this. Her diligent reading of the various drafts has been invaluable. Indeed she has been totes amazeballs.

I would like to thank everyone at Palgrave Macmillan for their guidance and patience along the way. I should not forget those involved in the copy-editing process. Again, many thanks. This has been a thrilling experience.

I should also offer my thanks to my trusty espresso maker, without which this book would not have been possible.

CHAPTER 1

Introduction

In this chapter we shall look at some important contextualizing elements within which research on ageing takes place. From the definition (or not) of concepts, through research design and methodology, this chapter will provide an overview of this particular field of study. This is by no means a comprehensive chapter on methodology or analysis. Instead, it provides the bedrock from which to explore subsequent chapters. The most important aspect of this chapter is that it identifies some of the main issues associated with research in this area, issues that will be picked up at various points throughout the book. The final section provides an account of what is covered in the subsequent chapters.

The field of ageing research is large and is continuing to expand. As such, the scope of this book reflects this, albeit with a clear focus on the psychological aspects of ageing. In addition, it is a highly politicized field of study with much potential for theory and research to exert its influence on attitudes and policy that will not only affect the current generations but those yet to come. Issues surrounding our ageing demographic are with us to stay for the foreseeable future. To begin this chapter we will take a brief tour of how the study of the psychology of ageing has developed over time, from its inception up to the present day.

The history of the psychology of ageing

It may seem strange to consider now the fact that the scientific study of ageing is a relatively recent phenomenon. Much focus was on child development rather than older adults. A couple of key texts appeared during the first few decades of the twentieth century that attempted to bring to light the importance of studying older adults (Buhler, 1933; Hall, 1922). This lack of scientific enquiry into ageing more than likely stemmed from the assumption that development was something that occurred in children and adolescents, not in older age groups where one saw only a predictable decline in function. Interest in ageing grew until it became a specialist discipline.

There has been a real boom in ageing research during the last 30 years. The field of geriatrics focuses on the diseases of ageing, whereas gerontology looks to the study of healthy older adults. From out of this grew a desire to examine the psychology of ageing. Increasingly it became clear that there was no inevitable decline. Instead development across the lifespan differs greatly across individuals as the result of numerous unique interactions between organism and environment that act to shape who we are.

The study of adults across all age ranges is vital to our understanding of the psychology of ageing. It is a plausible premise to assume it unlikely that young adults and older adults function comparably at a cognitive level. Memory would seem to be an obvious topic of choice, as would attention. There are clear everyday examples where cognitive function differs across the age spectrum. This conjecture of age differences in function holds for all aspects of behaviour.

The study of older adults is important in terms of notifying us in advance of the potential changes that may occur as we age. Knowing what may happen can help people devise more appropriate plans for their future, especially at pivotal moments such as the onset of retirement. It also informs our interactions with older adults, making us more sensitive to potential issues. Given the rise in numbers of this section of the community, knowledge and understanding of the needs and desires of older adults among professionals and laypersons alike is essential.

So far in this book terms such as adults and older adults have been used. Indeed, the book is imaginatively titled *The Psychology of Ageing*. It is important to consider what is meant by age. Who in fact are these older adults we shall be referring to time and again throughout this text?

Defining age

There are a number of different ways to define age. We are most familiar with the concept of chronological age. This refers to the elapsed time from birth. However, chronological age may not always be the best predictor of someone's behaviour and level of ability. You only have to look around you to see that vitality and age do not necessarily go hand in hand.

Biological age reflects a person's relative position along their own personal lifeline – their longevity, in other words. A person who will live until they are 100 will not be considered biologically old at the age of 65, whereas someone who lives only until the age of 70 will. This is because in the first instance the individual has yet to live another 35 years, whereas in the latter case they will merely live for another five years. Clearly, there is no tried-and-tested method of determining how long someone will live for. So, age here is relative to lifespan.

A more contextually based assessment of age reflects how well we are able to perform everyday activities. This is referred to as a person's functional age. Comparing mobility for two older adults of the same age will invariably identify clear differences in the sense that one might find moving around more difficult than the other. In this sense relative functional ages will differ. However, because of the vast individual differences both across older adults and within each person, functional age may be comparably lower for some activities yet higher for others (Siegler, 1995). A person may have good mobility but may suffer from poor eyesight, for example.

Perhaps a more familiar conception of age is that of psychological age. The ability to adapt to age-related changes has a major impact on psychological age. Those who show that they can adapt effectively to such challenges by deploying a range of cognitive, behavioural, and social skills are deemed psychologically younger than those who do not possess the same range of competencies.

Society as always exerts a strong influence here. Social age is indicative of assumptions about what is appropriate behaviour for people in different age groups. Such expectations, whether appropriate or not, pervade the world in which we live. No doubt you can think of a number of examples. Looking across the board it is clear that there are a number of stages deemed common for each different age band. For example, it is assumed that we complete our education in our twenties. A person who continues education in their forties or fifties would be classed as socially younger than someone who completed their education at the age of 21. The concept of life-long learning is being assimilated into our culture. Last year the University of the Third Age (U3A) celebrated its thirtieth anniversary. This is a UK-based self-help organization that provides educational opportunities for older adults.

Age, we can conclude, is largely subjective. It is clear that people in their early twenties see the age of 50 as the marker for old age, whereas people in their fifties may consider themselves middle-aged (Goldsmith & Heiens, 1992). To adapt (and in the process ruin) a line from one of Shakespeare's Sonnets, one's age is not 'an ever-fixed mark' but one that across the lifespan 'alters when it alteration finds' (Shakespeare, Sonnet 116).

Ageism

When looking at the role of society we see that there are forces at work. People have conventions as to what are appropriate behaviours for specific age groups.

Some are clearly based on physical ability. Others are steeped in prejudice and misunderstanding. In the previous section we looked at how age can be defined. It is obvious that, however we conceptualize age, a very real issue for many societies is that of ageism. It refers to discrimination faced by many older adults as a result of inaccurate assumptions about their capacities and capabilities (Quadagno, 2008). It is hoped that over time this may change to reflect the shifting demographic as more people live to an older age. The impact of the baby boom that occurred at the end of World War II and continued until the mid-1960s is becoming increasingly apparent. Combined with a decrease in birth rate since 1964, the increased number of older adults as a result of this period will continue to exert a large effect on society until 2030. This period will likely lead to many changes in policy relating to this age group, largely in terms of healthcare and housing among other things. A more persistent trend is the increasing longevity of older adults. With time there are more and more of us continuing to lead our lives past the age of 85. The political, economic, and social ramifications are yet to be experienced. The third age is upon us.

The changing demographic

There is a global rise in population size with more and more people living a lot longer. Recent figures in the United Kingdom showed that between 1985 and 2010 those aged 65 and over increased 20 per cent, reaching a total of 10.3 million. In 2010 roughly one-sixth of the population was aged 65 and over; those above the age of 85 reached 1.4 million. Over the same period of time the percentage under the age of 16 fell 2 per cent to only 19 per cent (Office for National Statistics, 2012).

The median age for women was higher than for men – 41 and 38 years respectively – indicating a gender difference in life expectancy, albeit one that is slowly reducing. This has resulted in a rather asymmetrical population profile. Population ageing is predicted to continue for some time. It is projected that in the UK around 5 per cent of the population will be over the age of 85 by 2035, an estimate of 3.5 million; the proportion aged between 16 and 64 is expected to reduce over the same period (Office for National Statistics, 2012).

When looking at marital status, again for the UK, we can see that by 2033 the proportion of the population of England and Wales who are married is anticipated to decrease, and that the proportion of both men and women between the ages of 45 and 64 who have never married is predicted to rise. With the escalation in life expectancy comes a decline in the proportion of older adults who are widowed. Fewer males are widowed compared to females due to a combination of a longer life expectancy among women and the fact that men often marry women who are younger (Office for National Statistics,

2010). Where men do lose their spouse, there is an increased likelihood they will remarry, when compared to women who lose their husbands. Because of this there is an imbalance in the number of widows who continue to live alone – a predicted 39 per cent for women and 18 per cent for men by the year 2033 (Office for National Statistics, 2010). The implications of this in terms of well-being in later life are something that will be picked up again in a later chapter when we look at the role of carers (see Chapter 12).

Influence on development

Throughout this book we shall see how our own biology as well as the way we interact with the environment help shape our development across the lifespan. Menopause is a good example here, as is the age we formally attend school. Both are events associated with specific chronological age ranges. This is referred to as normative age-graded influence (Baltes, Reese, & Lipsitt, 1980). Yet more influence on development is a result of major historical events, such as wars, and how they affect expectations about roles and behaviours. Such normative history-graded influences are common to specific cohorts. Events unique to our own lives – non-normative life events – impact only on our development; a good example here would be those fortunate enough to win a large sum of money on the National Lottery.

Theories of ageing

A great deal of the research in the field of ageing, as is the case for research in general, is driven by the individual researcher's view of a particular topic – their metatheory – and as such acts to select aspects of behaviour that best fits with these assumptions (Elias, Elias, & Elias, 1977). Such models influence also the type of methodology used to test hypotheses. Various perspectives have emerged over the years.

One view, the mechanistic perspective, sees the human body as a machine enabling us to disassemble it in order to study the function of each component (Pepper, 1942). The information-processing approach is a classic example of this way of thinking. This is where brain function is broken down into its constituent parts, thereby allowing researchers to focus on different stages of processing. The organismic perspective, on the other hand, offers a more organized view of human development. This approach focuses on stages of development, each of which proceeds in a structured way. A third overarching metatheory is the contextual perspective. This emphasizes the dynamic nature of behaviour, one where we act on as well as react to the environment.

This approach acknowledges individual differences rather than seeing development as a rigid set of stages through which we all progress.

The ecological model of ageing

The main assumption behind this model is that whenever we interact with the environment some adaptation in our own behaviour will occur. Individual competencies are important here. These reflect an individual's capacities across a number of different domains of functioning and include physical, cognitive, and social elements. Each environment we encounter presents a challenge in one or more of these domains. This is sometimes referred to as environmental press. Adaptation occurs when there is a good match between individual competencies and environmental demands (Lawton & Nahemow, 1973). Maladaptive behaviour occurs as the result of a mismatch between these two competing demands such that competence far exceeds environmental press, or environmental demands exceed individual capabilities. The buffer zone of adaptive behaviour is greater for individuals who have high levels of competence. For these individuals environmental demands need to be higher in order that adaptive behaviour can occur. Those with high competence retain the ability to adapt across a wider range of situations exerting various levels of environmental press. Lawton (1999) also argues that adults with higher competence will be able to interact with their environment and so better utilize resources that are available to them.

The lifespan approach

Intimately linked to the early development of the field of the psychology of ageing is the work of Baltes and colleagues (Baltes, 1983). The lifespan approach has been hugely influential and so will be referred to at various stages throughout this book. This approach differed from the gerontological approach which focused largely on decline in functioning as the result of age, emphasizing instead the potential for growth. Indeed, most texts of ageing do often read as a manifesto declaring decline and despair presaged by old age. Although to some extent inevitable, it is my intention not to communicate to the reader that ageing is necessarily all about loss, but to instead raise awareness of how we are able to adapt to the multidimensional and multidirectional nature of ageing, a view that reflects that of the lifespan perspective described previously (Baltes, Freund, & Li, 2005).

Central to this lifespan approach is the concept of developmental bio-cultural co-constructivism (Baltes & Singer, 2001) which acknowledges the centrality of biological history and cultural context in influencing our inter-actions with the world. It is important, therefore, to conceive different levels of analysis to the psychology of ageing. At a macro level there is the biocul-tural architecture of lifespan development (Level 1). This level attempts to identify exactly how society and biology interact to affect our own develop-ment. From an evolutionary perspective the biological advantage of selection declines as we grow older largely as the result of individuals exceeding the age of reproductive fitness, as well as the fact that in our distant past few adults reached old age.

Neither the evolution of our species (phylogenesis) nor our development as individuals (ontogenesis) occurred in a vacuum but can instead be seen as being the net result of interplay between our biology and the culture in which we live. Our expectation of extending life, and a well-lived life on top of that, demands cultural resources that facilitate this process. This is particularly pertinent when one considers the biological changes that occur throughout the ageing process, necessitating increasing support to prolong functioning (Nelson & Dannefer, 1992).

The next level to consider is how resources are allocated to various func-tions (Level 2). Such allocation is largely determined by considerations of progress, conservation, and forfeiture (Freund & Ebner, 2005). These pro-cesses reflect our ability to adapt to different situations in order to satisfy our desire for improvement and higher functioning, for maintenance of function in the face of a challenge, and for regulating loss that better mirrors decline in functional capacity.

The concept of adaptation driven by decline often leads to a range of compensatory strategies that not only neutralize deficit but may be seen to enhance level of functioning in some instances. The third level of analysis then is to examine an overarching theory of successful ageing. The theory of 'selective optimization with compensation' (Baltes, 1996) focuses on three major components for psychological adaptation in the older adult.

The process of selection refers to a capacity to assess viability of particular actions from within the context of our innate capability to perform those actions. This selection process inevitably results in a paring down of potential options. This process can be goal-driven (elective selection) or it can be in response to some loss (loss-based selection) (Freund & Baltes, 2002). In both instances our aims and objectives are reorganized to better match resources available at that point in time.

The second component of this model is optimization. This reflects the processes required to attain the targeted level of functioning in as efficient and effective a manner possible. This draws upon both internal and exter-nal means with optimization being achieved through a series of iterations whereby resources are coordinated and refined.

Compensation occurs when previously available means are no longer present, requiring instead the search for alternative resources that would enable a person to retain the same goal-state objective.

The selective optimization with compensation model views successful ageing as reflecting maximal gains with minimal loss. This model can be applied to a range of settings – social, behavioural, or cognitive (Baltes & Carstensen, 1996) – and the processes of selection, optimization, and compensation may operate at different levels, be they active or passive, conscious or automatic, internal or external (Baltes, Freund, & Li, 2005). This approach offers much in terms of modelling everyday behaviour. In the case of osteoarthritis, selection is used to restrict the type of activities people engage in, optimization is brought into play when actions are practiced, and compensation is evident with the use of devices to assist daily living (Gignac, Cott, & Badley, 2002). Studies have shown that adults who engage in selective optimization with compensation evidence higher levels of well-being and overall life satisfaction (Freund & Baltes, 2002).

Having explored some of the main theoretical approaches to ageing, the next thing to consider is how one should develop and test hypotheses in this field. A number of established research designs are used to address different components of the literature on ageing. These range from the small scale, such as case studies, through to large-scale longitudinal designs. There is also a range of methodologies that can be used to obtain the information required, be it observational or neuropsychological. As we shall see, each provides a unique insight into specific components of ageing.

Research design

Central components of all research designs are age, cohort, and time. Age effects refer to individual differences that are the direct result of physical, psychological, and social changes experienced by those recruited rather than merely being residue left by the passage of time itself. Cohort effects reflect differences as a result of experiences of a particular generation. A cohort refers to the recruitment of individuals who were born around the same time. As a result, members of each cohort would have shared common experiences throughout their development. Of particular relevance is the state of medical knowledge during that time as well as structure of the education system. Of course, just because people are born in the same year, it is rather unlikely they were each presented with the same opportunities in life. Time-of-measurement effects denote contextual elements, be they sociocultural or environmental, experienced at the time of testing that may impact on data collected.

Cross-sectional design

Various research designs are used in the study of ageing. The cross-sectional design operates by recruiting two or more groups of differently aged participants at one point in time. With cross-sectional designs there is no concern that significant changes occur to the participants over time as each will be tested only once. The issue of retention is not an issue here either for the same reason. The main advantage of this design is that it is a quick and efficient means of collecting data. The main problem with this type of design is that differences between age groups may not actually reflect age but instead be the result of a cohort effect.

Longitudinal design

Longitudinal designs address a number of the limitations associated with the cross-sectional design approach. In longitudinal studies the same individual is assessed on two or more occasions over a specified period of time. With this type of design all participants are recruited at the same age and so form a cohort. One problem with this design is that of practice effect, although this may be minimized if follow-up intervals are sufficiently spaced far enough apart.

The major issue with this type of design is that of attrition or dropout as the same individuals are being called upon over an extended period of time. The main problem with this is that attrition tends not to be random. It is often the case that those who remain part of the study are the ones who perform at a higher level (Siegler & Botwinick, 1979). This will produce a huge bias in the data set collected. In addition, longitudinal designs are expensive and extremely time consuming.

However, although there are limitations, there is a real need to conduct longitudinal studies in the field of the psychology of ageing. Baltes and Nesselroade (1979) identified that it was not only important to identify differences between people (interindividual differences) but to also explore within-person differences (intraindividual differences). A great deal of current theories are based on cross-sectional studies, so research in the future should instead examine within-person changes using longitudinal design (Hofer & Sliwinski, 2006).

Time-lag design

In addition to both cross-sectional and longitudinal studies, there are time-lag designs. This is where the same age group is compared across different time periods. So groups consist of different cohorts of the same age but born in different years. Such studies allow researchers to look at differences in the profiles of the same age groups across decades.

Sequential design

Sequential designs are an advance on these in that it can combine elements of cross-sectional, longitudinal, and time-lag designs (Schaie, 1965). In doing so it attempts to get around some of the issues associated with research on ageing, namely effects of age, cohort, and time of measurement. Designs of this type allow different combinations to take place, such as a cross-sectional study being carried out at two or more different time points. This would allow the researcher to tease out age-related effects from potential confounds of particular periods in sociocultural history.

Experimental studies

Experimental studies focus on the examination of both dependent and independent variables. Dependent variables are the measures of interest. The experimental components refer to any manipulation of the independent variable. The preferred design is a random allocation of participants to these different experimental conditions. In doing so, it is possible to examine the impact of different levels of the independent variable on the chosen outcome variables. A good example of this type of design is to compare performance on a range of cognitive tasks of two groups of older adults, where one of the groups received a drug believed to enhance performance, the other receiving a placebo.

Quasi-experimental studies

With the quasi-experimental approach there are the same components of dependent and independent variables, except that in this case participants are not allocated to groups randomly. Instead, the researcher makes use of the participants' own situation to monitor impact on dependent variables. For example, they may want to compare quality of life of older adults living in their own home with those living in a nursing home. Participants are not in this case assigned randomly to groups. Because of that the same cause-and-effect statements cannot be made.

Correlational studies

In correlational studies there is no experimental manipulation of variables. Instead the researcher is interested in how variables relate to each other naturally in the real world. Although such studies do not allow one to make claims about cause and effect, they do identify how strongly variables relate to each other. This type of design is particularly prominent in the field of ageing as the key variable, age, cannot be manipulated experimentally given our current level of technology.

Case studies

Case studies are particularly useful in instances where there is a need to study a rare condition. In-depth study of someone with a unique combination of symptoms can lead to the identification of a new syndrome that demands further investigation.

Methodology

Some of the main methods of collecting data include diary data, self-report measures, interviews, as well as behavioural measures. To some extent collecting diary data is relatively unobtrusive. The diaries may take the form of an everyday log through to more structured entries where sections are identified by the experimenter. Questionnaires are quick and easy to administer and may be conducted remotely. As with all self-report measures there are concerns over accuracy. In addition, unless completed in the presence of the experimenter, questionnaires are often returned incomplete. Sometimes this is due to the person not understanding what is required of them, whereas it may in some cases be a genuine mistake such that they had intended to finish answering all sections but forgot to do so. Interviews may take place face-to-face or via the telephone. These can be either structured sessions, where each participant receives a fixed schedule of questions and prompts, or they can be open-ended where there is greater flexibility. Focus groups – a small cohort who are brought together to discuss a specific topic – are increasingly used as an initial stage in the exploration of a research topic, and so data gathered may be used to inform the construction of a more topic-specific questionnaire.

It is argued that behavioural measures offer more accuracy (although my own biases here as a hard-nosed cognitive type are at play). These can take the guise of formal assessments of intelligence or neuropsychological measures of functioning. I shall refer you here to Chapter 8 which is dedicated to assessment of cognitive function and turn, instead, to observational studies.

Observations are another key method and may be either naturalistic or laboratory in nature. Naturalistic observations are made within the context of the real world where no manipulation of any form takes place. Systematic yet unobtrusive study of behaviour can reveal much and so inform further research as well as complementing current understanding in a particular area. Laboratory observation refers to a situation where individuals are observed under controlled conditions, be it inside a laboratory or in a real-life setting. Manipulating the environment allows the researcher to observe impact of a particular variable on behaviour. Observational methods provide much in terms of identifying important aspects of study, but they do not provide explanations why various behaviours occur. There is always a concern over observer bias, where the researcher's theoretical assumptions drive the types of observations made. In addition, unless the observer has been present for an extended period of time, or are unobservable, their presence will likely influence how those under study behave.

Summary

This chapter has presented a range of material that is fundamental to one's conceptualization of how research into the psychology of ageing is conducted. The fundamental issues with definition are an important context within which to view much of the literature. How age is defined can have major implications both to the individual and society. We also looked at theories of ageing and demonstrated how models inform what research questions are asked and which designs and methodologies one should use. The spread of approaches in this increasingly multidisciplinary field is very large indeed, and as such the scope of this chapter has been to merely present a brief overview of some of those available. As with all research it is important to consider the same question from a number of different angles. Only in doing so do you obtain a fully rounded (or at least a clearer) picture of what is going on.

Overview of this book

Before leaving this chapter, let me present a concise overview of what will be covered in the remainder of this book. You will notice that there is quite a strong emphasis on cognitive functioning. This is not merely a result of my own professed bias, but it is a conscious attempt to redress the balance of other texts on the topic of ageing. More of that later.

To follow on from this introductory chapter, Chapter 2 presents an in-depth account of the biological changes that occur as we age. Alterations in our biological functions, alongside changes in cognitive functioning, undoubtedly underpin all our behaviour. We cannot consider how someone can adjust to a change in lifestyle without referring to either of them. Obviously other factors are at work, our personality traits and so on, but if you chip away you will find that supporting all behaviour is a biological and cognitive infrastructure that is ever-changing, albeit at varying degrees both within the individual and across individuals. In this chapter we look at physical changes in the body and how these impact on behaviour, specifically those occurring in the brain, heart, kidneys, and lungs.

Chapter 3 focuses on how basic cognitive processes are affected by many of the changes that were detailed in the previous chapter. Here we look at basic sensory and perceptual functions, as well as exploring our attentional capacity in terms of efficiency and effectiveness. Linking with the biological component, the last part of this chapter will focus on the role neurotransmitters have to play in all this activity. There follows next two chapters on memory. This may seem like overkill. However, when you once again consider the fundamental nature of memory to the lives we lead, this additional space is justified.

Chapter 4 deals with the concept of short-term memory. In doing so the focus is on the concept of working memory. This is the approach or model that is predominantly used in research to look at how we are able to manipulate and store information for brief periods of time. It is a development from earlier models of short-term memory. Working memory, as you will soon see, refers to something far more flexible and fundamental. Because of the nature of the research, much of our current understanding of working memory is enriched by the use of imaging technology. Although the next chapter focuses on long-term memory, it is clear that there is a link to working memory. Working memory does not operate in isolation. Not only does it require that you sense and attend to environmental events, it also entails access to stored knowledge. These systems are interconnected even though they are dealt with in separate chapters.

In Chapter 5 we shall examine the different subtypes of long-term memory. Long-term memory – and one component in particular, autobiographical memory – is closely linked to our sense of identity. Our understanding of memory did not really gather much momentum until pioneering research conducted in the 1950s using case studies of patients with amnesia. From this early research we have been able to separate out and classify different types of long-term memory, be they memories that are explicitly retrieved at our behest or memories that affect our behaviour even though we are not aware of it. The effects of age are often first noticeable when we find our memory is not what it once was. These are tangible effects that resonate across all aspects of our lives.

Keeping with the cognitive theme, Chapter 6 examines metacognition. We shall see that by metacognition we mean our ability to think about our own thought processes. There are various sub-themes within this literature, such as how well we can assess our own memories or how effectively we are able to regulate our emotions, but sustaining it all is the cognitive infrastructure discussed in Chapters 3 through 5. Of particular focus in this chapter is social cognition. Our ability to manage our own behaviour determines to a great extent our ability to perform in social situations. Not only do we need to understand our own thoughts and feelings, we need to have an accurate account of how others are feeling and what they are thinking (although if you have studied psychology before then the latter is already second nature to you – we can, after all, read minds). One facet of this is the concept of theory of mind, an aspect of cognitive functioning that develops relatively early on in childhood.

Chapter 7 homes in on everyday functioning. By that we mean how the types of reasoning and decision making processes we make impact on our ability to lead the lives we desire. Of particular importance are the decisions we make in terms of our own health. Again, we shall pick up on issues relating to social cognition, although this time the emphasis will be on the influence of personality traits. The final section of this chapter focuses on language. Where would we be without the ability to speak and comprehend language? Again changes in biological and cognitive functions have a major bearing here.

Before finally laying the cognitive theme to rest, Chapter 8 presents an overview of some of the key tools used to assess cognitive function in older adults. Cognitive psychologists are a particularly inventive breed, such that for almost every conceivable aspect of function, there is a corresponding measure to assess that function. Also considered are some of the rudimentary components to any neuropsychological assessment, each of which is vital in constructing an accurate account of a person's level of ability.

In Chapter 9 we shall tackle the mountain of literature looking at the impact of age on personality and intelligence. This chapter begins with a short account of key personality theories before considering how one's personality changes across the lifespan. Indeed, does our personality change? We will then examine what is meant by the term 'intelligence' and how once again age exerts an influence on functioning. Our conceptualization of intelligence has grown since earlier rather restrictive accounts to embrace a range of different capabilities as personified in the notion of multiple intelligences. Linked to this is the growing appreciation of creativity and wisdom and how these play a role in our later years. We shall see that, as foretold by one of the forerunners of the New Wave of British Heavy Metal, 'You don't have to be old to be wise.'

It is the job of Chapter 10 to address the issue of change. Just how capable at adapting are we? Throughout our lives there are a number of pivotal moments, each of which requires some element of adjustment. For older adults key moments include the change of role from person-in-employment to person-in-retirement. For some this change is almost imperceptible, whereas for others this opens a major rift in a once comfortable routine. There are also the issues of losing friends and family and how one learns to deal with this. An increased dependency on others and how this impacts on the type of care one receives is examined here also. Appropriately enough the final section of this chapter explores various issues associated with the final stages of a person's life, in particular how we need to address ethical issues associated with different practices that are becoming increasingly available.

One of the major changes that can hit someone in their later years is a decline in health. Chapter 11 looks at the major health conditions associated with older adulthood both in terms of the identification of potential risk factors and in terms of strategies for prevention and treatment. This chapter will also develop further some of the personality aspects introduced in Chapter 9, although this time the focus is on factors that influence quality of life. Some key concepts to be discussed include optimism, hope, and resilience in the face of stress or trauma, all of which are associated with increased sense of well-being. This chapter then examines how an individual's response can have an effect on one's health status, often for the better.

Whereas the previous chapter concentrated on medical complaints, Chapter 12 presents the most prevalent psychiatric conditions associated with older adults. In this chapter we shall cover depression, anxiety, insomnia, and delirium, as well as dementia in its many forms. We have all heard of these yet our true understanding of what these conditions mean to the person with the diagnosis is probably at best sketchy unless we have had first-hand experience of someone with them. Much is made of dementia in the media, in particular Alzheimer's disease, a specific form of dementia. It is therefore important that we appreciate more fully the severity of these conditions given the rise in number of those at risk from these disorders. Substance abuse is also covered as this is increasingly an issue of concern for this age group. As we shall see many successful treatments for the conditions covered involve the use of drugs. How drugs work within the body will form the final section here.

Chapter 13 is dedicated to neurodevelopmental disorders. This is a much overlooked topic in many texts on the psychology of ageing, often as the result of a misconception that autism spectrum disorder and attention deficit hyperactivity disorder stop being an issue once one has reached adolescence. This is clearly not the case, and we shall see that, although problems may manifest differently for adults, they still pose a significant challenge. The same is true for intellectual development disorders such as Down's syndrome. The combination of increased life expectancy and subsequent risk of developing Alzheimer's disease is a real concern here. We shall also see that for many of these disorders comorbidity with other medical or psychiatric conditions is reasonably common.

The final chapter, Chapter 14, is an attempt to end on a positive note with a speculative look at what the future holds in store for older adults. Much has been made of brain training and how it can reverse cognitive decline. While these claims may not be as positive as one may wish them to be, there is growing evidence that a range of activities can help slow down the signs of cognitive ageing. Linked to this is the section that examines the use of technology to augment therapy and improve an older adult's independence. Having first looked at what can be done to offset changes in cognitive function, the final section looks at what medicine can offer to halt or reverse physical signs of ageing. The chapter ends by identifying some of the key ethical issues that need to be addressed as the result of our continuing success at extending and enhancing the lives of the current and future generations.

Further reading

BBC World Service (2009). Third Agers, BBC. http://www.bbc.co.uk/programmes/ p0027v64 [This is a four-part documentary that was first broadcast on the BBC World Service in 2009. Over the course of the programmes a range of key issues concerning the ageing population is discussed. This is a really insightful programme.]

Robson, C. (2011). *Real world research: A resource for users of social research methods in applied settings*. Oxford: Wiley-Blackwell. [This book is to be found on many an academic's bookshelf and for good reason. It is a great source of information for those interested in conducting research in the real world.]

Saracci, R. (2010). *Epidemiology: A very short introduction*. Oxford: Oxford University Press. [This is a great introduction to epidemiology. It is short as its title suggests and an easy read.]

CHAPTER 2

Biological Changes

This chapter will focus on the biological changes that take place as we age. Any foray into the literature will lead to the discovery that there is a huge range of theories about ageing, each competing to provide the most coherent and complete account of typical ageing. The physical structure of our bodies often determines how we lead our lives, from muscular strength and skeletal integrity to cardiovascular and respiratory systems. We shall examine also how hormonal and immunologic functions change as we age. Closely linked to this is the role of the senses. Changes in how we see, hear, feel, taste, and smell impose limits on how well we are able to function on a daily basis. The final section will explore age-related neurological changes and the role played by advancements in neuroimaging technology in helping us understand how we each adapt to deal with the vicissitudes of the ageing process.

It is important to remember that whatever happens at the level of our physiology impacts on all other domains of our lives. Biological changes exert both a direct and an indirect effect on our psychological well-being, be it in terms of declining neurological functioning or confidence in our ability to carry out everyday activities that were previously taken for granted. Our social lives are also affected in a number of ways as the result of changes in our ability to function physically as well as mentally.

Theories of ageing

There have been a number of different theories that attempt to explain the ageing process, each with varying degrees of success.

Metabolic rate

One particular theory of ageing that appears commonsensical is that organisms have a finite amount of energy to last them a lifetime. Once capacity is reached, life is expunged. There would appear to be a relationship between how long animals live and their metabolic rate, such that animals with a high metabolic rate tend to lead much shorter existences. Indeed, the manipulation of basic behaviours has been shown to have knock-on effects in terms of life expectancy, such that certain mammals live longer after being induced to hibernate (Cristofalo et al., 1999).

Caloric intake

Caloric intake appears to exert an effect here also. A reduced calorie diet has led to longer life spans for both rodents and rhesus monkeys, apparently by slowing down certain expected age-related changes (Hayflick, 1996). Similar findings have been seen with humans. Among Japan's Okinawan population the proportion of centenarians is 40 times greater than the rest of Japan. The incidence of cardiovascular disease, diabetes, and cancer among this group is also halved (Monczunski, 1991). When looking at the diet of the Okinawans, they consume merely 60 per cent of calories forming part of the average Japanese diet. Although intriguing, there is no conclusive evidence to suggest any direct relationship between metabolism and longevity (de Magalhaes, Costa, & Church, 2007).

Telomeres

What happens at the cellular level naturally has an impact on the ageing process. An organism's lifespan is partly determined by the number of times cells are able to divide. Cells grown *in vitro*, in other words outside the host organism, appear to undergo a fixed number of divisions before they eventually die. The number of divisions appears to be affected by the age of the donor, such that cells from an older donor undergo fewer divisions before dying. This is referred to as the Hayflick limit (Hayflick, 1996). Human foetal cells can divide up to 60 times, whereas human adult cells only undergo this process around 20 times. An important determinant seems to be the physical structure of the chromosomes, more specifically the tips of the chromosomes called telomeres.

Telomeres are positioned at both ends of eukaryotic chromosomes (humans are eukaryotic organisms as our cells contain a nucleus and mitochondria that is bound by a plasma membrane). They consist of multiple repeats of a short DNA sequence. With age the number of these DNA repeats decrease ('Telomere', 2007). Telomeres assist in regulating cell division. To allow these telomeres to reproduce in the divided cells, the enzyme, telomerase, is needed. This enzyme is not, however, present in somatic cells (cells not involved in reproduction); rather it appears only in germ cells (either the egg or the sperm cell) and some adult stem cells (an undifferentiated cell) (Kirkwood, 2005). Because of this, when somatic cells divide, with each replication the telomeres become progressively shorter. Following a number of such divisions, the telomeres become too short, causing instability within the chromosome (Saretzki & Von Zglinicki, 2002). This loss of telomeric DNA acts to prevent cell division from becoming excessive, preventing the runaway process that occurs in cancer (Campisi, 1997).

Cross-linking

An alternative explanation of ageing based on cellular changes concerns a process called cross-linking. This is a process whereby specific protein molecules within human cells, called collagen, interact in such a way that the resultant molecules have the effect of reinforcing soft body tissue; a higher rate of cross-linkage results in stiffer body tissue (Galetti, 1995). Cross-linking increases as we age, and this may account for the fact that the heart muscles and arteries become less elastic with age. Apart from these structural changes, there is no evidence of a more intrinsic role for cross-linking in the process of ageing.

Oxidative stress

It has also been suggested that ageing is caused by free radicals – unstable molecules that occur through the breaking of a bond in a stable molecule thereby resulting in two fragments, each fragment possessing an unpaired electron (Cristofalo et al., 1999). On interaction with other molecules free radicals can result in some dramatic cellular changes, such as causing a change in a cell's oxygen level, leading to localized damage (Lu & Finkel, 2008).

The greatest evidence of a link between free radicals and the ageing process comes from observing the effects of antioxidants including Vitamin A, Vitamin C, and Vitamin E. As discussed already, free radicals react with other molecules within the body, a process called oxidation. Antioxidants help to keep this process in check. Oxidative stress occurs when this neutralization process is inadequate.

It has also been shown that regular dietary ingestion of antioxidants seem to delay the onset of certain age-related conditions and diseases, including cancer and cardiovascular disease (Lu & Finkel, 2008). However, although this does appear to be the case, no evidence yet exists that indicate antioxidants in any way increase a person's lifespan (Miwa, Beckman, & Muller, 2008).

Programmed cell death

With our ever-growing understanding of the impact of genetics on our lives, the role played by programmed cell death in the ageing process may prove to be vitally important (Pankow & Solotoroff, 2007). Programmed cell death, or apoptosis, refers to the innate capacity for cells to self-destruct. This is something that occurs as part of the normal process of development. When tissues and organs initially form, more cells are produced than are actually needed. These structures take on their end form through a process of apoptosis ('Apoptosis', 2003). This can be seen in the formation of the hand. In embryonic form, it appears shovel-like, with no observable fingers. Such definition occurs as cells between the proto-fingers undergo apoptosis. Little is currently known about this process. Apoptosis, or rather the lack of apoptosis, has been linked to the development of cancers. However, with increasing evidence to indicate a role for genetics in many conditions and diseases, there is a clear need to further our understanding of this phenomenon.

Before moving on, from an evolutionary perspective it makes little sense to search for the cause of ageing as natural selection has resulted in all our physiological systems deteriorating at roughly the same rate. The amount of cellular repair and bodily maintenance occurs at a rate that makes practical sense in terms of our own survival. An analogy often made is that it would be unlikely if we had evolved in such a way that costly repairs are carried out on one system while other systems deteriorate at a faster rate (Diamond, 1991). Repairs, after all, require a great deal of energy. The body needs around 1600 calories each day to maintain itself. That means that we will never isolate a single cause for ageing, so there will be no single cure. However, attempts to interfere with the natural ageing process will be explored in Chapter 14.

Observable changes

This section focuses on the main physical changes that occur in our bodies as we grow older. I shall be focusing here on observable changes. In other words, changes that we can see with the naked eye. Such physical signs of ageing are the focus of many a media campaign. These surface changes can have a dramatic effect on how we lead our lives.

A recent novel by Pascal Mercier, *Night Train to Lisbon*, contains a wonderful passage about who we really are (Mercier, 2009). It questions the notion as to whether the way we appear to others accurately reflects our true nature. Are we able to view our own reflection and see ourselves as others do? How we perceive the person starring back at us in the mirror is particularly apposite as we grow older. We can observe the indelible marks etched on our bodies by the march of time in a way that is accepting and positive, helping to maintain a burgeoning sense of overall well-being, or we can view such change as a harbinger of inevitable decline. Our sense of command over our bodies, our confidence in our capabilities and competencies, will determine to a large extent our ability to adapt to change, be it internal or external. When looking in the mirror, the first indicator of age confronting us is our skin.

Skin

What happens to skin as we age is a complex process (Wulf, 2006). As a result of progressive cell loss over time, the outer layer of skin becomes much thinner. This makes it much more fragile and prone to damage. The connective tissue, consisting of collagen fibres, loses its elasticity. Because of this skin is less pliable. Elastin fibres located in the middle layer no longer keep the skin taut, with sagging being the resultant effect. Finally, the fat layer that provides padding becomes thinner and so stretches of skin are no longer contoured.

Such changes to the skin have a number of knock-on effects. Skin becomes less effective as a regulator of body temperature. As already mentioned, it is more fragile, and so it is likely to cut, bruise, and blister more easily than a younger person's skin. Age spots and moles become more prevalent. These are areas of intense pigmentation. Varicose veins may also begin to appear due to increased dilation of blood vessels near the surface of the skin (Wulf, 2006).

Facial appearance is influenced a great deal by what we have allowed our faces to be exposed to. Being a smoker and sitting in the sun are two major factors that appear to impact on facial appearance. Ultraviolet radiation present in sunlight acts to break down the collagen fibres in the skin. The appropriate use of sunblocks, as well as restricting exposure to the sun, reduce the speed of wrinkle formation. Smoking acts to reduce the flow of blood around the lips (Wulf, 2006).

Hair

Both men and women experience a gradual thinning and greying of the hair. Loss of the germ centres that produce hair follicles lead to hair loss. A halt in pigment production causes grey hair to appear. Men, however, retain facial hair integrity, and often increased production of hair in hitherto barren areas. Women, on the other hand, due to hormonal changes, may start sprouting patches of facial hair (Aldwin & Gilmer, 2004).

Height

Common observations to be made when witnessing someone age is that there are quite pronounced changes in weight and height. Between the ages of 50 and 70 men lose on average around one inch in height, women two inches (de Groot, Perdigao, & Deurenberg, 1996). Loss of height is more often than not due to spinal compression as the result of reduction in bone strength and physical changes in the intervertebral discs. Loss of height can be influenced by postural changes as we age as well (Deal, 2004).

Weight

When looking at patterns in weight across the lifespan, weight is generally gained during middle age, then lost again in our later years. Such fluctuations are largely as the result of metabolic changes occurring in the body. A combination of a slower metabolism and a reduction in the level of exercise means that fewer calories are demanded by the body. Much needed adjustments to one's diet rarely occur, resulting in weight gains around the abdomen for men and around the hips for women. Later in life weight drops due to loss of both muscle and bone (Yang, Bishai, & Harman, 2008). The health of adults aged 65 who have normal body weight is comparably better than those who do not, and life expectancy is also higher (Yang, Bishai, & Harman, 2008).

Muscle

Muscle tissue is gradually lost over time – a process called sarcopenia. This reduces both the number and size of muscle fibres. Peak muscle strength occurs around the age of 20. Following a plateau period lasting until the age of around 50, muscle strength begins to decline rapidly (Kostka, 2005). Muscle endurance, on the other hand, is reasonably protected (Lavender & Nosaka, 2007).

Reductions in strength as we age are often thought to be the result of decreases in muscle mass (Raj, Bird, & Shield, 2010), but neurological disruption (Klass, Baudry, & Duchateau, 2007) and growing tendon stiffness (Carroll et al., 2008) also contribute to this effect. Exercise becomes increasingly difficult as the result of the cumulative effects of sarcopenia, thereby contributing to the overall effect (Lang et al., 2010). Consequences can be exacerbated by excessive weight gain, a condition referred to as sarcopenic obesity (Zamboni et al., 2008).

There are clear practical issues to consider here. With a decline in lower body strength, risk of falls increases considerably, as do mobility problems. Balance becomes impaired and further compounds these problems. Our ability to retain mobility is vital if we are to maintain a sense of independence. Although mobility issues will affect us all, for the majority of us these changes will have minimal impact on how we lead our lives.

Bones

Bone tissue is lost as we get older. This process generally begins around the age of 30, becomes more pronounced in our fifties, and then slows down again when we reach 70 (Parker, 2009a). There is a large gender difference here, with the rate of loss being higher in women. This is in part due to lower levels of oestrogen following menopause. Oestrogen has been shown to reduce the level of demineralization that occurs in bones following menopause ('Menopause', 2010), so reduced levels following menopause often lead to problems in this area. The impact of such loss is greater at an earlier stage in women compared to men. This is because women have less bone mass compared to men, so when depletion commences, there is less of a buffer with which to withstand the loss.

When looking at the structure of bones as they age, it is clear that they appear increasingly hollow because of reductions in bone mass. They become more porous as well. Such structural changes increase the likelihood of fractures occurring. The structural changes in older bones mean also that when they do fracture, the split is likely to be clean. Clean breaks present a greater challenge to the healing process. A reduction in the collagen content of bones has the effect of reducing bone flexibility when pressure is exerted on them, thereby increasing the potential for fractures to occur (Saito & Marumo, 2010).

Aside from the usual changes associated with age, a number of degenerative processes have a pronounced effect on our bones, most notably osteoporosis and arthritis. These changes are linked to a range of chronic health conditions that are prevalent among adults and older adults.

Osteoporosis

Osteoporosis is more prevalent among women. This is a severe condition that causes further degeneration of bone tissue to that expected from normal ageing. Bones lose extra mass and become excessively porous. With time, this leads to a stooping posture in the sufferer.

In terms of the causes of the condition, a number of factors seem to play a role. These include deficiencies in calcium and Vitamin D, high protein diets, and low levels of oestrogen. Individuals receiving medication for asthma, cancer, rheumatoid arthritis, thyroid problems, and epilepsy are at a greater risk of developing osteoporosis because such medications reduce bone mass.

Arthritis

Arthritis is common among older adults. From early adulthood onwards, the protective cartilage between joints begins to deteriorate. The two most common forms of arthritis are osteoarthritis and rheumatoid arthritis.

Osteoarthritis. Osteoarthritis occurs when deterioration in cartilage results in bone damage through a process of wear and tear. This condition progresses gradually, leading to escalating pain and increased difficulties with movement and mobility. Osteoarthritis becomes increasingly disabling with time. It occurs more frequently in those who have led highly demanding physical jobs. The main sites affected are the hands, spine, hips, and knees, with the wrists, elbows, shoulders, and ankles being relatively unaffected. Pain is experienced most intensely when the affected joint is in use. There tends to be no redness or swelling around the affected site. The most effective treatment strategy for this condition consists of anti-inflammatory medication and the use of steroids, a combination of rest and exercise, and appropriate adjustments to diet.

Rheumatoid arthritis. Rheumatoid arthritis instead targets fingers, wrists, and ankles. Unlike osteoarthritis there are clear external indicators of the condition, such as swollen joints. This is because the synovial membrane becomes inflamed. This membrane usually protects and lubricates joints. Treatment of this condition includes the use of aspirin or other non-steroidal anti-inflammatory drugs (NSAIDs) or disease-modifying anti-rheumatic drugs (DMARDs). Again, a combination of rest and exercise appear therapeutic for this condition, although here the exercises prescribed are more passive in nature. There are often fluctuations in symptom severity which, if one is not mindful, may disrupt care and management of the condition.

Psychological impact

The changes that occur with age impact greatly on how a person perceives themselves – their self-concept, in other words (Aldwin & Gilmer, 2004). To some extent, this change in a person's self-concept is a reflection of how society views ageing, with its various prejudices and stereotypes that result in the type of ageism that is all too often present (Clarke & Griffin, 2008).

Although our bodies, and specifically our appearance, stand testament to the ravages of time, and that this effect is comparable for us all, the psychological impact, and indeed the societal impact, appears to differ for men and women. Something as innocuous as greying hair affects men and women differently. Although often seen as a negative thing for women and, therefore, something to hide, for men grey hair suggests experience with a hint of distinction.

Although predominantly the domain of women until relatively recently, techniques that aim to offset the impact of the ageing process increasingly attract a mounting wave of concerned men. However, even with plastic surgery, the effect at its best is merely to delay the inevitable. At some stage it becomes all too clear that a person is old. I address appearance issues further in Chapter 14 within the context of technological advancements.

It is not just changes in physical appearance that has implications for our psychological outlook. Changes in how we are able to move around, our physical endurance, and so on have a major effect on how we are able to lead our lives. It determines the extent to which we have to reassess our capacities for different activities. However, in the absence of some debilitating condition, physical fitness can be improved at any age. Aerobic exercise, in fact, is hugely beneficial in combating cognitive decline (Andel et al., 2008) as well as enhancing physical ability. This is something that I will come back to in Chapter 14.

As already seen the impact of conditions such as osteoarthritis and rheumatoid arthritis on everyday functioning is substantial. By the very nature of the difficulties experienced, there are psychological effects as well as physical challenges. Among other things such conditions reduce the sufferer's feeling of independence. In addition, the relative frequency with which pain is felt also has an effect. On the whole, however, older adults tend to employ a whole range of adaptive behavioural and psychological strategies to offset some, if not all, of these difficulties (Gignac, Cott, & Badley, 2000).

Sensory systems

Having explored some of the more obvious observable changes age has in store for us, this next section examines how our senses cope with the ageing process.

Sight

One of the most obvious things to be affected by age is eyesight. Almost everyone at some stage reaches the conclusion that their arms are no longer of sufficient length to allow them to focus on the book they are reading (or rather attempting to read). Although often a source of mirth for those witnessing this ritual, there are very important psychological effects associated with failing eyesight. Very often feelings of sadness are associated with increasing deterioration in vision (Mojon-Azzi, Sousa-Poza, & Mojon, 2008).

There are broadly two physical changes that occur to our eyes over time. The first consists of structural changes occurring within the eye itself. One change involves the amount of light gaining admittance into the eye. Less light is able to pass into the eye largely as the result of a reduction in pupil size (senile miosis). There are clear practical difficulties associated with this, although the most obvious is poorer visual acuity in the dark. However, the converse of this is that older people are also more sensitive to glare (Aldwin & Gilmer, 2004). Linked to both of these is an inability to adapt to changes in lighting – a process referred to as dark adaptation (Charman, 2008). There are obvious implications here in terms of driving behaviour.

The lens of the eye also undergoes change (Charman, 2008). It acquires a yellow tint, thus making discrimination between certain colours more difficult. Colour perception is also impaired as the result of a reduction in short-wavelength-sensitivity cones. The lens' ability to adjust its shape is more restricted because its elasticity is gradually lost over time, thereby producing problems with focusing. The typical effect is a condition referred to as presbyopia. This refers to the situation where individuals find it very difficult to focus on objects up close. The ability of the lens to adapt to changes in focal point decreases, and so it takes more time to change our focus from near objects to those further away, and vice versa. Contrast sensitivity is also affected. This measures our ability to detect spatial information.

Other changes may befall us as we age. Cataracts may perhaps develop. These occur as cloudy formations on the lens. The amount of light thus entering the eye is greatly reduced. Glaucoma is another common condition. This is where aqueous humour in the eye fails to drain properly, resulting in an increase in internal pressure. If left untreated this condition causes internal damage and loss of vision in the affected eye. Both of these conditions can now be treated with high degrees of success.

Age-related macular degeneration may also occur (Margrain & Boulton, 2005). The macula lutea is the region of the retina where the focal point of vision occurs. Compared to the rest of the retina, the macula contains the highest density of rods and cones, the specialist receptor cells required for vision. At the centre of the macula there is the fovea. Visual acuity is highest at this point. With macular degeneration irreversible damage occurs to the receptor cells contained in this region. Following such damage the ability to see detail is lost.

Diabetes can also affect vision. Diabetic retinopathy causes fluid retention in the macula (macula oedema), retinal detachment, as well as haemorrhaging and risk of aneurysms in the eye (Margrain & Boulton, 2005). This condition develops slowly, and so most at risk are those who develop diabetes early on.

Changes in vision impact greatly on how well a person is able to function on a day-to-day basis and, as a result, is an important determinant of their sense of well-being (Mojon-Azzi, Sousa-Poza, & Mojon, 2008). To a large extent a great many of the conditions identified previously can be rectified successfully with minimal intervention. In addition, physical changes can be made to make environments safer for older adults.

To a certain extent, personality characteristics can influence how individuals cope with such changes. Those who score more highly on conscientiousness tend to see such age-related changes in vision as a challenge that needs to be overcome (Casten et al., 1999): something to master rather than submit to.

Smell and taste

Smell and taste are both affected as we age (Margrain & Boulton, 2005). The threshold for taste sensitivity increases. A number of physical changes account for this loss, including altered function in taste receptors and tongue structure. Changes within the olfactory system contribute to loss of sensitivity to different smells. This is largely due to structural changes within the olfactory epithelium. How such change manifests differs greatly across individuals. It does appear that smell is affected to a greater extent than taste. Changes to both sensations can be worsened if the individual is a smoker, and some medications impede sensitivity here as well.

Such loss can prevent individuals detecting noxious tastes and smells either in their food or in the environment. Both taste and smell play a major role in nutritional habits, especially in terms of choices made and overall appetite. Loss of these senses can result in poor nutrition (Schiffman, 1997).

Touch

Sensitivity to touch is reduced, with the resultant effect that threshold for pain increases (Meisami, 1994). Touch refers to the ability to detect changes in pressure as well as temperature. Impact on sensitivity differs depending on location. Detection threshold is lowest at the fingertips, lips, and tip of the tongue. The ability to detect movement and limb position is also reduced. This has important implications when considering the incidence of falls among older adults.

As mentioned pain detection is affected. There is a great deal of individual difference here, not only in the actual ability to detect such physical sensations, but also in a person's willingness to report pain (Harkins & Scott, 1996). A degree of habituation may have taken place, thereby reducing disruption from pain. With age there is the increased likelihood that people will experience chronic pain as a result of an ongoing health condition. Obesity is a particular concern here (McCarthy et al., 2009). This may make the detection of additional pain from an entirely unrelated, acute condition very difficult.

The need to cope with chronic pain is relatively common among older adults. Despite this, the majority of these individuals are able to maintain an independent existence, although performing everyday tasks does become more of a challenge (Covinsky et al., 2009). Pain has a strong effect on cognitive functioning, producing a number of noticeable deficits (Weiner et al., 2006). It is again important to take this into consideration when cognitive functioning is assessed, as pain, like many other health-related conditions, exerts an independent effect, thereby confounding performance.

Hearing

Hearing loss is common as we age (Aldwin & Gilmer, 2004). One of the most widespread complaints is a reduced sensitivity to higher pitches – a condition called presbycusis. Presbycusis can occur as the result of a number of changes occurring in the inner ear (Margrain & Boulton, 2005): sensory (degeneration of receptor cells in the cochlea), neural (loss of nerve fibres, including spiral ganglia), metabolic (strial atrophy), or mechanical (atrophy of inner-ear structures). The cause of the condition is important as it determines what aspects of hearing are affected (Whitbourne, 1996): sensory presbycusis has the least impact; neural presbycusis makes it very difficult to understand speech; metabolic and mechanical presbycusis causes reduced sensitivity across all pitches.

There are important quality of life issues associated with varying degrees of hearing loss. Among those with some form of hearing impairment, performance of everyday tasks and activities becomes increasingly disrupted (Dalton et al., 2003). Of greatest concern is the impact of hearing loss on a person's ability to communicate (Fook & Morgan, 2000). Older adults tend to express increased difficulty understanding speech. Often words are misheard or confused, and this can lead to speech being misinterpreted. One only has to imagine having a conversation with one's doctor to appreciate how such problems may raise levels of anxiety. Misunderstanding what has been said compounded by a lack of an appropriate response on the patient's behalf due to lack of clarity can quickly lead to the formation of an inaccurate clinical picture.

Independence is also likely to be affected. Among other things, the individual will be less responsive to potentially aversive events occurring in their environment and will be unable to respond appropriately to auditory prompts, such as fire alarms. Emotional responses to changes in day-to-day functioning are important when considering the impact on a person's quality of life. Depression and loss of self-esteem are linked to hearing loss, as is an increased likelihood of growing social isolation.

Tinnitus is reasonably common too. This refers to the condition where noises are perceived by the individual in the absence of external stimulation. Certain medications can induce this state, as can the build-up of wax in the ears. Often it is the result of exposure to loud noise or head injury. The noise experienced is possibly the result of increased bursts of neural firing or hyper-sensitivity (Cacace, 2003), although it is still poorly understood.

Balance problems become more of an issue as we get older. Balance is regulated by the vestibular system in the inner ear. Older adults frequently report feeling dizzy (light-headedness) or experiencing vertigo (spinning sensation). These feelings increase the likelihood of falls (Dickin, Brown, & Doan, 2006). Some age-related changes to the vestibular system may account for some of this, but such feelings may also occur because it takes longer for older adults to integrate various streams of sensory information (Aldwin & Gilmer, 2004).

Cardiovascular system

Major changes occur to both our cardiovascular and respiratory systems as we grow older. Both systems provide vital functions, damage to which will greatly impede our ability to function in the manner to which we are accustomed.

Taking first the cardiovascular system, fatty deposits occur around the heart. At the same time muscle tissue and heart valves are slowly becoming replaced by stiffer connective tissue. The wall of the left ventricle thickens, thus resulting in a reduced capacity to pump the same volume of oxygenated blood as it used to (reduced diastolic function). That means the remaining muscle tissue has to work harder to maintain the same activity (Nikitin et al., 2006). Changes occur throughout the circulatory system. Arterial wall, for example, become less elastic as the result of calcification and deposits of cholesterol.

In combination, such changes greatly reduce the amount of physical exertion a person is capable of carrying out. By the time we reach 65, our aerobic capacity (the maximum amount of oxygen able to be transported by the blood) and our cardiac output (volume of blood pumped per minute) have dropped extensively; roughly 40 per cent below that of young adults (Betik & Hepple, 2008). This is dependent to a great extent on our physical fitness throughout our adult lives.

Cardiovascular disease

The risk of developing cardiovascular disease increases as we age, with higher rates occurring in men up to the age of 75. Two of the main risk factors associated with this condition are also on the rise, namely diabetes and obesity.

Congestive heart failure

Cardiovascular disease can take many forms. Congestive heart failure occurs as the result of a reduction in the heart's capacity to contract ('Congestive heart failure', 2008). It is no longer able to meet the demands made by the body. Heart muscle may enlarge (described as being hypertrophic). The inevitable end result is failure of either one or, as is common, both ventricles. Angina pectoris occurs when insufficient oxygen reaches the heart, producing the characteristic referred pain in the chest. It is classified as referred pain because pain is experienced at a site that is different from the actual damaged organ. This happens usually in response to physical exertion.

Myocardial infarction

When the supply of blood to the heart is cut off completely, or at least greatly reduced, a person experiences a myocardial infarction. Although symptoms are comparable to those experienced with angina, they are more severe. However, chest pain may not always presage a heart attack. Individuals may suffer 'silent' heart attacks. This occurs more commonly in older adults.

Atherosclerosis

With age fatty deposits build up in arteries, and the arterial walls calcify. This is a condition known as atherosclerosis. Such deposits may hinder blood flow through the arteries. The condition is made worse as a result of an unhealthy lifestyle, such as a poor diet and smoking.

Cerebrovascular accident

When atherosclerosis affects blood supply to the brain a person may experience a cerebrovascular accident (CVA). This occurs because blood flow is prevented from reaching a section of the brain. CVAs may be caused by a blood clot which acts to block arteries in the brain. Blood vessels may also rupture, causing a cerebral haemorrhage. Depending on the severity of the CVA, and the site affected, various problems may arise. Two of the most common are aphasia and hemiplegia, problems affecting speech and paralysis of one side of the body respectively.

Hypertension and hypotension

Hypertension increases the risk of a CVA occurring. This rise in blood pressure is often the result of age-related structural changes within the cerebrovascular system. Apart from increasing the chances of cardiovascular disease, hypertension also impairs cognitive performance and kidney function among other things. This condition is often the result of chronic stress and high levels of sodium in the diet.

Hypotension may also occur, often as the result of anaemia (lower than normal level of red blood cells). The most common form is postural hypotension. Symptoms manifest if a person moves suddenly following a period of rest. The cardiovascular system is not able to respond with sufficient swiftness to deal with the change in position. As a result, not enough blood makes it to the brain in time, resulting in dizziness and nausea, and sometimes fainting. Because low blood pressure can lead to dizzy spells ('Hypotension', 2010), there is an increased vulnerability among older adults to more serious accidents as the result of fainting.

Respiratory system

A number of changes to our respiratory system go undetected as we age. The capacity of a single intake of breath decreases by around 40 per cent by the time we reach the age of 85. The efficiency with which carbon dioxide is replaced by oxygen reduces due to deterioration within the alveoli (air sacs of the lungs) (Pride, 2005).

Chronic obstructive pulmonary disease

A common respiratory complaint experienced by older adults is chronic obstructive pulmonary disease (COPD). This is an irreversible condition that leads to reduced capacity for both inspiration and expiration. Included in this are chronic bronchitis and emphysema. One of the main causes of COPD is smoking, although pollution is also implicated.

Emphysema

Emphysema develops as alveolar walls over-inflate and become damaged. Elasticity within the lungs is greatly reduced – the inevitable effect of this being a greatly compromised ability to exchange oxygen for carbon dioxide. In more serious cases sufferers can become greatly confused and disorientated as a result of the lack of oxygenated blood.

Chronic bronchitis

Chronic bronchitis often develops as the result of prolonged exposure to high levels of dust and pollution in the environment. Asthma is another condition of the respiratory system, and one that is on the increase.

Urinary system

In terms of functioning within the urinary system, glomerular filtration rate is slower in older adults (Sun et al., 2009). Glomerular filtration rate refers to the removal and reabsorption of material before it is excreted as urine. This has an important knock-on effect in terms of the metabolism of medication. It is, therefore, of increasing importance to monitor doses prescribed to older adults in order to avoid the possibility of overdosing (Wyatt, Kim, & Winston, 2006).

A common complaint among older adults concerns bladder function. The bladder increasingly becomes both less able to hold and release urine. Although the bladder does not change size, there is a change in perception such that there appears to be a need to micturate with greater frequency. Enlargement of the prostate occurs in many older males, a condition referred to as benign prostatic hypertrophy. As a result of its location it exerts more pressure on the bladder, thereby increasing frequency with which urination is deemed necessary. Mild urinary incontinence may be experienced by some, which in many cases follows a sudden urge to micturate that then results in seepage. Physical exertion can also bring about leakage of this kind.

Despite common stereotypes, little change occurs within the digestive system of older adults. Saliva production slows, as does the release of gastric juices. As with most aspects of ageing a great deal of variation occurs across individuals (O'Donovan et al., 2005).

Reproductive system

There are large and very obvious gender differences in terms of changes that occur to the reproductive system as we get older. For men change occurs gradually. This is not the case for women. The perimenopause (sometimes called climacteric) usually begins around the age of 40. During this phase menstruation become irregular and many women experience night sweats. Completion of menopause occurs around the age of 55, although there are large individual differences. This is the point when a woman's ovaries no longer produce eggs. Levels of both oestrogen and progesterone also decrease at this time. These hormonal changes often herald the onset of a range of physical and psychological symptoms, including hot flashes, headache, sleep problems, fluctuations in mood, and cognitive difficulties among other things.

The negative effects of menopause are largely due to the drop in the levels of oestrogen. Levels of this hormone (in conjunction with progestin) can be raised artificially through hormone replacement therapy (HRT). Although once seen as a way to counteract some of the more serious effects associated with this transition, HRT is now generally adopted to treat initial symptoms using the lowest effective dose in the short term only. This is because HRT does not appear to decrease the risk of developing heart disease as previously thought. However, it is still highly effective as a method of preventing osteoporosis following menopause (Marshall, 2004).

For men, as already mentioned, change is gradual. The main process involves a drop in testosterone levels (Seidman, 2003), a phase referred to as andropause. Sperm production also declines (Parker, 2009b). Changes to the structure of the prostate gland result in its enlargement. With this comes the possibility that the urinary tract becomes obstructed. Prevalence of prostate cancer is also higher in middle age.

Endocrine and immune systems

Endocrine system

The endocrine system is responsible for controlling many bodily functions. It achieves this through the secretion of hormones into the bloodstream. The system itself is controlled by the hypothalamus and the anterior section of the pituitary gland. Foremost among the endocrine glands are the pituitary gland (located in the brain), the thyroid gland (found in the neck), the adrenal gland (situated in the abdomen), and the sex gland ('Endocrine system', 2008). Hormones are involved in a number of processes, from digestion through to bodily growth. They also contribute to homeostatic function.

Age impacts on this system by altering the level of hormones secreted by different glands. Activity of both growth hormone and insulin-like growth factor-1, a related hormone produced in the liver, result in what is called somatopause of ageing. This is linked to the various physical changes that occur with age, such as loss of bone minerals, decreased muscle mass, and so on (Lombardi et al., 2005). Cortisol, produced by the adrenal gland, is secreted during times of stress. Cortisol helps mobilize the body for action. There is some evidence to suggest that cortisol levels rise as we grow older – the glucocorticoid cascade hypothesis – which result in a loss of neurons in the hippocampus (Angelucci, 2000). This has a negative effect on the cognitive function of older adults (Comijs et al., 2010).

Under the control of hormones located in the thyroid gland, the basal metabolic rate slows once we reach middle age. This is the causal mechanism behind the much vilified middle-age spread that occurs, where weight is gained even though caloric intake is unchanging. The condition, subclinical hypothyroidism, found in a small proportion of older adults results in a range of cognitive deficits (Hogervorst et al., 2008).

Sleep wields much influence over many activities. The hormone melatonin plays a fundamental role in controlling the sleep–wake cycle. This hormone is secreted by the pineal gland situated in the brainstem. This then impacts on the body's circadian rhythm, which is known to fluctuate as we age (Mahlberg et al., 2006). Melatonin supplements may have a role to play in treating sleep problems (Gubin et al., 2006), although there is a need to examine its effects further before it is widely adopted.

Immune system

The immune system is an essential part of the body's ordnance against disease and infection. With age this line of defence begins to break down as the result of immune senescence (Dorshkind et al., 2009). Both T cells and B cells become less effective at destroying antigens, the result of which is heightened sensitivity to infection (Grubeck-Loebenstein, 2010).

The brain

This next section explores some of the main changes that occur in the brains of all of us as we age. Our understanding of what goes on has been enhanced by the continued advancement of neuroimaging technology. Techniques such as magnetic resonance imaging are non-invasive and allow us to explore the functions associated with specific brain structures. Structural changes within the brain, along with potential concomitant changes in function, influence behaviours across a person's lifespan, affecting the entire spectrum of human behaviour, be it cognitive, social, or emotional. Neuroscience is useful as a tool to evaluate the effectiveness of different intervention strategies alongside behavioural measures (Colcombe et al., 2003). I shall, therefore, describe some of these changes and in doing so refer to specific technologies that have facilitated our knowledge and understanding in this field. To begin with I shall provide a brief overview of some of these tools.

Neuroimaging

Structural imaging techniques work by making use of the fact that different tissues consist of different physical properties. Techniques such as computerized tomography (CT) and magnetic resonance imaging (MRI) produce a range of static images of these structures. Functional imaging techniques work by making use of the postulation that localized changes in physiological activity is the result of neural activity. Techniques such as positron emission tomography (PET) and functional magnetic resonance imaging (fMRI) enable the production of real-time dynamic images of brain activity so that we can see what is happening when the brain is engaged in a range of different tasks. PET focuses on the change in blood flow to a specific region, whereas fMRI examines the concentration of oxygen in the blood. Although both techniques provide an indirect indicator of activity, not neuronal activity per se but change in blood flow or oxygen levels, they do offer a great deal of flexibility as both a research and a diagnostic tool. In contrast, techniques such as electroencephalography (EEG) and magnetoencephalography (MEG) measure activity (electrical and magnetic respectively) generated by the actual neurons.

Different perspectives

As with other disciplines a number of different approaches to neuroscience exist (Cabeza, 2004). The neuropsychological perspective concerns itself with comparing brain activity and function in patient groups of any age with those of healthy older controls. Abnormal changes in brain structure as the result of pathological disorders produce changes in cognitive functioning. Should the cognitive deficits apparent in the healthy control group be comparable to the patient sample, it is possible to argue that such behavioural changes reflect the same changes to underlying brain structure. An alternative to this is the correlational approach. This is where attempts are made to associate a specific cognitive function with a specific region or structure. As the name suggests this perspective attempts to find associations and so there is often uncertainty surrounding the validity of such links. The activation imaging approach aims to make explicit the link between a particular behaviour and a specific underlying brain activity. This technique measures changes in brain activity whilst a range of cognitive tasks are carried out.

The impact of age on cognitive function is something that affects us all, thus, there has been a real focus on exploring this through research, not only in terms of abnormal changes within the brain but also changes in the typically ageing adult. Advancements in imaging technology now act to inform existing cognitive theories of functioning. Amid growing concern regarding an ever-ageing population, there is a vanguard of research exploring ways to identify abnormal changes in brain pathology early on in order to better diagnose conditions, such as Alzheimer's disease, thereby widening treatment options (Leveroni et al., 2000). More of this, however, in Chapter 12.

Cerebral cortex

Having briefly looked at the main tools on offer to help explore changes within the brain, we shall turn our attention to changes in specific regions of the brain. The first to consider is the cerebral cortex.

Changes in the cerebral cortex have been much studied. The cortex comprises two separate hemispheres linked by the corpus callosum. Research has identified a number of specialities associated with each hemisphere, thereby indicating asymmetry of function. Language is primarily a left hemisphere activity, although this appears to be related to handedness. The majority of right-handed individuals show left hemispheric dominance over language. In contrast, the right hemisphere seems to be dominant for the processing of visual-spatial information (Filley, 2002).

As a result of a number of physiological changes that occur in the brains of older adults – such as loss of neurons, loss of white matter, increase in neurofibrillary tangles, and beta-amyloid plaques – brain functioning is less efficient. In order to compensate, specialization within hemispheres decreases (Cabeza, 2002). Asymmetry is no longer as defined. This is because comparable structures in the contralateral hemisphere are recruited in order to stave off potential decreases in functioning that would be present in the normal asymmetrical brain.

The role of the frontal cortex has intrigued researchers, especially in relation to age-related changes in cognition. The frontal lobes are essential for higher-order cognitive functioning. Such executive functions allow us to plan, modify, and monitor our actions across the entire gamut of human behaviours.

Frontal lobe theory of ageing

Research that explores age-related changes in brain functioning has tended to focus largely on frontal lobe activity – the frontal lobe theory of ageing

(Buckner, 2004). The main finding from this research shows a lower rate of activity within both the prefrontal and medial-temporal regions of the brain (Grady et al., 1995); regions of the brain intrinsically linked to a range of cognitive activities. Such under-recruitment of the prefrontal cortex is evidenced by a failure to adopt effective encoding strategies as a means to improve recall. It is important to note that, although such under-recruitment does occur on recall tasks, when advised on the use of strategies to improve the encoding of material, age differences disappear (Logan et al., 2002).

When comparing the performance of younger and older adults across a range of cognitive tasks, it is clear that, rather than age being associated only with decreased frontal activity, patterns of neural activation in different regions also differ. When examining performance on tasks that involve verbal working memory, for example, scans of younger adults show focused activity in the left prefrontal cortex. Scans of older adults during the performance of the same task highlight bilateral activation rather than unilateral activation, meaning both left and right prefrontal cortices are being recruited to perform the same task that required only the left hemisphere in younger adults (Buckner, 2004; Park & Reuter-Lorenz, 2009). This, therefore, results in an increase in frontal activity as opposed to a reduction in activation as previously seen. An explanation for such bilateral input continues to elude researchers. A plausible reason is that older adults recruit more sites as a way to compensate for deteriorated performance as the result of age.

Default network

A recent approach to this body of research has demonstrated that there are age-related differences in brain activity during rest compared to activity during the performance of a specific task. The pattern of brain activity observed at rest is referred to as the default network (Park & Reuter-Lorenz, 2009). Activity within this default network is suppressed in younger adults when faced with a challenging task to complete. This appears not to be the case with older adults (Grady et al., 2006). As a result, there is an overall increase in frontal activation when active processing is required (Reuter-Lorenz & Cappell, 2008).

An influential model here is that of the scaffolding theory of ageing and cognition (STAC) (Park & Reuter-Lorenz, 2009). It is hypothesized that high functioning is maintained despite age-related decline in various systems as the result of a variety of compensatory mechanisms. Additional brain areas are recruited to compensate for age-related decline in functioning in order to improve efficiency of functioning and maintain performance. Although such fluidity in response may be positive as a means to offset decline, scaffolding in this manner is less efficient, and may eventuate in poorer overall performance. It is posited that this is evidence of brain adaptation.

We shall return time and again to how age-related changes in cortical function impacts on our behaviour. Subsequent chapters will examine in more depth other changes to brain structure that affect how older adults function.

The nervous system

This next section focuses on changes that occur within the nervous system. It has long been acknowledged that there is an important interplay between the nervous system and the immune system (Lupien et al., 2009). The field of neuropsychoimmunology is growing in our quest to better understand the role of mind and body in establishing our overall health and wellbeing. Vitamin E and protein appear to improve immunologic functions in older adults, as does regular exercise (Aoi, 2009; Mocchegiani et al., 2008; Senchina, 2009). Prolonged stress has the opposite effect (Gouin, Hantsoo, & Kiecolt-Glaser, 2008).

Much of what occurs within the brain as a result of age happens at the neuronal level. Neurons transmit and receive information throughout the body. Information is received first by dendritic processes before being relayed to the cell body. On conversion into an electrochemical impulse, this impulse is transmitted down the axon towards the synaptic bouton. Because there is no physical connection information is passed on to the next neuron through the release of neurotransmitters into the synapse.

Neurotransmitter pathways

Age-related changes occur within various neurotransmitter systems. One such system is that of the dopamine pathway. With age, levels of dopamine decrease. Excessive loss of dopamine-producing neurons is linked to the development of Parkinson's disease. Parkinson's disease is a movement disorder that is characterized by tremors, rigidity, poor balance, and a shuffling walk. This condition will be explored in greater detail in Chapter 12.

The acetylcholine neurotransmitter system also undergoes change, again with a decline in production occurring over time. Most common of the problems associated with this decline are memory difficulties (Katz & Peters, 2008). There is a great deal of interest in this neurotransmitter system, largely because of the role it plays in both Alzheimer's disease and Huntington's disease.

White matter hyperintensity

As we have seen, structural changes in the brain include changes in brain volume and density. Another indicator of age is changes in white matter hyperintensity (WMH). The white matter consists of myelinated axons. Myelin improves both the speed and the efficiency with which neural signals are conducted. WMH reflects demyelination and/or neural atrophy (Nordahl et al., 2006).

Shrinkage clearly occurs. However, such loss of volume does not occur equally throughout the brain. Instead, areas particularly affected are the prefrontal cortex, the hippocampus, and the cerebellum. The sensory cortices, on the other hand, are relatively preserved (Raz & Rodrigue, 2006). White matter deteriorates also. Diffusion tensor imaging (DTI) is a technique that measures water diffusion throughout the white matter. In doing so it provides an index of structural integrity within the white matter (Park & Reuter-Lorenz, 2009). WMH is associated with deficits in cognitive performance (De Groot et al., 2002). Changes in hippocampal volume affect memory (Rosen et al., 2003). In addition, loss of volume in the frontal lobes is linked specifically to impairment of executive function (Buckner, 2004; Raz & Rodrigue, 2006). By comparing the findings from both cross-sectional and longitudinal studies of ageing there is good evidence to show that increases in WMH result in poorer executive functioning (Cook et al., 2004).

Intra-individual variability

When looking at within-person variability white matter is of particular importance. Within-person variability, or intra-individual variability, refers to examining variation within individuals across trials. It is thought that intra-individual differences reflect neurophysiological integrity. Damage in such areas, as detected by WMHs during MRI scans, impact greatly on performance efficiency (Kivipelto, Soininen, & Tuomilehto, 2002). These changes often result in slowed reaction times and an increase in within-person variability. Bunce et al. (2007) provide evidence to show that deterioration in nerve transmission within the frontal cortex is associated with greater intra-individual variability.

Intra-individual variability decreases from childhood to adolescence, then increases once more during late adulthood. These reductions during adolescence and early adulthood reflect a concomitant reduction in the density of grey matter and the process of synaptic pruning (Gogtay et al., 2004; Sowell et al., 2003). These morphological changes in the brain likely eventuate in improved efficiency within the nervous system. Changes in grey matter in older adults may also have comparable effects (Raz et al., 2004). Changes in white matter volume also follow the same inverted U-shaped development curve (Paus, 2005; Williams et al., 2005) with higher levels of degradation being associated with higher levels of variability.

The efficiency of neural transmission through noise attenuation is important also, again leading to a more efficient system. Age-related changes in the modulation of neurotransmitter systems, including the cholinergic and dopaminergic systems among others, add to this level of neural noise, contributing as a result to greater levels of intra-individual variability (Backman et al., 2006; Cohen & Servan-Schreiber, 1992; Hultsch, MacDonald, & Dixon, 2002).

Cholinergic pathways are seemingly responsible for efficient inhibitory control (Edginton & Rusted, 2003). The type of variability observed in cognitive performance, including among other things lapses of attention, suggest a deficit in inhibitory control, thereby hinting at the involvement of the cholinergic system. Dopamine is involved in a number of different domains, including the performance of cognitive tasks (Backman et al., 2006), especially higher-order cognitive processing activities (Park & Reuter-Lorenz, 2009). Numerous techniques have indicated that there is a decline in functioning within the dopaminergic neurotransmitter system as we age (Backman et al., 2006). The resultant effects of such decline manifest as poorer recall of personal memories (episodic memory) (Backman et al., 2000) and problems with short-term (or working) memory (Erixon-Lindroth et al., 2005). Performance on tasks that require fewer attentional resources remain relatively intact.

Plaques and tangles

Age exerts a number of effects on our nervous system, although in the majority of cases, behavioural changes are subtle in the typically ageing adult. One characteristic of normal development involves the production of neurofibrillary tangles in certain regions of the brain. These are intracellular clusters of neurofibrils consisting of insoluble tau protein. These tangles are believed to act as a barrier to energy metabolism, the transportation of nutrients, as well as cellular communication. Difficulties often arise when attempts are made to delineate normal from abnormal ageing. The presence of neurofibrillary tangles is a case in point as, although they occur in the typically ageing adult, they also form an essential component for a positive diagnosis of Alzheimer's disease *post-mortem*.

Amyloid plaques, often called neuritic plaques, may also develop in the synapses. These plaques comprise an accumulation of degenerative neuronal tissue. At its core is beta-amyloid. Plaques therefore interfere with neural transmission and may also be the cause of localized cell death. A high concentration of such plaque formation is not evident until advanced age is reached.

Up to that point a high concentration of amyloid plaque is indicative of neu-rodegenerative disease (Nordberg, 2008).

To compensate for loss of neurons, there is both a lengthening of and an increase in the number of dendritic processes in surviving neurons (Matus, 2005). In addition, neuronal plasticity reduces the impact of structural change on everyday functioning (Goh & Park, 2009).

Body temperature

As a whole little change occurs within the autonomic nervous system. However, the regulation of body temperature and frequency of sleep complaints do become more apparent with age.

It becomes increasingly difficult to gauge our body's core temperature the older we get (Van Someren, 2007). This means people often fail to notice they are actually cold. To compound this our ability to raise core body temperature – the vasoconstrictor response – is greatly reduced (Degroot & Kenney, 2007). Conversely, when the temperature is high, less notice is taken largely due to a reduced sweat gland output in response to heat (Kenney & Munce, 2003). Thirst sensitivity is reduced so that, under such conditions, older adults are less inclined to rehydrate with water (Phillips et al., 1991). This means that older adults are more at risk from both hypothermia and hyperthermia during extreme weather conditions (Kenney & Munce, 2003).

Sleep

Although there is little truth in the myth that older people require less sleep (Ancoli-Israel & Cooke, 2005) – in fact, extensive sleep (in excess of nine hours) has been associated with higher risks of mortality (Chen et al., 2008) – it is clear from evidence that sleep problems are reasonably common among older adults and manifest as difficulty falling asleep, nocturnal awakening, waking early, and subjective feelings of a poor night's sleep (Wolkove et al., 2007). EEG sleep patterns change such that a longer time is spent in Stage 1 sleep (the transitional stage into sleep) at the expense of both Stage 4 (slow-wave) and rapid eye movement (REM) sleep (Kamel & Gammack, 2006).

When looking at the endocrine system it was indicated that age affects a body's circadian rhythm. Studies have demonstrated a clear shift among older adults to seeing themselves as 'morning people', in the sense that they have a preference for carrying out chores and activities during the day rather than in the evening (Hasher, Goldstein, & May, 2005). This subjective shift obvi-ously reflects a physiological shift as a result of changes in sleep and arousal patterns (Benloucif et al., 2004). Such a shift in arousal among older adults is important to consider when assessing cognitive functioning to ensure no systematic bias occurs that work against this population (Rowe, Hasher, & Turcotte, 2009).

The impact of poor sleep on everyday functioning is well established. All aspects of our daily routine are affected. The symptoms of poor sleep include lowered mood, poor concentration, fatigue, and poor motivation (Ancoli-Israel & Cooke, 2005). These subjective complaints mirror physiological changes that occur with age. The sleep–wake cycle changes from a two-phase pattern – where one is awake during the day and asleep during the night – to a multiphase pattern – where a person takes a number of naps during the day and spends less time asleep during the night.

Sleep apnea may also occur. Sleep is disturbed as a result of this condition because a person momentarily stops breathing during sleep as the result of a partial obstruction to airflow during inhalation as the result of snoring. This can occur many times during the night. Under these conditions there is a need for the heart to work harder to compensate for the cumulative lack of oxygen that occurs with each obstruction in airflow. The resultant effect being that there is a rise in blood pressure during the night. There is often a concomitant rise during waking hours. This increases risk from heart attack and stroke. Other factors that degrade both sleep time and sleep quality include mood disorders and poor physical health.

Summary

What happens to us physically as we age is fundamentally important to how age affects us psychologically. A number of theories exist that attempt to explain why we age. Which provides the most likely explanation is debateable. One thing that is clear and undeniable is the transformation our body undergoes over time. Changes in our physical size and shape impact on our health, both physical and mental. It is also, as we shall see in a later chapter, an area of much controversy with society's ever-growing obsession with appearance issues (see Chapter 14).

Our senses are something we all take for granted and as such their centrality to our lives rarely provokes comment until these systems begin to decline in function. Decline in sight and hearing in particular influence our ability to effectively register and process information we receive across a vast range of situations. The impact here on cognitive functioning cannot be underestimated.

Loss of capacity or functioning may occur across a number of different vital functions, including the cardiovascular, respiratory, urinary, endocrine, and immune systems. These have major implications again in terms of a person's overall health and well-being and can be a major source of impediment for many older adults, especially in terms of one's ability to continue leading the life one is used to. Enforced changed is, as we will see in Chapter 10, a source of much consternation in this population.

The final sections of this chapter looked at changes within the brain and the nervous system. As with all other systems described earlier, subsequent chapters will continue to refer back to biological changes in order to provide a context for the various psychological aspects of ageing we shall consider. This is especially the case for neurological changes. The impact of age here has a profound effect in terms of a person's ability to function on a day-to-day basis. There are also clear links here when considering the impact of disease processes on behaviour, as in the case of dementia (see Chapter 12).

Further reading

Farley, A., McLafferty, E., & Hendry, C. (2011). *The physiological effects of ageing.* Oxford: Wiley-Blackwell. [For those looking for a comprehensive guide to the physical effects of ageing this is ideal.]

Greenfield, S. (1997). *The human brain: A guided tour.* London: Weidenfeld & Nicolson. [An excellent and engaging account of the human brain. A must for those interested in the neural underpinnings of behaviour.]

Kirkwood, T. B. L. (1999). *Time of our lives: The science of human ageing.* London: Weidenfeld & Nicolson. [An interesting and very readable account of the ageing process.]

CHAPTER 3

Basic Cognitive Processes

In the previous chapter age-related changes to sensory systems were discussed. This chapter will, in part, focus on the role of cognitive processes that relate to the processing of sensory information. In particular there will be a focus on basic perceptual and attentional processes. A number of theories exist that attempt to link sensory detection and cognitive processing. Some argue that this link becomes increasingly strong as we move into older adulthood (Baltes & Lindenberger, 1997). Others have argued that the type of cognitive impairment observed cannot be explained purely on the basis of a decline in sensory function (Anstey, Luszcz, & Sanchez, 2001; Lindenberger, Scherer, & Baltes, 2001). However, regardless of just how much sensory systems contribute to these problems, it is clear that such organs of detection are vital for a range of both simple and complex cognitive operations, from basic sensory processing through to memory and language (Schneider & Pichora-Fuller, 2000; Wingfield, Tun, & McCoy, 2005), as well as contributing to independence and well-being (Marsiske, Klumb, & Baltes, 1997). It, therefore, provides the background material that will be needed when we consider more intricate cognitive operations later on.

Before focusing on attention it is important to consider again what happens at the cellular level and how this determines cognitive processes. One question to consider here is whether ageing is merely development in reverse or whether it is more complicated than that.

Development in reverse

A paper by Craik and Bialystok (2006) examined the changes in cognitive functioning that occur across the lifespan and compares those to the physical changes that take place. Physically we are more vulnerable at the two extremes of our lives: infancy and older adulthood. In contrast, our youth and adulthood are times of independence and vitality. When looking at structural changes within the brain, as seen in Chapter 2, there is an increase in weight and size until maturity is reached. This reflects the proliferation of synaptic connections between neurons (grey matter) as well as an increase in myelination of nerve tissue (white matter). On reaching adolescence grey matter begins to reduce as the result of synaptic pruning. This is because learning is taking place. The individual is developing more effective and efficient ways of doing things through continued interactions with their environment. The ages at which grey matter volume changes occur differ across the various regions of the brain, with peak volume appearing at the age of 12 in the frontal and parietal lobes, at 16 for the temporal lobe, and age 20 for the occipital lobe (Giedd et al., 1999). From early adulthood, then, grey matter volume starts a steady decline, initially as the result of pruning, but later due to neural atrophy.

Changes in white matter as the result of myelination are largely controlled by genes. This process occurs first in the brainstem and spinal cord before propagating into subcortical and cortical areas. Again this process of myelination differs across brain regions. Indeed, myelination within the frontal cortex continues through a person's late twenties and early thirties. In conjunction with the lateral temporal regions, the prefrontal cortex is closely connected to higher-order thinking (Casey et al., 2005). Although it is the last area to develop, the frontal cortex is the first to be hit by age-related decline (Raz, 2000; West, 1996). The white matter in this region is at higher risk from damage from lack of blood supply as well as neural atrophy. White matter integrity alongside the combination of profuse synaptic connections and appropriate pruning are important determinants of processing efficiency.

It has been suggested that what happens to the brain as the result of the ageing process conforms to this same pattern and is, in fact, the development process in reverse. However, this fails to do justice to the changing dynamics of cognitive functioning over time. Rather it would be more accurate to conceive deficiencies in performance to be the result of an incomplete attainment of knowledge in children, whereas for older adults deficits arise because of difficulties accessing stored knowledge (Craik & Bialystok, 2006).

Sensory processes

In Chapter 2 we examined the physical changes that may occur to various sense organs. Our ability to respond and adapt to our environment is something we all take for granted and, indeed, perform on a daily basis. In order to carry this out effectively and efficiently we need highly responsive sensory organs. These organs provide us with the much needed information concerning vision, hearing, touch, smell, and taste. The accuracy with which this information is picked up, and the proficiency with which it is processed, has major implications further down the line in terms of cognitive functioning.

Signal detection theory

Sensory organs each have a threshold at which information is registered. Too little stimulation means the signal goes undetected. Organs differ also in terms of sensitivity. The greater the level of sensitivity to a particular stimulus, the lower the threshold required to detect a stimulus. The intensity of stimulation required for a stimulus to be detected 50 per cent of the time is referred to as the absolute threshold.

It is not just intensity of a stimulus that affects thresholds, however. For example, pitch and frequency influences thresholds for auditory stimuli: the threshold for low-pitch tones is less than for high-pitch tones in older adults. In terms of vision, colour plays a role here: older adults show lower thresholds for red, orange, and yellow compared to other colours.

When assessing sensory activity it is important to consider individual response styles as these play a major role where information processing is concerned. The signal detection model is important here (Green & Swets, 1966). There is a tendency for us to become more cautious as we grow older (Botwinick, 1984). Using the terminology of signal detection, older adults are less likely to detect a signal that is not present; in other words, they make fewer false alarms. However, it is likely that some target items will pass undetected; therefore increasing numbers of misses are made. Because of this, sensitivity to specific stimuli could be underestimated in certain circumstances.

Perception

Many things happen following the initial registration of a stimulus by a sensory organ. The process of perception refers to how the brain interprets a particular stimulus. It may be defined as the process whereby information received is organized and interpreted ('Perception', 2008). Perception is not only influenced by the intensity of the stimulus, but also by how much attention is directed towards the stimulus, our store of knowledge, our expectations, and also our emotional state. Perception then informs what happens next in terms of further processing and action. This entire process takes place out of sight, reflecting as a result the complex inner workings of our brains.

However, various methods have been developed in an attempt to at least quantify some of these hidden processes.

Reaction time

One vital measure is that of reaction time. This is a measure of the elapsed time between the onset of a stimulus and our response (Townsend, 2005). A number of different versions of reaction time measures have been devised, each exploring different aspects of our response system. Simple reaction time tasks present a single stimulus which requires only one response. With choice reaction time tasks, participants are presented with two stimuli, with a separate response required for each of these. Complex reaction time tasks extend this further by presenting three or more stimuli, with each item requiring a different response.

There are two component processes behind all reaction time measures: premotor time and motor time (Botwinick, 1984). Premotor time reflects the length of time between stimulus onset and the point at which a motor response is initiated. Motor time is the amount of time from the point of response initiation to completion of the response. Premotor time is largely hidden, whereas motor time can be accurately measured though electromyographic measurements (Kausler, 1991). It has been estimated that reaction time comprises mainly premotor time (84 per cent), with only 16 per cent reflecting motor time (Botwinick, 1984), thereby indicating that reaction time assesses central processing operations in the brain.

Level of complexity

As you might expect, reaction time becomes slower the older we get. Such changes provide a great deal of insight into cognitive functioning (Salthouse, 2007), especially in terms of everyday behaviours. An important determinant of this slowing in response time is the inherent complexity of the task. The more complex the activity, the more time needed to respond (Verhaeghen, 2006). Salthouse (1991) proposed the age-complexity hypothesis. When comparing performance of young and older adults across a range of reaction time measures, the relative slowing shown by the older adults increases with growing complexity, from simple reaction time measures to complex reaction time tasks, thereby mirroring the level of central processing required.

The factor determining increasingly slower response on reaction time measures may be general cognitive slowing, although it is likely that a number of factors play a part in such age-related changes as seen in, for example, perceptual processing and memory (Cerella, 1994; Salthouse, 1996).

Stimulus persistence

A highly influential theory, the stimulus persistence theory (Birren, 1974), argued that cognitive slowing was the result of a slowing down in the speed with which information is processed centrally in the nervous system. Once registered by a sensory organ, the time needed to process this information takes longer in the older adult. Subsequent stimuli occurring close to the initial stimulus would be processed in a less efficient manner because the individual would still be processing the initial stimulus.

One method for exploring this is to measure critical flicker fusion threshold (Botwinick, 1984). When presented with a series of light pulses where rate of presentation is manipulated, rather than seeing a series of individual pulses, there comes a point when the participant reports seeing a continuous light. In other words, the pulses are presented so quickly that they blend into each other. This is referred to as the critical flicker fusion threshold. With age, this threshold has been shown to decline (Kline & Scialfa, 1997).

Attention

Having looked at sensory processing and perception, it is now time to turn our attention to, well, attention. How empty our lives would be if the processes of attention did not take place. As we shall see, some of these functions occur with little or no conscious awareness; other activities require us to consciously determine where our attention should be targeted. Attentional processing will affect how quickly we are able to register and respond to stimuli in the environment. Age exerts a considerable effect here.

There are a number of different ways to consider cognitive slowing among older adults. An often used method is to graph response times of older adults against those of younger adults. These are called Brinley plots (Brinley, 1965). On the whole, the relationship is a linear one (Verhaeghen, 2006). Age-related slowing in cognitive function is in fact proportional, such that estimates of performance for an older adult group can be predicted from the response times of a younger group by multiplying these scores by a specific constant. Constants range from around 1.2 up to 1.8 depending on how complex the activity is, indicating that older adults are around 40 per cent slower than young adults. This means that as tasks become more demanding, and more processing time is needed, the gap between younger and older adults becomes ever wider.

Information processing

An information-processing approach is often adopted when looking at cognitive function. A computer metaphor is used to provide an account of how we deal with multiple sources of data. Within this metaphor we are seen as being receivers of information from our surroundings. This information is then transferred to the brain for transformation and subsequent encoding. Information processing occurs in a number of different stages. A key component process is that of attention. One of the founding fathers of cognitive psychology, and one of the most eloquent writers in the field, William James (1907, p. 265), captured what is meant by 'attention' when he explained that

> Every one knows what attention is. It is the taking possession by the mind, in clear and vivid form, of one out of what seem several simultaneously possible objects or trains of thought ... It implies withdrawal from some things in order to deal effectively with others, and is a condition which has a real opposite in the confused, dazed, scatterbrained state which ... is called distraction.

A number of models of attention have been offered to account for the changes that occur as a result of ageing. Attention refers to our capacity to filter out certain information and instead to focus on specific stimuli of our choosing. Such a mechanism is needed as it would be impossible to process everything that our senses receive (Vecera & Luck, 2002), even though there is a self-serving, evolution-driven temptation to try to do so in order to maintain vigilance and make use of appropriate opportunities when they arise. Instead we need to focus on what is relevant to our current goal-state in order to ensure efficiency and coherence of activity over time (Allport, 1989; De Pisapia, Repovš, & Braver, 2008). Rather than there being one central reservoir of attentional resources, research has shown there to be multiple stores of attentional resources, each with its own domain of operation (e.g. Cowan, 1995).

Bottom-up and top-down processing

The concepts of both bottom-up and top-down processing are prevalent within cognitive psychology. In the instance here presented, bottom-up processing, sometimes called data-driven processing, refers to the situation where what we attend to is determined by the environment, in this case, sensory stimuli. Top-down processing refers to the situation where there is a conscious decision about what should be attended to and what should be filtered out. Under such conditions our mental representation of objects and situations come into play helping us make sense of the stream of information being presented, and thereby assisting us in determining what to focus on in order to fulfil our current goal. Because top-down processing relies on stored information our expectations about what is and what is not appropriate in the current situation exerts a major influence.

Reduced capacity or deficit in inhibition?

The reduced attentional resources/capacity model argues that there are fewer attentional resources available as we grow older (Salthouse, 1991). This would explain why deficits only become apparent as task complexity increases. Processing becomes less efficient and more errors are made due to the fact that the individual's processing capacity has been exceeded.

Hasher and Zacks (1988) proposed an alternative account – the inhibitory deficit model. Rather than there being a decline in available resources, deficits observed in older adults are the result of a reduced ability to inhibit irrelevant information when performing a task. Because vital attention is allocated to the processing of distractors, insufficient capacity remains to process the target activity.

Experimental examination of attention has concentrated on three broad categories of activity, namely sustained, divided, and selective attention (Kausler, 1994).

Sustained attention

Sustained attention is often referred to as vigilance. Such activity requires an individual to monitor a situation without a break, being always ready to detect a change that may occur in a largely unchanging environment. Such activity takes its toll leading inevitably to states of fatigue. Due to their repetitive nature and fatigue-inducing character, errors occur with reasonable frequency. When looking at age differences on vigilance tasks, there is little to define a difference between older and younger adults on simple tasks. In fact, less mind wandering occurs in older adults (Giambra, 1989). When task complexity is increased, or when the frequency of change increases, older adults start to make more mistakes (Rogers & Fisk, 2001).

Divided attention

When attention is required to be split between different activities it is said to be divided. Divided attention is typically assessed using the dual-task paradigm. This is where participants are required to perform two tasks at the same time, thereby ensuring that they attend to both activities constantly. A good example of this would be talking on a mobile phone whilst driving. Because there is a finite supply of attentional resources, when attention is divided between two concurrent activities, performance on one of the tasks will suffer. Older adults tend to perform less well in such situations (Verhaeghen & Cerella, 2002).

Where performance is affected, it is referred to as a dual-task cost. This effect has been observed among older adults when they are required to learn a list of words whilst simultaneously standing still. Shifts in a person's centre of gravity corresponded to fluctuations in the attentional demands of the task (Rapp, Krampe, & Baltes, 2006); the more demanding the task, the more unstable the person becomes maintaining their position. The evidence from most studies shows a shift in priority where effort is expended in order to maintain balance as the cognitive load increases. This is likely because the actual costs of falling far outweigh the cost of forgetting the odd item.

Task switching

Divided attention can also be assessed in tasks where participants are required to shift attention from one task to another. Such task-switching activity is common to us all. In an age of burgeoning multimedia it is not uncommon to switch attention from reading a book to respond to an email or a text and back again. We do this type of activity all the time with little awareness. However, each time we make such a switch there is a small cost in terms of response time.

There are various ways of measuring this cost. If one were to measure the cost in terms of calculating the difference in time taken to switch between two activities and the time taken to perform each activity in isolation, this would be an assessment of the global cost. This then provides an indication of the effort needed to perform both activities. An alternative would be to assess local cost which is where one focuses on performance under the task-switching condition only, comparing response time when a shift is made with response time when no shift was required. In this sense, this provides a measure of the demand as a result of correctly selecting the target task and inhibiting the non-target task. When looking at age differences here discrepancies are larger for older adults compared to younger adults in terms of global costs, with little difference evident when comparing local task-switching costs (Verhaeghen & Cerella, 2002).

Selective attention

Although dual-tasking is an intrinsic part of everyday life, there are times when we need to focus on one thing (the target) without this focus being disrupted by other things occurring around us (distractors). This is called selective attention. Our capacity to do this does appear to be affected more as we grow older, especially when presented with more difficult situations where attentional demands are high. One explanation for this is a greater proneness to interference as a result of a deficit in inhibitory control. In other words, older adults often find it increasingly difficult to constrain behaviour, and as a result they are susceptible to external distraction.

Intra-individual variability

Most research looking at cognitive function compares performance across a variety of participant groups. Data are analysed in terms of changes in mean scores, sample variances and covariances. Change in mean scores is ideal when comparing, for example, patient groups where cognitive deficits occur with a control group where performance is unaffected. However, focusing on mean scores may not be particularly informative when the emphasis of the study is change within the individual over time. At a sample level there may be no significant difference in performance over time. This is not to say that there are no changes in the performance of individuals, only that when viewed as a group changes average out across the sample – increases cancelled out by decreases – resulting in them not being significant.

There are a number of alternative ways of exploring such data. One way is to look at the degree of divergence within samples. This can provide an indication as to whether groups become more similar with time or whether they tend to diverge (Preece, 1982). In other words, do groups become more homogeneous or more heterogeneous? It has been demonstrated that variations in processing speed diverge during middle age (Martin & Zimprich, 2005).

A method particularly suited to the study of cognitive functioning in older adults is that of intra-individual variability. The neurophysiology relating to this was discussed in Chapter 2. An example of intra-individual variability would be an examination of trial-by-trial changes in a measure of reaction time within each individual. Such analysis, in contrast to means-level analyses, provides a more accurate estimate of performance (Hultsch & MacDonald, 2004; Jensen, 1992). Among older adults levels of intra-individual variability are higher (Hultsch, MacDonald, & Dixon, 2002; Rabbitt et al., 2001). This is most pronounced in perceptual motor tasks.

A number of studies have linked intra-individual variability to, among other things, biomarkers of ageing (such as visual acuity) (Anstey et al., 2005; Li et al., 2001; Strauss et al., 2002), as well as showing a clear predictive capability in terms of risk of mortality (Shipley et al., 2006). This all suggests that such variation provides an accurate index of central nervous system integrity (Hedden & Gabrieli, 2004; Hultsch & MacDonald, 2004). Greater levels of intra-individual variability are shown on tasks mediated by the frontal cortex (Bunce, Warr, & Cochrane, 1993; West et al., 2002).

This metric is useful when looking at the performance of individuals with mild cognitive impairment, as well as for those diagnosed with dementia (Christensen et al., 2005). There are clear patterns of variability also for different subtypes of dementia, thereby reflecting varying involvement of the frontal cortex (see Chapter 12).

Visual attention

The previous sections have looked at attention in general. This section will focus solely on visual attention. Visual attention is of fundamental importance in terms of everyday cognitive functioning. A great deal of cognitive activity occurs automatically, with little, if any, conscious thought. Visual attention is no exception. The underlying mechanisms become increasingly apparent when demands of the task exceed our ability to process the information. When this happens, we have to consciously direct our attention to specific activities whilst at the same time inhibiting responses to others.

An important component process of visual attention is selection. This involves focusing attention only on specific stimuli whilst also integrating important components for additional processing. Visual orientation refers to our ability to make use of our capacity to predict events before they unfold in order to better focus attention on the intended target. Target detection is quicker and more accurate following the presentation of a cue indicating the position of the target – an example of covert orienting.

Field of attention

An important contributor to cognitive functioning is the size of one's attentional field. An often used measure to assess this is the visual search task. Age effects become increasingly apparent when there is an increase in the number of distractor items. This would indicate that the attentional field is slowly shrinking as the result of age. Such changes in field size have clear implications for the performance of everyday activities. A good measure of this is the useful field of view task (Owsley et al., 1998). This task requires participants to first fixate on the middle of the screen. They are then instructed to detect changes occurring within their visual field – namely registering the presentation of either target or distractor stimuli. Results from this task indicate clear age differences such that older adults perform less well than younger comparison groups. Indeed, performance on this task demonstrates predictive capability when compared to the frequency of car accidents experienced by this age group (Owsley et al., 1998).

Detecting movement

When looking at the perception of movement, it is clear that it requires a whole host of complex cognitive operations. This level of complexity aptly mirrors its importance in terms of our everyday life. The need to accurately perceive and process motion underpins almost all tasks carried out on a daily basis. It is not surprising then to find that a great deal of the visual sensory cortex is given over to the processing of motion. As motion processing is clearly fundamental to how we are able to deal with a range of daily activities, there are understandable repercussions in terms of quality of life when the processing of such activity declines. Advancing age is associated with increasing impairment in motion perception (Hutchinson et al., 2012). Among older adults visual impairment has a number of real-life implications, including among other things increasing the likelihood of suffering falls and the subsequent risk of serious injury (Harwood, 2001).

When examining such things in real-life settings an important concept to consider is that of global motion. Global motion refers to an overall perception of motion in a group of objects regardless of the individual trajectories of component items. In other words, it is a perception of coherent movement. A swarm of bees may be seen to head off in a particular direction, although on closer inspection individual members of this swarm may in fact be on opposing trajectories at any particular moment. The higher the coherence, the more likely one will detect global motion.

There is much evidence to show older age is associated with a reduced ability to detect motion (Ball & Sekuler, 1986). There is some evidence to suggest a gender difference here also such that older women are more susceptible to problems of motion detection (Gilmore et al., 1992). Such motion studies generally use random dot kinematogram (RDK) patterns. These comprise individual dots. Depending on the experimental condition, varying numbers of these dots move in the same direction (signal), whilst the remaining dots move randomly (noise). Studies that have focused on age effects have tended to use one specific type of RDK stimuli, specifically where signal dots move along a translational trajectory (up/down or left/right). Few such studies have examined complex optic flow where, for instance, signal dots move radially (towards the edge of the circumference or towards the centre) or rotate (clockwise or anti-clockwise). Where studies have used these techniques there is little agreement in the findings. It has been argued that complex motion stimuli are not appropriate for older samples because processing changes may reflect age-related changes in contrast sensitivity rather than reflecting changes in global motion perception (Allen et al., 2010).

Perceptual learning

A number of physical changes occur to the eye as the result of age as has been discussed in the previous chapter. However, it is often the case that such physical changes prove insufficient as an explanation for such myriad visual problems experienced by older adults, suggesting instead deficits within the visual pathway.

Studies such as those presented previously indicate the need in some instances for interventions to help older adults deal with the visual problem they face. One way would include visual perceptual learning. Perceptual learning leads to an improvement in how a person perceives and reacts to visual stimuli as a result of specific training (Fahle, 2005). This results in task-relevant information being selected more efficiently (Gibson, 1969). Such training has been shown to improve visual performance. Indeed, there is adequate plasticity within the adult visual system to benefit from such training (Sagi, 2011), and there is indeed evidence of this in samples of older adults. However, few studies have been conducted in this area (Ball & Sekuler, 1986).

I shall end this chapter with a little digression into the role that neurotransmitters play in attention. Although briefly described in Chapter 2, I would like to expand a little here on the role of two key neurochemicals that are behind much cognitive functioning, namely acetylcholine and noradrenaline. They are in no way the only neurotransmitters to impinge on cognition; however, they are the most relevant to the material presented in this chapter.

Neurotransmitter function

Neurotransmitters underpin a great deal of cognitive function, be it in terms of mechanisms of attention or the impact of mood on performance. In fact, they provide the premise for the use of various drugs to treat a range of conditions from depression to dementia. Neurotransmitters are a basic component of information processing in that they transmit information by traversing the synaptic cleft as part of the nerve impulse. Once across the gap these neurotransmitters then bind to the appropriate receptors on the post-synaptic neuron. A number of key neurotransmitters have been isolated. These include acetylcholine, noradrenaline, dopamine, and serotonin. When examining visual processing, it is the first two that appear vital.

Cholinergic neurons occur throughout the body. When stimulated these neurons release acetylcholine. One such class of neurons only appear within the peripheral nervous system, such as within the autonomic division, thereby affecting the innervation of sweat glands. Other classes of cholinergic neurons occur within the central nervous system. The central nervous system consists of the brain and the spinal cord. Some of these neurons are located in the striatum and retina. Others appear in the basal forebrain, a cluster of subcortical nuclei that project to cortical and limbic areas of the brain. The presence of cholinergic neurons in the basal forebrain is significant here because they develop axonal projections to the hippocampal formation via the medial septum. Similarly, the nucleus basalis magnocellularis is also situated in this area, and it too innervates the amygdala and neocortex (De Rosa & Baxter, 2005; Wenk, 2005). Cholinergic pathways support a great deal of high-level cognitive functions, in particular attention and memory.

Psychopharmacological research has demonstrated memory to be impaired when participants receive a drug, such as scopolamine, which is known to decrease cholinergic activity. In addition, drugs such as caffeine have been shown to improve vigilance on cognitive tasks that are dependent on the basal forebrain cholinergic system (Christopher, Sutherland, & Smith, 2005; Sarter, Givens, & Bruno, 2001). Cholinergic neurotransmitter pathways are also affected by Alzheimer's disease and are, therefore, implicated in the marked cognitive decline associated with this condition. Indeed, there is growing awareness that some of the higher-order deficits associated with Alzheimer's disease may be the result of degraded visual information processing (Tales & Porter, 2009).

Noradrenaline is another important neurotransmitter here. Again, it occurs both peripherally and centrally. Within the central nervous system clusters of noradrenergic neurons populate the lower brainstem and pons, the largest of which is the locus ceruleus. From here noradrenergic cells innervate all regions of the brain (Wenk, 2005). As with acetylcholine, noradrenaline is implicated in higher-order processes such as learning and memory, and also in more basic, low-level functions such as arousal. Evidence from psychopharmacological studies again demonstrates the important of this neurotransmitter in everyday cognitive operations. Administration of the drug clonidine induces states that mimic sleep deprivation (Smith et al., 2003). This is because clonidine is a noradrenaline antagonist – in other words, a drug that reverses the effects of noradrenaline. When clonidine is administered, reaction times are seen to increase dramatically. Because caffeine exerts an effect on both the cholinergic and noradrenergic neurotransmitter systems, it is able to reverse such low arousal states (Christopher et al., 2005).

Summary

This chapter has focused on emphasizing the importance of basic cognitive processes in our everyday lives. Indeed, there has been a recent shift of focus in Alzheimer's disease research such that researchers are now examining basic cognitive processing in addition to higher cognitive function in this patient group. This is because there has been growing evidence of clear deficits in these fundamental processes (Tales & Porter, 2009). Impairment at this level cannot fail to impact on higher-order operations.

The field of cognitive psychology has contributed considerably to our understanding of the ageing process. The types of basic sensory and perceptual processes described are often the building blocks of more complex functions. We have seen how deficits in function here impact on a person's ability to deal with everyday tasks and activities, be it in terms of slowed reaction times or a lessened ability to deal with increasing task complexity.

Attention is vitally important to many, if not all, the processes we shall be exploring shortly in Chapters 4 to 7. If you were to reflect on many of the activities you perform on a daily basis, you will soon discover that pretty much all involve, either singly or in combination, some element of sustained, divided, or selective attention. The most obvious example would be the increasing expectation for multitasking. For example, just typing this paragraph I have had two email prompts (it is marking season), a calendar reminder (albeit to remind to do what I am actually doing), and a message from my computer informing me that something or other is using a great deal of my PC's resources. In fact, it is becoming increasingly clear that people very rarely do one thing at a time anymore. The all-pervasive presence of technology has ways of making you attend.

The final section was a tiny foray into the importance of neurotransmitters to such basic cognitive operations. I focused here on two neurotransmitters that play a major role in attentional processes. The whole field of psychopharmacology will be explored further in Chapter 12 when looking at how drugs are used to control and treat a range of conditions.

Further reading

Johnson, A. & Proctor, R. W. (2004). *Attention: Theory and practice.* London: Sage [This is a great general text on attention and is an excellent resource for those interested in cognitive psychology.]

Pinker, S. (1997). *How the mind works.* London: Allen Lane, 1997. [For a more relaxed read, Pinker's excellent tour of the mind is highly recommended.]

Salthouse, T. A. (2010). *Major issues in cognitive aging.* Oxford: Oxford University Press. [This is a recent text from one of the major figures in the field of cognitive ageing. A must for those interested in this area.]

CHAPTER 4

Short-Term Memory

A great deal of research focuses on problems with long-term memory – our ability, in other words, to access a lifetime's acquired knowledge, to recall important events in our lives, and so on. Before tackling this, however, it is important to explore how short-term memory is affected. For the purpose of this chapter the models of working memory will be used primarily to explore the type of problems associated with normal ageing. Working memory may be conceptualized as dealing with the manipulation, integration, and short-term storage of information. The previous chapter on basic cognitive processes is important here. Without such mechanisms active working memory operations would suffer greatly. We need effective sensory systems and intact attentional control mechanisms for working memory to operate effectively.

At the end of this chapter I shall focus a little more on the frontal lobes. This region of the brain is intimately involved in many working memory activities and is central to all higher-order executive functions. It is key also in terms of our ability to function successfully in everyday life (see Chapter 7). The final section will focus on some recent research that has examined executive function in older adults using neuroimaging technology.

Working memory

To begin with, then, it is important to consider what we mean by short-term memory. When talking about short-term memory we are referring to discrete cognitive systems that have limited storage capacity – limited both in terms of how much is stored and how long it is stored for. Early pioneers of cognitive research demonstrated that the capacity of short-term memory is finite. The most elegantly simple demonstration of this was presented in the classic paper by Miller (1956) 'The Magical Number Seven, Plus or Minus Two: Some Limits on Our Capacity for Processing Information'. It was clear also that there is a time limitation to storing such material. Unless appropriate

58

rehearsal strategies are deployed, information will be permanently lost (Atkinson & Shiffrin, 1968).

Much more common now is the concept of working memory. Working memory not only reflects the type of temporary storage of information in limited capacity systems described in the previous paragraph, but it also concerns the active manipulation and integration of data streams, as well as more higher-order self-monitoring operations (see Chapter 6).

The Baddeley and Hitch model

There are a number of competing theories of working memory. However, for the purpose of this chapter, and indeed this book, I shall largely be referring to the model proposed by Baddeley and Hitch (1974). The Baddeley and Hitch model advanced our understanding of short-term memory. Rather than it being a set of passive stores, Baddeley and Hitch argued that one function of working memory was to enable multiple streams of information to be held in our mind so that the material could be analysed and manipulated. In doing so this argument better reflected the complexity of human cognitive processing, be it in terms of reading and comprehending written text, attempting to find a solution to a puzzle, and a host of other dynamic thought process that occur throughout each day of our lives. The original 1974 model has undergone a number of revisions over the past 40 years.

Phonological loop

Working memory, therefore, consists of components that process domain-specific information, specifically verbal and visual–spatial information. The phonological loop is concerned with processing auditory material. It offers the capacity for the transient storage of material. Unless refreshed, through the process of sub-vocal rehearsal, all trace will be lost. The role of the phonological loop is wide-ranging. One of its main functions lies with the processing of language. It also plays a central role in performing mathematical operations (Gathercole, Lamont, & Alloway, 2006). Areas within the parietal lobe are associated with storage and maintenance of information required for online processing (Thompson & Madigan, 2005). Tasks requiring input from the phonological loop activate the left temporal lobe as well as parts of the frontal lobe (Baddeley, 2006).

Visuo-spatial sketch pad

A similar component was proposed for the temporary storage and processing of information concerning visual appearance and location of objects in space.

The visuo-spatial sketch pad is involved a great deal in day-to-day cognitive activities. One obvious area is that of navigation (Logie & Della Sala, 2005). There are strong links with the phonological loop, such that verbal information is often encoded as mental imagery (Baddeley, 2006). Tasks with a strong visual component activate regions within the occipital lobe (Baddeley, 2001). It is clear also that visual and spatial processing often requires input from the frontal lobes (Logie & Della Sala, 2005).

The proposition that there are separate processing domains within working memory provided an explanation as to why it is possible to perform a verbal task and a visual–spatial task simultaneously without hindrance (Baddeley & Hitch, 1974). It is equally clear that performance can quickly become disrupted if we attempt to execute two very similar tasks at the same time. In the first instance the two tasks activate two separate components, each drawing upon their own pool of attentional resources. This refers to the concept that there are separate attentional resources for different modalities of task activity (Navon & Gopher, 1979). However, when two tasks compete for the same limited pool of resources evidence of our limited finite capacity become all too apparent.

Central executive

The ability to direct and juggle different processing tasks concurrently reflects the operation of a third component, the central executive. The central executive oversees all cognitive activity. It integrates information from both the phonological loop and sketch pad, as well as from the episodic buffer and long-term memory (see later section). It does not act as a memory store itself. The central executive is responsible for directing attention, for planning, and for coordinating behaviour (Baddeley, 2001). Part of this process is the inhibition of irrelevant information. The concept of higher-order executive function is something that will be examined at different stages throughout this text. Underpinning a great deal of this activity are the frontal lobes (Baddeley, 2006). This will be explored further near the end of this chapter. As a proviso it is important to remember that, although frontal activity is often linked fundamentally with executive function, other regions of the brain are involved in such activity, thereby reflecting the complexity of these operations. The frontal lobes act to orchestrate this activity in order to produce appropriate coherent action.

Episodic buffer

As mentioned, although the central executive is concerned with manipulating and combining information, it does not act as a store. The episodic buffer, on the other hand, does. It provides the nexus for information processed in the phonological loop and visuo-spatial sketch pad, as well as material from long-term memory. The buffer, therefore, provides a mechanism for such integration of information from different modalities (Baddeley, 2000).

Having described the working memory in some detail, the rest of this chapter will focus on how advancing age interferes with its operation. In doing so we shall examine each component of Baddeley and Hitch's model in turn.

Working memory and age

Phonological loop

There is a decline in both verbal and visual–spatial memory span due to age. However, taken in the wider context of cognitive decline, this is a minute change (Parkinson, Inman, & Dannenbaum, 1985; Spinnler et al., 1988). What does become apparent is that, as tasks increase in complexity and cognitive demand, age-related deficits become more prominent (Craik, 1986). Such tasks require the type of active manipulation of information that occurs within working memory.

Research has indicated that working memory is indeed affected as we grow older. However, what is not clear is exactly how it is affected. One example is that of digit span. In this task participants are presented with increasing numbers of digits which they are required to recall in the correct serial order. On average older adults have been shown to have a digit span of 7.1 items, whereas younger adults are slightly higher with 7.6 digits (Bopp & Verhaeghen, 2005).

In the sentence span task participants are presented with a series of sentences which they are asked to verify in terms of credibility and then, on completion of this phase, they are required to recall the final word from each sentence. There does appear to be age-related effects associated with this task, although the magnitude of the effect is quite small (Verhaeghen, Marcoen, & Goossens, 1993). It has been suggested that the age-related effect is not in fact due to either the processing or storage components of working memory, but is instead the result of a reduced ability to inhibit irrelevant information (Hasher & Zacks, 1988; May, Hasher, & Kane, 1999), a process that reflects involvement from the central executive.

Visuo-spatial sketch pad

Obtaining evidence of visuo-spatial span can be problematic. This is largely because, although on the surface the task may appear visual or spatial in nature, there is a cultural bias in Western societies to encode such information verbally. In comparison to studies focusing on age effect with verbal working memory, few to date have focused on visuo-spatial working memory. One study did show age-related effects similar to that seen in verbal working memory (Park et al., 2002). However, it was not possible to separate visual working memory from spatial working memory in this instance.

A more recent study found there to be only a weak relationship between age and performance on either visual or spatial working memory measures (Shaw, Helmes, & Mitchell, 2006). In the case of visual working memory the relationship was not statistically significant. When comparing this performance to that on a verbal working memory task, it was found that there was a significant age effect on the verbal task. It was noted that performance on the verbal task was, however, better than on either the visual or spatial measures. One potential explanation for this is that the visuo-spatial tasks were more demanding of the central executive. Because of this they were more difficult to perform, thereby explaining poorer comparative performance overall.

One task that seems to be particularly effective in assessing the visuo-spatial ability of older adults is the jigsaw puzzle task (Vecchi & Richardson, 2000). This task involves presenting fragments of a picture which are individually numbered. Participants are required to indicate on a grid where each piece should appear. The focus is on active manipulation of the fragments presented such that participants attempt to reconstruct from them the original picture. Memory load is minimized as the various fragments are visible to the participant throughout the task. When comparing performance on this task across different age ranges, clear differences were apparent. On the whole the older participants tended to make more errors and took longer to respond in each instance than the comparison groups. Performance here indicates that there are problems with the manipulation and integration of information as a result of age (Cornoldi & Vecchi, 2002).

An area of growing interest in this field looks at the effects of age on a person's ability to bind related material. Binding refers to the process that allows us to develop a cognitive representation of a particular stimulus. For example, such representations contain various components of information, such as colour, shape, orientation, and so on. Accurate recall of information requires that all this information about an object is readily accessible. Previous research has identified that binding of surface features is relatively intact as a result of age (Brockmole et al., 2008), whereas object-location binding is affected (Cowan et al., 2006). Comparable findings were seen in a more recent study (Brown & Brockmole, 2010).

Central executive

A reduced ability to inhibit irrelevant material may be related to an observed decline in their ability to maintain concentration on a specific activity

(Backman & Molander, 1986). Other studies have shown that older adults experience greater difficulties when they are required to keep track of multiple streams of information (Charness, 1985). There is a great deal of evidence demonstrating impairments under dual-task conditions (Riby, Perfect, & Stollery, 2004). A range of tasks has been used. Good indicators of overall working memory span are tasks where digits or words are presented for recall, but interspersed within this presentation is an additional task, such as assessing the accuracy of a mathematical statement or grammatical precision of a presented sentence. Age differences occur here such that working memory span for older adults is around three items, whereas younger adults retain around four (Bopp & Verhaeghen, 2005). Such tasks are dynamic, requiring the processing of different streams of information.

Dual-task activity is under the aegis of executive control processes (Baddeley, 1992). The extent to which executive control is required depends on the characteristics of the individual tasks, as well as the degree of overlap between primary and secondary tasks. Older adults experience greater problems with dual-tasking than do younger adults (Tun & Wingfield, 1995). This is backed-up by objective experimental data (Hartley & Little, 1999). The ability to dual-task has important implications in terms of a person's ability to maintain independence into older adulthood.

Early studies looking at age-related differences in dual-task performance utilized cross-sectional designs. When comparing performance of each task separately, then again when both tasks were combined, clear age differences were detected (Broadbent & Gregory, 1965). Such differences were largely the result of older adults focusing on one task and neglecting the other (McDowd, Vercruyssen, & Birren, 1991). Age effects were generally larger with tasks of increasing complexity (Wright, 1981), although other studies have failed to support such findings (McDowd & Craik, 1988). When accounting for age differences in single task performance, Salthouse, Rogan, and Prill (1984) showed that there was again evidence for age-related impairment. Being asked to perform concurrent activity during encoding seems to be more detrimental in older adults. This may be because encoding is in itself cognitively demanding (Anderson, Craik, & Naveh-Benjamin, 1998). Similarity between both tasks also has an impact on retrieval (Fernandes & Moscovitch, 2000).

One argument put forward to explain poorer dual-task performance in older adults is that of lack of practice. However, a number of studies have been conducted where both younger and older adults engage in a variety of training sessions in dual-task activities. The general finding is that age differences remain despite such training (McDowd, 1986).

Li, Krampe, and Bondar (2005) explored an ecological approach to study dual-task performance in older adults. This account draws inspiration from Baltes and Baltes (1990) selective optimization with compensation (SOC) model. From this perspective we constantly adapt to the various changes in the environment, be it an opportunity to develop, or a need to respond to a particular restraint. Such changes differ across the lifespan. The SOC model is concerned with the selection of appropriate goals, optimizing performance, and compensating in the face of loss. The SOC model is particularly helpful when looking at changes in cognitive and motor functioning with increasing age.

It has been argued that, in order to offset some of the deficits that occur with motor function as the result of age, such activity comes increasingly under the control of cognitive processes. Sensorimotor activity such as maintaining balance, a highly automatized action sequence, has been shown to demand increasing cognitive resources as we age (Woollacott & Shumway-Cook, 2002). On the whole, sensorimotor functions are given priority, often at the expense of cognitive performance (Li, Krampe, and Bondar, 2005). Such prioritization is particularly prominent under dual-task situations. This then can be seen to form the basis of a more ecologically valid method of exploring dual-task performance among older adults. When older adults are required to perform a demanding cognitive task, as opposed to a less demanding task, whilst at the same time swinging their arms, it takes longer for postural stability to be regained (Stelmach, Zelaznik, & Lowe, 1990). Comparable findings have been demonstrated in older adults when examining the impact of cognitive load on fluctuations in weight distribution when asked to stand still (Maylor & Wing, 1996). Through various manipulations of difficulty of both cognitive and sensorimotor task, it is clear that the priority given to sensorimotor activity is not the result of a failure to grasp the cognitive task (Li, Krampe, and Bondar, 2005). In terms of one's overall safety and well-being such prioritization is highly adaptive.

Falls among older adults is particularly prominent. Most falls occur when performing normal everyday activities (Tinetti, Speechley, & Ginter, 1988). There is a large cost associated here also, with falls often resulting in injury, fear, even death on occasion (Simoneau & Leibowitz, 1996). Studies have demonstrated that reduced blood flow within the frontal cortex is associated with posture and gait problems in patients with Alzheimer's disease (Nakamura et al., 1997). There is also a higher incidence of falls in Alzheimer's patients (Buchner & Larson, 1987). Teasdale has argued that a lack of postural stability in older adults is the direct result of an inability to direct appropriate attentional resources to overcome any disturbance in balance when under dual-task conditions (Teasdale et al., 1992).

Age-related deficits in executive function have been demonstrated on a range of tasks including, among others, the Wisconsin Card Sorting Task (see later for more details) and the Stroop test (Mittenberg et al., 1989). It has been argued that tasks requiring some form of executive control are affected by an overall decline in the speed with which information is processed (Salthouse, 1996). When processing speed is taken into consideration, age effects largely disappear on such tasks (Salthouse, Babcock, & Shaw, 1991). However, this is not the case for all tasks. There is good evidence that improved speed of processing through explicit training leads to enhanced overall performance (Ball, Edwards, & Ross, 2007). The issue of cognitive training will be examined in more detail in Chapter 14.

Executive function can be subdivided into a number of related yet discrete activities. This is often referred to as fractionation (Baddeley, 1996). Various accounts of how such activity is subdivided appear in the literature. Miyake argues that executive function comprises three separable activities: the ability to allocate attention to different sub-tasks (shifting); ensuring the accuracy of material processed in working memory (updating); and preventing the intrusion of irrelevant responses (inhibition) (Miyake et al., 2000).

Research focused on the effect of ageing on executive function has indicated that a process of dedifferentiation may occur with age. Indeed, structural equation modelling approaches – a method of statistical analysis where the effects of a construct are evaluated through the combination of proxy measures – indicate a model containing two sub-component processes to best fit data under these conditions, with shifting and updating forming one latent variable, and inhibition the other (Hedden & Yoon, 2006). Both latent variables were independent from memory and speed of processing.

A great deal of research exploring the effects of age on working memory has focused on inhibition as a potential indicator of individual differences in performance. The argument is that inhibitory processes prevent irrelevant information from entering working memory and thereby prevent the limited attentional resources and capacities associated with this system being directed to processing material that does not relate to the task at hand (Harnishfeger & Bjorklund, 1993; Hasher & Zacks, 1988).

A similar model to that described previously was identified using structural equation modelling (Adrover-Roig et al., 2012), although this time inhibition was not identified as a separate factor. Instead a two-factor solution was suggested consisting of (1) maintaining information in working memory and (2) access to long-term memory. Speed of processing was identified as a mediating variable. The implication is that inhibition is not a single, easily identifiable operation (Friedman & Miyake, 2004).

The process of dedifferentiation may be delayed in some individuals as the result of various adaptive or compensatory mechanisms, such as cognitive reserve – the notion that decline in cognitive function can be offset by tapping into a buffer zone of spare capacity (Reuter-Lorenz & Cappell, 2008). The concept of factors that offset the impact of cognitive ageing is discussed further in Chapter 14.

Before moving on to look at long-term memory, a number of times I have referred to executive function. An area of the brain that is unquestionably entwined with this activity is the frontal lobes. This next section will explore this region in more depth.

Frontal lobes

In terms of explanations based on neuroanatomical changes, it is clear that the frontal lobes play a fundamental role in attention and how it is allocated to different tasks. However, although the last to develop, the frontal lobes are highly susceptible to the effects of normal ageing (Craik & Bialystok, 2006). In this way, they are the most evolutionarily advanced sections of the human brain (Kemenoff, Miller, & Kramer, 2002). This area of the brain allows us to regulate our behaviour, to interact at a social level, and to develop a sense of self-awareness (Stuss & Floden, 2005).

The frontal lobe model developed out of studies utilizing neuroimaging techniques that show cerebral blood flow in this region to decline earlier than in other parts of the brain. Regional cerebral blood flow is taken as an indicator of neural activity in different areas of the brain. A reduction in blood flow to a specific area would indicate loss of function. In conjunction with this, the rate at which neural tissue is lost is higher in this region of the brain compared to others (Kramer et al., 1994).

Although the role the frontal lobes play in cognition will be addressed at various points throughout this book, it is important to acknowledge here their central involvement in almost all aspects of everyday life, be it planning, making decisions, juggling more than one activity, or preventing an impulsive action. The frontal lobes are essential for all forms of higher-order, or executive, functions.

The frontal lobe model argues that performance difficulties will occur on tasks that require some degree of frontal involvement. Indeed, evidence does seem to suggest this. A good example is performance on the Wisconsin Card Sorting Test (Grant & Berg, 1948). Each card has printed on it a different shape, and the number of same shapes appearing on each card also differs. The shapes are printed in different coloured ink. Participants are initially instructed to sort the pack of cards either by colour, shape, or number. Once the participant shows they have successfully acquired that rule by not making errors, the rule is then changed. In this type of card sorting task, older adults made more errors when instructed to change the criteria for sorting a set of cards. Rather than changing their mode of response, they continued sorting according to the previous criteria (Kramer et al., 1994). In other words, they were unable to inhibit a previous pattern of responding in order to adopt the new rules. This is an example of perseveration. A related finding is that of 'off-target verbosity' that is observed often in older adults (Arbuckle & Gold, 1993). This refers to a tendency for verbal responses to lose focus. One explanation of this is that individuals are unable to suppress task-irrelevant thoughts due to a deficit in executive control. These thought intrusions then act to divert a person's train of thought, thereby making their responses less coherent.

Our understanding of how different areas of the brain relate to specific cognitive functions continues to grow as the result of continued advancements in neuroimaging technologies. The final section looks specifically at how imaging techniques have facilitated the development of cognitive models that better describe the impact of age on executive function.

Imaging studies

With the increasing complexity of imaging techniques there has been a rise in the number of studies exploring neurocognitive aspects of ageing. In particular, a great many studies have focused on executive functions (Spreng, Wojtowicz, & Grady, 2010). Generally, studies have demonstrated clear age differences on such tasks, especially those where cognitive load is high (Jonides et al., 2000).

Studies show a general tendency among older adults for increased activation of lateral prefrontal cortical structures when asked to perform executive function tasks (Jonides et al., 2000). Such activity likely reflects a lower signal-to-noise ratio, where there is more noise than signal, thereby necessitating increased modulation of processing activity (Persson et al., 2006). Such inefficient processing is the direct result of a number of changes that occur with age including changes in white matter, cortical thinning, and lower activation levels within the hippocampus. With age there is a shift away from automatic processing for some activities, and so there is a need for greater conscious control of attention, and as such more need of executive control. This is manifest in the posterior-to-anterior shift seen in older adults (Davis et al., 2008). This is often referred to as neural scaffolding as these lateral prefrontal regions of the brain are needed to assist with learning new material and to sustain cognitive activity when demanded by tasks (Erickson et al., 2007; Park & Reuter-Lorenz, 2009).

When using imaging techniques to examine performance on a range of working memory tasks, there are clear age differences. Among younger cohorts there tends to be increased lateral activation of the prefrontal cortex (Smith & Jonides, 1998). Among older adults, the level of activation is greater and bilateral even under low task-demand conditions (Jonides et al., 2000). This pattern of activity is thought to reflect reduced ability among older adults to enlist appropriate processing resources in order to perform a range of activities (Cappell, Gmeindl, & Reuter-Lorenz, 2010).

A recent meta-analysis carried out by Turner and Spreng (2012) focused on exploring the impact of age on functional brain changes across a range of executive function tasks. Their findings indicate that there may in fact be domain-specific changes in executive function as a result of age. Whereas some executive control tasks do result in increased dorsolateral prefrontal cortex involvement, inhibitory control does not necessitate such over-recruitment. This means processing is less efficient during this type of activity.

Summary

The development of models of working memory increasingly allows us to better comprehend the complex and dynamic system that operates when we process and manipulate information. It is clear that, far from being a passive store of items in memory for short durations, our working memory is involved in the web of processes whereby new and old information is activated, disassembled, juxtaposed, reintegrated, and generally operated upon in order to deal with the varying demands of everyday life, be it in terms of merely attempting to remember a telephone number someone has relayed to you (a ritual that is becoming increasingly rare these days) or a more complex activity such as trying to solve a particular problem that one faces.

Changes to these operations can have important implications in terms of a person's ability to live independently. It is clear that cognitive slowing is not the only force at work here. Instead a reduced ability to inhibit the intrusion of material that is irrelevant to the task at hand seems to account for some of the difficulties faced by older adults when attempting to deal with competing demands.

This chapter ended with a focus on frontal lobe activity and how vital this region of the brain is to working memory operation. Neuroimaging studies have shown that at times older adults mobilize resources to process tasks in an inefficient manner, emphasizing consciously controlled behaviour when more automatic processing would be appropriate. Here, as in later chapters, there is good evidence to show that, even though performance across a range of activities may not be as good as it once was, older adults activate a variety of strategies that compensate for such decline, thereby maintaining a respectable degree of functioning.

Further reading

Baddeley, A. D. (2007). *Working memory, thought, and action.* Oxford: Oxford University Press. [This needs no introduction. It is a highly readable text on Working Memory by the man who developed it (along with colleague Graham Hitch). Highly recommended.]

Rose, S. (2003). *The making of memory: From molecules to mind.* London: Vintage. [Another great book from the pen of Steven Rose, this time on the biological basis of memory.]

Ward, J. (2010). *The student's guide to cognitive neuroscience.* Hove: Psychology. [This is recommended to those who want to delve a little further into the neuroscience of the mind.]

CHAPTER 5

Long-Term Memory

The two previous chapters have focused on basic cognitive processes and short-term memory. As we have seen, short-term or working memory depends on a combination of basic sensory, perceptual, and attentional processes to feed its activity. Such activity is essential also for long-term memory. A stimulus needs to be sensed, perceived, and attended to before it can be processed and stored in long-term memory.

Since the 1950s, a revolutionary time for memory research, researchers have identified a number of discrete elements to long-term memory, each reflecting core aspects of a person's everyday functioning. A great deal of our understanding in this field developed from research with patients who experienced amnesia of one form or another. Many hundreds of papers have been published on individual case studies. Although now out-of-date, a most readable book by Parkin (1997) provides a comprehensive account of how research on amnesia led to our appreciation of different forms of memory systems. Such subdivisions include our capacity to store autobiographical information, retain knowledge about complex sequences of action, and to remember to do things at particular times. We also need to consider how we are able to retain facts and figures that comprise our accumulated knowledge across the lifespan.

One of the main distinctions to make is between declarative and non-declarative memories. Declarative memory refers to memories that require some form of conscious recollection. This can be further subdivided into episodic and semantic memory. Non-declarative memory on the other hand concerns memories that do not involve conscious recollection but nonetheless influence our behaviour. Examples here include procedural memory.

Episodic memory

The ability offered by episodic memory was likened by Tulving to mental time travel (Tulving, 1972). It allows us to not only relive previous experiences but to also use past knowledge to guide future behaviour. Episodic memory, as its name suggests, comprises a host of specific individual memories. It is our memories for events that occurred at a specific time in a specific place, each time with our self as the point of reference. Each experience is encoded in a manner that ensures it can be distinguished from other similar memories. Each episodic memory is also highly robust. In this sense, such memories are rich in contextual information. Episodic memories form the basis for autobiographical recall (see later section).

As we age our memory for specific events in our lives declines. The severity of the decline depends on the exact nature of the memory task performed, as well as the specific way in which memory is assessed. Not only is episodic memory as a whole compromised with age, but also processing capacity and environmental support influence the extent of the deficits experienced (Craik, 2005). Deficits in older adults are more apparent when, for example, to-be-learned material is presented for a limited duration. This is largely because cognitive processing is slower in this group and so more time is needed to perceive and adequately process material before performance compares comparably to a younger group.

When talking about any form of memory three discrete stages of processing are implied. These are encoding, storage, and retrieval. Integrity of memory will be affected should error occur at any of these stages.

The encoding phase is important as it determines the quality of the material to be retained. Various approaches can be taken at this stage. The repetition of to-be-remembered material may be sufficient for storage, a process known as rote learning. This process does not produce a distinctive memory trace as it lacks any element of further processing whereby meaning is attached to the source material.

An alternative to rote learning is that of elaborative encoding. With this approach a more distinctive trace is generated, thereby reflecting the unique qualities of the material albeit through supplementary visual or verbal embellishment. This could take the form of enhancement through visual imagery or semantic clustering of the material: for example, forming a clear picture of the item in your head or linking items in terms of specific categories. Often when presented with a list of words to remember, older adults tend to recall fewer words than a sample of younger adults. When looking at the type of strategy adopted older adults generally opt for a rote-learning approach. The result is a less distinctive memory trace that may be more prone to error later during recall.

When cued to use a more sophisticated encoding strategy, performance improves accordingly. Because older adults spontaneously choose rote over elaborative encoding they may be described as showing a production deficiency. If it were the case that they were unable to elaborate to-be-remembered material it would be an example of mediation deficiency. Production deficiency among older adults may be due to reduced cognitive resources. Adopting a more parsimonious encoding strategy is less challenging overall and less of a drain on a person's capacity (Light, 1991).

Following encoding the material enters the storage phase. Once in storage information is retained. Typical ageing does not adversely impact on the long-term storage of information, although the ability to access this material may be reduced somewhat. Future retrieval of information is greatly improved if the memory traces are organized appropriately.

Retrieval from memory can take many forms. A recall task requires a conscious attempt to retrieve specific items from long-term memory storage. Recall involves an active search of memory followed by a decision making process that ensures only relevant information is produced (Watkins & Gardiner, 1979). Cued recall again requires a conscious retrieval attempt, although this time an appropriate hint is provided in order to assist this process.

Unlike recall, recognition memory requires only the decision making phase. This is because participants are presented with the stimuli. The test of recognition memory consists of correctly identifying that the item presented formed part of the original list, for example. This decision making process relies on both recollection and familiarity. The ability to recollect an item indicates that the item is available in memory, whereas a sense of familiarity indicates a recent exposure to the material.

When comparing age groups it is usually recall memory that differentiates groups such that performance declines as a function of age. This could in part be explained by the relative cognitive load imposed by recall tasks over tests of recognition memory (Smith, 2006). The superior performance on tests of recognition memory may be explained by reference to the theory of encoding specificity (Tulving & Thomson, 1973). This states that performance will be improved if contextual information present during encoding is also present at retrieval. With tests of recognition memory the presence of previously presented stimuli provides this needed context. Such support is not available when recall is tested. Instead the person attempting to retrieve specific information must try to generate the necessary contextual information to achieve recall. This process is highly demanding of processing resources.

When comparing recognition memory for semantically related and semantically unrelated word pairs in both young adults and older adults, differences occurred in the accuracy for unrelated word pairs but not for related word pairs (Naveh-Benjamin, 2000). Such differences were not the result of attentional deficits in the older adult group but instead due to a reduced capacity to form associations between presented stimuli – the associative deficit hypothesis. This performance gap is narrowed when the memory component of the task is combined with some active manipulation of the to-be-remembered object. Participants are required to remember a list of objects, and along with each object there is a specific instruction. When comparing the performance of those who merely listened passively to the items to those who actually performed the activity, recall performance was greatly improved when the activity was carried out (Backman & Nilsson, 1984). Improved performance can be linked to the rich, multimodal encoding of material.

The impact of age on performance is generally greater in tests of recall than recognition. To some extent, this could be because of the relative paucity of environmental cues present in recall memory tasks (Craik, Byrd, & Swanson, 1987). However, recognition tests are less demanding than tests of recall.

Semantic memory

Semantic memory refers to our knowledge of facts and figures about the world in which we live. It incorporates our knowledge of language, our understanding of mathematical operations, and a host of other rules and regulations. Unlike episodic memory, semantic memories are not tied to a specific location either in time or place, and so contain no specific contextual elements.

Semantic memory is on the whole preserved as we age. In fact, it may even develop as the result of age (Giambra et al., 1995). Indeed, vocabulary is often assessed as a matter of course in studies examining the impact of age on functioning as an indicator of premorbid general ability. What does decline is the speed with which such information can be accessed (Burke et al., 1991).

Autobiographical memory

Autobiographical memory consists of memories of ourselves and how we relate to the world which we inhabit. It incorporates elements of both episodic and semantic memory, such as facts about who we are and specific episodes in our lives. It has been described as the psychological history of the self ('Autobiographical memory', 2006) and so forms a vital component of our sense of identity.

A general finding here is that older adults have rather good memory for events that took place in their life between the ages of ten and 30. This is referred to as the reminiscence bump (Rubin, Rahhal, & Poon, 1998). This effect appears to be particularly strong for positively valenced memories (Gluck & Bluck, 2007). One explanation that has been advanced relates this relative period of lucidity as being central to a person's unique identity and associated, therefore, with deeply encoded memories (McLean, 2008). These memories form part of our life narrative – the account that we each create of our journey through life, thereby reflecting what we perceive our true selves to be (Baddeley, Eysenck, & Anderson, 2009).

Procedural memory

Procedural memory reflects our ability to develop and retain a variety of skilled behaviours across our lifespan. Unlike memories discussed previously, procedural memory is not open to conscious inspection. In this sense, where the memories discussed previously may be referred to as declarative, procedural memories are non-declarative.

As we have seen, we often make the assumption that with advancing age comes general decline, and memory is a prime example. However, we have also seen that this may not always be the case. Take as an example procedural memory, such an assumption here would be fallacious. Not only are a lifetime's skills retained but also new ones can be developed (Smith et al., 2005). Retention of procedural memory often acts as an effective compensatory mechanism, offsetting deterioration in psychomotor speed and working memory functionality to ensure maintained performance (Mireles & Charness, 2002).

Implicit memory

When talking about procedural memory a distinction was made between it and the types of memories previously discussed. The difference concerned the subjective experience of these memories. Procedural memory occurred outside of conscious awareness. Implicit memory shares this same feature such that previous experience affects performance even though the individual is not aware that this is happening. This type of memory is often demonstrated by word stem completion tasks. Such tasks require participants to study a list of words and, rather than being instructed to recall as many words as possible from the original list, participants are presented with word fragments which they have to complete. Participants are more likely to complete the word fragments using one of the words to which they were exposed originally.

There does appear to be a clear age-related decline in how people are affected by priming activity, such as that assessed by stem-completion tasks. In the case of stem completion, participants study a list of words. The test phase consists of the first few letters from each stimulus item followed by a blank space. Participants are required to complete each stem as they see fit. Fewer completions made by older adults involve items that were part of the original list, demonstrating a weaker priming effect. Fewer age differences are observed in tasks where, for example, participants are required to decide whether the stimulus is a real word or a non-word (Light et al., 2000), indicating the importance of elaborative encoding.

In some situations implicit memory effects appear to be stronger. One such task where this effect is prominent requires participants to process a list of unfamiliar names. This list is then superseded by another. Instructions this time inform the participant to indicate which of these names belong to someone famous. This produces what has been called the false fame effect. Older adults make the mistake of judging as famous those names that were part of the first list of names processed (Dywan & Jacoby, 1990). However, it may be argued that this does not, in fact, reflect implicit memory. Rather, it merely indicates poor episodic memory. Responses are influenced by the greater sense of familiarity imbued by the names that formed part of the initial list.

Source memory

Being able to recall both the spatial and temporal contexts during which a particular piece of information was learned are important aspects of memory. This is referred to as source memory. Performance on such tasks does seem to be affected by age. In one study participants listened to sentences spoken by a range of male and female narrators. During the presentation the written text was also presented, as was a picture of the person narrating the material. When later asked to identify who read which sentence, retrieval of that information was poorer among the older age group (Simons et al., 2004). When emotional salience of the material is manipulated, performance of the older adult group has been shown to improve (Rahhal, May, & Hasher, 2002). Similar studies have indicated that older adults may in fact encode contextual information but experience problems utilizing that material at retrieval (Thomas & Bulevich, 2006).

Of particular importance here is memory for taking medication. It is vital that one is able to distinguish between an actual memory of taking medication at a specific time from an intention to take the medication. There is evidence also that a phenomenon occurs where there is a memory of something that did not happen (Dodson, Bawa, & Slotnick, 2007). Such illusory memories reflect poor source memory.

Because of this older adults are more amenable to the creation of false memories. Using the Deese–Roediger–McDermott (DRM) paradigm participants are presented with a list of words that are from the same semantic category (Roediger, McDermott, & Robinson, 1998). There are, however, no overt instructions informing them of this. Participants are then presented with a test of recognition memory. Among the distractors is the name of the semantic category describing the previously presented items. Because the original list acts as a prime, participants believe that the distractor term that defines the original list's semantic category was indeed part of this original list (Roediger & McDermott, 1995). It appears that when presented with this standard paradigm, older adults are less able to prevent a false memory from developing. The explanation offered being that older adults are less able to link content to context (Dehon & Bredart, 2004). There is evidence from imaging studies that indicate this effect to be strongest where frontal lobe functioning is impaired (Roediger & Geraci, 2007).

Impairment in source memory can have important implications in terms of being able to cope in everyday life. Problems with this form of memory would make a person more susceptible to various deceptive practices. An example of how this failure of memory could be exploited is through telephone scams (Jacoby, 1999). As part of the trick an initial call would be made during which as much personal information as possible about the individual would be gleaned. This initial call would then be followed up at a later date. The caller would refer back to previously obtained information. In doing so, they would gauge how much the person remembered of the previous conversation. If it is clear the person does not recall this conversation, the caller initiates the scam.

Discourse memory

Discourse memory is an important element of everyday life. This reflects our ability to construct a mental model of written or spoken communication. A number of physical constraints can affect this type of memory, such as hearing impairment. Controlling for obvious deficiencies invariably produces findings that show older adults to perform reasonably well on activities of this type. A number of compensatory strategies are likely mobilized to offset potential performance decline as a result of age-related changes. Knowledge of language structure offers one such advantage. This is supported by findings that show discourse memory to worsen when presented speech is manipulated in such a way as to remove any natural language-based cues (Stine-Morrow, Noh, & Shake, 2006).

When asked to provide information about previously presented narratives, older adults perform at a similar level to the age comparison groups for general thematic information, often referred to as the story's gist. However, memory for specific detail is often reduced in older adults. This drop in performance is more pronounced when the material presented is not familiar, more grammatically complex, and when rate of presentation is fast (Stine, Soederberg, & Morrow, 1996). With more complex material there appears to be a deficit in the ability to inhibit information that is of less relative importance (Hartley, 1986).

An interesting finding, and one that is important in the context of health-related behaviour, is that older adults are less likely to accurately recall information that contradicts previously held knowledge or beliefs (Rice & Okun, 1994). The relevance here in terms of learning accurate information about a medical complaint is something that should be taken into consideration when talking to patients about their condition. It is important, therefore, to accurately assess what information they currently have about the condition, evaluate its accuracy, and then identify aspects of understanding that are not accurate.

Sense of familiarity

Clear age-related differences occur when considering both a person's ability to remember items and their associated context and also their sense of knowing or familiarity with the material. This difference between 'remember' and 'know' has been replicated many times (Parkin & Walter, 1992), such that comparisons between younger and older adults show comparable performance in the 'know' condition but poorer overall performance in the older adult group for the 'remember' condition.

The remembering or recollective process degrades as we age (Light et al., 2000). Remembering is a complex process involving the ability to recall the appropriate association between the to-be-recalled item and the context in which it was learnt. This, again, reflects the associative deficit hypothesis described earlier (Naveh-Benjamin, Guez, & Marom, 2003). These metacognitive aspects to memory will be explored in more detail in Chapter 6.

Prospective memory

Our ability to remember to do something at a particular time is a facility we rely on every day of our lives. It is, therefore, unfortunate that prospective memory is particularly prone to decline with age. To perform well on prospective memory tasks, it is first necessary to remember the action that needs to be performed. Then a person is required to remember when that action needs to be carried out. This information then has to be retained over a period of time whilst carrying out some unrelated concurrent activity. It may be possible that, under certain well-controlled laboratory conditions, participants may be able to rehearse the prospective memory task if the concurrent activity is not too demanding of attentional resources. In the real world the potential for such rehearsal activity is unlikely. In everyday life such memory tasks may span several days. Because of competing demands rehearsal of the intended action would occur only intermittently.

Prospective memory can be separated into time-based tasks and event-based tasks. Time-based prospective memory requires the individual to remember to perform a specific action at a specific time. Event-based prospective memory entails a person remembering to perform a particular action in a precise situation. Although research has shown time-based prospective memory appears to decline to a greater extent in older adults (Park et al., 1997), some studies have found that, in fact, older adults perform less well on event-based tasks (d'Ydewalle, Luwel, & Brunfaut, 1999). However, such ambiguity may suggest that time-based versus event-based distinction may not be particularly useful when trying to identify age-related effects on prospective memory (Baddeley, 2009).

The lack of clarity surrounding the performance of older adults on such tasks is ameliorated to some extent when one examines findings from studies that explore prospective memory performance when embedded in a more realistic context. Under such conditions, where the intended action is included as part of a person's everyday life – such as remembering to post a card – older adults perform at a higher level than the younger controls (Rendell & Thomson, 1999). When a comparable activity was carried out under controlled laboratory conditions, the opposite pattern of results was observed.

The finding that older adults demonstrated better prospective memory in real-life situations than did the younger controls cannot be due to a greater reliance on memory aids, such as diaries, as a way to compensate for declining memory. Indeed, studies have provided explicit instructions for participants not to use such *aide-mémoires* (Rendell & Thomson, 1999). An alternative explanation for superior performance under such restrictions could be that we lead more structured lives as we grow older, thereby providing an environment more conducive to such activity. Motivation is also likely to play a role. The vagaries of our memory increasingly become a matter of intrinsic importance with age, such that performing well on these activities is assigned a higher priority among older adults than in younger controls (Baddeley, 2009).

A great deal of research into prospective memory has focused on older adults. Unfortunately, there is much variation in the findings of these studies, with some providing evidence of decline in prospective memory as a result of age, whereas others show age-related improvements (Maylor, 1996). A highly generalized explanation for such polar findings is that older adults tend to perform worse in laboratory-based studies of prospective memory, whereas performance seems to be better under more naturalistic conditions (Henry et al., 2004).

More recently Logie and Maylor (2009) conducted a large-scale Internet study of prospective memory across adulthood. The prospective memory task required participants to click on a particular image when it appeared on screen – a smiley face in this instance. The stimulus appeared 20 minutes into the session. The session comprised a range of questionnaire and cognitive performance tasks measuring retrospective memory. When presented with the initial task instructions, some participants were shown the smiley face during the instruction phase, whereas others were not. An additional manipulation presented some participants with instructions stating that the smiley face would appear 'at the end of the test' (temporal certainty), whereas others were told that it would appear 'later in the test' (temporal uncertainty).

The findings from this study showed prospective memory declined at a comparable rate to working memory span. The group who had been shown the smiley face during the instruction phase performed comparably better, but the effect was the same for both younger and older adults. Knowing when the stimulus would appear had a negative effect on performance, a finding that was particularly marked in the older adult group. One explanation could be that, when uncertain about the appearance of the target, one is more conscious of what is needed, and so there is likely to be a higher level of task monitoring during the activity, thereby increasing the likelihood that the smiley face will elicit a response. Evidence for this effect was seen in the concurrent performance task data, with drops in performance indicating a heavier cognitive load for the group who were informed only that the stimulus would appear 'later' in the session.

Summary

Over the last few pages we have identified the ways in which long-term memory can be compartmentalized into discrete subtypes. As with the previous chapters, here too we can see the all-pervasive nature of long-term memory. Indeed, although presented in separate chapters, to some extent perception, attention, working memory, and long-term memory are inseparable. The more recent accounts of the working memory model specifically draw attention to the direct input of long-term memory to working memory operation. Where would we be without our store of knowledge after all?

We have seen age to have a detrimental effect on episodic memory, whereas semantic memory is spared (Park et al., 2002). A likely reason for this difference is that semantic information is not stored in one location within the brain, rather storage of such material is spread throughout the cortex (Eichenbaum, 2003) and so is less likely to be lost as the result of structural changes in the brain that occur as a result of ageing. Episodic memory, on the other hand, is localized as it requires input from the hippocampus.

When looking at long-term memory a number of key components manifest. These include depth of processing, encoding specificity, and organization. Depth of processing reflects the fact that remembering material depends a great deal on how much one has processed that information during the encoding phase. The more new information is integrated into existing knowledge, the better we can recall it later. Encoding specificity has been shown to be important such that retrieval of information is better when it matches the conditions in which the information was encoded originally. It is the case also that the better organized information is the easier it is to remember. Age does not appear to adversely affect the benefit of such encoding strategies.

Memory is central to our perception of self and is, therefore, a greatly cherished faculty. In later chapters we shall examine instances where rather more extreme forces exert their effect on these systems, and in the aftermath of their attack a mere shadow of one's former self is all that remains.

Further reading

Draaisma, D. (2013). *The nostalgia factory: Memory, time and ageing*. Yale: Yale University Press. [At the time of writing, I am eagerly anticipating it, and so should you if you are intrigued by the impact of age on memory.]

Kandel, E. R. (2006). *In search of memory: The emergence of a new science of mind*. New York, NY; London: W. W. Norton & Company. [This is part memoir and part science. In this book Eric Kandel takes the reader on a journey that examines how memories are formed.]

Park, D. C. & Schwarz, N. D. P. (2000). *Cognitive aging: A primer*. Hove: Psychology. [A detailed account of how age impacts across a range of cognitive functions.]

CHAPTER 6

Metacognition

Until relatively recently any hint of introspectionist tendencies was met with disdain by experimentalists within psychology. Introspectionist accounts epitomized early psychological research. Through the work of Wundt and Titchner our understanding of the inner workings of the human brain expanded greatly. This early pioneering work provoked many criticisms. One such denunciation arose within the psychotherapeutic community arguing that Freud's theory of the unconscious indicated that not all mental activity was open to conscious inspection. Such unconscious mental activity clearly affected a person's overt behaviour.

Probably the most damning attack originated from the then growing school of behaviourism, with the new breed of psychologists, such as Watson and Skinner, arguing that overt behaviour should be the sole focus for psychological research and that introspectionist accounts were irrelevant to the growing science of psychology.

Largely as the result of the cognitive revolution, which took place during the middle of the twentieth century, there was a renewed interest in introspection, this time with an emphasis on objective assessment based on experimental paradigms. This new strain of research focused initially on states of 'feeling of knowing' which can be described as a belief that a piece of information is known even though it cannot be retrieved at the time of questioning (Hart, 1965). Such feelings of knowing appeared to accurately predict whether or not a person actually knew the information.

Linked to this is 'judgement of learning' (JOL) and reflects the capacity for a person to accurately gauge whether a period of prior study has been sufficient to ensure accuracy in an examination (Dunlosky & Nelson, 1992). Judgements of this type can be assessed on an item-by-item basis whereby individuals are asked to designate which items from a previously learned set will be recalled correctly and which will not under subsequent examination conditions. Such judgements of relative accuracy can be complemented by judgements of absolute accuracy where predicted recall is directly mapped onto to objective test performance. Someone who demonstrated perfect absolute accuracy would be incorrect for all answers they judged they would not recall, correctly recall 30 per cent of the items to which they had allocated a JOL of 30 per cent, and so on.

What is metacognition?

Regardless of a rather tainted history within the field of psychology, research exploring subjective accounts of thinking continues. The study of metacognition – the ability to think about what goes on when we think – has continued and is now increasingly becoming the focus of attention for many sub-disciplines within psychology, including cognitive neuropsychology. This is because there is a range of techniques that allow subjective accounts to be assessed against objective indices of accuracy.

The term 'metacognition' was first introduced by Flavell in the 1970s (Flavell, 1971) when discussing how children develop an awareness of what information they have stored in their memory. Metacognitive processes underlie much of the activity we carry out on a daily basis. One could broadly split metacognition into two components: one that is concerned with knowledge and one that deals with behavioural regulation. Metacognitive knowledge reflects our understanding of how we think, what we have stored in our long-term memory, and our ability to reason (Flavell & Wellman, 1977). Such knowledge aids our study and improves our ability to learn new material. Metacognitive monitoring and regulation underpins our capacity to scrutinize our behaviour and modify our actions when needed across a range of situations (Flavell & Wellman, 1977).

A common conceptual framework in this area was proposed by Nelson and Narens (1990) which suggested that one could classify cognitive processes into two main types; those that occur at the object level and those that occur at the meta level. Object level processing consists of basic information processing such as encoding, retrieval of material, and so on. The meta level operates by supervising this activity and taking control when required in a typical top-down fashion.

As we have seen, metacognition permeates the majority of human behaviour. It brings together a range of cognitive processes into one unified whole. Because of its all-encompassing nature, the term 'metacognition' is used to reflect a number of distinct behaviours. Metacognition concerns knowledge of our own thought processes (or cognition). It is also concerned with how we monitor our behaviour (Hertzog & Hultsch, 2000). The research on ageing has to date focused largely on metacognition and memory, or metamemory.

In the case of older adults, how well we assess our own memory, for example, will have a major impact on our daily lives.

Metamemory

Older adults often present at clinic complaining of memory problems. This goes hand-in-hand with a shared belief that memory deteriorates as we grow older (Hertzog & Hultsch, 2000). However, we need to consider how good we are at assessing our own memories. We need to consider also how this accuracy changes as we age. This is important because such beliefs about our own ability influence the way we perceive both self and others, thereby exerting a strong influence on a person's quality of life (Langer, 1989; McFarland, Ross, & Giltrow, 1992).

Changing perception of memory ability

In order to explore beliefs about memory, a number of measures have been developed. Such measures require participants to rate their memory ability, both in terms of global ability, and also in terms of ability related to specific types of situations. In addition to personal beliefs about memory participants are asked to reflect on how much control they have over this process. One study required participants to rate the memory ability of the average adult at different ages, from the age of 20 through to age 90 (Lineweaver & Hertzog, 1998). Participants were grouped according to their own age: young, middle-aged, old. This then provided an indicator of their implicit beliefs about memory. From the findings it was clear that all participants believed memory declined with age. It was also interesting to note that the young and middle-aged groups believed the decline in performance accelerated once a person reached the age of 50. The older adults in the study, on the other hand, held an implicit belief that memory performance was maintained a little longer. In addition, belief in how much control the average adult has over their memory was similarly pessimistic (Hertzog, McGuire, & Lineweaver, 1999).

A shared belief in the negative impact of age on memory functioning is likely to cloud, or at the very least colour, our perception of our own abilities later in life. This is because we assume that what happens to others will also happen to us (Elliott & Lachman, 1989). On comparing a group of older adults who believed in the inevitability of decline as the result of age to those who believed that memory functioning remained unaffected, it was clear that the former group attributed performance to their own ability and were less likely to make use of effortful strategies to aid accuracy. This is not unsurprising considering the mindset which considers poor performance to be a function of age (Devolder & Pressley, 1992).

There is much evidence to show that there is often disagreement between subjective accounts of performance and objective indices of behaviour (Dixon, Bäckman, & Nilsson, 2004). The Cognitive Failures Questionnaire (CFQ) (Broadbent et al., 1982) is a standard indicator of cognitive functioning, focusing particularly on instances of everyday slips of action as well as general memory. The CFQ has proved useful across a number of areas, including high correlations with road traffic accident frequency (Broadbent, Broadbent, & Jones, 1986). The ability to report such cognitive failures reflects an individual's capacity for metacognitive awareness. There was a high positive correlation between scores on the CFQ and ratings of the Meta-Cognition Questionnaire (MCQ) (Cartwright-Hatton & Wells, 1997). Mecacci and Righi (2006) found that with higher ratings of cognitive failures individuals were conscious of the need to minimize worry that may be associated with such failures, thereby indicating a high level of metacognitive awareness and control. In a study comparing self-reports of cognitive functioning in both younger and older adults Mecacci and Righi (2006) replicated earlier findings by Rabbitt and Abson (1990) such that older adults were seen to report fewer problems than the younger group.

Regardless of how such measures relate to objective test scores, subjective reports of functioning are important as they provide insight into self-representation of ability (Schwarz, 1999). In order to make sense of the previous finding, it is highly likely that older adults are less concerned with cataloguing such errors because of changing expectations about which aspects of functioning they deem to be important in their lives as they grow older (Schwarz, 1999).

There is a great deal of concern about what deficits will appear with age. An ever-growing fear among ageing adults is that they will develop Alzheimer's disease in their later years (Cutler & Hodgson, 1996). In addition to specific memory problems as a result of age, anxiety exerts an independent effect, acting to further worsen, or heighten, any age-related decline. Ratings of anxiety among older adults are much higher than younger adults in situations that require information to be remembered (Cavanaugh, Grady, & Perlmutter, 1983). A fear of cognitive failure inevitably leads to deficits in performance. This, naturally, fuels any anxieties a person may have, and so increasing the likelihood of experiencing more impairment in the future. This self-perpetuating downward cycle of dysfunction can have quite serious consequences in terms of an individual's well-being and ability to function on a day-to-day basis.

Although such beliefs in memory functioning, this implicit theory of memory change, does exert an influence on how people lead their lives, longitudinal studies have shown that perceived changes in functioning do not actually match objective measures of performance (McDonald-Miszczak, Hertzog, & Hultsch, 1995). On the contrary, subjective complaints of memory problems correlate positively with depression scores (Niederehe & Yoder, 1989).

The fact that older adults often hold inaccurate beliefs about their own ability has major implications in terms of their general well-being. The expectation of general cognitive decline, combined with the worry that such failures may be indicative of the onset of Alzheimer's disease, may lead to depression (Cutler & Hodgson, 1996). With depression and, indeed, anxiety, impairments in cognitive functioning proliferate (Christopher & MacDonald, 2005), thereby creating a self-fulfilling prophecy (Levy, 1996).

A number of possible explanations for this mismatch abound. One explanation is individual differences in what is perceived as being good or bad memory. It has also been argued that older adults are less accurate at judging cognitive failures. In fact, they often report fewer lapses when compared to a younger adult group. This could be because demands made upon us as we age diminish, often before lapses in cognition become apparent (Rabbitt et al., 1995). On the other hand, older adults may simply have forgotten many of the problems they had experienced, therefore presenting an over-optimistic picture of functioning.

It could also be the case that the objective tasks used lack sufficient ecological validity, thus explaining why there is a weak correlation with questionnaire ratings of everyday cognitive failures (Bruce, 1985). Taking this one step further, the behavioural specificity hypothesis argues that, in order to obtain an accurate picture, it is necessary for questionnaire items to focus on specific behaviours, with the appropriate cues forming part of the question. In addition, the specific behaviour stated in the question should also be assessed as naturally as possible (Hertzog et al., 2000). Although there are many practical issues to be considered here, in certain instances, where there are clear concerns about well-being, such an approach would be extremely useful. Medication adherence would be a prime example (Intons-Peterson & Fournier, 1986).

A study by Hertzog and colleagues (Hertzog et al., 2000) explored medication adherence in patients suffering from rheumatoid arthritis. A comprehensive battery of measures was taken, including questionnaires and cognitive performance tasks, and also an interview was conducted. Medication adherence was assessed using specially constructed bottles that contained a microchip in the lid. This chip recorded the date and time of every occasion the bottle was opened. The model arising from this study identified poor performance across a range of retrospective memory tasks to be predictive of complaints of memory problems. In addition, evidence of actual errors in medication adherence was successfully predicted by subjective complaints of such errors.

These findings are in line with the predictions of the behavioural specificity hypothesis. Interestingly, ratings of depression did not weaken such relationships. It was also shown that older adults were better able to stick to a medication regime than middle-aged adults.

Sense of control

Our memory and how well it functions is a highly emotive subject. It is a vital component of our self-image. Knowledge of our own memory processes is referred to as metamemory. There is evidence to indicate metamemory becomes less accurate the older we get. This has been demonstrated by examining how people revise material on which they will be later examined (Murphy et al., 1981).

Personal beliefs about the competence of our own memories impact greatly on how we function in our daily lives. Self-efficacy relating to our own memory is therefore important (Berry, 1999). The impact here often begins in middle age. This is a time of heightened sensitivity to minor changes in cognitive functioning. Instances of memory failure are often met with a growing concern and dread of an inevitable decline (Whitbourne & Collins, 1998). This implicit theory of ageing, and the apprehension surrounding it, will exert a negative effect on a person's sense of self-efficacy concerning their memory (McDonald-Miszczak, Hertzog, & Hultsch, 1995).

An important factor to consider here is to what extent we feel we have control over how we perform on cognitive tasks. Studies that have focused on this sense of control have shown there to be a positive relationship between control and performance (Lachman & Andreoletti, 2006). Where individuals feel they have control over their performance more effort is expended to ensure accuracy at retrieval.

It is interesting to note that subjective reports of memory function do not always reflect performance on more objective measures. In some instances older adults report substantial memory problems even though objective test performance fails to back up this claim. In such instances there is a concern that a heightened perception of memory failure is the result of depression.

The extent to which one attributes memory failures to either internal stable or internal unstable factors impacts greatly on our perceptions. Internal stable factors are usually assigned to the memory failings of older adults, with the related assumptions that it is a far more serious and long-term problem. The same errors made by younger adults are often assigned an explanation based on internal unstable factors, such as a lack of effort or attention on the individual's behalf. The assumption is that we have little control over internal stable factors. It has been shown that people have more sympathy in instances where memory difficulties are attributed to internal stable factors (Erber, Szuchman, & Prager, 1997).

Emotion regulation

A great deal of research has explored the role of emotion in cognition. Neuroscientific techniques allow us to further understand why this occurs. Two distinct neural processes appear to be at play here. When presented with a highly arousing negative stimulus, amygdala activation automatically occurs to process the material for memory encoding in conjunction with the hippocampus. When the stimulus is less arousing, although still of an emotional nature, activation of the prefrontal cortex is required. This reflects a more consciously controlled process for encoding the material (Kensinger & Corkin, 2004).

Emotion plays a central role in the way we adjust to growing older and is linked invariably to our sense of overall well-being. There are clear links here with resilience which will be discussed further in Chapter 11. The regulation of emotion can be utilized to maintain positive affect whilst being cognisant of objective reality (Labouvie-Vief, 2005). The interplay between primary emotions and higher-order cognitive operations has led to a great deal of attention being focused on the impact of ageing on the limbic–cortical networks (Labouvie-Vief, 2005).

Development of emotion regulation

Throughout development, emotion processing and response become increasingly mental events rather than merely knee-jerk reactions to events happening in the now. Emotion is increasingly used to guide behaviour through complex planning operations. New secondary emotions develop as a result of this process of abstraction from the present (Lewis, 2000). During adulthood there is greater flexibility in how emotions are processed as well as greater complexity in the internal representation of emotion. Such complexity declines once late adulthood is reached (Porter & Suedfeld, 1981). As a result, emotive situations no longer elicit a complex weighing up of competing emotions (Blanchard-Fields, 1999). This finding would seem to reflect declines in higher-order cognitive functioning associated with older adulthood (see next section).

Responding to everyday situations

An important aspect of metacognition concerns the regulation and suppression of emotions. Emotion regulation is an important determinant of how successfully we function and adjust to the stresses and strains associated with our day-to-day lives. Poor emotion regulation is implicated in a number of conditions including the development of mood disorders. There are repercussions in terms of general physical health as well. This is particularly pertinent as we grow older. These shall be discussed in more detail in later chapters. As is invariably the case we can turn to Ancient Greece to provide an apt description of this. Plato (427–347 BC, 1994) expressed that

> He who is of a calm and happy nature will hardly feel the pressure of age, but to him who is of an opposite disposition youth and age are equally a burden.

Emotion regulation can be utilized in order to anticipate and respond appropriately to affect-laden experiences in order to either avoid them altogether or to attend only to selected aspects, thereby making the experience more manageable. Alternatively, emotion regulation can occur once an emotion has been elicited in order to modify a particular behavioural or psychological response (Niedenthal, 2005).

It has been argued that older adults adjust and adapt their environments in order to maintain an overall positive affect whilst minimizing negative mood states. Socioemotional selectivity theory suggests the drive to achieve this is because of a person's awareness that time is limited and, as a result, various goals and expectations may need to be rationalized and restructured accordingly (Carstensen, Fung, & Charles, 2003). Other studies have suggested this effect is only evident among women and not men. In addition, the effect is apparent in women largely because levels of emotional reactivity among older women is in stark contrast to levels evident in young adulthood, reflecting growing confidence in their ability to judge how they are feeling themselves rather than reflecting on the reactions of others (Labouvie-Vief & Marquez, 2004).

Still other studies have shown that, rather than less reactivity, older adults often show heightened reactivity to situations, especially when the nature of the event rates high in terms of personal relevance (Kunzmann & Grun, 2003). It would appear then that characteristics of the event eliciting the emotion are the important factor in determining the level of emotional reactivity. It may be argued that how well an older adult responds to such a situation depends on whether they responded appropriately to similar situations in the past and, therefore, hold the relevant schema in order to respond efficiently and effectively (Gross, 1998).

Complexity of emotion and emotion regulation

Emotion regulation allows individuals to control the way they respond in different situations, be it in terms of mood, overt behaviours, or physiological reactions (Gross, 2001). To some extent older adults effect emotion regulation through the careful selection of what to do and who to share experiences with (Aspinwall & Taylor, 1997). To compliment this, older adults believe they have comparatively more control over their emotional responses (Gross et al., 1997). Because of this they tend to adopt more flexible and targeted coping strategies (Blanchard-Fields, Mienaltowski, & Seay, 2007).

One possible mechanism for greater emotion regulation as a function of age is an increase in emotion complexity (Gruhn et al., 2013). One element of this complexity is the older adult's ability to experience contrasting emotions at the same time – co-occurrence (Ong & Bergeman, 2004). In addition, older adults are able to differentiate emotional responses more effectively – structural complexity (Carstensen et al., 2000). Each encounter initiates a physiological response. The individual then interprets this change in state, assigning it a particular emotion label (Barrett, 2004). This labelling or categorization process is highly individualistic, reflecting our own unique developmental experiences.

During stressful periods negative moods become more prevalent and there may also be a correspondent drop in positive mood (Mroczek & Almeida, 2004). Having access to greater emotion complexity is likely to help individuals regulate their emotions when faced with an aversive situation. This fine-grained approach would enable individuals to better comprehend the situation and to be more eloquent in their interactions with others regarding the situation (Barrett, 2004). With such capabilities individuals are less likely to exhibit extreme emotional responses (Larsen & Cutler, 1996). However, a recent study has not supported the argument for age-related increases in emotion complexity (Hay & Diehl, 2011). However, they did provide evidence to support the argument that emotion complexity does help with emotion regulation.

Self-concept incoherence (SCI) refers to the situation where one's self-concept varies depending on the situation and the role one finds oneself in (Donahue et al., 1993). A high level of self-concept incoherence is associated with labile emotional states and negative affect (Diehl & Hay, 2007).

Social cognition

Having looked at how metacognitive processes infuse much of our behaviour, this next section focuses specifically on the impact of cognition on social behaviour. Just as you cannot separate emotion from cognition, we cannot get away from the fact that we are social animals. The innate skill that allows us to understand mental states in other people provides the foundation for our ability to predict how people behave and so forms the basis of social cognition. This reflects the fact that there is clearly something different in the way we process information relating to other people when compared to how we process information about objects. This difference is apparent from a very young age. Indeed, it has been shown that we are born with a natural talent for processing human faces and voices. This predilection clearly formed a major component in the evolution of our species (Schaffer, 2006).

Social cognition can be seen to develop in three stages. The first stage reflects our innate ability to perceive and mimic human actions. The next stage concerns the ability to link both physical expression and body posture to different states of experienced emotion. The final developmental phase reflects our capacity to attribute internal states to others based on how we felt when carrying out the behaviour observed in others (Meltzoff, 2010).

Social cognition is achieved partly through the selection and utilization of mental structures based on previously experienced events. These schema are generalized representations that can be used to guide the way we process social information (Quinn, Mcrae, & Bodenhausen, 2005).

Theory of mind

Theory of mind refers to our ability to reflect on both our own and other people's state of mind. The capacity to understand that another person can maintain a belief or view of the world that is not shared by oneself forms an important stage within the development of any child. This illustrates a definite move away from egocentrism seen in young children. It is an important mechanism that allows one to make inferences about someone else's behaviour (Mitchell & Lewis, 1994). This capability appears once we have developed the facility for metarepresentation.

Theory of mind is fundamentally important for all forms of social interactions. The role theory of mind plays in regulating behaviour underpins social cognition (Beer & Ochsner, 2006). As we have seen, social cognition refers to how we perceive other people, our stored body of knowledge relating to social norms, and so on. The majority of research exploring theory of mind has focused either on children or atypically developing groups (Baron-Cohen et al., 2001; Perner & Davies, 1991) or those with psychiatric conditions (Shamay-Tsoory, Aharon-Peretz, & Levkovitz, 2007).

In the developing child, theory of mind appears around 18 months. At this stage children engage in activities that involve shared attention and proto-declarative pointing (Baron-Cohen, 1995). Between 18 and 24 months of age children can participate in pretend activity (Leslie, 1987). By the time they are 24 months old, children are able to understand the concept of desire as a mental state (Wellman & Woolley, 1990). By the time the child reaches the age of four they are able to comprehend that another person may hold a false belief (Gopnik & Astington, 1988). By the age of seven children cultivate more advanced metacognitive abilities (Perner & Wimmer, 1985). Advanced social behaviour occurs between the ages of nine and 11, allowing children to recognize instances when a social faux pas occurs. This is a particularly complex skill as it requires the observer to recognize that another person has said something that should have been left unsaid and that the interlocutor may feel hurt as a result.

Theory of mind may be conceptualized as consisting of two broad aspects. One aspect reflects a cognitive approach comprising intentions and beliefs concerning other people (Coricelli, 2005). This cognitive component to theory of mind is assessed using tasks of false belief, attribution of intention, and social faux pas. The representation of socially relevant material can be based either on inferences about the perspectives of others (first-order representations) or a more meta-level of representation taking into consideration multiple viewpoints (second-order representations) (Morin, 2006).

In contrast to this cognitive component of theory of mind there is an affective element. This constituent is concerned with the feelings of others (Brothers & Ring, 1992). Affective arousal is important as a mechanism by which different stimuli can be separated – hospitable versus hostile, for example. Understanding of emotion develops between the ages of two and three and links to our understanding of theory of mind. Following this is the ability to regulate emotional responses which continues to develop into adolescence. Our ability to control and regulate emotion mirrors closely the development of executive functions.

Various measures are used to gauge this component, including among others the *Reading the Mind in the Eyes* test (the Eyes Test) (Baron-Cohen et al., 1999). Although often confused with empathy, affective theory of mind is a distinct construct. Empathy, on the one hand, refers to the subjective state of feeling someone else's emotion without necessarily understanding why that person is feeling that way; whereas affective theory of mind reflects an appreciation why someone is feeling a particular way without concomitantly experiencing that emotion (Baron-Cohen, 1988). Of course, empathy can be subdivided into emotional and cognitive components also; in which case, affective theory of mind would be most closely related to cognitive empathy (Shamay-Tsoory et al., 2005).

Executive function

There is a great deal of research interest in exploring the links between theory of mind and executive function. There are a number of studies that present findings showing an overlap here, especially in terms of cognitive control. Development of executive function provides the necessary cognitive complexity for theory of mind to grow (Pellicano, 2007).

Regarding the few studies that have examined theory of mind in older adults, findings are mixed. Some studies show a decline in function with age (Maylor et al., 2002), whereas others have failed to find any such effect, instead showing improvement (Happe, Winner, & Brownell, 1998). More recent studies have revealed that individual components of theory of mind are affected differently as the result of age. Although the ability to infer different mind states in others may remain intact, the ability to process and manipulate such information does appear to be reduced (German & Hehman, 2006).

Age-related decline in cognitive theory of mind is most likely the result of deterioration in executive function (German & Hehman, 2006). Bailey and Henry (2008) stress the importance of inhibitory control mechanisms here. Most studies that have examined theory of mind in older adults to date have focused almost entirely on this cognitive component as opposed to affective theory of mind.

A recent study examined the impact of age on both cognitive and affective theory of mind (Duval et al., 2011). Across all objective measures of theory of mind, older adults performed at a significantly lower level than the younger comparison groups. Group differences failed to occur when such ability was assessed by means of subjective rating scales. To some extent, the failure of the subjective measure to capture age effects has been demonstrated in other areas of cognitive functioning, including memory (Rabbitt & Abson, 1990), with fewer cognitive failures being reported even though objective performance was clearly impaired. This apparent mismatch between subjective and objective measures may be seen to reflect poor metacognitive awareness (Koriat & Ackerman, 2010; Lysaker et al., 2011).

Duval and colleagues (2011) found impairment in the older adult group but not in the young or middle-aged groups for cognitive theory of mind, thereby supporting previous findings in this field (Charlton et al., 2009).

There is evidence also for age effects in terms of first- and second-level theory of mind (Duval et al., 2011) where effects are mediated by integrity of executive functions. Age-related effects for second-level theory were not mediated by processing speed, executive functions, or memory. These findings reflect varying demands made by the different activities. First-order representations demand much from the limited pool of attentional resources as a result of the level of manipulation of information required here to adopt the perspective of another (Bull, Phillips, & Conway, 2008). Second-order theory of mind – as characterized by its higher-order, metarepresentation of information – makes heavy demands on executive functions as well (Miller, 2009; Stuss, 2007).

When looking at affective theory of mind, using the Eyes Test (Baron-Cohen, Wheelwright, & Jolliffe, 1997), Duval et al. (2011) did not observe any age effects relating to basic emotions, although differences were seen with the processing of complex emotions. This test presented participants with photographs of the eye region in which actors were instructed to adopt specific emotions, either basic or complex. Identification of basic emotions is relatively automatic and so does not require a great deal of attentional resources (Coricelli, 2005), whereas processing complex emotions do as additional reasoning is needed to make sense of them. In addition, for complex emotions to be processed effectively, some form of context is needed. This was not provided in the Eyes Test. Age effects were also observed in the performance of the Tom's Taste Test (Duval et al., 2011). This task requires participants to assess the taste preference of another individual given a particular context (Snowden et al., 2003). To perform this task successfully participants needed to process both the cognitive and emotional states of the character involved. This test also included a social context within which the scenario took place.

Neural underpinnings of social cognition

Findings from behavioural studies showing an enhanced ability to regulate emotional responses have been replicated using scanning technology. The field of social cognitive neuroscience is an ever-expanding one. It allows us to explore in greater depth how we react in social situations.

When looking at the types of causal judgements people make, it has been shown that such social judgements occur relatively automatically, involving very little, if any, conscious control. This often leads to errors. Such errors of judgement become more frequent when there is a greater degree of ambiguity as to the causes of a person's behaviour. In addition to the usual structures involved in social cognition – namely the lateral temporal cortex, amygdala, and basal ganglia (Adolphs, 1999) – research has shown that the prefrontal cortex, anterior cingulate, and the hippocampus to be activated when making complex social judgements (Lieberman et al., 2002). Both the amygdala and the basal ganglia are integral to emotion processing. These structures are less affected by the effects of ageing, especially when compared to deterioration within the prefrontal cortex as a whole. However, less deterioration occurs within the ventromedial section of the prefrontal cortex when compared to the whole. The ventromedial prefrontal cortex plays an important role in emotional processing. The net result is a relative sparing in a person's ability to process emotion material throughout their mature years.

Neurodegenerative disorders

Not many studies have explored social cognition in older adults. However, assessment of social cognition may help in the early detection of Major Neurocognitive Disorder (as classified in the DSM-V) – an increasing problem as the result of an ageing population. An effective way to assess social cognition is through measures of theory of mind.

When looking at how social functioning is affected by different disease states, poor functioning in this area is particularly characteristic of Alzheimer's disease. Such difficulties may contribute to reductions in both independence and quality of life during the middle stages of the disease (Piquard et al., 2004). Particularly affected is performance on second-order false belief tasks (Fernandez-Duque, Baird, & Black, 2009). This may in part reflect poorer overall working memory functioning in such patients (Cuerva et al., 2001). In terms of the few studies conducted to date, there is evidence for some impairment in cognitive theory of mind in Alzheimer's disease cases, but not for affective theory of mind (Gregory et al., 2002).

Among other things, being able to accurately assess a person's emotional state from their facial expression is an intrinsic component of social cognition (Ekman, 1997). This ability is linked directly with affective theory of mind as we have seen already. There appears to be important differences that occur as a result of age. Older adults generally find identification of negative emotion in the faces of others to be much more difficult (McDowell, Harrison, & Demaree, 1994).

The ability to accurately assess the facial expressions of others is for the most part affected in Alzheimer's disease (Hargrave, Maddock, & Stone, 2002). There is some evidence to suggest problems also occur in patients with relatively mild dementia (Bucks & Radford, 2004). Deficits are more apparent for more subtle facial expressions (Phillips et al., 2010). There appears to be a valence effect also, such that positive emotional expressions are more accurately assessed (Guaita et al., 2009). There is evidence to also suggest impairments in empathic responses among such patients (Fernandez-Duque et al., 2010).

It is interesting to note that there does not appear to be any impairment in emotion recognition among patients who have received a diagnosis for mild cognitive impairment (MCI) – the prodromal state of Alzheimer's disease – when the emotion expressed was intense (Teng, Lu, & Cummings, 2007), but there does appear to be some impairment when the emotions were more subtle (Spoletini et al., 2008). This may be indicative of the spread of neuropathology into regions of the brain associated more closely with recognizing emotion, such as the superior temporal sulcus. Impairments are evident in patients with multiple-domain MCI as opposed to single-domain MCI (Markesbery, 2010).

The findings from both Alzheimer's disease and MCI patients suggest that cognitive impairments are paramount and that any theory of mind deficits are secondary to these changes in functioning. In other words, difficulties experienced are the result of a general decline in cognitive function rather than because of a specific deficit in social cognition. This is likely due to the fact that the frontal lobes are relatively unaffected by either MCI or Alzheimer's disease.

Summary

In this chapter we have developed our understanding of how aspects of executive function pervade most of the behaviours we perform each day. The concept of metacognition refers to our capacity to reflect on our own thought processes. Part of this reflection concerns the extent to which we can accurately assess our memories for various things. Metacognitive processes are involved when we perform actions, ensuring that we remain on track and that we adapt should the situation demand it.

The monitoring and regulating of emotion is also a component of metacognition. As such, these processes play a vital role in our daily lives. The section on social cognition and theory of mind examined the role of executive function in determining the extent to which we can successfully integrate and interact in social situations. Success here depends to a large extent on our ability to infer different thoughts and feelings to other people. Linked to this is our capacity to respond appropriately in emotional situations. This chapter ended with a look at how metacognitive functioning is affected by different neuropathology.

Further reading

Gross, J. J. (2007). *Handbook of emotion regulation.* London: Guilford. [For those interested in emotion regulation, this handbook presents a great overview of this growing field of study.]

Perfect, T. J. & Schwartz, B. L. (2002). *Applied metacognition.* Cambridge; New York: Cambridge University Press. [An authoritative text that examines all aspects of metacognition. A very good introduction to the topic.]

Ward, J. (2011). *The student's guide to social neuroscience.* Hove: Psychology Press. [This text presents a highly approachable account of the neuroscientific approach to social cognition.]

CHAPTER 7

Everyday Functioning

Of overriding importance to most adults is the desire to maintain independence for as long as possible. Given the many changes associated with ageing this can be challenging given the demands associated with independent living. Being able to care for both oneself and one's material goods are but two examples. Everyday functioning can be used to refer to a person's competence in dealing with the various problems encountered on a daily basis (Schaie, Boron, & Willis, 2005).

In this chapter we shall explore the processes of decision making and problem solving that occur in everyday lives. These are fundamental cognitive operations that influence a wide range of commonplace behaviours such as how we make decisions concerning our health and how we deal with problem situations that arise through our interactions with other people. Linked to this are the sections on social cognition (a topic first introduced in the previous chapter) and moral reasoning, both of which inform a number of important decisions and social interactions.

The final section in this chapter focuses on language and speech. Language is what distinguishes humans from our ancestors and, as such, plays a pivotal role in who we are and what we do. We shall explore some of the ways age-related changes impact on this most singular capacity.

Decision making

The way we extract information from our environment, and the way we process that information when faced with dilemmas, has a bearing on how people make decisions. The types of decisions we make concerning our health and well-being becomes more of a concern the older we get.

It is interesting to note that older adults tend to show a bias for positive information – the positivity effect (Kennedy & Mather, 2007). When comparing how younger and older adults assessed healthcare plans, more positive information was used to inform the final decisions of older adults (Lockenhoff & Carstensen, 2007). Negative information was largely ignored. When explicit instructions to focus on facts and details were given, a more balanced assessment was made, thereby overriding the positivity bias.

Treatment options

Increasingly medical practitioners share the decision concerning which treatment option to choose with patients. A good example here is in the treatment of cancer where often there are a number of treatment alternatives. This is a shift away from the orthodox position where all decisions were previously made by the physician. Research has indicated a positive effect in instances where patients have been involved in this process (Davison et al., 1999).

One study examined the decision making process in healthy women who were required to make a choice concerning treatment for breast cancer based on accurate case histories. Various treatment options were presented, with each one being backed up by expert opinion. When comparing different age groups, it was found that younger women tended to seek new information, weighing up the pros and cons of the different treatment options. In this sense, they adopted a bottom-up processing strategy. Older women, on the other hand, relied more on their prior knowledge, and thus failed to fully explore the various options – an example of top-down processing strategy. The top-down approach is quicker, less cognitively demanding, and can be accurate, assuming one's knowledge is up-to-date. However, on the whole, a bottom-up strategy is preferable. These findings were replicated in a sample of women who had been diagnosed with breast cancer in the previous three years (Meyer, Russo, & Talbot, 1995). Men also showed a comparable pattern when needing to make decisions about prostate cancer (Meyer, Talbot, & Ranalli, 2007).

Sources of (mis)information

Studies have also explored the sources that people use to inform their decisions over healthcare. Older people predominantly make use of newspapers, television, and friends to obtain information, rather than seeking advice from medical professionals. There may be a number of reasons for this, one being reluctance to burden healthcare providers unless invited to do so (Turk-Charles, Meyerowitz, & Gatz, 1997). Another major source of information, often misinformation, is the Internet. With access to such a vast array of data, there is an ever-greater need to sift validated sources of medical information from spurious opinion.

Moral reasoning

The types of decisions we regularly make, and the judgements formed, emerge from a host of complex cognitive operations. These processes do not occur in isolation either. The context in which events occur have a strong influence on the final conclusion. The importance of contextualization is especially important when examining whether an action is right or wrong. An influential model here is that of Kohlberg, who proposed a three-tier cognitive developmental model for moral reasoning (Kohlberg, 1969). The basis of this model was inspired by the work of Piaget (Piaget & Gabian, 1977).

Kohlberg, and indeed Piaget, argued that moral reasoning could only occur if the necessary cognitive architecture was in place. In Piagetian terminology, there should be decreased egocentrism where there is a developing ability to understand the perspectives of other people, and also a growing adoption of formal operations enabling abstract and hypothetical thinking to occur.

Kohlberg's model

Kohlberg's theory consisted of three levels of development, with each of these comprising two discrete stages (Kohlberg, 1976). The initial, or pre-conventional, stage is characterized by egocentric thinking. At this stage punishment to the self is the only indicator of what is right or wrong, and there is no ability to appreciate the effect of one's own behaviour on another individual. Egocentrism declines allowing the child to develop a rudimentary appreciation of someone else's point of view. This largely individualistic way of thinking is replaced by a wider acceptance of the views of society in general (the conventional stage), although the thinking at this stage is by and large dichotomous. With the emergence of the principle level of development (the post-conventional stage) abstract theorizing over ethical issues is possible (Grimm & Thompson, 2007). At this stage the individual cultivates his or her own unique set of ethical principles. Moral judgements are based on deep-seated ethical codes. Indeed, such principles may conflict with what society expects. The core constructs here are justice, compassion, and equality.

Kohlberg believed that each stage had to be attained in strict order and that these stages were universal. However, the most advanced stage, post-conventional morality, is not always achieved. In addition, the post-conventional stage of moral development appears to be a Western construct as it does not appear in many societies. This is because individualism is not favoured in many cultures as subjugation of the individual for the benefit of the collective is often emphasized (Shweder, Mahapatra, & Miller, 1990).

Perspective taking

In terms of age, as we have seen before, the manner in which the dilemma is presented influences how different age groups respond. On the whole, participants scored higher on moral maturity when they responded to situations where the characters matched their own age group (Chap, 1985).

An ability to adopt the viewpoint of others is a necessary skill for effective problem solving and decision making. It plays a vital role here too in terms of the formation of moral judgements. Chap presented a model describing four levels in moral perspective taking (Chap, 1985). In the lowest level, only one viewpoint is acknowledged and considered. Those who show the greatest level of sophistication acknowledge and consider two or more perspectives.

Some evidence suggests that older adults were inclined to believe there to be only one legitimate perspective (Chap, 1985). These findings were replicated in a longitudinal study conducted over a four-year period (Pratt et al., 1996). Although moral maturity did not appear to change with age, the level of moral perspective taking did. A more restricted use of perspective taking would reduce the overall cognitive load when evaluating situations. Indeed, higher levels of educational status, health status, and social support acted as a buffer in terms of reducing the overall level of decline in the formation of moral judgements.

Social problem solving

Although there is a tendency to think of both emotion and cognition as separate entities, as I have stressed before, it is really impossible to consider one without the other. There is no greater evidence of their interconnectivity than in everyday life (Labouvie-Vief, 2003). Models of social problem solving focus on, among other things, the emotional salience of situations and the type of strategies adopted to deal with those situations. When looking at the solutions produced by participants to a range of dilemmas, a number of discrete categories of responses emerged (Blanchard-Fields, Jahnke, & Camp, 1995). Problem solving strategies were apparent where clear attempts were made to deal with the situation. Thinking through the various aspects of a problem reflects a cognitive–analytic strategy. On the other hand, rather than attempting to deal with the problem either practically or cognitively, some preferred to remove themselves from the situation, adopting instead a passive–dependent strategy. Others used avoidant strategies to deny the actual existence of a problem.

When looking at age-related changes in strategy use, regardless of age, where problems were low in terms of emotional impact, a problem-focused approach was generally taken. This comparability across age groups changed when the problem under consideration rated high on emotional significance. Instead, older adults were least likely to address a situation using direct problem-focused strategies, preferring rather passive–dependent or avoidant strategies. Part of an explanation for this could be that older adults exert more emotional control than the younger groups, and in doing so reducing the likelihood of conflict and other stressors (Magai & Passman, 1997). There is a sense here of holding off unless absolutely essential (Birditt, Fingerman, & Almeida, 2005).

Older adults are often less inclined to indulge in impulsive behaviour (Labouvie-Vief, 1997). Should a negative event present itself, attempts are made to reinterpret the situation so that it is less confrontational, thereby minimizing the need for emotional conflict. Behaviour, as we have seen, is more regulated (Blanchard-Fields, 2007).

Everyday competence

Given the weight of evidence presented in previous chapters demonstrating a decline in cognitive functioning as we age, one might be tempted to assume that perceived quality of life might drop as a result of this change. Issues surrounding quality of life will be examined in depth in Chapters 10 and 11. However, leading on from the previous section on social problem solving, a number of studies have examined the impact of cognitive functioning on a person's quality of life and have produced counterintuitive findings showing no such link (Argyle, 1999). The likely explanation for this rather odd finding is that the nature of the tasks used were not good at assessing how well one functions on a day-to-day basis. It is more likely that tasks resembling the type of activities performed as part of everyday life may be a better indicator of retained capacity and, therefore, a better predictor of quality of life.

The types of abstract measures often used to access functioning generally are well defined, with one correct answer, devoid of context, and not reliant on one's store of knowledge. This is in marked contrast to the types of problems we all face in our daily lives. Such problems are rarely well-defined, and you are only presented with partial information, for a problem that is multifaceted, emotion laden, and context-bound. What is more, it is doubtful there will be a single correct solution unlike for many standard measures of intelligence as we shall see in Chapter 9 (Sternberg et al., 1995). Solving the types of problems we encounter in our daily lives requires one to access one's store of knowledge and experience (Baltes & Staudinger, 2000). Using more concrete measures of everyday problem solving ability, there is evidence that performance here does reflect a person's assessment of their own quality of life (Gilhooly et al., 2007). Being able to effectively solve real-life problems likely bolsters beliefs about one's ability to deal effectively with whatever life throws at you, enabling one to maintain independence.

Social cognition

In the previous chapter we examined social cognition from a cognitive perspective, identifying the types of processes underlying this activity. Here we shall focus instead on how social cognition is an intrinsic part of everyday functioning.

The role of schema

How we function in social situations is hugely influential on our sense of well-being. Throughout our lives we meet people, instantaneously form impressions of them, and interact with them. Underpinning this everyday behaviour is an integrated cognitive infrastructure that allows information to be processed efficiently and, on the whole, effectively. One element of this infrastructure is schemas: these are cognitive constructs that guide action based on stored knowledge and past experience.

As with many processing operations there are top-down (goal-driven) approaches as well as bottom-up (stimulus-driven) approaches. In the case of schema-based processing, a top-down approach is referred to as category-based operation. This is where impressions are based on a previously formed schema. Oftentimes, such an approach is accurate, whilst at the same time making minimal demands of cognitive resources. However, if our schemas are no longer accurate, our responses may be inappropriate. A more bottom-up approach, or piecemeal operation, is needed so that a new schema is constructed based on current information. This active processing of online information is highly demanding although obviously more accurate (Cuddy & Fiske, 2002).

Trait diagnosticity

Trait diagnosticity is important when forming impressions of people (Hess, 1999). Behaviours high in trait diagnosticity inform the perceiver about the presence of a specific personality trait in the other person. Take, for example, lying. This might be seen as being high in diagnosticity for the trait of moral behaviour as it confirms dishonesty, thereby implying moral turpitude; an honest act does not offer the same level of diagnosticity as it is not always possible to glean the drive behind such acts. Trait diagnosticity becomes increasingly important as we get older. When presented with a description of an individual, impressions are gleaned largely dependent on information that is high in trait diagnosticity. This may merely reflect a lifetime of experience, with people showing a keener sense of what really is important when meeting someone new – a prime example of adaptive functioning.

Causal attribution theory

An important element of social cognition is our belief in what causes specific events in our lives. This is referred to as causal attribution theory. We all utilize causal analysis in our everyday interactions, attributing the behaviour of others to either situational factors (e.g. high work demands) or behavioural dispositions (e.g. being a highly anxious individual). In this sense we weigh up how much a person's personality traits are driving their behaviour compared to the control imposed by the situation in which they find themselves (Heider, 1958). In other words, we weigh up the role of dispositional attributions (internal factors) and situational attributions (external factors). Such attributions influence how we respond in social situations. Again, schema are important here. These contain our knowledge of specific situations, and as such act to guide our behaviour. They are based on prior experience and are deeply rooted in our own culture and society.

Causal attributions can take many forms. Such attributions are measured by presenting participants with vignettes, with instructions to determine what caused the dilemma or outcome. There can be dispositional attributions, where the main factor in determining the outcome is personality characteristics of the interlocutors. In some instances, the specific context is seen as the causal agent, and so there is a situational attribution. Sometimes people believe that there are both dispositional and situational determinants, thereby making interactive attributions (Peng & Nisbett, 1999).

With age we tend to make more interactive attributions. This to some extent reflects the years of experience we have of such situations, where there is, more often than not, a need to consider various perspectives. However, it has been shown that this is not always the case. Older adults make more interactive attributions when presented with accounts concerning relationships, but not when the scenario depicts achievement (Blanchard-Fields, 1994). Age of the characters in the story also influences the approach adopted (Blanchard-Fields, Baldi, & Stein, 1999).

When the presented situation depicts the outcomes of other people, participants mainly emphasize dispositional factors rather than situational. In other words, the observed person's behaviour is caused by personal characteristics rather than by external factors. The person being observed, however, believes that their behaviour is caused by the situation they face. In this instance too much emphasis is placed on the impact of personality traits in determining someone's behaviour. This is called the fundamental attribution error (Gilbert & Malone, 1995). It is also referred to as actor–observer asymmetry. When comparing age groups, older adults were even more inclined than younger adults to commit the fundamental attribution error, especially when the outcome was negative (Blanchard-Fields, 1994). Age of the characters was important, such that dispositional attributions were associated with younger individuals in the vignette, but more situational attributions were made for older characters.

Language and speech

Having looked at reasoning and decision making, this next section explores the role of language and speech in everyday life. It goes without saying both are intrinsic aspects of our lives, be it in terms of conversing with others, reading for pleasure, or writing an email. When competency in one or more of these areas is challenged, there are immediate repercussions in terms of our sense of well-being.

Word recognition

Sensory deficits, such as presbycusis (loss of hearing), impact greatly on a person's ability to identify words (Humes, 1996). Other changes also occur that make word recognition more difficult, including among other things slowed processing of speech (Pichora-Fuller, 2003). When given basic word-recognition tasks the performance of younger and older adults appear not to differ (Dunabeitia et al., 2009). It is only when complexity is increased that age differences become apparent (Ratcliff et al., 2004). These differences were more obvious when stimuli were manipulated to make them more difficult to encode compared to manipulations of word frequency (Allen et al., 1993).

Spelling

The ability to spell is a relatively preserved ability and as such is largely protected against the effects of age. Older adults appear just as accurate as younger adults at detecting misspelt words (Shafto, 2010). However, when older adults are considered in isolation, there appear to be age-related effects such that the older age groups do indeed show reduced accuracy at spotting errors in spelling (Abrams, Farrell, & Margolin, 2010). In addition, when asked to spell words, the fact that errors do start to creep in is suggestive of the cognitive demands imposed by both recall and recognition memory tasks (MacKay & Abrams, 1998).

Pronunciation

Pronunciation is also preserved across the lifespan. To some extent pronunciation is indicative of general attainment of education and so forms part of what can be considered crystallized intelligence, our store of acquired knowledge (see Chapter 9). To reflect this, a standard measure used in clinics – the National Adult Reading Test – assesses this very skill (see Chapter 8 for more details).

Word meaning

Retention of word meaning forms part of the battery of tools to measure crystallized intelligence. Unlike some of the other abilities, discussed before, that are preserved, changes are evident when older adults are presented with tasks measuring semantic processing, with evidence for both slowed production of word meaning as well as reduced precision in definitions (McGinnis & Zelinski, 2000). Performance on measures such as the Boston Naming Test drops as a function of age (Connor et al., 2004). Specifically, older adults appear less able to utilize contextual information to inform definitions, demonstrating a reduced ability to make inferences (McGinnis & Zelinski, 2003).

Two often cited explanations for deficits in retrieval of word meaning are that, with age, we are less able to suppress the retrieval of information that is not relevant to the task at hand (the inhibition deficit model; Hasher & Zacks, 1988); alternatively, it has been proposed that deficits occur as a result of attenuated connections among the mental representation of knowledge (the transmission deficit model; MacKay, Abrams, & Pedroza, 1999).

Tip-of-the-tongue phenomena

A much studied topic is that of tip-of-the-tongue phenomena. Tip-of-the-tongue phenomenon refers to the cognitive state where one is unable to retrieve a word whilst at the same time knowing that the word is in the fringes of their mind, tantalizingly close but at that moment unobtainable. The feeling has been likened to being on the brink of a sneeze (Brown & McNeill, 1966). The tip-of-the-tongue phenomenon is, therefore, a good example of metacognition in action, with the overwhelming sense of knowing being combined with interrupted recall.

Tip-of-the-tongue states are experienced more frequently the older we get (Burke et al., 1991). In older age groups such errors centre around the recall of names of acquaintances whom they had not conversed for some time (Burke et al., 1991). Given time and the necessary encouragement, tip-of-the-tongue states often dissipate (Kausler, 1994).

A number of different factors seem to be associated with these states. The number of phonologically similar words to the target (neighbourhood density), as well as their frequency of use (neighbourhood frequency), seems to be important here. Low neighbourhood frequency appears to increase the likelihood that tip-of-the-tongue states will occur (Vitevitch & Sommers, 2003). If one were to adopt the transmission deficit explanation, because there are fewer neighbouring words that are connected to the target the overall level of activation would be lessened, and so one might expect tip-of-the-tongue states to be more prevailing.

There is also evidence that older adults experience more difficulty identifying low frequency words where neighbourhood density is high (Sommers, 1996). From the perspective of the inhibition deficit model, low frequency words in such circumstances would be more difficult to identify due to an inability to inhibit the activation emanating from the profusion of high frequency words that are phonologically similar to the target.

Story comprehension

The efficiency with which one is able to read and comprehend text is reliant on domain-specific knowledge – at least that is the case for older adults (Miller et al., 2004). The ability to comprehend and recall elements of prose is also highly dependent on working memory. In instances where working memory span is limited, a person allocates more time and resources to processing individual word meaning. Increases in working memory span acts to enable the individual to allocate more resources to processing meaning of the overall text.

When asked to recall information based on a previously read passage of prose, performance of older adults is poor. Accuracy declines further when instructed to produce a précis of the story. This requires additional processing and as such evidences deficits in cognitive functioning (Byrd, 1985).

It is interesting to note that recall by older adults of items presented as part of a radio news broadcast was highly accurate, offering a finding much at odds with the bulk of research findings (Bonini & Mansur, 2009). This implies functioning to be less impaired in real-life situations compared to more contrived laboratory experiments, thus highlighting the importance of studies that attain a reasonable level of ecological validity.

Understanding speech

Of increasing importance to older adults is the impact of processing speech from more than one speaker. The vagaries of everyday conversation bring with it many fluctuations in speech patterns, what may be termed 'acoustic realizations'. This is especially true when comparing different speakers. In order to try to overcome these transformations the receiver attempts perceptual normalization (Pisoni, 1993). As a result, accuracy in correctly identifying words presented by different speakers is poor when compared to processing the speech of just one individual (Yonan & Sommers, 2000).

Attempting to listen to a speaker in situations where there is background noise also poses a problem: in other words, where there is a poor signal-to-noise ratio (Frisina & Frisina, 1997). Performance impairments are reduced when words form part of highly predictable sentences compared to less predictable ones (Frisina & Frisina, 1997). Prosody or intonation is also important such that accuracy in processing material presented with list intonation is poorer compared to normal prosody (MacKay & Miller, 1996).

A plausible explanation for many of these deficits is that older adults focus heavily on contextual information to compensate for sensory deficits in an attempt to glean additional information in order to correctly identify the meaning of words presented. As a result of this, the higher level processing required to assimilate various components of speech is unable to take place due to insufficient resources remaining (Pichora-Fuller, Schneider, & Daneman, 1995).

Speech production

When comparing younger and older adults on the complexity of spontaneous speech, clear age effects are observed. With age utterances tend to be less varied, to contain fewer clauses, and to be increasingly prone to error (Kynette & Kemper, 1986). An explanation often tendered is that older adults are aware of their declining abilities and make adjustments necessary to give the appearance of maintained functioning.

As seen throughout the literature, use of compensatory strategies abound. In keeping with this is evidence to suggest that older adults allocate more time to processing text at the point where one grammatical structure terminates and another begins, a process called 'wrap up' (Stine-Morrow, Noh, & Shake, 2010). The time taken here depends entirely on the complexity of the material presented and can be seen as indicative of the degree of processing required to make sense of the material previously presented before being able to move on. This inflated use of such strategies may indeed reflect a conscious effort to compensate for other failings.

When analysing spontaneous speech it is important to also assess the prevalence of off-target verbosity. This is a measure of how well a person is able to maintain the focus of a specific conversation. A high level of such activity is symptomatic of a reduced inhibitory response (Arbuckle, Nohara-LeClair, & Pushkar, 2000). This behavioural manifestation is most apparent when older adults are asked to relate accounts of particular times in their lives (Gold et al., 1988).

There are a number of important implications to consider here regarding how others perceive someone who regularly goes off target. Interactions with these individuals are generally rated lower on satisfaction (Pushkar et al., 2000), and also inferences are made regarding overall intellectual competence (Ruscher & Hurley, 2000).

These findings are not universal and may be open to an alternative explanation. By deviating off topic the accounts regaled by older adults are rated as being higher in overall quality and in terms of how informative they are (James, Burke, & Austin, 1999). It has been suggested that older adults focus more on imaginative interpretation of experienced events as opposed to providing concise accurate accounts (Boden & Bielby, 1983).

Elderspeak

Misconceptions surrounding the level of both speech production and comprehension among older adults often lead younger adults to adopt 'elderspeak'. This is characterized by adopting a speech pattern more reminiscent of vocal utterances a parent makes when communicating with an infant (Ryan et al., 1986). Sentences thus constructed tend to contain fewer clauses, to be shorter in duration, to contain words with fewer syllables, to be spoken at a slowed rate with longer pauses.

If one were to filter out the stereotypical assumptions nourishing such patronizing affectation, it is possible to examine how modifying speech pattern and structure can improve communication with older adults whilst protecting their dignity. Where attempts to do this have been made, it appears that increased semantic elaborations (expansion, repetition, and comprehension checks), as well as reductions in embedded clauses, enriched overall communication. The other characteristics of elderspeak did not convey any positive impact on the communication process (Kemper & Harden, 1999).

Reading for pleasure

Reading as a pastime activity is one indicator of a person's willingness to participate in activities that are cognitively challenging (Dellenbach & Zimprich, 2008). There are a number of claims about how such activity is important in preventing or diminishing the effects of age-related decline. However, I shall suspend discussion of this hotly debated area until Chapter 14.

Aside from reading as a form of mental stimulation, it is a principal source of information, thereby playing a major role in supplementing a person's store of knowledge. Of particular relevance to older adults is the accuracy of knowledge concerning health issues and the impact then on health and well-being (Perlow, 2010), a topic discussed in an earlier section of this chapter.

Reading not that long ago conjured up images of books and libraries. Cosy evenings inside by the fire reading M. R. James (or indeed James Herbert) while Jack Frost does his worst outside. Nowadays, of course, such gewgaws of antiquity are referred to as physical books, being instead replaced by e-books that are downloaded onto one's Kindle™ or iPad™. However, when we consider reading for pleasure for the current generation of older adults, the transition from reading paper books and newspapers to reading from a computer monitor or e-reader can be problematic.

However, e-books certainly offer more flexibility for the older reader. For one they are much lighter and easy to handle, especially if one has musculoskeletal problems. Many e-readers now offer non-reflective screens thereby enhancing visibility. In addition text size and font style can be manipulated to optimize the reading experience. There is no longer the need to rely on specially printed texts with large typefaces and the restricted range of titles they offer. To some extent e-readers are likely to take over from audiobooks which were once the only real alternative to off-the-shelf books. The experience of listening to an audiobook and actually reading it for oneself is in no sense comparable. The way the material is processed is completely different. Listening to a narrated text does not afford the same mental shortcuts and cognitive tricks that make reading a pleasure (such as parsing, skimming, and re-reading to name but three).

Summary

The chapter began with a look at how decision making processes impact on the types of choices one makes regarding treatment. A number of biases were identified in the way such information is handled. Some of these issues are compounded when one considers the sources people use to try to obtain a better understanding of their condition. Although a wonderful resource on the whole, the Internet can offer much information that is of poor quality.

What we perceive to be right or wrong determines many of the decisions we make throughout our lives. This sense of morality has a direct feed into the choices we make when faced with problem situations in our interactions with others. A person's ability to regulate their behaviour exerts a huge influence on how well we function in everyday situations. In addition, the topic of social cognition was picked up again. This time the emphasis was on the types of mental shortcuts we all make use of in order to be efficient in the way we process information. Here we examined the role played by both personal disposition and environmental factors in determining a particular outcome.

The final section on language and speech showed just how important these skills are. Some of the main problems experienced by older adults were discussed, such as tip-of-the-tongue phenomenon. Not only is an older person's ability to produce and comprehend speech of importance, but also how others interact with them. False assumptions abound here. It is abundantly clear that there are minor modifications that we can all make to improve how we communicate with older adults if only we could strip away the element of condescension.

Further reading

Kahneman, D. (2012). *Thinking, fast and slow*. London: Penguin. [A readable introduction to the study of human rationality (or, indeed, irrationality).]
Pinker, S. (2008). *The stuff of thought: Language as a window into human nature*. London: Penguin. [An enjoyable account of the evolution of language.]
Sahakian, B. J. & LaBuzetta, J. M. (2013). *Bad moves: How decision making goes wrong, and the ethics of smart drugs*. Oxford: Oxford University Press. [A highly topical book that looks at how we make decisions and how those decisions impact on our behaviour.]

CHAPTER 8

Assessment of Cognitive Function

The aim of this chapter is to introduce the reader to some of the key principles underlying good clinical practice in the assessment of cognitive function. The need for testing of this nature is becoming increasingly apparent given the fact that we are living longer with expectations of continued independence into older adulthood. As we have seen in previous chapters, cognitive function exerts a major influence across many domains. As such, accurate assessment of deficits will enable appropriate interventions to be enlisted early on so that, even though a person may be experiencing cognitive failures that result either from the normal ageing process or are the consequence of disease, their ability to function effectively in everyday situations is protected for as long as possible. What follows is a list of some of the most widely used tests available to the clinician. It is by no means a prescriptive selection but merely indicative of the range of measures out there. Kipps and Hodges (2005) present an excellent overview of cognitive assessment for clinicians. In addition, Hebben and Milberg's text provides an insightful and comprehensive account of neuropsychological testing (Hebben & Milberg, 2010), as does Lezak's book (Lezak, 2012).

Neuropsychological testing

Hebben and Milberg (2010) set out the main uses of neuropsychological assessment. Probably the main function is to provide a profile of a person's strengths and weaknesses across a range of measures that assess different components of cognitive function, mood, and behaviour. Assessment of cognitive function straddles two camps: those of a cognitive bent who are concerned with understanding the psychological mechanisms involved in a particular task, against a more diagnostic approach where the aim is to predict performance.

It is essential that cognitive functioning be assessed regularly over an extended period of time in order to fully develop an accurate prognosis. Amassing data of this type provides the clinician with the material to develop rehabilitation strategies for each individual. Educating both family and carer is a core aspect of the overall treatment package in many instances. This will enable more effective support mechanisms as there will be a raised awareness concerning the condition itself, especially the potential presence of challenging behaviours, as well as clear expectations about outcome. Among all this is the need to consider the likelihood that individuals will adhere to a specific treatment plan, part of which will be to decide how much supervision will be needed to maximize the chance that this will happen.

Background information

An essential component of any clinical assessment of cognitive functioning is a full history of each participant. Test results from someone who did not perform well at school and who then went on to work as a manual labourer may be expected to rank below the norm on certain measures that are geared towards academic performance. Compared to someone with a university education who has worked in professional posts, their performance on some measures could potentially be seen to indicate impairment were it not for the knowledge gleaned from the initial personal history. In such cases more caution would be needed to diagnose with more confidence impairment in these domains. This is one reason why normative data is essential when assessing performance across a range of individuals.

Aside from basic demographic information, there is a need to collate information concerning current diagnosis of a medical complaint and/or psychiatric disorder, details of any accidents or trauma experienced, particulars about medications past and present, and also information pertaining to current levels of exercise and diet (especially intake of alcohol or use of recreational drugs). The clinical interview is an effective medium for obtaining a great deal of rich data concerning an individual through both direct interaction and observation of behaviour.

There is a need to identify potential confounds that may interfere with the accuracy of any diagnosis (Kipps & Hodges, 2005). They emphasize the importance of ruling out the presence of delirium in those undergoing clinical assessment. This condition, as we shall see in Chapter 12, is associated with extreme cognitive confusion. Observing how alert the person appears is an effective indicator as to the manifestation of delirium. In some cases they may appear restless, in other instances withdrawn. Alertness can also be used to gauge potentially confounding effects due to the experiencing of side effects caused by prescribed medication.

Format of the assessment

Before beginning any form of assessment it is important to pose a series of fundamental questions. Is the test or battery of tasks appropriate to the individual being tested? Do they exhibit difficulties that might invalidate test results? Does it reflect the reason for their referral? Are there good levels of both test validity and reliability? Will the selection provide insight into a person's ability to function in everyday life? Is it comprehensive enough to yield relevant data?

Building a picture

It is usual for any neuropsychological assessment to begin with some measure of a person's premorbid ability, often as an index of intelligence (Hebben & Milberg, 2010). This is because it is often unlikely that there already exists objective evidence on how they function across a number of cognitive domains. A post hoc index of functioning is achieved by looking at a person's level of education, the type of work they carried out, in addition to how well they perform on objective measures that are on the whole unaffected by disease or injury. Such tests might include measures of vocabulary and general knowledge. Measures of intelligence are multidimensional in the sense that they provide a snapshot of functioning across a wide range of activities. Performance on such measures provides a fixed point against which other tasks are compared. Where time is restrained, the use of brief screening measures of intelligence may be justified.

Early on an assessment of general orientation both in terms of time and place is administered. Of the two, orientation in time is of most use clinically. Knowing what the date is, or indeed, not knowing what the date is, does not offer much information to the clinician as it is reasonably common for people to be less accurate here.

Attention and memory

Cognitive function should be assessed through a combination of measures that assess basic and higher-order processes, from measures of attention to measures of general working memory and executive function. Aspects of attention that can be measured include a person's ability to focus their attention on one activity, to divide their attention across different tasks, and to sustain their attention on one task over prolonged periods of time. The impact of interference or distractor activity on performance of the target task can also be assessed. It is important to reflect here that attention underpins all other cognitive activity.

By using a combination of such measures the clinician or researcher will be able to identify where functional deficits occur. Identification of a specific area of impairment can be explored further by an additional selection of tasks that focus on a precise domain of operation, thereby providing evidence for the reliability of a particular deficit.

Measures of working memory provide an indicator of how well the dorsolateral prefrontal cortex operates (Levy & Goldman-Rakic, 2000). Working memory underscores a wide range of activities, and just as wide ranging are the tests used to assess its function. Working memory impairment often manifests as losing track of what one is doing, not remembering what one was planning to do next, and so on.

More complex and higher order forms of cognitive function can be assessed using measures of executive function. Executive function as we have seen comprises a number of demanding activities concerning how attention is allocated to competing tasks, how focus is changed, how we plan and organize sequences of actions, how we reason and judge, and also how we regulate our behaviour. Executive dysfunction is quickly detected when there is a noticeable decline in such activities.

Fluency tests are commonly used to evaluate executive function, with poor performance indicative of dysfunction in this realm. Simple measures of response inhibition can be used to provide evidence for impulsivity that may be suggestive of executive impairment. Variants of the Go/No-Go task can be deployed, with the clinician instructing participants to tap the table once in response to a single tap initiated by the clinician, and not to tap when the clinician taps twice. Changes in rules can also assess a person's ability to switch tasks; poor executive functioning will likely result in perseverative behaviour on measures such as this (Goldman-Rakic, Cools, & Srivastava, 1996).

Assessment of memory can take many forms, with different tasks focusing on the various component stages of memory: encoding new material, retention of information, retrieval of stored items. Other assessed aspects may include rate of forgetting, the effect of interference, as well as different modes of assessing memory, such as comparing recall with recognition.

The hippocampal-diencephalic system can be assessed with measures that focus specifically on episodic memory. Episodic memory can be measured in terms anterograde memory (recently acquired information) and retrograde memory (material acquired in the distant past). In the majority of cases anterograde and retrograde memory loss occur together, such as in Alzheimer's disease, although this is not always the case. Pure anterograde amnesia may occur as a result of tumour (Aggleton & Brown, 1999).

Integrity of the anterior temporal lobe is assessed through tests of semantic memory. Problems with semantic memory are apparent when a person's vocabulary begins to diminish, with the participant often substituting required words with non-specific nouns.

Language

Potential issues with both language production and comprehension need to be identified early on in order to diagnose the presence of aphasias among other things. Language problems become evident when individuals are asked to provide background information about themselves and the difficulties they are facing. Such problems reveal themselves when they demonstrate poor articulation and verbal fluency.

The ability to name items involves a range of processing activities covering visual, semantic, and phonological aspects. The clinician may point to items on their desk, for example, to try to elicit how accurate a person is at naming everyday items. Impairments here include phonemic and semantic paraphasias: these are sound substitutions or additions and substitution of a semantically related word respectively.

Comprehension may be assessed by seeing how accurately the individual is able to follow a series of instructions that range in terms of semantic complexity. The use of deceptively simple phrases such as, 'No ifs, ands, or buts' can be effective here to see how effectively a person can repeat material accurately. Reading comprehension can be assessed quickly by observing how they respond to a written command such as, 'Close your eyes'. Writing is often disrupted to a greater extent than reading because it involves both spelling and formation of letters in order for it to be executed accurately. It is, therefore, open to disruption as the result of dysgraphia (inability to express oneself through writing) and dyspraxia (disorder of movement and coordination).

General neurological functioning

Acalculia refers to an impairment in a person's ability to comprehend and deal with number. It can reflect a complete loss in the conceptual understanding of number (primary acalculia) as well as an inability to perform mathematical calculations (secondary acalculia).

Apraxia refers to a predominance of spatial and sequencing errors occurring when instructed to make a particular movement with a specific body part in the absence of either motor or sensory impairment. Assessments include a request for participants to imitate specific gestures, to pretend to use objects, and to perform sequencing tasks.

Visuo-spatial function can be determined a number of ways. Neglect often occurs as a result of lesions in the right hemisphere. Such deficits can be unmasked by presenting bilateral tasks, either visual or sensory, as well as using letter cancellation tasks. Asking participants to copy geometric shapes or draw a clock face are also informative here. A failure to accurately identify an object may be suggestive of visual agnosia (Ino et al., 2003).

General considerations

Important to any assessment of cognitive function is a consideration of how much effort a person is expending in performing the tasks, how motivated they feel, and also what their underlying mood is (Hebben & Milberg, 2010). Finally, the test battery has to be honed so that it is devoid of filler measures that do little to add to the overall clinical picture. It is always important to remember that not only are there physical constraints imposed on any formal assessment, more often than not the issue of time, but also constraints imposed by the individual you will be assessing. Their physical ability to perform the tasks as well as their stamina are fundamental points to consider in any formal assessment situation (Hebben & Milberg, 2010).

Selecting a test

Aside from a range of individual tests and measures available to select from, there is a large number of fixed test batteries that can be used. It is clearly not possible to provide details of all measures out there. Instead, I shall present a small selection that is illustrative of the type of measures used to assess a range of cognitive functions in older adults.

Psychopathology

Before obtaining test data it is essential for the clinician or researcher to collect measures of the participant's current mood as performance on such tasks are greatly influenced by both depression and anxiety. Both the Beck Depression Inventory (BDI-II) (Beck, Steer, & Brown, 1996) and the Beck

Anxiety Inventory (BAI) (Beck & Steer, 1993) are useful here. The Minnesota Multiphasic Personality Inventory (MMPI-2) (Butcher et al., 1989) is a standard way to test for maladjusted behaviour, including hypochondriasis, hysteria, and paranoia.

Test batteries

Mini-Mental State Examination

The Mini-Mental State Examination (MMSE) (Folstein, Folstein, & McHugh, 1975) is by far the most often used screening tool to assess cognitive functioning in older adults. The focus of this examination is on assessing a person's orientation, attention, short-term memory, and also language processing. It does not include an assessment of executive function, and there is little assessment of visuo-spatial processing, so additional measures are needed to supplement the battery (Kipps & Hodges, 2005). One of the main limitations of this measure is the length of time needed to administer it. Screening tools should preferably be short in duration. The current updated edition of the test includes among other things a brief screening version that is available for tablet PCs and smartphones and also an expanded version for more in-depth assessment of conditions such as subcortical dementia.

Cambridge Cognitive Examination

The Cambridge Cognitive Examination (CAMCOG) forms part of the Cambridge Cognitive Examination for the elderly (CAMDEX) and focuses on neuropsychological functioning including orientation, language, learning, memory, and thinking (Roth et al., 1986).

Montreal Cognitive Assessment

The Montreal Cognitive Assessment (MoCA) (Nasreddine et al., 2005) fills an important gap in the clinician's armoury. There is a growing need to assess individuals who present with symptoms indicative of mild cognitive impairment (MCI), a condition that as we shall see in Chapter 12 often precedes dementia. Screening tools of this nature are available, such as the MMSE described previously, but timely access to services providing such assessment cannot always be obtained, so tools that are available through primary care is of strategic importance in the campaign to detect and treat memory impairments early on. Importantly this measure can be administered in around ten minutes. Studies have indicated excellent test–retest reliability and high sensitivity in detecting MCI.

Addenbrooke's Cognitive Examination Revised

The Addenbrooke's Cognitive Examination Revised (ACE-R) (Mioshi et al., 2006) is another brief screening tool often used to assess cognitive functioning. Reliability is very good and there is a high correlation with the Clinical Dementia Scale indicating sensitivity to early detection of cognitive impairment. As mentioned previously, there is a need for more readily available measures of cognitive dysfunction, ones that are not only sensitive but also ones that are quick and easy to administer. The ACE is soon to be made accessible as a freely obtainable computer package for clinicians. ACEmobile lends itself to be administered on tablet PCs, thus making it easy to implement using readily available resources (ACEmobile, 2013).

Cambridge Neuropsychological Test Automated Battery

The Cambridge Neuropsychological Test Automated Battery (CANTAB®) is a computerized test battery that assesses a whole range of cognitive functions including visual memory, attention, and planning. This test battery has been used extensively in neuropsychological studies as it comprises a standardized suite of informative measures. There is now CANTAB®mobile that can be used for quick assessment of memory functioning, thereby offering greater flexibility and accessibility to healthcare professionals.

Premorbid ability

National Adult Reading Test

The National Adult Reading Test (NART) (Nelson, 1982) is a standard measure of premorbid intelligence that can be used from adolescence to older adulthood. Participants are presented with a list of 50 words with irregular spellings and are instructed to say how they think the word is pronounced. The assumption of this test is that reading ability is independent of changes within the brain. However, there is some evidence to suggest this measure may only prove accurate during the early stages of dementia (Fromm et al., 1991).

Wechsler Test of Adult Reading

The Wechsler Test of Adult Reading (WTAR) (Wechsler, 2001) is an alternative measure of premorbid intelligence that again presents participants with a list of irregularly spelled words that are read aloud. Although the NART is often used up to age 70, the WTAR allows testing to occur up to the age of 89. This measure is co-normed with the Wechsler Adult Intelligence Scale

(WAIS-IV; for details see later section) (Wechsler, 1981) and the Wechsler Memory Scale (WMS-III) (Wechsler, 1997) and so it provides a good prediction of both general ability and memory performance.

Wide Range Achievement Test 4 – Word Reading

The Wide Range Achievement Test 4 – Word Reading (WRAT-4) (Wilkinson & Robertson, 2006) measures word reading ability and can be used to assess participants from one end of the age spectrum to the other. Participants are instructed to read aloud from a list of words that become increasingly rare in their frequency of usage.

Intelligence

Raven's Progressive Matrices

The Raven's Progressive Matrices (Raven, 1995) assesses non-verbal intelligence through a variety of abstract reasoning and problem solving tasks. Designs are presented in a matrix and participants are required to identify the missing element that completes a particular pattern.

The Wechsler Adult Intelligence Scale

The Wechsler Adult Intelligence Scale (WAIS-IV) (Wechsler, 2008) can be administered to all ages across the adult lifespan. This measure includes a number of indices. The Verbal Comprehension Index comprises Information, Vocabulary, and Similarities sub-tests. The Working Memory Index consists of Arithmetic and Digit Span sub-tests. The Perceptual Reasoning Index includes Block Design, Matrix Reasoning, and Visual Puzzles sub-tests. The Processing Speed Index contains Coding and Symbol Search sub-tests.

Attentional processing

Trail Making Test

The Trail Making Test (McLean & Hitch, 1999) provides participants with instructions to connect a series of stimuli in a predefined sequence under the pressure of time. There are two parts to this test, Trail Making A and Trail Making B. Trail Making A consists entirely of numbers, whereas Trail Making B demands that the participant alternates between sequencing numbers and letters. This task taps into multiple aspects of attentional processing such as sustained attention, visual scanning, and switching mode of response.

Digit Vigilance Test

The Digit Vigilance Test (Lewis, 1995) is a measure of sustained attention and psychomotor speed as it requires the participant to scan the presented stimuli quickly to locate and cross-out target items. A number of scores can be calculated including overall time to completion and prevalence of errors of omission.

Paced Auditory Serial Addition Test

The Paced Auditory Serial Addition Test (PASAT) (Gronwall, 1977) measures both sustained and divided attention in addition to proving an index of speed of processing. Participants are presented with a series of single digit numbers and are instructed to sum the most recent two on each occasion.

Test of Everyday Attention

The Test of Everyday Attention (TEA) (Robertson et al., 1994) contains eight different sub-tests that map onto aspects of everyday living. These include assessments of selective attention, sustained attention, and also the ability to switch processing between tasks or modalities. An important aspect of this test is that all the materials relate to real-life situations. Examples include a map search task and a telephone directory search task.

Executive function

Behavioural Assessment of the Dysexecutive Syndrome

The Behavioural Assessment of the Dysexecutive Syndrome (BADS) (Wilson et al., 1996) focuses on elements of executive function that impact on a person's ability to function in their everyday lives. It covers elements measuring the ability to plan and organize, problem solve, and the capacity to effectively allocate attention, all of which may act as barriers to both recovery and rehabilitation. There is an accompanying questionnaire, the Dysexecutive Questionnaire, which assesses emotion, motivation, behaviour, and cognition, all of which are likely affected by executive dysfunction.

Verbal Fluency Test

The Verbal Fluency Test (Spreen & Benton, 1977) is a timed task that requires participants to volunteer as many words as they can within a 60-second time limit based on a particular criterion set by the clinician or researcher. In one condition the instructions are to say as many words belonging to a particular semantic category, such as animals; another condition requires responses beginning with a particular letter.

Stroop Color and Word Test

The Stroop Color and Word Test (Golden, 1978) is a reliable measure of our ability to inhibit default modes of responding and demonstrate cognitive flexibility. There are three conditions to this task. The initial condition instructs participants to read aloud the colour word presented. Participants are then asked to name the colour of the stimulus strip that they see. Following this, instructions to name the colour in which the stimulus word are presented. In this latter condition participants are again presented with colour words, although this time there is a mismatch between the colour word itself and the colour of the font used to present it.

Tower of London-Drexel University

The Tower of London-Drexel University task (TOL-DX) (Culbertson & Zilmer, 2000) assesses planning and problem solving skills and is based on the original Tower of Hanoi puzzle. There are two sets of pegboards and beads. The instructor arranges a prearranged pattern and requests that the participant matches this configuration without violating the rules relating to acceptable moves.

Wisconsin Card Sorting Test

The Wisconsin Card Sorting Test (WCST) (Grant & Berg, 1993) provides clinicians with a measure of abstract reasoning ability and provides an effective way of identifying evidence of perseverative behaviour in the participant. There are different forms of this task. In the conventional form participants are instructed to identify through trial and error the correct sorting rule. The classification may relate to either the colour, form, or number of geometric shapes presented on each card.

Memory

Doors and People Test

The Doors and People Test (DPT) (Baddeley, Emslie, & Nimmo-Smith, 1994) enables an assessment of both verbal and visual memory to be made using tests of recall and recognition, such as instructions to memorize a series of coloured photographs of doors.

Rivermead Behavioural Memory Test

The Rivermead Behavioural Test (RBMT-3) (Wilson, Cockburn, & Baddeley, 2008) is an assessment of everyday memory functioning. As a result there are a number of component tests that cover a range of activities including a person's ability to remember specific appointments, recall of names, the ability to remember to deliver a message, recall of prose material, a face recognition task, as well as a measure of implicit memory among others.

Language

Boston Naming Test

The Boston Naming Test (BNT) (Kaplan, Goodglass, & Weintraub, 2001) assesses a person's ability to correctly retrieve and name a range of line drawings. In instances where participants show evidence of problems with perception, various prompts in the form of categorical or semantic cues can be provided.

Academic achievement

Nelson-Denny Reading Test

The Nelson-Denny Reading Test (Brown, Fishco, & Hanna, 1993) provides a two-part assessment of academic achievement according to measures of vocabulary, comprehension, and reading rate. It consists of multiple-choice items with a range of short prose passages on which to assess ability.

Visual–spatial processing

Clock Drawing Test

The Clock Drawing Test (CDT) (Royall, Cordes, & Polk, 1998) presents individuals with a sheet containing a circle. The instructions direct them to fill in the numbers and set the time such that it reads the time specified by the person administering the test. In addition to assessing visuo-spatial processing, this measure offers insight into planning and abstract thinking.

Indeed, a variant of this measure, CLOX, specifically focuses on assessing the degree of executive impairment an individual is experiencing. Participants are initially asked to draw the clock freehand. In instances where they are unable to achieve this, they are instructed to copy a drawing of a completed clock. Those able to successfully complete the copying task but who fail to draw it freehand demonstrate a level of executive dysfunction.

Widening choices made by clinicians

A relatively recent paper has shown that clinicians tend to choose the test they use to screen patients from a relatively small selection (Shulman et al., 2006). The most frequently used measure here is the MMSE. Other frequent tools are the CDT, Delayed Recall, Verbal Fluency, Similarities, and the Trail Making Test. More recent measures such as the MoCA (Nasreddine et al., 2005) are increasingly being adopted. With the growing availability of tablet PC-based applications, the range of options available to healthcare professionals will hopefully proliferate.

Obtaining normative data for older adults

In the previous section we identified some of the most used assessment tools of cognitive function. As with all tests, it is important that an individual's score is placed in some meaningful context in order to see how they perform in relation to others. Most clinical measures have been used across a range of situations and so there is a repository of normative data whereby meaningful comparisons can be made.

One of the main problems when attempting to collect normative data for older adults is how to define 'normal' performance in such a heterogeneous population. Often data collected are obtained from studies utilizing a cross-sectional design. The biggest problem here is that one is then comparing performance across different aged samples whose educational and occupational experience probably varied significantly, and as a result potentially inflating perceived differences. This is referred to as a cohort effect. Another consideration to make here is to what extent the older sample comprises individuals who are exhibiting symptoms of different disease processes. Longitudinal studies help to reduce such biases.

Aside from the problems associated with sampling, at the individual level problems may also arise. A sample of older adults will vary a great deal in terms of their level of enthusiasm to partake in such activity (Hebben & Milberg, 2010). Older adults will tire more easily, so fatigue will be a major confound to consider when planning an assessment.

Their ability to co-operate will be affected by the presence of either medical or psychiatric symptoms. Loss of motor function and persistent pain are particularly relevant for consideration here. Bearing in mind a great deal of assessment requires reasonably extensive periods of time filling out pencil-and-paper measures or focusing on a computer monitor whilst having to make various button responses, physical constraints such as hearing impairment and problems with vision will exert an independent negative effect on task performance (Hebben & Milberg, 2010).

The preferred approach when assessing older adults is to select short but highly accurate measures. Unfortunately very few of the measures available were designed specifically to be administered to older adults and as a result there may be implications in terms of sensitivity to changes in functioning within this group – evidence then of a floor effect.

Before leaving this chapter it is important to consider the use of computer-based assessment tools. From the previous section we have seen that computers provide a useful platform from which tests can be administered. However, as we shall see, there are some important issues to consider when using such an approach.

Growing use of computer-based assessment

The focus of a great deal of interest is developing tools to detect and track dementia as well as MCI (Woodard, 2010). Early detection is seen to be crucial in the treatment and management of these conditions, especially in terms of a propensity to predict dementia in currently healthy individuals. Current tests do allow clinicians to predict later onset of Alzheimer's disease in individuals who are currently diagnosed with MCI (Albert et al., 2001).

Although many measures are in a pencil-and-paper format, more and more tasks are being designed to be implemented on a computer. In some instances, levels of anxiety may be higher when asked to interact with unfamiliar technology. Although given these reservations, there are many unique advantages to computer-based testing. Computers allow testing to be administered in a standardized format each time, with scoring being carried out automatically. Among other things, automatic scoring eliminates the influence of subjective bias. Increasing use of web-based assessment packages now eliminates the need for dedicated computers for testing, thereby side-stepping the need for compatible operating systems.

However, there are a number of disadvantages with computer-based testing. Differences in processing speed may bring with it the perennial issue over accuracy of timing. Differences in monitor size, whether the computer is a desktop or a laptop, whether the respondent uses a mouse or keyboard to register responses, and many other factors will confound a study's findings unless accounted for. Some of these issues may be eradicated through the use of dedicated button response boxes and the inclusion of a calibration routine as part of the software to ensure comparability of timings across devices. Standard computer-based test batteries can also prove expensive, with many companies requiring annual licensing. However, as we have seen earlier freely available assessment tools are becoming available to clinicians and researchers alike.

Summary

Accurate assessment of cognitive function is much needed for both clinicians and researchers. The standard format of clinical assessment has been described, from initial information gathering concerning education status and general health to the implementation of specific tests. Along the way we have considered some of the main tools available: some that provide measures of specific function, others that offer a comprehensive assessment of function. We have also examined why it is important to collect normative data. The final section considered the growing use of computer-based assessments. Although there are many positive arguments for using technology from a methodological point of view, there are clear considerations to make when administering tests to older adults using such an approach.

The growth of formal assessments of function is mirrored to some extent by a growing market for informal assessments, epitomized by a variety of brain training packages. The validity of such claims will be examined in Chapter 14 when we consider what we can do to minimize the impact of age-related changes in cognitive function.

Further reading

Hebben, N. and Milberg, W. (2010). *Essentials of neuropsychological assessment*. Chichester: John Wiley [An indispensable guide for those involved in administering tests of cognitive functioning.]

Hodges, J. R. (2007). *Cognitive assessment for clinicians*. Oxford: Oxford University Press. [This text provides some excellent case study material.]

Lezak, M. D. (2012). *Neuropsychological assessment*. Oxford; New York: Oxford University Press. [This is a comprehensive handbook covering all forms of neuropsychological assessment.]

CHAPTER 9

Personality, Intelligence, and Individual Differences

The study of personality is thriving especially in connection with health outcomes and life expectancy (Wilson et al., 2004). There is now a good understanding of how age affects personality, be it in terms of aspects that remain stable compared to those that change (Mroczek et al., 2006). We will be exploring health and ageing in Chapter 11. However, we shall now look first at different accounts concerning personality across the lifespan, along with a consideration of how stable our personalities actually are. After a brief overview of two key theories of cognitive development, we shall examine intelligence. For most people intelligence is something that is measured by such things as the dreaded 11-Plus. However, as we shall see, it is restrictive to think of intelligence in this way. Instead, intelligence consists of many things relating to ability across a range of domains. This chapter will end with a look at two related concepts, namely those of creativity and wisdom.

Personality

Psychodynamic perspective

Many contemporary models of adult development are based to some extent on the psychodynamic perspective. Freud believed that once we enter the adult phase our personality remains unchanged. The shaping of our personality occurred largely during the *sturm und drang* of childhood, a time of great conflict between behavioural instincts, thoughts, and feelings. Indeed, Freud claimed that due to inflexibility of thought, psychotherapy is not a plausible option once one reaches the age of 50 (Freud, 1957). To cement this claim even further Freud argued that the much needed libidinal drive that fuels change is absent after a certain age (Freud, 1957).

However, evidence from Freud's own life and the lives of his followers demonstrate clearly that this age restriction was not a central tenet of the psychodynamic approach as evidenced by the fact that many of Freud's disciples were actively engaged in their own personal analysis around this pivotal age. Abraham argued that more important to change is the age at which neurosis manifested (Abraham & Jones, 1979). Unfortunately this ambiguity over age resulted in many older adults being dissuaded from embarking on psychotherapy until the final half of the twentieth century (Biggs, 2005). Modern development of Freud's theory has led to a consensus that personality is a great deal more malleable than was once thought.

Freud believed that the aspects of personality that were of greatest importance in terms of behaviour were hidden within the unconscious mind. The id is concerned with satisfying desires. The ego reigns in the demands of the id, thereby preventing the types of transgressions that would occur should the id be allowed to dominate behaviour. Defence mechanisms are erected to prevent id demands reaching conscious awareness, thus allowing us to function in normal society without unnecessary conflict. The super-ego symbolizes a personification of authority figures and operates as censor. The id, the ego, and the super-ego comprise Freud's Structural Theory (Freud et al., 1961). This structural theory encapsulates the dynamism between the drive of the id and the mediating effects of the ego and super-ego.

Ego psychology

Whereas Freud believed the ego merely served the id, others argue instead that the ego is the conscious mind where information is integrated, analysed, and synthesized. The ego is used to direct our everyday behaviour. To some extent, the ego is the self. Erikson developed a highly influential theory of psychosocial development in which the emphasis was no longer on libidinal drive but instead harnessed the entire lifespan. This theory emphasized the impact of the environment on a person's development.

Erikson proposed eight stages to his life cycle, of which three focused on adulthood and older adulthood (Erikson, 1982). Each life stage comprised a specific conflict that needed to be resolved before moving on to the next phase. The stages that make up this cycle are as follows:

(i) *Basic trust versus mistrust* occurs during infancy and centres on the ability to develop trust.
(ii) *Autonomy versus shame/doubt* reflects the period when a child may gain a sense of independence.

(iii) *Initiative versus guilt* occurs around the age of four and consists of attempts to identify behaviours to emulate.
(iv) *Industry versus inferiority* occurs with the child's attempt to master their environment.
(v) *Identity versus identity confusion/diffusion* refers to the stage during which an individual makes choices about who they are and what their plans will be.
(vi) *Intimacy versus isolation* is the first adult-life stage and concerns the development of intimate relationships.
(vii) *Generativity versus stagnation* reflects a period of time during which personal growth and productivity is possible.
(viii) *Integrity versus despair* focuses on attempts to maintain a sense of self-worth in the face of growing challenges as a result of old age.

A theory closely related to that of Erikson is that of Loevinger's conceptualization of the ego (Loevinger & Blasi, 1976). Loevinger argued that the ego is responsible for regulating behaviour, relating to other people, and achieving a true understanding of the self. At the earliest stages in ego development, referred to as the conformist stage, there is only a fundamental understanding of self and society. There is little comprehension of why others behave the way they do. As a development of this, the conscientious-conformist stage sees an internal representation of right and wrong. Insight into both our own and others' behaviour is achieved at the conscientious stage. Respect for the individual is attained during the individualistic stage. The full complexity of human behaviour is realized during the autonomous stage, as well as a capacity to deal with uncertainty. The final stage, the integrated stage, reflects a time when we are master of the inner self.

This theory, then, is a combination of both ego psychology and moral development. It has been demonstrated that high scores on Loevinger's scale relate to better cognitive functioning, as well as higher scores on personality variables such as assertiveness, conformity, and fearfulness (Cohn & Westenberg, 2004).

Defence mechanisms

The concept of defence mechanisms is important from a psychodynamic perspective. Contrary to Freud's view, Vaillant argues that defence mechanisms change over the course of our adult lives (Vaillant, 2000), allowing us to adapt and cope with the types of challenges we face in our daily lives. We find increasingly more mature ways to deal with the anxiety resulting from such stressors. Immature responses such as acting out, where anger is relieved through action, provides only temporary relief, and may be injurious to oneself and others. More mature strategies, such as the use of humour, have more long-term benefits, as well as fewer social and psychological costs.

In a longitudinal study of men and women it was found that, as we age, we adopt more mature defence mechanisms (Cramer, 2003). Narcissistic personality types, those whose experience with others vacillates between over idealization and devaluing, use more maladaptive strategies, often to the detriment of their own psychological health (Cramer & Jones, 2008). More adaptive strategies result in a greater control over one's emotions and an ability to reframe the situation to make it manageable (Diehl, Coyle, & Labouvie-Vief, 1996). A more rational approach is taken, acknowledging the importance of persevering in order to achieve an improved outcome. It is interesting to also note that, independent of age, gender differences occur. Women show a greater tendency to avoid stressful situations, internalize blame, and turn to others for support, whereas men externalize their feelings, making use of reaction formation. Reaction formation refers to the process whereby intolerable desires are controlled by overtly behaving in a manner diametrically opposed to these feelings. Repression of the urge, however, means that it will likely surface at some stage.

Jungian psychology

For Jung adult existence consisted of a time of adjustment and consolidation during which we try to find our fit in society (Jung, 1967, 1930: IX, 771). This process continues until we reach middle age. For the latter half of life Jung argued that we commence a journey of self-discovery, a process referred to as individuation. The drive is no longer conformity but rather an unearthing of potential.

Adult attachment theory

Theories of adult attachment explore the way in which the relationship we experienced as children with our parents or caregivers influenced our adult existence. A major proponent of this theory was Bowlby. His theory developed out of his experiences observing children in orphanages but was indebted to accounts of primate ethology. Although physical needs were met, Bowlby argued that emotional needs very rarely were, thereby explaining some of the behavioural problems observed in these children (Bowlby, 1969). The success of attachment, specifically in this instance maternal attachment, influences greatly the development of the self. Poor caregiving is believed to lead to feelings of insecurity and a negative self-concept later in life (Bowlby, 1973).

The issue of attachment style concerns how we interact and relate to our principal attachment figure, be it our mother during childhood, or our partners in later life. In a classic experiment of attachment based on the work of Bowlby, Ainsworth measured how young children reacted to their mother leaving and then returning in various controlled situations (Ainsworth, 1978). They identified a range of attachment styles reflecting behaviour following separation from and on returning to their mother. Those children with a secure attachment style cope well with their mother leaving the room. On her return, the child turns to her and seeks out contact. At no time does the child display any negative emotions. Instead, they seek only to reinforce the positive relationship they enjoy with their mother. In some instances, on returning, the mother faces a child who actively resists all forms of contact from her. In such cases the child is showing evidence of an avoidant attachment style. Those with an anxious attachment style appear to want contact with their mother, but when proffered, they reject her. An additional classification, disorganized/disoriented, was included to reflect children who failed to fit into one of the existing styles (Main & Solomon, 1986).

Although there is a great deal of research looking at attachment style in both children and young adults, the same cannot be said for the literature on older adults. The studies that have been conducted show that adult attachment styles are more secure, thereby reflecting their greater ability to manage relationships as evidenced by the adoption of a variety of defence mechanisms. In particular, there is a lower prevalence of anxious attachment styles in older adults (Segal, Needham, & Coolidge, 2009). Secure attachment at a young age has been shown to be associated with greater feelings of happiness in later life (Consedine & Magai, 2003). However, there does seem to be greater resilience to negative parenting as we grow older, such that less secure attachment styles cease to exert such a strong effect for older adults (Magai et al., 2004).

Trait approaches

From a trait perspective personality is seen to comprise a series of stable and enduring personality characteristics. These qualities lead us to behave in idiosyncratic ways. A number of models of personality exist, although probably the most influential is the Five Factor Model (McCrae & Costa, 1997). The five factors are Openness, Conscientiousness, Extraversion, Agreeableness, and Neuroticism. Openness to experience reflects a person's interest in art, imagination, enthusiasm for new experiences, tolerance, and understanding of emotional responses. It is also highly correlated with crystallized intelligence (see later section for more details) (Ashton et al., 2000).

Conscientiousness concerns attention to detail, a sense of order, restraint, and prudence. Extraversion is linked to sociability, assertiveness, and active engagement. It has also been shown to significantly predict well-being and happiness (Stewart, 2006). Agreeableness is indicative of someone who is trusting, humane, and supportive. High scores on neuroticism are linked to someone who doubts, who is prone to extreme changes in emotion, and is shy. There is a strong link between high scores on neuroticism and clinical mood disorders. Our own unique set of personality characteristics guides our behaviour, and so, to a large extent, the choices we make are a function of our personality, rather than life events determining specific personality traits.

It was generally believed that such personality traits appear consistent over time (Roberts & DelVecchio, 2000). However, more recent studies have shown this was not necessarily the case. More sophisticated statistical modelling techniques enable us to examine changes across time, not only at the level of the five main factors, but also in terms of the individual facets within each factor. Such studies have shown that self-discipline, a component of conscientiousness, drops with age. This suggests that older adults shy away from activities that are not intrinsically appealing to them. On the other hand, the deliberation component increases, with behaviour becoming less impulsive with age (Terracciano et al., 2005).

Social cognitive approaches

Social cognitive approaches focus to a large extent on the interplay between motivation and emotion and how they relate to everyday life. How ageing affects this relationship is increasingly becoming the focus of research, especially in terms of how a person's needs, desires, and goals change across the lifespan.

Socioemotional selectivity theory argues that we each build relationships so that risks are minimal and rewards maximized (Charles & Carstensen, 2010). The type of rewards we desire change as we become older, thereby fuelling different forms of interactions with others. This approach sees relationships with others as providing either an informational function or an emotional function. A relationship that provides an informational function provides a person with knowledge that was previously unavailable to them. Relationships that provide an emotional function add to one's sense of well-being. The drive is to maximize positive emotional experiences by reducing the range of an individual's social network so that it comprises those to whom they feel closest. In this sense emotion regulation occurs through exposure to only highly selective social interactions.

Considered within the framework of ageing, this theory proposes that there is a shift from relationships that provide an informational function to those that provide instead an emotional function. The reason for this shift, it is suggested, is the growing awareness of one's own mortality. Linked to this yearning for familiar relationships is the much needed emotion buffer such relationships afford (Lang & Carstensen, 2002).

Structure–process model

It has been argued that the trait approach does provide an effective framework for personality but in doing so many other aspects have been excluded (McAdams, 1992). As an alternative aspects from both the trait and social cognitive models are combined to produce a two-dimensional model of personality consisting of structure and process (Hooker & McAdams, 2003). Structure reflects elements from the trait approach, whereas process consists of facets of the social cognitive model. Each dimension houses three distinct aspects of personality. The structural component comprises traits, characteristic adaptations, and life stories; the process component consists of states, self-regulation, and self-narration. In an attempt to capture the effects of age on one's personality, this model reflects both aspects of personality that do not change (structural dimensions) and those that do in response to situational characteristics (process dimensions). This change is transient so that once the eliciting situation has resolved behaviour reverts back to normal.

Cognitive perspective

Cognitive self theories argue that events are assessed in terms of their relevance to the self. A large part of the cognitive perspective is given over to mechanisms for coping. People generally view themselves as unchanging: the same person they have always been. However, this is often inconsistent with reality (Baumeister, 1996). In addition to this, people generally appraise themselves in a positive way (Baumeister et al., 2001).

Possible selves theory

One approach, the possible selves theory (Markus & Nurius, 1986), suggests that how we view ourselves, our self-schema in other words, guides the way we behave and the choices we make. The concept of possible selves refers to the notion that one appraises one's current self, and then reflects on how one would like to actually appear. Any discrepancy between the actual and desired self would then act to guide behaviour in order that the desired self is obtained. Conversely, a person will strive to avoid becoming their feared possible self. In order to achieve a positive outcome, one's desired self must be achievable. A realistic desired self will eventually increase satisfaction with one's lot (Cheng, Fung, & Chan, 2009). This process continues throughout our lives, even in late adulthood (Smith & Freund, 2002).

Identity process theory

Identity process theory argues that our lives consist of an everlasting attempt to maintain a consistent sense of self (identity assimilation) in an ever-changing world (identity accommodation) (Whitbourne, Sneed, & Skultety, 2002). We all strive to make sense of events based on how we view ourselves. However, on occasion, an event occurs that fails to make sense in terms of how we view ourselves at that moment in time, and so necessitates degrees of accommodation in order to do so. With age, the process of identity assimilation becomes increasingly important. Without this, experiences accumulated throughout one's life may act to lower perceived self-esteem. The process of assimilation enables a consistent positive self-image to be maintained. If assimilation is misjudged, our assessment of ourselves may no longer marry with that of reality. Self-esteem is higher among those who predominantly adopt the approach of identity assimilation (Sneed & Whitbourne, 2003). The opposite is seen in those who generally adopt identity accommodation.

Evidence suggesting identity assimilation has positive health effects can be seen in a study which showed that, among adults who avoided a negative perception of ageing, life expectancy was over seven years greater than in the comparison group who did not show the same resistance to age (Levy et al., 2002). A similar finding is observed when psychological health is the outcome studied (Cramer & Jones, 2007).

Midlife crisis theories and findings

The use of the term 'midlife crisis' began in the 1970s in an attempt to encapsulate often noted changes in personality as adults make the transition into middle age. It was at this juncture that an appraisal of one's achievements and goals was carried out. Any future plans were unavoidably tarnished by one's own impending death (Jaques, 1965).

An influential theory to develop in this field was that of Levinson and colleagues (Levinson, 1978). Central to this approach is the concept of life structure – the blueprint of a person's life. Levinson believed that as adults we each progress through different stages, flitting from periods of calm to times of intense change. Periods of transition that follow a reappraisal of one's current situation are characterized by an exploration of alternatives. The period of transition occurring during middle adulthood often reflects a sense of disillusionment in the realization that youthful hopes and aspirations have failed to materialize. It is a time for self-examination, a time to plan for the future.

In terms of empirical support for such a transition phase, there is very little (Lachman, 2004). The concept of midlife crisis suffers with an issue of definition: if it is such a universal phenomenon, when, in fact, does it occur? Of those studies that have been conducted, one of the most psychometrically robust studies failed to replicate the findings of Levinson (1978). There appeared to be no change in scores on personality (McCrae & Costa, 2003). In fact, one of the only tangible findings associated with high scores on measures of midlife crisis occurred in men who had scored high on neuroticism in the previous decade. This would suggest, then, the state of flux associated with midlife crisis is associated more with a history of psychological problems rather than it being representative of the average adult.

Does personality change with age?

There has been much debate as to whether personality remains fixed as we age or whether in fact it is in flux as a result of changing demands and experiences. A seemingly flippant response would be to say that the weight of evidence suggests that some people's personality does indeed remain stable, whereas other people's personality does not (Mroczek, Spiro, & Griffin, 2006). More sophisticated statistical modelling techniques have allowed researchers to explore in more depth the individual differences component of personality across the lifespan. It appears that there is a great deal of variability across individuals. Studies have also indicated that, in addition to variation over long periods of time, there are fluctuations on a daily basis in terms of how people see themselves, reflecting intra-individual variability (Jones, Nesselroade, & Birkel, 1991).

Why some people change and not others can be explained with references to a host of psychological, biological, and environmental influences, all of which interact to produce a unique life experience (Caspi et al., 2002). Life events play a major role in eliciting personality change, such as marriage which leads to increased conscientiousness and reduced neuroticism (Neyer & Asendorpf, 2001). Changes in health are important here also. Deterioration in health may result in social withdrawal. This may then lead to diminished extraversion and higher levels of neuroticism (Mroczek, Spiro, & Griffin, 2006). This is a two-way process such that health changes may result in the altering of personality as well as personality shifts impacting on health. For example, diminishing health may make one less extraverted. This in turn may lessen one's drive to maintain healthy behaviour patterns and so worsening health even further. Of course, the converse it true also, with certain changes in personality being linked to greater resilience (Aldwin & Levenson, 1994; Ryff & Singer, 1998). We shall explore the impact of personality on health a little more in Chapter 11. The next section will look at what we mean by intelligence and how age influences functioning within this domain. Before doing so, however, there is a small section describing the work of both Schaie and Piaget. Both models present accounts of how cognitive development takes place: from the most basic operations that progress from birth through to complex abstract processes we carry out as adults.

Cognitive development

One influential model here is that of Schaie (1977). This model categorizes our lifespan into discrete stages. At each of these stages our cognitive abilities are concerned primarily with activities that are meaningful for that particular time of life. During childhood and adolescence we are fuelled to acquire knowledge and skills that we will need to function in society further down the line. This acquisitive stage leads into the achieving stage of development that takes place during early adulthood. Our motivations during this stage reflect the desire to become competent, independent social beings, each with his or her own goals and objectives. The middle years of adulthood are characterized by demands made of us to act responsibly, both in the home and at work. We need to develop the skills necessary to care for our family; we also need to adapt to increasing responsibilities at work. This stage is referred to as the responsible/executive stage. The final reintegrative stage experienced during older adulthood reflects the need to be more selective in how we expend our time and energy. This may in part reflect changes in the demands made upon us, but it may also be in response to changes affecting cognitive functioning.

Later versions of this model added two further stages. A reorganization stage was included to reflect the changes associated with retirement. Retirement is a time when a great deal of change occurs to our daily routine. It is a time also to contemplate one's level of independence. The second stage to be added concerned our final years: a time when we contemplate our own end. It is during this time that people review their lives and final revisions to wills are made. These are topics we shall return to in Chapter 10.

Although such an approach is useful in terms of examining the motivational changes that to some extent drive our cognitive activity across our lives, there are clear and obvious limitations when attempting to apply this structure across cultures. An individual's state of health will also be a deciding factor as to whether every stage is experienced.

The classic Piagetian approach also conceptualizes humans as progressing through discrete stages of cognitive development (Piaget, 1952). He assigned an active role to the child in his or her contact with the environment, emphasizing not merely biological maturation but adaptation also. As children, we soon develop cognitive representations of the objects with which we interact. From birth until around the age of two a child is seen to enter the sensorimotor stage of development. During this time the child is learning to explore his or her environment through both movement and senses. From this rudimentary language and problem solving skills develop between the ages of two and seven. The preoperational stage sees children begin to use words to communicate, from one- or two-word utterances to much longer sentences. They also develop the concept of object permanence, where it is understood that even when the movement of a previously detected object is not observed, the object continues still to exist. The child develops the capacity to form mental representations of external events allowing them to think about things without their actual occurrence.

During late childhood our evolving ability to manipulate mental representations reflect a period called the concrete operational stage. This occurs between the ages of seven and 11. Such concrete operations include among other things an appreciation of the conservation of quantity. This is where the child understands that properties of concrete objects are not affected as a result of some form of transformation. An example often provided is that of conservation of volume. This is where water from one container is poured in to a different-shaped receptacle whilst a child observed. The usual response from a child who has successfully completed this stage is that the volume of water has not changed even though the height of the water observed in the vessel has altered.

The final stage of cognitive development during childhood links with our shift into adulthood. This period reflects such higher cognitive functions as logical reasoning required to solve abstract problems. This is referred to as the formal operations stage and occurs from between the ages of 11 and 15 and continues through adulthood. Once this stage of development has been reached the child is able to develop and test hypotheses about the way the world operates. Abstract thinking is possible using symbolic representations of reality. Knowledge is built upon with increasingly complex interactions with the environment through a process of adaptation. Knowledge structures are applied to different situations (assimilation) and are then modified to reflect reality (accommodation) (Torres & Ash, 2007).

Piaget's theory has been very influential. However, it is clear that, as adults, we do not always use logical reasoning to solve problems we face in everyday life. Often, everyday situations do not lend themselves to such an approach. Although formal reasoning forms the backbone of many psychometric tests, everyday life requires something more creative (Sinnott, 1996). To this end, a postformal thinking stage has been offered as following Piaget's original formal operations stage. Postformal thinking reflects a need to tolerate ambiguity and adopt a flexible way of responding when faced with a problem to solve. Unlike psychometric tests, the types of problems we encounter in life rarely require a single correct response. Instead, various solutions may be possible, each with varying degrees of success. This will be explored in more depth later in the chapter.

Intelligence

How intelligent (or not) we perceive ourselves to be acts as a major influence on our lives. It forms an intrinsic part of the self (Leonardelli et al., 2003). The impact of age on intelligence, real or imagined, is something that is rapidly becoming a major concern to older adults, largely due to the media representation of age-related decline in mental ability.

The historical development of psychometric measures of intelligence started with the Stanford-Binet test (Thorndike, Hagen, & Sattler, 1986). This was a measure of child intelligence. The need to develop adult measures quickly led to the development of the Wechsler Adult Intelligence Scale (WAIS; Wechsler, 1955), a measure that continues to exist today, albeit the product of a number of iterations. The WAIS breaks down into two main scales: verbal and non-verbal. Performance on verbal scales generally remain stable across our lifespan (Kaufman et al., 1991).

Early pioneering work on intelligence led to the notion that there existed a general capacity in each of us that reflected intelligence: in other words, a general factor of intelligence, or 'g' (Spearman, 1904). Since then, rather than intelligence being a single entity, the general consensus is that there are many different facets or dimensions of intelligence. An example of this approach is referred to as the primary mental abilities framework (Thurstone, 1938). Instead of there being only one unitary intelligence there is a range of intelligences associated with verbal meaning, word fluency, number, spatial relations, memory, perceptual speed, and general reasoning.

Fluid and crystallized intelligence

Rather than being primary abilities, Cattell later argued that Thurstone's list reflected secondary mental abilities (Cattell, 1963), and that intelligence should instead be seen to comprise two sets of capacities: fluid intelligence (Gf) and crystallized intelligence (Gc).

Fluid intelligence reflects a person's innate ability to perform a range of higher-order cognitive activities involving the manipulation and integration of information, often of an abstract nature. Crystallized intelligence, on the other hand, involves acquired knowledge and skills. In combination, both fluid and crystallized intelligence provide an index of ability that takes into consideration biological, psychological, and social aspects of functioning. Although originally considered as separate entities, it is clear from more recent research that how crystallized intelligence develops is to a large extent dependent on fluid intelligence (McArdle & Hamagami, 2006).

Stability of intelligence

In longitudinal studies exploring the impact of age on intelligence, it is generally the case that most abilities do decline after the age of 60. However, the age at which people peak at different type of abilities is not uniform. Aside from numeric ability which peak early on, other abilities peak much later in life, such as verbal ability, and even perceptual speed. It is clear that there is no set pattern to how age affects intelligence (Schaie, 2005). There is a great deal of individual difference in terms of which aspect of intelligence is affected. Looking at the samples as a whole, Schaie showed that very few of the oldest adults demonstrated impairment across all aspects of intelligence measured. When reassessed, it appears that fluid intelligence – the ability to manipulate information – generally reached its zenith in early adulthood then declines with age, whereas crystallized intelligence peaks in older age and so does not suffer the same decline (Salthouse, 1991). Although decline does occur in some areas, the degree to which it impacts negatively on a person's life may be ameliorated to some extent by controlling the environment, such that greater competence is demonstrated by those older adults who remain in familiar surroundings (Schaie & Zanjani, 2006). Indeed, people remain highly competent in abilities intrinsic to their well-being.

There are, of course, a number of factors that may impact on how intelligence changes across a person's life. Cognitive functioning can be affected both by the onset of a particular disease or by the treatments used to manage or eradicate it (Tabbarah, Crimmins, & Seeman, 2002). In addition to neurodegenerative disorders, medical conditions such as diabetes, heart disease, and chronic obstructive pulmonary disease can seriously affect cognitive function (Almeida & Flicker, 2001; Fioravanti et al., 1995; Jackson-Guilford, Leander, & Nisenbaum, 2000). Other health conditions also affect cognitive function, such as arthritis. Such deficits among this patient group include impairments in verbal comprehension, spatial processing, and inductive reasoning (Schaie & Zanjani, 2006). Various treatments also impact here, such that regimes to control heart disease, cancer, and diabetes have all led to impaired functioning (Abayomi, 2002; Drexler & Robertson, 2001; Stanley et al., 2002).

When looking at the influence of health-related behaviour on cognitive functioning, it is important to consider whether behaviour results in a decline in functioning, or whether a person's cognitive ability determines the behavioural choices made. A recent longitudinal study has produced findings that suggest that it is cognitive functioning which largely determines physical function (Elovainio et al., 2009). The mechanism of this change may be as a result of a decline in physical activities due to deteriorating cognitive function.

There are gender differences at work here also. Men and women differ in terms of how well they perform on various measures of intelligence (Kaufman et al., 1991). It is also the case that decline in fluid intelligence hits women sooner than men, whereas crystallized intelligence is compromised earlier in men (Dixon & Hultsch, 1999).

In addition to gender, socioeconomic status influences intelligence, such that higher groupings offer some protection against the decline associated with age (Aartsen et al., 2002). Environmental factors play a substantial role, especially the home environment of the retired individual: the more stimulating the environment, the smaller the decline in intellectual functioning (Schaie et al., 2001).

Personality is important in the sense that, more confident individuals who adopt a more open-minded approach to life retain greater competence across a range of intellectual abilities (Schaie, Willis, & Caskie, 2004). High anxiety is also linked to poorer performance on a range of measures (Wetherell et al., 2002).

Multiple intelligences

Although the bedrock of much research, the concept of fluid and crystallized intelligence is often thought to be too restrictive, and as such not reflecting the true breadth of human intelligence. The theory of multiple intelligences proposes, instead, eight forms of intelligence (Gardner, 1983). These are verbal–linguistic intelligence (our ability to use language and acquire knowledge), logical–mathematical intelligence (manipulation of abstract symbol systems), auditory–musical intelligence (appreciating and generating music), visual–spatial intelligence (utilizing mental imagery), kinaesthetic intelligence (knowledge and control of one's body), intrapersonal intelligence (handling one's own emotions), and interpersonal intelligence (ability to communicate with other people). From this perspective, each of us consists of a range of strengths and weakness across a variety of domains.

Another approach to incorporate non-academic ability into their conception of intelligence is the triarchic theory of intelligence (Sternberg, 1985). Sternberg proposed that the three components reflected basic academic qualities, such as the ability to analyse and evaluate information (analytic intelligence); practical skills (practical intelligence); and the ability to think, conceive, and imagine (creative intelligence) (Sternberg, 1999).

These approaches shift the balance away from purely academic indices of intelligence, arguing instead that a more accurate gauge of how successful we are as individuals is mirrored in abilities that encompass biological, psychological, and social components (Sternberg, 1999). This approach has been influential in reconceptualizing how adult intelligence is conceived, informing a growing understanding of what we mean by wisdom (Sternberg's balance theory of wisdom; Sternberg, 1998). We shall pick up on the topic of wisdom shortly.

In his conceptualization of intelligence Sternberg (Sternberg et al., 1995) distinguishes between formal knowledge and tacit knowledge. The difference between the two is that tacit knowledge refers to that which is not openly expressed and is not acquired as the result of explicit instruction. Tacit knowledge underpins practical intelligence, which is the ability to acquire and utilize this knowledge in order to cope more effectively with everyday problems when they arise (Sternberg, 2000). Formal knowledge is assessed through standard psychometric tests. Tacit knowledge, on the other hand, can be portrayed as 'knowing how' as opposed to 'knowing that' (Sternberg & Lubart, 2001). Tacit knowledge tends to increase with age. Such knowledge is often linked to how well a person is able to cope with everyday problems. As such, tacit knowledge would appear to be an important factor associated with successful ageing.

Creativity

A linked construct to what we have been discussing is that of creativity. In his conceptualization of intelligence, Sternberg (Sternberg, 1996), as seen previously, proposes there to be analytic, practical, and creative components to intelligence. Analytic intelligence is comparable to the abilities assessed by psychometric tests – ones that focus on assessing convergent thinking where attempts are made to find the single best solution in each case. Practical intelligence involves the use of tacit knowledge to inform actions. Creative intelligence largely reflects more divergent modes of thinking where a range of plausible solutions to a problem is generated. However, it poses a number of complications when trying to assess it objectively.

Various attempts have been made to monitor changes in creativity across the lifespan. Some have found creativity to dwindle once we reach

30 (Lehman, 1953), whereas others provide a more encouraging picture (Dennis, 1966; Simonton, 1990). To some extent, the level of creativity apparent as we age depends on our occupation (Dennis, 1966) and also the age at which we embarked on a career (Simonton, 1990). Those who enter a career later in life experience a peak of creativity.

When attempting to assess creativity, it is important to consider both quality and quantity of output. Peaks in creativity often go hand in hand with peaks in productivity. This is reflected in the constant-probability-of-success model of creativity (Simonton, 1990). This model proposes that individuals who produce more have a greater likelihood of finding success.

Productivity often declines as we get older. However, sometimes there is a final flurry of activity in those in their sixties and seventies: the swan-song phenomenon (Simonton, 1990). What is apparent is that, in the final outputs of composers, writers, and artists, regardless of styles developed early on in their lives, works of great clarity are produced; pieces that are elegant in their simplicity. The final symphonic output of Sibelius is a shining example of this process of integration and precision.

Wisdom

Following on from the previous sections about intelligence and creativity, this final section will focus on 'wisdom'. It is a term that is used in common parlance. There are many ways to define wisdom. However, each definition usually refers to wisdom being an accumulation of expert knowledge and insight about life (Baltes et al., 1995). However, wisdom is not merely obtained through the accumulation of knowledge. Wisdom concerns a person's ability to identify where there are gaps in their knowledge, and making more effective use of the knowledge you do have (Birren & Fisher, 1990).

Wisdom offers much when one is faced by the types of problems that present themselves every day. Problems where there is an element of uncertainty, where there is some form of interpersonal dilemma to address (Baltes et al., 1995). Wisdom is also passed on to others through sage advice (Baltes & Smith, 1990).

The picture presented of wisdom so far is that it is the pinnacle of cognitive development. One element that has been missing is that of emotion. Wisdom refers to the tricky balance between our thoughts, actions, and emotions (Birren & Fisher, 1990). A wise person never acts impulsively. Instead, they calmly consider the options available, making the best choice possible in the given situation.

When thinking about what is meant by wisdom, there is an automatic tendency to associate it with advancing age. We require time in order to build up this repository of knowledge and abilities (Baltes & Smith, 2008). Although some support this, other research has shown that this may not necessarily be the case. It is certainly the case that wisdom is not a given regardless of our age. Indeed, the variability of wisdom in older adults is great (Ardelt, 2000), and linked to overall satisfaction with life.

One view then is that with increasing knowledge comes an increased tendency to err (Percy, 1975). Knowledge is fundamentally imperfect and so wisdom is needed to mediate feelings of suspicion and conviction that arise as a result (Meacham, 1990). Because we do inevitably acquire knowledge throughout life, our ability to make such distinction lessens due to the fact that we feel more confident or certain of our ability to choose the appropriate response.

A competing theory mirrors the general belief that wisdom can only be developed as a result of life experience and advancing age. Theories that uphold the belief that wisdom increases with age generally adopt a neo-Piagetian approach, thereby proposing a stage-like rise in abilities that foster wisdom (Kramer, 1990). However, not everyone attains wisdom as a result of not developing prerequisite cognitive abilities or personality integration.

A key figure associated with a life-stage approach is Erikson (Erikson, Erikson, & Kivnick, 1986). The next phase of development is attained through the resolution of a specific crisis that occurs at each stage. Middle age brings with it a series of challenges, a key one here being generativity – one's contribution to the world, be it through procreation or professional contribution. During older adulthood a key crisis to resolve is the coming to terms with the successes and failures of one's life, bringing with it a sense of ego-integrity. Mastery of both these stages can be associated with increased wisdom (Orwoll & Perlmutter, 1990).

The dynamic between the complexity of cognitive and emotion processing plays a substantial role here also. In a similar vein to Meacham's proposition that all knowledge is imperfect (Meacham, 1990), these accounts argue that wisdom reflects the ability to form conclusions from information that is inherently fallible based largely on a person's ability to utilize and integrate cognitive and affective processing in decision making processes (Kramer, 1990).

One approach that attempts to integrate earlier theories proposes five criteria associated with wisdom (Baltes, Smith, & Staudinger, 1992). These are rich factual knowledge, rich procedural knowledge, lifespan contextualism, value relativism, and awareness and management of uncertainty. Both factual and procedural knowledge refer to one's knowledge base for a range of situations as well as awareness of appropriate strategies. As such they are heralded as necessary but not sufficient for wisdom (Pasupathi & Staudinger, 2000). The last three are designated meta-criteria and refer to our understanding of how the past, present, and future are intertwined, how values vary from one individual to the next, and how we are able to deal effectively with uncertainty.

Important in relation to who may develop wisdom are one's motivation to strive and excel as well as exposure and response to relevant experiences. Existential confrontations are particularly important in developing this type of higher-order thinking style. Indeed, it is not only the case that experiencing such events are important, but also one's reflection upon what happened and how that knowledge is then integrated into one's belief system are just as important too (Staudinger, 2001). The concept of positivity following adversity has been shown to be influential in terms of how one adapts to the challenges of ageing (Davis, Nolen-Hoeksema, & Larson, 1998). This model enforces the argument that there is no linear relationship between age and wisdom. Instead, wisdom emerges through one's interaction with the environment in which we live based on antecedent capacities available to us.

Differences in underlying cognitive style works to either foster or stifle wisdom. Positive effects occur with a style that focuses on trying to understand behaviour and its implications as opposed to attempting to categorize behaviour as right or wrong (Sternberg, 1990). Creativity appears important also as might be expected (Staudinger, Lopez, & Baltes, 1997).

One of the main difficulties with this field of research is how wisdom is actually measured. The predominant approach at the moment is to present individuals with vignettes that depict a particular hypothetical dilemma. Participants respond by providing details of the advice they would give to the fictional character in the story. As with real-life situations, rarely is there a single correct solution. What this approach allows is for each individual's advice relating to a particular scenario to be rated in terms of its perceived wisdom. In order to achieve a high score on wisdom responses needed to encompass all aspects of the dilemma, with a number of plausible actions being stated. Each action should be presented in terms of its pros and cons, and in particular an evaluation of the risks associated with each one. Finally, emphasis should be given to the monitoring and evaluation of whichever action is chosen as a way to establish how appropriate it is.

The findings of such studies indicate that only five per cent of those sampled achieved high scores on wisdom (Baltes & Smith, 1990). In addition, this sub-sample did not solely comprise older adults. Instead, high wisdom scores were evenly distributed across young, middle-aged, and older adults. It was also apparent that insight was greatest when a person was presented with dilemmas where respondents had to engage with somebody of a similar age. It is important to note here that, although a great deal of the literature focuses on the cognitive decline associated with age, the type of cognitive operations associated with wisdom appear intact.

Summary

We have seen that the stability of one's personality varies across individuals. To some extent we all have a sense of self that remains constant. However, this sense of self has to do battle with many demands that challenge our current view of ourselves. As we have seen time and again, individual differences proliferate the older we get. As personality research, with its focus on individual differences, continues to be integrated into studies within the field on topics as diverse as health, cognition, reactions to life events, and physical changes, greater understanding will be gained about how people vary in their reactions to the ageing process. Such work will help further the development of the field in terms of biopsychosocial processes, leading both to a richer theoretical understanding of ageing and practical implications for intervention.

The second main section of the chapter focused on intelligence. Although there is evidence for a decline in some domains of functioning, individuals vary in their capacity to compensate for this deterioration. It was suggested that the standard view of intelligence may be too constricting and that we should instead widen the net to encompass the whole range of capabilities individuals possess. The concept of multiple intelligences is something that makes intuitive good sense. The concept of creativity is important here also and can be seen to have a major role to play in many areas of our lives. The final section on wisdom related to many of the topics addressed earlier on in this chapter. It also has implications in terms of later chapters that focus on change. What is clear is that the higher-order cognitive processes that underlie wisdom exert a major influence on our lives, not least in terms of perceived quality of life and overall well-being.

Further reading

Gardner, H. (2006). *Multiple intelligences: New horizons*. New York: Basic Books. [A great introduction to the concept of multiple intelligences.]

Hall, S. S. (2010). *Wisdom: From philosophy to neuroscience*. New York: Alfred A. Knopf. [An extremely readable account that explores wisdom from a range of viewpoints. Well worth reading.]

Whitbourne, S. K. (2002). *The aging individual: Physical and psychological perspectives*. New York: Springer. [A good account of the highly influential identity process model.]

CHAPTER 10

Adjusting to Change

This book has focused so far on changes in how a person is able to function as a result of increasing age. In most cases there is very little, if anything, we can do to prevent this from happening. However, within our power is the ability to adjust to and deal with such changes in an appropriate manner, thereby increasing our chances of leading a more fulfilling life. Beginning with changes that occur to one's life as the result of leaving employment, we will then go on to examine the importance of different types of relationships, especially when considered within the context of increasing dependency and need for care. The final sections here focus on loss, be it in terms of one's friends and loved ones, or contemplation of one's own mortality.

The lead up to adulthood, with all the trappings that go along with it, is to a large extent focused towards work and the attainment thereof. For the vast majority of us work is an essential component of our lives. It provides the means enabling us to lead our lives in the manner we desire. Because of this, work is so central to our lives that, when it is time to retire, a great deal of fine-tuning is needed to replace the void that had once provided structure to one's day for many years.

Work

The number of individuals who continue to work past the age of retirement is increasing. The highest proportion in this group comprises males with both higher achieved education and higher employment status (Duchesne, 2004). Quality of the spousal relationship is important here. Where the relationship is close, with a strong desire to spend time together, there is a stronger urge to retire. In relationships where there is a high level of conflict, retirement is delayed (Henkens, 1999).

We all perceive work differently. Work may bring with it a sense of self-worth and prestige. It is a way of giving something back to society. Whichever way you look at it, for the majority of individuals, work is a means to an end, a way to cover the cost of living. A person's occupation exerts a major influence on one's life. It, to some extent, determines where you live, who your friends are, how you dress, and so on.

Increasingly, workforces across the world are becoming older. The labour market is awash with older adults aged 50 and above who are eager for work. Because of this, alongside the continuous advancements in technology, there is a need to address the changing demands of the workplace. A major barrier here is age discrimination. Because there is a prejudice against employing older workers, there are longer periods of unemployment or forced early retirement among this age group (Butler, 1969).

Some organizations are beginning to appreciate that older workers are, in fact, a valuable resource in terms of expertise and as a result are taking steps to integrate them into the workplace (Frerichs & Naegele, 1997). This may take the form of retraining. The process of retraining is just one way in which our working lives differ now. It was not uncommon for people to choose an occupation and steadfastly stick with it throughout their employment. It is increasingly the norm now to change occupations, even to make substantial career changes. Such change can be seen as evidence of an employee's flexibility (Havighurst, 1982).

Many organizations now offer in-house skills training, or they may subsidize employees to attend external courses. Such courses help offset any mismatch between current skills base and the new demands imposed by advances in technology. Holding back many older workers is a lack of self-efficacy. In this instance, older workers often do not believe they have the capability to develop new skills (Maurer, Weiss, & Barbeite, 2003).

Anxiety over one's job security adversely affects both mental health and behaviour, even when the worry is not founded in reality (Roskies & Louis-Guerin, 1990). Loss of employment has far-reaching consequences. How people respond to unemployment varies greatly. In fact, four groupings have been identified (Wanberg & Marchese, 1994): those who are confident but with concern about securing another job; those distressed as a result of their status; those who are indifferent to their unemployment; those who are optimistic about their future.

Retirement

Retirement is something we will all face given sufficient time. There comes a time when one's day is no longer controlled by those who employ us. Retirement is often associated with the need to systematically rid the labour force of older adults in as efficient a manner as possible. It is also synonymous with the final phase of existence. It is one's pension (or lack of one) then which largely determines quality of life for this age group (Wise, 1993). It is also clear that we are also faced with the situation where people are living longer with the added expectation of doing so free from disability for many years (Fries, 2003).

Retirement may occur for a number of different reasons: it may naturally occur once one reaches the designated age; in other cases retirement may be enforced by one's employer; still others may be required to retire through declining health. The amount of perceived control over retirement is important such that those who were given no option but to retire experienced lower physical and psychological health (Gallo et al., 2000). Findings similar to this have been replicated by other studies (De Vaus et al., 2007). However, it is indeed the case that in many instances ill health is often the main driver behind early retirement (Hansson et al., 1997). However, the nature of the condition is important, with conditions such as lung disease and cancer being major reasons for retiring early (Wang, 2007).

How successfully one copes with retirement is to a great extent dependent on how much preparation one has made for it. Greater preparation means a more fruitful retirement (Sterns & Gray, 1999). Finance can be a large barrier to rewarding retirement. This is because retirement brings with it a drop in income. Even though this is the case, many do not plan for such change (Ferraro & Su, 1999). Retirement is generally seen as positive when there is financial security, good health, and friends and family who are supportive (Gall, Evans, & Howard, 1997).

Of course, the aftershock of retirement touches the behaviour of our friends and family. Most affected are our partners. Long-established routines are disturbed. This compels couples to initiate a period of readjustment (Pearson, 1996), although not always with ease. Interactions with friends change little with retirement, unless ill health prevents the individual from maintaining the relationship (Bosse et al., 1993). Friends are another source of compassion and companionship, both of which are vital during this period of change.

Nevertheless, for many people retirement is something to look forward to, especially if it coincides with receiving a pension. Much disturbance ensues if governments make moves to adjust the age at which pensions are received (Davies & Cartwright, 2011). The shift in demographic now means that our older constituents wield an increasingly powerful political strength due to sheer numbers alone.

Leisure

How one decides to spend one's leisure time becomes of paramount importance when faced with retirement. Loss of occupational identity is often a severe blow to the individual. In many cases, retirement means that all links to one's previous work are now severed. For others, retirement may be partial, choosing instead to work part-time (Henretta, 1997).

In contrast to our working life, it is important that we engage in leisure activities. These can be cultural, physical, social, or solitary (Bosse & Ekerdt, 1981). Such activities can be assessed in terms of the cognitive, emotional, and physical demands made on the individual. Many external factors exert an influence on which activities we choose to pursue. These include one's income, health, capability, and education to name but a few (Lawton et al., 2002). To some extent health is the major determinant of leisure activity in older adults (Duke et al., 2002). However, engaging in pleasurable leisure activities improves well-being (Lawton, Moss, & Fulcomer, 1986).

Attitude

When looking at how Western society views ageing, in particular its less than sympathetic attitudes towards older adults, we cannot help but feel disappointed. However, what was once heralded as a major divide between the East and West, rising globalization brings with it increasingly negative attitudes towards ageing across the globe (Ingersoll-Dayton & Saengtienchai, 1999). Stereotypical beliefs about ageing not only taint the perceptions of the current young generation, but also lead individuals who themselves age to form an imperfect view of their abilities, impacting hugely on self-image, thereby heightening the likelihood of poor physical and psychological health (Aiken, 1989).

There has been much research over the years on how people deal with negative events in their lives. The approach of Masuda and Holmes (1967) emphasizes how life events differ in terms of impact, but that this effect is a constant. This perspective also argues that events rarely happen in isolation. Yet such an approach offered no explanation about how people deal with such losses. This was the domain of Lazarus's model (1976). This model focused on how people cope with isolated negative events.

How people deal with more than one negative event has been less effectively studied. When faced with multiple challenges, the likelihood is that people will opt for an emotion-focused approach to deal with the situation. Age is an important determiner also of how different coping strategies are utilized (Boerner & Jopp, 2007).

Brandtstadter (1999) discusses the use of assimilative strategies which focus on problem solving strategies and also accommodative strategies that are more emotion-focused. Both assimilative and accommodative approaches attempt to obtain the best fit between the demands imposed by the situation one is faced with and the characteristics of the individual (Brandtstadter & Renner,

1990). Again, age is a major determiner of which strategy is adopted, with younger adults opting mainly for assimilative strategies whereas older adults select accommodative strategies. The tendency to adopt accommodative strategies with increasing age may be seen as a reflection of diminishing resources available to cope with negative events. It is also likely that such negative events are concerned with irrevocable loss.

The concept of personal resources is an important one (Hobfoll, 1989). Well-being is often associated with a surfeit of such resources because individuals are better able to deal with potentially ego-threatening situations (Jopp & Smith, 2006), whereas a dearth of resources can result in depression (Hobfoll et al., 2003). The availability of resources lends itself to the adoption of active problem solving strategies (Holahan & Moos, 1991).

Sense of control plays an important role here as well. As seen with availability of resources, control is often associated with subjective well-being (Krause & Shaw, 2000). This notion of control links to the concept of self-efficacy, where belief in one's ability determines how one is able to deal with a negative situation (Bandura, 1997). It is plausible, therefore, to suggest that individuals who believe they are able exert control over a situation tend to use assimilative strategies.

A recent study by Jopp and Schmitt (2010) examined the interplay between beliefs about both personal resources and control and the types of coping strategies people adopt when faced with multiple negative life events. Their study focused on adults who were middle-aged. This can be a particularly turbulent time, often characterized by major life-changing events, be it personal, economic, or indeed health related. It is also a time when functional capacity and availability of resources is relatively high (Lachman, 2004). This study highlighted the need to further explore in detail the complexities inherent when faced with multiple negative life events within the context of individual differences. Such studies will lead to a more realistic understanding of how people deal with these life events.

Relationships

Although our lives are peppered with episodes of change, a source of stability for many lives is one's friends and family. Friendships play a dominant role throughout our lifespan. Friendship may be defined as a relationship where one person influences the other's behaviour and beliefs. Friends also offer support (Arnett, 2006).

When looking at how friendships grow, distinct stages of development are discernible. Friendships start as acquaintanceships. Depending on compatibility, acquaintances may develop into friends. It is inevitable, in many cases, for friendships to deteriorate and ultimately end. Many factors influence this, including the availability of alternative relationships (Levinger, 1980).

The pattern of friendships changes across our life. The number of friends and acquaintances is highest during early adulthood (Sherman, de Vries, & Lansford, 2000). Because of numerous transitions that take place in our lives, we tend to retain fewer friends as we grow older. One explanation for this is that our requirements change as we age (Carstensen, Isaacowitz, & Charles, 1999). In early adulthood, friendships are often a source of information about the world and our place in it. For older adults the predominant motivation for friendship is to provide support and help regulate our emotional responses. A combination of greater selectivity and diminished opportunity to meet new people provides an explanation why we have fewer friends as we grow older.

The qualities of our friendships become increasingly important with age. A strong friendship is a much needed pillar of strength in times of change (Adams & Ueno, 2006). Adult friendships are characterized by a sense of trust and commitment, mutual interest, and compatibility (de Vries, 1996).

When looking at romantic relationships, we see again that patterns change across the lifespan. In an attempt to define the indefinable, Sternberg (2006) suggests that love consists of three main components. Such relationships are characterized by an intense passion for someone, a sense that one is able to share intimate thoughts and feelings with another, and a desire for commitment whatever happens.

When looking at lifestyle choices, increasing numbers of adults choose to remain single (see Chapter 1 for more information on the changing demographic). However, there still seem to be biases against individuals who make this choice (DePaulo, 2007). Women, on the whole, face a stronger pressure to marry, often leading to a great deal of ambivalence about their situation (Lewis & Moon, 1997). The decision not to marry is often slow in coming, invariably the result of changes occurring in their lives rather than a conscious lifestyle choice, thereby diverting attention away from goals related to marriage among other things (Connidis, 2001).

The choice not to marry does not mean living on one's own. Cohabitation is common and is becoming increasingly so. Cohabitation may be limited, and seen as a lifestyle choice of convenience, with no intention to marry. On the other hand, it may, indeed, be a precursor to marriage, whereas in some instances it may also be a substitute for marriage. This arrangement often brings with it financial benefits, especially for older couples (King & Scott, 2005).

For those who do decide to marry, the average age at which this occurs has risen 2.5 years since 1996 (*The Guardian*, 2012). In terms of successful marriages, a number of key factors have been identified. Marriage between more mature adults is more likely to succeed, as is that between partners who are financially secure. Shared values and interests are important as one would expect.

It is also important that couples feel that their marriage is equal, with each person making a comparable contribution to the situation. A similar pattern is seen when looking at dependence. Couples who share a mutual dependence tend to remain together. An imbalance in dependence leads to conflict. The balance of dependence may change through loss of work or ill health. A spouse may find themselves taking on a carer role and all the adjustments associated therein; however, more on that topic shortly. Adaptability within relationships is, therefore, essential for the success of the relationship (Karney & Bradbury, 1995). The issue of dependency will be explored further in the next section.

During the early stages of marriage adjustment occurs in both parties regarding both perceptions and expectations. Conflict resolution within any relationship is pivotal to the success of that partnership. Satisfaction with married life appears quite high among older couples (Henry et al., 2007). Satisfaction often increases after retirement but does tend to drop as one might expect with the onset of increasing health problems (Miller, Hemesath, & Nelson, 1997). Over time many older married couples feel almost detached happiness within their marriage (Connidis, 2001). Recall of events concerning their partner sometimes has a positive bias (O'Rourke & Cappeliez, 2005). On the whole, couples who remain together grow more alike and have developed successful strategies to deal with conflict should it arise.

The ability to deal with whatever challenge life throws at us is key to a strong marital relationship. However, being diagnosed with a long-term condition or life-threatening illness exerts an enormous pressure on a marriage. Caring for one's spouse, then, can completely alter the dynamics of a marriage. Following a lifetime together where responsibilities have been shared equally, the spouse now has to assume the principal role of caregiver. Depending on the condition, this may reduce or, indeed, eliminate any intimacy between partners, thereby putting additional stress on the relationship. The role of the carer will be explored again in more detail in Chapter 12.

Having talked about what makes a successful marriage, an all too inevitable outcome to many marriages is divorce. Divorce rates are rising. Many studies have been conducted in order to predict divorce. Gottman and colleagues developed two such models: one predicting divorce within the first seven years of marriage, the other predicting divorce later on (Gottman & Levenson, 2000). Conflict awash with negative emotional reactions predicted early divorce. Interestingly, divorce later in the marriage was predicted by a lack of positive emotion being expressed when discussing day-to-day activities.

A marital partnership can also be brought to an end through the death of a spouse. Widowhood has far-reaching consequences. Friends and family often find it difficult interacting with the widowed spouse, increasing further their sense of despair and isolation (Martin-Matthews, 1999). The surviving spouse very often faces financial difficulties during this time of increased need (Lee et al., 2001).

Dependency

Already this chapter has considered dependency as an inevitable end result for lots of people entering older adulthood. Loss of independence is a real fear for many as they grow older. Realizing the need to become increasingly reliant and so dependent on others is a moment of significant change within the individual. Many things may necessitate this transition, such as decline in both physical and psychological functioning.

Being dependent on others is often seen as demeaning (Cordingley & Webb, 1997). Local governments and charities offer much in terms of assistance for older adults who require support to maintain their independence. Where such offers of helps are not taken up, the opinion often formed is that the individual is at fault by not accepting the aid rather than them being encouraged to maintain independence (Cordingley & Webb, 1997).

In some cases dependency may be imposed by institutions that reject any form of autonomy. On other occasions dependency may be encouraged as the result of overzealous healthcare workers offering packages that fail to take into consideration the actual capabilities of the individuals they are interested in helping. Dependency can be seen as a boon to one's life as it frees that individual from having to battle activities that are beyond their functional capacity. The degree to which experienced dependency is seen to be either functional or dysfunctional has an impact on one's health, with higher instances of depression and hypertension for those experiencing dysfunctional dependency (Fiori, Consedine, & Magai, 2008).

A growing dependence on others is often the first sign of a burgeoning need for care. Care can take many forms. The following section explores how both informal and formal care can enrich a person's life if used effectively.

Provision of care

Either as the result of retirement or growing frailty, older adults often experience a reduction in their level of social engagement. If ignored, loneliness and feelings of social isolation develop (Higgs et al., 2003). As a result, there is a greater need for informal support networks. Walker (2005) presented evidence that quality of life is enhanced through social contact, and that it was the quality rather than the quantity of contact that was most important. Social engagement is less among those who make more frequent visits to their general practitioner (Bowling, 2005). There also seems to be a link with the ability to maintain activities of daily living (Bowling & Browne, 1991).

Social care can comprise both formal and informal aspects. Formal care consists of government-sanctioned organizations, including some voluntary organizations, whereas informal care recruits from family, friends, and self-help groups (Froland, 1980). There is a general policy to allow older adults to remain in their own home, and under these circumstances, care is usually provided by formal support networks as well as informal care from family members. This type of mixed care approach is referred to as social care (Cantor, 1991) and comprises both functional care and emotional support.

Although there are many advantages to informal care, there are clear limitations. Not everyone is inclined to participate in such groups. There is also the issue of limited knowledge of particular conditions often in conjunction with a lack of resources. There are changes in work patterns such that more married women hold down full-time jobs, thereby making them less available to take on the role of caregiver that once was associated with them (Ngan, 2011). Dual-earner families are becoming more prevalent to combat increasing cost of living and the desire to maintain a chosen lifestyle (Bell, 1976).

From the caregiver's perspective there is a great deal of stress in terms of physical and psychological strain, as well as financial pressure (Kosberg, Cairl, & Keller, 1990). There are likely to be issues concerning adequacy of the care they provide necessitating a need to address the dilemma as to either continue providing care themselves or to send their relation to a care institution (Buhr, Kuchibhatla, & Clipp, 2006).

Litwak (1985) proposed a theory of shared functions in instances of informal care, such that neighbours become a source of support in the case of emergencies when an immediate response is needed, relatives then being sought to provide long-term care, with friends then being ideally suited to offer emotional support at different stages.

An important development is that of improving quality of life whilst simultaneously extending it. This is referred to as 'ageing well' (Bowling, 2005). Alongside both mental and physical health, social well-being is also important (Bowling, 2005). This notion of social capital reflects resources available through social connections, especially community resources (Kawachi & Berkman, 2000). A UK-based programme, *Growing Older*, highlighted a number of factors that influence overall quality of life, including good social relationships, being involved in voluntary activity, feeling safe, and good functional ability ('Quality of life in older age: Messages from the Growing Older Programme', 2005). Another important finding from this and other studies is that self-rated independence is a priority.

Methods for assessing quality of life are fraught with a number of problems. The general focus of such measures has been on objective symptoms rather than a subjective sense of one's current state, or subjective well-being (Cummins, 1997). One measure to include this subjective component is the Personal Well-being Index (Lau, Cummins, & McPherson, 2005).

The issue of social care for older adults is even more pertinent when one considers the growing incidence of dementia as the result of the ever-ageing population. Caring for someone who has been diagnosed with dementia brings with it even greater challenges. Among these being severe behavioural disturbances (Teri, Larson, & Reifler, 1988). It is often felt that a purely medical model of care fails to meet the needs of such individuals. Instead, a more holistic approach is needed to fully appreciate the insecurities experienced and needs required by patients (Kitwood, 1997).

Grief following bereavement

The process of bereavement touches on many areas of one's life. At the most fundamental end are the physical symptoms often experienced during grief. These include among other things shortness of breath, tachycardia, problems with the digestive system, as well as general restlessness and muscle tension (Parkes, 1996). Physical symptoms may also be accompanied by indicators of psychological distress, such as depression and anxiety.

Whereas the severity of these symptoms abate given time, in the majority of cases a reasonable percentage do go on to experience more longer-lasting disturbance. In some instances severe and prolonged distress resulting from a bereavement may increase mortality among these survivors during the six months following the loss (Osterweis, Solomon, & Green, 1984). These deaths are often linked to heart disease and cancer, as well as to liver damage as a result of abuse of alcohol.

Episodes of complicated grief often follow the death of a loved one that was either sudden, unexpected, or traumatic. Another predictor is proneness to depression in the survivor (Worden, 2009). Criteria proposed for the DSM-V include a chronic longing for the departed, plus a number of additional symptoms including among other things a lack of trust of others, disproportionate anger, and detachment (Prigerson & Jacobs, 2001; Prigerson & Maciejewski, 2006).

Over the years there have been many theories about how to best cope with grief. Early psychoanalytic theories emphasized the need for 'grief work' whereby contemplation of the events leading up to the death, as well as those proceeding it, should be the focus for contemplation with the ultimate aim of gradually experiencing detachment from the deceased (Stroebe, Schut, & Stroebe, 2007).

This approach fails to take into consideration the complexity of the griev-ing process. It is a time of adaptation and change affecting every aspect of a person's life and, as such, cannot be tackled all at once. More modern accounts accept the need to take small steps in an attempt to reduce the dis-crepancy between environmental demands and the person's capacity to cope, thereby minimizing the amount of stress experienced (Folkman et al., 1986). Strategies to combat each aspect of the grieving process vary. In addition, strategies used to deal with the short-term amelioration of grief may be mala-daptive if used for long periods of time and so may need to be replaced by different strategies for long-term adaptation.

Maintaining a focus on negative emotions and their consequences, a pro-cess of rumination, has been identified as maladaptive during grieving as it prolongs grieving by making it more difficult for the individual to adapt (Nolen-Hoeksema, 2001). However, suppressing such thoughts may also be potentially problematic (Folkman et al., 1996).

A more recent approach – the Dual Process Model of Coping with Bereavement – characterizes stressors as being either loss-oriented or res-toration-oriented (Stroebe & Schut, 1999). The former reflects a person's need to process information concerning the actual bereavement, and so to some extent reflects grief work as described previously. On the other hand, the latter type comprises stressors that develop as a result of losing the loved one, and include among other things concern over how one will now cope on their own, thereby providing distraction from the grief. The Dual Process Model also emphasizes that some regulatory process is needed to ensure the most adaptive method for coping. Such regulation acknowledges the need to sometimes avoid active engagement with stressors, as a result acknowledging the dynamic and exhausting process of grieving.

A recent study, Changing Lives of Older Couples, has shown that older adults are quite successful at adapting to loss (Carr, Nesse, & Wortman, 2006). In almost half the cases spouses demonstrated a resilient pattern to their experienced grief with only a short-lived mild drop in mood following the demise of their spouse. A subset of those who survive their spouse show improvements on ratings of distress following the event, thereby suggesting a repressive marital relationship or a release from demands imposed on them whilst caring for their partner.

Taking a constructivist approach, Neimeyer argues that grief is a process whereby a person adapts by reconstructing their world and the meanings attached to it in order to compensate for their loss (Neimeyer, 2001). This process of revision allows one's self-narrative to take account of the changes that have occurred (Neimeyer, 2004). Failure to do so will lead to the type of fragmentation of the self evident in those who experience complicated grief (Boelen, Van den Hout, & Van den Bout, 2006).

Having looked at how grief affects the individual, we shall turn our attention to how a person attempts to deal with their own inevitable demise, as well as investigating what options are available to people nearing the end of their lives.

Preparing for the end

A much criticized theory of the 1960s was that as we age we reduce our interaction with the outside world, be it the result of the death of family and friends or the product of conscious choice. As a result disengagement theory argued that such change allows individuals to prepare for the inevitable (Cumming & Henry, 1961). There was little evidence to back this theory up, however. Instead a number of factors appeared to play a key role in the process of gradual disengagement, such as financial hardship and a tendency to be reclusive (Magai et al., 2001).

A posited alternative to this theory focused on levels of activity. It argued that social activity buffered against any negative effect experienced (Holtzman et al., 2004). However, if taken to the extreme, with regimens of enforced social interaction, activity theory may be seen as equally reprehensible as that of disengagement theory (Mor et al., 1995). Again, this issue of causality may be an issue here. To be able to participate in social activity effectively one has to be relatively healthy, so it may be argued that it is no surprise that the healthiest older adults are those who appear to engage in such activity (Everard et al., 2000). Indeed, when health is factored out of the analysis, social activities were not the best predictors of well-being and life expectancy. It was found instead that solitary activities were (Lennartsson & Silverstein, 2001).

When examining death and our personal thoughts and feelings about our own mortality, it is clear that there are lifespan changes in our responses. As young adults death is feared because it effectively ends a life where there was so much potential (Attig, 1996). When we reach middle adulthood we are forced to face the prospect of our parents' death. On the death of a parent, hidden within the maelstrom of emotion, there is the realization that we must face our own inevitable end at some future date. When alive one's parents' existence almost negates the need to consider our own death as we are expected to outlive them. When they are no longer there, time's arrow points inexorably towards our own demise. With age, often as the result of losing friends and family, death becomes an inevitability that no longer compels the same sense of dread.

The subjective experience of dying was investigated by Kübler-Ross during the 1960s. She recorded five individual reactions, namely denial, anger, bargaining, depression, and acceptance (Kubler-Ross, 1969). Denial time and again impels individuals to seek second opinions. Anger frequently develops out of frustration. Often patients attempt to bargain for more time by professing they will mend their ways. Throughout this process it is important for patients to express their feelings. Depression is prominent during this time, and is often the result of an acceptance that the sufferer can no longer deny the severity of their situation. With acceptance comes peace. Sequencing of these responses differs across individuals. Indeed, not all may be experienced.

A more holistic approach argues that we need to address issues such as physical demands, psychological well-being, friends and family, and spiritual beliefs (Corr, Nabe, & Corr, 2004). When faced with death, both patients and families often experience fear, grief, and resistance which act as barriers to change (Parkes, 2007).

Fear is a natural response to any situation that threatens us. One characteristic of fear, hyperalertness, may accentuate current concerns and symptoms and so eventuate a vicious cycle of increasing dread (Parkes, 2007). Aggression often develops to help individuals deal with their ensuing demise, as does substance abuse. Attention may turn to eliciting advice from sources outside the medical profession in instances where orthodox approaches appear not to be working.

There is a tendency among some to deny the reality of the prognosis they have been given. Denial is often communicated when either the patient or the survivor persists in daily habits and routines that are no longer appropriate in the sense they do not take into consideration changes that have occurred. In other words, there is incongruity between the reality of the situation and our previous existence. Our world-view is revised each time such divergences from previous behavioural routines are experienced (Parkes, 2007).

For a person who is nearing their own death, a number of options are available to provide the needed care and support prior to their passing. This last section of the chapter then looks at end-of-life issues and the role of bioethics in determining the final stages of an individual's life.

End-of-life care

A change that has occurred largely as a result of advancements in medical technology is a shift from death as a result of infectious disease to death from degenerative disease. The resultant effect of this is to extend the dying trajectories which take into consideration both the duration and shape of the decline (Seale, 2005). Medical advancements allow us to identify early on various disease processes and thus predict their course. Provision of care for terminal illness has expanded as a result.

The General Household Survey conducted in the United Kingdom has given evidence for a gradual rise in chronic conditions that have led to a reduction in daily functioning (ONS, 1998). There is evidence of this across the world (WHO, 2000). Because greater numbers of us are living to 75 and beyond symptoms such as cognitive failures, depression, and incontinence are increasingly experienced for longer periods of time (Seale & Cartwright, 1994).

Along with the prospect of longevity is the predicted concomitant rise in chronic illness. Because of this, although death is some way off, the preceding period can be blighted by a drawn out process of decline and impairment. The concept of palliative care is, as a result, of huge importance when considering the tail end of a person's life. Palliative care reflects attempts to relieve suffering of those with a serious illness, as well as a way to improve quality of life for patients and their families. Palliative care is not just dealing with end-of-life issues, it is concerned with how a person is able to live their life in the shadow of a serious condition (National Health Service, 2013). This realization that one will no longer be able to achieve all that had been planned, or more to the point, 'the fear of not being able to become whom one had planned to be' (Mercier, 2009), is a pivotal moment in a person's life. Often such care tackles the huge array of symptoms experienced by older adults in these conditions. The most common symptoms are restricted activity, fatigue, physical discomfort, as well as general cognitive impairment associated with a variety of conditions (Walke et al., 2004).

Patient accounts of their own suffering have been shown to be relatively accurate, although there is a tendency to under-report pain (Parmelee, Smith, & Katz, 1993). In instances where pain is under-reported, a more accurate assessment of the severity and frequency of pain may be obtained through close observation of mood fluctuations and noticeable changes in behaviour (Ferrell, Ferrell, & Rivera, 1995). In instances where patients are non-verbal, difficulty arises in trying to assess experienced pain. Often behavioural cues provide this information, such as increased agitation, decreased mobility, and also severe confusion (Pautex et al., 2006).

Bioethics

There has been a recent growth in the provision of hospice care and training in palliative care among healthcare professionals not only in an attempt to manage physical symptoms but to also provide the much needed psychological and social support for those who are nearing the end of their lives (Seale, 2005). Such opportunities fit with the growing desire to plan and control events in our lives, with death being no exception (Giddens, 1991). Linked to this is a growing wish to take even more control over events by choosing when to end one's own life.

For most conditions palliative care can be provided to offer relief from a variety of symptoms. Psychological concerns are more difficult to address effectively. Fears concerning loss of both autonomy and dignity are paramount among those facing death, as is fear of becoming a burden to family and friends (Werth, Gordon, & Johnson, 2002). Linked to this are concerns over loss of mental perspicacity and awareness, largely because of the implications in terms of being unable to make one's own decisions.

Bioethics is impacting on the lives of more and more people every year. Bioethics addresses the issues raised when weighing advancements in technology against human lives and values. Bioethics emphasizes individual freedom of choice. The most important issue surrounding bioethics is euthanasia. Before one is able to even begin to contemplate under which circumstances such an act is acceptable, it is necessary to attach a specific value to the life of another person (Eliott & Olver, 2008). This is the form the dilemma takes for many who have been diagnosed with a terminal illness, and in some instance by family members faced with a relative on life support.

Euthanasia may be initiated in compliance with an unambiguous statement from the patient themselves or independently from someone in legal authority. Such active euthanasia generally involves the administration of a drug overdose or the removal from life support. Euthanasia may be more passive, involving instead the withdrawal of treatment or medication.

Summary

This chapter has focused on how people adjust to changing life experiences. The shift from work to retirement is an important and life-changing step. For around four decades your job has provided the main structure to your life. Suddenly, all that changes when retirement occurs. How successfully individuals adjust to this has a major impact on a person's quality of life. We explored in this chapter leisure activities and relationships with other people, and considered the nature of their importance in contributing to a person's sense of well-being.

We also looked at the changing role of key relationships as the result of a transformation in health status whereby a person may become increasingly dependent on the care and support of another. Families are often the first port of call when an older relative requires help. However, there is a growing trend towards smaller family units and also a tendency for children to move far from their family home (Grundy, 1996). This naturally poses problems in terms of availability of care, with practical help being provided through healthcare organizations or institutions instead.

The final section looked at the impact of death, be it in terms of grieving for the loss of a loved one, or coming to terms with the prospect of one's own end. The need to comprehensively address the types of questions posed by bioethicists – those relating to among other things euthanasia – intensifies with each passing year. Technology advances in conjunction with the predictable rise in longevity, and so these issues will present themselves to increasing numbers of us as we head towards the final stages of our existence.

> Ah, Posthumus! our years hence fly
> And leave no sound: nor piety,
> Or prayers, or vow
> Can keep the wrinkle from the brow;
> But we must on,
> As fate does lead or draw us; none,
> None, Posthumus, could e'er decline
> The doom of cruel Proserpine.
> (Robert Herrick, 1648)

Further reading

Earle, S., Komaromy, C., & Bartholomew, C. (2008). *Death and dying: A reader.* London: Sage. [This work contains an interesting selection of readings both new and old related to death and dying.]

Milne, D. (2012). *The psychology of retirement: Coping with the transition from work.* Chichester: Wiley-Blackwell. [This book examines how to deal with retirement from the perspective of a clinical psychologist. A really interesting read.]

Quinodoz, D. (2009). *Growing old: A journey of self-discovery.* London: Routledge. [Quinodoz addresses many of the issues raised in this chapter from a psychoanalytical perspective.]

CHAPTER 11

Health and Ageing

Chronic illnesses can significantly interfere with the quality of a person's daily life, with far-reaching effects that often result in a constraint of activity, pain and anxiety, and difficulties in carrying out even the simplest cognitive tasks. In addition, for many older adults physical illness can also present complicating factors in the diagnosis and treatment of psychological disorders.

Previous chapters have identified some of the physical changes that occur as we age. This chapter will focus on how such changes impact on health and well-being. The first part will examine some of the main conditions associated with older adulthood, including heart disease and cancer. We will then pick up on ideas first introduced in Chapter 9 by once again reflecting on the role of personality, although this time the emphasis will be on how personality impacts on a person's health. The final sections will consider the linked concepts of optimism, hope, resilience, and quality of life. Before we do this it is important to first consider what is meant by health.

Defining health

When one considers what is meant by health, what we mean when we talk about being healthy, invariably we conceive an absence of illness. However, broader definitions are required to better reflect our conception of health. A much quoted definition was provided by the World Health Organization which suggests that, 'Health is a state of complete physical, mental and social well-being and not merely the absence of disease or infirmity' (World Health Organization, 1948). In addition to an absence of physical complaints, this definition also claims the need for both good mental health and a secure social environment. Such a definition acknowledges that someone may suffer from a condition yet still feel positive and contented. It, therefore, introduces a subjective component to the assessment of health.

To begin with we shall examine some of the main health-related conditions associated with older adults. Following this we will look at how people differ in terms of their response to these conditions and explore how such differences in response determines well-being.

Specific conditions

Heart disease

Some of the changes occurring within the cardiovascular system have been examined already in Chapter 2. It is clear that abnormal changes within the cardiovascular system can at one extreme lead to death. Less extreme changes may instead result in chronic disability. Coronary heart disease refers to a condition where coronary arteries become narrowed and in many cases blocked as a result of a build-up of plaque. A direct consequence of this is that blood supply to the heart is diminished or prevented altogether in some instances. Brief episodes result in angina pectoris which manifests as a referred pain in the chest, arm, back, and sometimes neck. If the supply of oxygen to the heart muscle is interrupted for a protracted period of time, tissue may be destroyed, with the patient experiencing myocardial infarction (heart attack).

A reasonable number of older adults develop congestive heart failure. This is where the heart is no longer able to meet the demands of the body, resulting in shortness of breath following minor exertion. In this condition the heart becomes enlarged and fluid builds up in a person's lungs.

Risk factors

Although there may be a strong influence of genetics on the development of such problems, a number of behavioural factors have been identified that act to increase the risk. One major risk factor is a lack of physical exercise (Yung et al., 2009). Regular exercisers greatly reduce their risk of suffering from myocardial infarction, and this reduction in risk is dependent on the level of exertion invested in the exercise routine (Lovasi et al., 2007). The unfortunate reality is that, those at greatest risk from such problems are the more elderly, and it is also the case that the proportion who engage in physical exercise declines as we grow older.

Smoking is another major risk factor. Smoking is believed to lead to arterial damage, thereby making them more susceptible to plaque formation among other things. In a similar vein, excessive ingestion of alcohol has negative effects, especially in terms of increasing the risk of stroke (Reynolds et al., 2003).

Being overweight is another major factor to be considered here also. There is a clear causal relationship between high BMI and death as a result of cardiovascular disease (Whitlock et al., 2009). This is largely due to ingesting foods that contain high levels of LDL cholesterol (low-density lipoprotein cholesterol). The obvious exception to this is foods that contain HDL (high-density lipoprotein cholesterol), the 'good' cholesterol, which is, in fact, associated with reduced risk of heart disease (Cooney et al., 2009).

Metabolic syndrome is associated with obesity (especially around the abdomen), high levels of LDL and low levels of HDL, hypertension, insulin resistance, high levels of triglycerides, raised levels of C-reactive proteins, and also evidence of coronary plaque formation. Three or more of these increases the risk of developing cardiovascular disease (Clarke et al., 2009).

Prevention and treatment

Having a better understanding of what causes heart disease has meant that our ability to treat such conditions has advanced a great deal over the years. One of the quickest and easiest preventative strategies is lowering levels of LDL cholesterol in the blood through the use of statins (lipid-lowering drugs). Medication aside, similar effects can be obtained through a modified diet and regular exercise. The use of relaxation strategies has been shown to be effective in individuals who suffer from hypertension (Tang et al., 2009).

Cancer

Following heart disease, cancer is the second biggest cause of death in many countries. Cancer occurs when unrestricted cell growth occurs. When this transpires a tumour (or neoplasm) forms. In some instances these neoplasms are benign and so offer no threat to the individual. However, in other cases these growths are malignant and so a diagnosis of cancer is made. Cancer can take many forms. Sometimes cancer cells spread to other sites in the body. This is because they do not adhere as strongly to each other as non-cancer cells do. When this does occur the process is called metastasis. On getting bigger each neoplasm incorporates into itself its own supply of blood through a process of angiogenesis in order to extract nutrients. Wherever located the tumour disrupts normal functioning. Death occurs either as the result of proliferation within vital areas leading to organ failure, or it weakens the individual so they are no longer able to fight infection.

Risk factors

Cancers are the result of damage to genes controlling cell replication. Some individuals are genetically predisposed to develop certain cancers, such as breast or colon cancer, although the majority of cancers are not the result of such hereditary factors. Random cellular mutations are due to either problems with cell division or as the product of exposure to radiation or hazardous chemical agents.

Cancer is generally a disease of old age, although there are obvious exceptions. This is because of the effect of cumulative exposure to a variety of carcinogenic components in our environment, be it in food, water supplies, or in the air we breathe. Such toxins include asbestos, arsenic, and cadmium to name but three. Respiratory cancer is increased through overexposure to substances such as silica and wood dust (Straif et al., 2009).

Lifestyle choices play a major role in the development of cancer. The highest risk is attached to smoking, poor diet, and overexposure to ultraviolet (UV) radiation. The latter, exposure to UV radiation, is the most common cause of cancer. Prolonged and chronic exposure to the sun leads to the development of melanoma (skin cancer). The next most common risk factor is cigarette smoking. The main effect of smoking is lung cancer, although smokers are also at risk from developing other forms of cancer, including cancers of the mouth, throat, and oesophagus. As with heart disease, diet is important here: high BMI is associated with higher death rates from diseases such as colon and rectal cancer. Stomach cancer is more common among those who ingest regular quantities of food that is preserved, either through smoking, salting, or pickling. Fresh fruit and vegetables may, on the other hand, protect against the development of stomach cancer.

Hormonal changes in testosterone and oestrogen may play a role in the development of prostate and uterine cancer respectively. Diabetes and high blood pressure among women has been shown to increase the likelihood of them developing cancer of the uterus, although this may be due to the fact that being overweight results in raised levels of oestrogen (Wedisinghe & Perera, 2009).

Prevention and treatment

Prevention is crucially important here. Regular health checks and screening play a vital role in this process. Should cancer develop, a number of treatment options present themselves. Most forms of cancer are treated through surgery, eventuating in the removal of the tumour. Radiation therapy is another option whereby higher-energy radiation is applied to affected tissue, thus preventing the cells from multiplying. Chemotherapy is another method used to combat the proliferation of cancer cells. Chemotherapy is most often the treatment of choice in patients where the cancer has metastasized.

Disorders of the musculoskeletal system

There are a number of disorders that target the body's muscles, joints, and connective tissue. These result in conditions that are frequently painful, with stiffness and inflammation occurring at key sites. In osteoarthritis deterioration of tissue occurs at the joints. This is the most common form of arthritis. Osteoporosis, on the other hand, is a condition that weakens bones, thereby making them more fragile and prone to fracture.

Risk factors

Osteoarthritis. Osteoarthritis generally develops as a result of chronic overuse of joints in the pursuit of some activities, typically job related. Obesity is an additional risk factor.

Osteoporosis. Women have a greater risk of developing osteoporosis because they have a lower bone mass compared to men. Cultural differences also occur, with White and Asian women being at greatest risk. Women who are small boned and have a low BMI are more at risk than women who weigh more. As with a number of other conditions, smoking and drinking alcohol also increase the risk.

Prevention and treatment

Osteoarthritis. Pain management strategies are used to treat this condition. This includes prescribing aspirin, ibuprofen, and non-steroidal anti-inflammatory drugs (NSAIDs). There is also the option of injecting corticosteroids directly into the affected joint. An appropriate exercise regimen has also been shown to be of benefit in terms of reducing pain in these patients (Kujala, 2009). Such treatment options are not curative. Instead, they only treat the symptoms of the disease. Interventions that do more than merely alleviate symptoms are available. It is possible to replace depleted synovial fluid with synthetic material in affected joints. A more drastic but permanent treatment option is hip or knee replacement surgery.

Osteoporosis. Risk of developing osteoporosis is greatly reduced if one's diet contains an adequate quantity of calcium through the consumption of dairy products, green leafy vegetables, salmon, bread, and the like, as well as regular quantities of magnesium, potassium, Vitamin K, Vitamin D, and several Vitamin B compounds (Tucker, 2009). Regular exercise plays a role in reducing risk here also.

The condition can be treated with a combination of food supplements and exercise as a way of restoring bone strength (Guadalupe-Grau et al., 2009). Medication is also available that slows down, and sometimes even stops, bone loss as well as improving bone density. This has the added bonus of reducing the likelihood that the bone will fracture if an injury occurs. Because oestrogen appears to play a role here, hormone replacement therapy may also be an option, although it is important to consider potential risks of this treatment against potential gains (Pietschmann et al., 2009).

Diabetes

Diabetes is a condition where the body is unable to regulate the levels of glucose in the blood, thus resulting in high levels accumulating. This occurs either because the body no longer reacts appropriately to the presence of insulin – the hormone responsible for controlling blood sugar levels – or because the pancreas fails to produce sufficient quantities. Diabetes can take on two forms. These are referred to as Type I and Type II diabetes. Type I diabetes develops at a young age and occurs as a result of the destruction of pancreatic cells due to an autoimmune response. Insulin injections are needed to counteract this. Type II diabetes is the most common form and describes a condition where the body is able to produce some insulin, albeit at a reduced level. Insulin injections are not required here. Instead glucose levels are often regulated through diet.

Risk factors

Obesity and lack of physical exercise are major risk factors for diabetes. Cultural factors are important, with Native Americans showing the highest rate of incidence. Chronic stress may also play a role in increasing an individual's risk for diabetes (Knol et al., 2006).

Prevention and treatment

One of the best ways to prevent Type II diabetes is through a controlled diet and reduced blood pressure. Regular moderate measures of alcohol show positive effects as well (Paulson et al., 2010). Regular blood tests are required to ensure that glucose levels are kept at an acceptable level. Insulin is taken in order to lower blood glucose levels. Physical exercise is an important adjunct to a well-regulated diet, largely as a way to manage weight and reduce blood pressure.

Respiratory diseases

One of the major forms of respiratory disease is chronic obstructive pulmonary disease (COPD). Individuals with this condition experience a permanently reduced flow of air into and out of their lungs, although problems are more evident when expelling air.

Risk factors

Cigarette smoking is a major risk factor for the development of respiratory disease. In addition, pollutants in the air and airborne toxins in work environments are additional factors leading to such conditions.

Prevention and treatment

For those who suffer from COPD, it is essential that those who smoke quit immediately. Inhalers can then be used to open the airways, allowing more oxygen to flow into the lungs, as well as reducing the level of inflammation. Lung surgery to remove affected tissue may be offered in certain severe conditions.

Personality, health, and illness

Having looked at a range of conditions associated with older adults, it is important to examine how individual responses to changing health influences outcome. A number of different theories have been proposed to explain the relationship between personality and health (Smith & Williams, 1992; Suls & Rittenhouse, 1990). It has been suggested that personality plays a direct causal role in health.

There has been a long history of research exploring the impact of personality on health. Probably the study that most readily comes to mind is Friedman and Rosenman's examination of the Type A behaviour pattern (Friedman & Rosenman, 1974). Individuals who embodied the pattern of personality traits specific to the Type A personality – in other words, individuals who are highly competitive, impatient, achievement-driven, and prone to be hostile – were associated with higher risk of developing cardiovascular problems.

Longitudinal studies have demonstrated a causal relationship, rather than a mere correlational one, between Type A personality and cardiovascular disease. Such individuals showed higher levels of mood disorder and anger. In addition, the levels of both C3 and C4 proteins were more pronounced (Boyle, Jackson, & Suarez, 2007). These proteins are indicators of risk for the development of heart disease. High trait anxiety is another clear risk factor for cardiovascular disease (Kubzansky et al., 2006).

The impact of personality on health seems to extend across the entire lifespan. Low scores on conscientiousness may lead to more negative lifestyle choices, such as a poor diet and lack of regular exercise, especially during adolescence and early adulthood. The resultant effect of which would be a BMI within the range indicating a health risk (Pulkki-Raback et al., 2005). The interaction between low scores on conscientiousness and weight gain continues throughout adulthood too. This appears to be most pertinent to women, especially in relation to high scores on measures of neuroticism (Brummett et al., 2006). This personality pattern is also linked to a tendency to smoke cigarettes (Terracciano & Costa, 2004).

Self-discipline, a component of conscientiousness, predicts lower rates of mortality in older adults (Weiss & Costa, 2005). It is likely that self-discipline acts to guide individuals in taking care of their own well-being by adopting a regimen of healthy activities and behaviours. Low levels of conscientiousness, in conjunction with high impulsivity, is associated with low levels of both high density lipoprotein cholesterol ('good' cholesterol) and interleukin-6, the latter being an antiviral protein and so plays an important role in terms of our body's immune response (Sutin et al., 2010a, 2010b).

Certain patterns of personality characteristics seem to predict time to mortality. These include a combination of low levels of both conscientiousness and extroversion as well as high levels of neuroticism (Almada et al., 1991). Neuroticism may influence life course by influencing a person's sensitivity to stress. Neuroticism is linked to increased reactivity to stressful events (Bolger & Schilling, 1991), and research has shown that chronically elevated levels of cortisol, the stress hormone, predict strongly decline in physical health (Kiecolt-Glaser & Glaser, 1986). The impact of emotion dysregulation here on the future well-being of individuals is clear (Kendler, Thornton, & Gardner, 2001).

It should be noted also that personality traits, such as high ratings on conscientiousness, may correlate negatively with the development of Alzheimer's disease. In a longitudinal study of Catholic nuns, priests, and brothers, lasting for up to 12 years in some instances, high scores on conscientiousness correlated with reduced rates of Alzheimer's disease (Wilson et al., 2007). Conscientiousness has been linked to higher levels of resilience which may then act to offset some of the negative fallout from aversive life events (Campbell-Sills, Cohan, & Stein, 2006). Resilience will be explored further later in this chapter.

High scores on hostility are important, not only in terms of Type A-related health risks, but also in terms of the development of mood disorders. Individuals who consistently rate high on hostility across their adult life are at higher risk of developing depression than those who are less hostile (Siegler et al., 2003).

However, before moving on, it is important to remember that although personality does exert a major influence on a person's health, health status can affect personality. It is clear that in many instances experiencing an illness leads to changes in personality. Such changes have been demonstrated in patients after experiencing a heart attack or following a diagnosis of a long-term health condition (Heckhausen & Schulz, 1995).

Key concepts

Having focused on specific personality traits, this next section examines other key concepts related to how a person responds to a change in health status.

Locus of control has been shown to influence how a person copes with an illness. Locus of control refers to the perceived source that is responsible for controlling one's behaviour. Having an internal locus of control is associated with better coping mechanisms and a greater understanding of the condition. The tendency is for the individual to try to take control of the situation that is facing them (Rotter, 1982). Levenson (1973) argued for two additional factors, namely the role of chance and the impact of powerful others on one's behaviour.

A related concept is that of self-efficacy which refers to a person's belief in their ability that when they perform an action it will eventuate in the expected outcome (Bandura, 1997). Self-efficacy works to some extent by increasing both motivation and persistence in the pursuit of a chosen goal. It is therefore associated with a wide range of health-related behaviours. Again, self-efficacy is linked to resilience by helping an individual deal with and overcome adversity (Bandura, 2004). The concept of resilience will be addressed shortly. Before doing so, however, we shall look at how two key concepts within positive psychology – optimism and hope – influences health.

Optimism

Learned optimism

A recent reworking of the learned helplessness model adopts the approach of positive psychology by showing how people can learn to become more optimistic (Seligman, 1991). According to the original model, learned helplessness (Abramson, Seligman, & Teasdale, 1978) develops when people are exposed to situations where a person has little control over what happens to them. Over time people expect future events to be similarly uncontrollable. The specific state of learned helplessness occurs when a person attributes failure to themselves, where there is the expectation that the situation will remain unchanging, and where the situation is all encompassing, pervading into every corner of their lives. In other words, one would be attributing internal, stable, and global factors at play.

Fundamental to this perspective is a person's explanatory style. One's explanatory style reflects how a person rationalizes and explains how one reacts to the vicissitudes of everyday life. Broadly speaking, explanatory styles can be either positive or negative: optimism or pessimism (Seligman, 1991). Remaining optimistic is often much more demanding (Seligman, 1991). In contrast to pessimism, optimism is characterized by a belief that negative events are circumstantial, temporary, and specific to a particular time and place. There is no sense of intrinsic causality here.

In order to combat pessimism and promote optimism, Seligman (1991) proposes two main mechanisms: distraction and disputation. Distraction is a mechanism whereby one focuses attention on an entirely separate matter so that one can return to face the dilemma afresh. Such an approach may help reduce the degree of emotional involvement when attempting to address a particular situation. It is important here to distinguish between temporary distraction and more permanent avoidance. Disputation, on the other hand, compliments distraction. It is a time to challenge the situation that currently presents.

Dispositional optimism

In the case of dispositional optimism, a person expects positive things to happen (Scheier & Carver, 1985). As a result, it is linked to higher levels of perseverance. A classic measure for this is the Life Orientation Test (LOT) (Scheier, Carver, & Bridges, 1994).

Our appraisal of a situation to varying extents determines the level of experienced stress. If initially deemed stressful, we first decide whether the situation has either positive or negative implications in terms of our own well-being. Following this, attempts are made to determine how best to address the situation – the development, in other words, of a coping strategy. These assessments form the basis of Lazarus and Folkman's (1984) model for coping. Two basic modes of coping operate – problem-focused and emotion-focused strategies. With problem-focused approaches the problem situation itself is the focal point. Strategies are developed in order to ameliorate the damage imposed by the stressor. Emotion-focused coping act to reduce the level of distress experienced by the individual involved rather making an attempt to minimize the source of the stress. In the majority of cases use of problem-focused strategies is the preferred option (Folkman, 1997). There are, however, instances where emotion-focused approaches are more appropriate, such as when the individual is unable to exert any control over the situation.

Optimism is associated with higher levels of perseverance and confidence in one's abilities when faced with a difficult situation (Scheier & Carver, 1985). Optimism is moreover linked to problem-focused coping strategies (Aspinwall & Taylor, 1992). Demanding situations are seen to be a challenge that, by overcoming them, will act to enrich one's existence (Carver & Scheier, 1999).

One clear way that optimism impacts on well-being is with a clear negative correlation with depression (Seligman, 1991). At the root of optimism is the belief that whatever difficulty one is faced with it is merely transient and that they have the power to do something about it.

Self-esteem refers to how one perceives oneself. In other words, how accepting are we of ourselves; optimism reflects one's relationship with the environment in which we live (Mäkikangas, Kinnunen, & Feldt, 2004). There is a strong correlation between self-esteem and optimism as one might expect, yet they remain separable constructs (Brissette, Scheier, & Carver, 2002). Those with high self-esteem and high dispositional optimism experience comparatively better physical and mental health (Mäkikangas, Kinnunen, & Feldt, 2004; Scheier & Carver, 1985). This is likely the effect of deploying more effective coping strategies (Schröder, Schwarzer, & Konertz, 1998) which boost levels of perceived well-being and greatly reduce levels of negative mood (Carver, Kus, & Scheier, 1994). Other likely mechanisms include improved functioning of the immune system (Segerstrom, Castañeda, & Spencer, 2003), as well as positive health behaviour (Mulkana & Hailey, 2001). Underlying this is the concept of resilience (Wanberg & Banas, 2000).

Although on the whole optimism is seen to be a positive state of being, it can be viewed as an entirely illusory condition, one not grounded in reality. Under some conditions the optimist's preference for problem-focused coping strategies may render them at a disadvantage. This is particularly the case when the problem situation consists of something over which we have no personal control. Under conditions where change is not possible, the only adaptive mode of responding is to accept the situation and deal with the emotional repercussions. In other words, engage in emotion-focused strategies (Peterson, 2000).

Situational optimism

The concept of situational optimism, as its name suggests, is an extension of dispositional optimism, and reflects situation-specific expectations about potential outcomes (Segerstrom et al., 1998). Rather than a global feeling of optimism, there is a sense of optimism attached to certain identifiable areas of a person's life. This concept is to some extent related to learned optimism, although learned optimism concerns itself only with a person's explanation for positive future episodes and not with their expectation for such events. Those who score high on situational optimism experience less stress and higher positive mood (Segerstrom et al., 1998).

Hope

A complementary approach to that described already concerns the concept of hope (Snyder, 2000). Hope refers to anticipation that one's aims and objectives will be realized. To begin with, there is a goal. Important here is a sense of agency – the resolve to achieve a particular end-state – and identified pathways – the generation of goal-specific action plans. Snyder's approach identifies that an important part of such positive thinking is accepting the need to devise plans to enable the successful completion of an objective. In this sense, what can be conceived as being a rather passive state of existence is transformed into one of active participation. The sense of agency here indicates that we should not expect a positive outcome unless we actively do something to enable it to happen. The probability that the desired positive outcome will occur is by no means certain; there would otherwise be no need for hope under such conditions. In this sense, hope is related to optimism. High levels of optimism would be associated with the sense of agency or desire to achieve a particular goal. However, optimism does not appear to be related to the identification of specific pathways in order to achieve that goal.

It has been shown that both academic and athletic ability positively correlate with hope (McDermott & Snyder, 2000). It is also related to better physical and mental health. In particular, there is a positive correlation with self-esteem – low scores being associated with depression (Snyder, 2002). In terms of physical well-being, those who score high on hope appear more knowledgeable about positive health-related behaviours and recover faster from illness (Snyder, 2002).

Resilience and health

The final topic to cover in this chapter is that of 'resilience'. The term has been mentioned a number of times already. The concept of resilience plays an important role in how people deal with stressful situations. Personality underpins this reaction. Some personality traits enable an individual to respond to a stressful situation without showing any adverse effects (resilience), whereas other traits may make a person more vulnerable under such conditions. The degree of personal control a person felt they could exert on a situation was believed to be only part of the explanation why some people fare better than others in stressful situations (Kobasa & Maddi, 1977). Kobasa and Maddi (1977) suggested that people who displayed high levels of hardiness under stressful conditions shared three key characteristics: there was a sense of personal control over the situation; they felt a high degree of commitment; any change was perceived as a challenge and an opportunity to develop rather than as a threat.

A related concept is sense of coherence (Antonovsky, 1979). A sense of coherence reflects a person's belief that their world is understandable, full of meaning, and, on top of that, controllable. There are fewer aversive health effects in individuals who have a strong sense of coherence (Jorgensen,

Frankowski, & Carey, 1999). Sense of mastery is also linked to this (Pearlin & Schooler, 1978) and reflects a belief that the situation is controllable.

As seen already, there is also a growing interest in the concept of optimism and its effect on health. Optimism is characterized by a pervading belief that positive outcomes will occur. Optimism has been linked to lower levels of distress when faced with a challenging situation, as well as better overall health and faster recovery following illness (Ouelette & Diplacido, 2001; Scheier, Carver, & Bridges, 2001).

The concept of resilience is itself thought to reflect high levels of self-esteem, personal control, and optimism (Major et al., 1998). Those high in resilience show attenuated levels of stress when faced with adversity. They also recover more quickly from such episodes. Problems are faced with a positive orientation, and there is a sense of growth as the result of having lived through the experience (Ong et al., 2006).

How people respond to stress has a direct effect on their overall health. Maladaptive strategies deployed in response to a stressor can lead to illness. Resilience is seen to intervene here, thereby protecting the health status of the individual. Optimism, for example, is associated with a reduced risk of illness, especially life-threatening conditions (Rasmussen, Scheier, & Greenhouse, 2009; Tindle et al., 2009).

It is clear that there is a great deal of overlap here in terms of what constitutes the various concepts. Because of that, it has been useful to categorize personality traits into those that provide resilience in the face of adversity and those that increase vulnerability under comparable conditions. The framework often used is that of Costa and McCrae's (1992) five-factor model of personality. The five factors refer to Neuroticism (emotional lability especially under stressful conditions), Extraversion (tendency to experience positive mood states), Openness (flexibility), Agreeableness (trusting), and Conscientiousness (being purposeful and controlled).

Resilience and related concepts most closely reflect traits associated with low scores on neuroticism – emotional stability as opposed to emotional lability (Smith & MacKenzie, 2006). Emotional stability is associated with good health (Chida & Steptoe, 2008). Extraversion, conscientiousness, and openness are important also (Taylor et al., 2009). The positive characteristics associated with extraversion may be related to a person's ability to perceive more options when they are faced with a challenging situation. This is related to the broaden-and-build model of adaptive behaviour (Fredrickson, 1998). Conscientiousness is important due to its association with goal-directed behaviour (Campbell-Sills, Cohan, & Stein, 2006). Two aspects of openness appear important here, namely emotional awareness and curiosity (Jonassaint et al., 2007). These would likely be associated with a more adaptive and flexible mode of responding to stressors. There has been little research focused on examining the role of agreeableness on health and well-being. From the research that has been conducted, there is little to support the notion that agreeableness plays anything more than a mere supportive role in determining health. Instead, it is associated with greater satisfaction in intimate relationships and may, as a result, exert an indirect positive influence on life expectancy (Malouff et al., 2010). Williams has shown that these traits influence health because they are associated with lower levels of occupational stress, better interpersonal relationships, a less extreme physiological response to negative events, as well as more effective recovery following adversity (Williams et al., 2011).

Resilience in older adults

Having seen how important resilience is in terms of a person's health, this section looks specifically at resilience as we age. The concept of successful ageing has been introduced in earlier chapters and appears to permeate much of the literature on ageing. It is generally associated with high-level cognitive and physical functioning, and low levels of disease or disability (Rowe & Kahn, 1987). However, this may not reflect exactly what older adults themselves believe successful ageing to mean (Montross et al., 2006). Most importantly, studies have highlighted that older adults may consider themselves to be ageing successfully even when they had experienced a serious condition in the past. The concept of resilience is important here.

Middle age

Before considering the older end of the age spectrum, how we deal with change during middle age can be seen to be of considerable importance. Midlife frequently brings with it a number of health problems that are associated with the ageing process. On occasion these conditions are chronic and, as a result, impact greatly on a number of areas of a person's life. At threat during this time is an individual's sense of self-worth because the realization of chronic health conditions results in diminished capacities as well as increasing dependence on support from others. Current and future cohorts are likely to be able to adapt more effectively to changing health status on entering middle adulthood because of a higher standard of general education and more effective healthcare systems (Broese van Groenou & Deeg, 2010). However, working against this is the ubiquitous notion of successful ageing which in turn exerts demands on individuals to sustain a healthy existence into their later years.

Illness is no longer expected by many as they head towards advanced age, indeed it is no longer an inevitable part of ageing. In a recent study to examine the impact on adaptation of a variety of health-related issues, it has been shown that illness characteristics are all important when exploring how an individual is able to deal with their condition (Deeg & Huisman, 2010). One example of this was seen when comparing adaptation to illness as a result of heart disease and cognitive impairment. For heart disease, a person's sense of mastery increased with time. This possibly reflected the predictable nature of heart disease and options to improve outcome. For cognitive impairment, sense of mastery decreased over time. This may be because there is an increasing reliance on technological tools. As a result, decline in cognitive functioning will become even more apparent and impose more barriers the older we get (Mikels, Reed, & Simon, 2009).

Older adulthood

There is growing evidence to show that resilience is important in influencing health-related behaviours in older adults (Perna et al., 2012) and to be linked to psychological well-being (Souri & Hasanirad, 2011). With age we increasingly experience challenging life events. The transition into older adulthood often heralds a reduction in disposable income, poor health and increasing disability, as well as the death of loved ones. It is likely that the personality factors discussed previously would prove beneficial in such situations. When looking at life expectancy, older adults who display such traits in the face of negative life events tend to live longer (Boyle et al., 2009).

Alongside recurrent or chronic health issues, a drop in financial resources, and loss of occupation, social differences between the advantaged and the disadvantaged become more prevalent (Dannefer, 1987). There is a growing mismatch between developmental gains and losses (Baltes, 1997). Although overall well-being does not drop merely as an artefact of getting older (Brandstadter & Wentura, 1995), self-esteem does seem to be affected (Ryff, 1989). It may not necessarily decline, but there does seem to be a great deal more variability among older adults (Trzesniewski, Donnellan, & Robins, 2003), and this seems to be the case in more instances at the oldest extreme. This has far-reaching implications when one takes into consideration the buffer role self-esteem plays in determining health and well-being (Levy, Slade, & Kasl, 2002; Murrell, Meeks, & Walker, 1991). Domain-specific self-esteem seems to be particularly variable. There is debate as to whether self-esteem can be considered a state or a trait (Crocker & Wolfe, 2001), so it may be the case that it is dependent upon various environmental factors.

With age health becomes increasingly an issue, especially the greater likelihood of developing a chronic condition. It is interesting to note that older adults, on the whole, are relatively resilient to stressors (Baltes & Baltes, 1990). Loss is an inevitable part of ageing, but dependent on how important that loss is, the negative impact varies greatly (Murrell, Meeks, & Walker, 1991). Loss may be compensated for through a number of strategies which act to protect, among other things, self-esteem (Heidrich & Ryff, 1993). Regarding social behaviour, older adults tend to focus on relationships that are emotionally rich as opposed to more affiliative relationships (Carstensen, 1995). Emotional disengagement takes place where a relationship is no longer satisfactory or, indeed, where acceptance or approval is no longer available (Crocker & Wolfe, 2001).

The role of carer

Before turning to the final section on quality of life, the issue of resilience is particularly relevant to those who find themselves in the role of carer. In Chapter 10 we looked at the important role played by informal support networks. There is a strong gender divide here also such that women are likely to experience being both care-giver and care-receiver at some time in their lives. Often the role of caregiver begins with caring for a child, then caring for ageing relatives, caring for their spouse also, then finally caring for grandchildren. Indeed, this gender difference has been supported by the statistic that only one quarter of all caregiving is provided by males (Wagner, 1997). The fact that women are more likely to care for their spouse reflects the fact that they experience longer lives. This is reflected in the finding that roughly 90 per cent of older adults are cared for in their own homes by members of their family. With this additional burden, older adults thrust into the role of carer are more likely to neglect their own health and well-being as a result (Connell, 1994).

Within this role of carer, resilience is all important in enabling the individual to adapt constantly to varying demands. Individuals who score higher on resilience maintain an overall sense of control and generate more support from others (Hildon et al., 2008). It has been suggested that rather than successful ageing being the goal, resilience is by far the better alternative as it represents a person's ability to reclaim levels of functioning following illness (Harris, 2008).

Quality of life

Another much used term is that of 'quality of life'. Indices of quality of life are used extensively within gerontology. Although useful, they often vary in terms of what is actually being assessed. Quality of life is a broad, multifaceted construct, encompassing among other things health, emotion, social, independence, and economic components (Baltes & Baltes, 1990). To a large extent, quality of life is a subjective assessment of one's current state within the context of societal expectations (Ring, 2007).

Quality of life can be broken down into two fundamental elements: cognitive and emotional (Diener & Lucas, 2000). These correspond to how one feels about one's current situation and one's judgement as to whether life is good or bad. A recent study by Holzhausen and colleagues focused on the cognitive aspects of this construct (Holzhausen, Kuhlmey, & Martus, 2010).

A few questionnaires exist that attempt to capture the truly subjective nature of quality of life. Such measures enable respondents to specify the elements of their life that are essential for an assessment of quality of life (e.g. Patient Generated Index; Ruta et al., 1994). These measures are tantamount to indices of life satisfaction. One criticism levelled at measures like these is that they focus on the negative, so that higher ratings are associated with a lack or minimization of a particular impairment or deficit (Ryff & Singer, 1998). Completing the measures can be quite complicated also, and many of them are not ideally suited to older adults. A measure that has developed out of this is the Quality of Life in Elders with Multiple Morbidities (Holzhausen, Kuhlmey, & Martus, 2010). This measure in a similar fashion requires individuals to specify elements in their life that are of paramount importance to their overall well-being. A number of examples are provided to help with this process of selection. Each are then rated in terms of how they currently feel about that domain – whether it could be improved or not. Finally, each domain is rated in terms of overall importance. Measures such as this have real practical significance as they provide individualized indices of quality of life and so would help identify the most appropriate healthcare support or intervention.

Summary

Although medical conditions do often develop as we age, with some becoming chronic complaints, it is clear that there are a number of factors at play which influence the development and impact of these conditions on our lives. Of particular focus in this chapter has been the role of personality and related behavioural characteristics. Aside from the main personality traits, self-efficacy has a major role to play, one that is linked to resilience. The rise of positive psychology has been slowly taking place over the last decade or so. Concepts such as optimism, hope, and resilience all contribute to enhancing a person's sense of well-being. Seligman (2011) proposes that the main purpose behind positive psychology is to increase flourishing which has at its core positive emotions, engagement with life, a sense of meaning, as well as self-esteem, optimism, and resilience among others (Huppert & So, 2009). With life expectancy increasing, the idea of maintaining, or indeed increasing well-being as we grow older is something to contemplate, especially when one takes into consideration mounting reliance on informal support networks. We shall see in Chapter 12 that physical and mental well-being of the carer is as important in many instances as that of the sufferer.

Further reading

Carr, A. (2011). *Positive psychology: The science of happiness and human strengths.* London: Routledge. [A comprehensive text on the scientific study of well-being.]

Dweck, C. (2012). *Mindset: How you can fulfill your potential.* New York: Ballantine Books. [A really interesting read and very practical.]

Seligman, M. E. P. (2011). *Flourish: A new understanding of happiness and well-being – and how to achieve them.* London: Nicholas Brealey Publishing. [If you are interested in positive psychology then you should read this recent book by Seligman.]

CHAPTER 12

Mental Health and Neurodegenerative Disorders

Much of the research conducted to look at prevalence of mental health issues in adults has been cross-sectional in nature (Gatz & Smyer, 2001). Such studies invariably use Diagnostic and Statistical Manual of Mental Disorders (DSM) criteria to identify conditions (American Psychiatric Association, 2000). Because of changes in diagnostic criteria and nomenclature made in each edition of the DSM, comparability of findings varies. With an ever-ageing population, incidence of mental health problems in older adults will increase. The current baby boom generation is experiencing high rates of mood disorders and related problems (Gatz & Smyer, 2001) and with increasing age dementias will become more and more of an issue as treatment options do not improve.

Three of the most prevalent conditions associated with older adulthood are depression, delirium, and dementia, and so an examination of these conditions will form a large part of this chapter. In addition to their pervasiveness, all three pose problems in terms of accuracy with which they can be differentiated (Ames et al., 2010).

One important way to achieve this is through history taking. Part of this process involves examining the onset of conditions: for dementia onset is usually insidious and progresses at a steady rate; onset is usually acute for delirium; and depression falls somewhere between these two extremes (Ames et al., 2010).

Because of the potential comorbidity of conditions, it is typically necessary to take note of how symptoms develop over the course of time. Dementia is progressive as we have seen. There are two outcomes associated with delirium: one is death; the other is complete re-establishment of normal functioning following recovery. The course of depression follows a pattern of recovery and relapse. In some instances clinical mood states persist without variation for long periods of time. Depression may also be seen as a major predictor for

178

later developing dementia (Jorm, 2000). In some instances of depression the decline in cognitive function is so marked that a diagnosis of pseudodementia is proffered. This condition is linked especially to later development of dementia (Shulman & Silver, 2006).

In addition to depression, delirium, and dementia, we shall also look at a range of other conditions including anxiety disorders, sleep disorders, as well as substance abuse. The final section of this chapter focuses on psychopharmacology. Drugs are successful in treating the majority of conditions laid out here in this section of the book. It is important, therefore, to have a basic understanding of how drugs work; in other words, what happens once they have been administered. There are a number of important factors that influence how effectively drugs work, but one over which we have control is adherence to a particular medication regime. To begin with, though, we shall turn our attention to depression.

Depression

Dysthymia is a condition in which patients experience subclinical symptoms of depression for a prolonged period of time. In some cases, patients with dysthymia will later develop depression. Depression can be defined as a condition where a depressed mood has prevailed for two or more weeks, with the patient deriving no pleasure from activities that they once enjoyed, a state referred to as anhedonia, as well as a lack of energy in general. Depression is particularly common among older adults. Other aspects that usually accompany this condition include a sense of guilt, sleep disturbances, and either psychomotor agitation or retardation (either excessive or slowed motor activity). There may also be psychotic features such as delusions and hallucinations (Alexopoulos, 2005). Marked cognitive difficulties, such as poor attention and memory, manifest, as well as general cognitive slowing (Christopher & MacDonald, 2005). Unipolar depression is more common than bipolar disorder in this age group (Gatz, Kasl-Godley, & Karel, 1996).

When looking at the performance of older adults with depression on a range of cognitive measures, it is clear that their results lie between a normal control and those diagnosed with dementia (Orrell et al., 1992). The diagnosis of either pseudodementia or reversible dementia has been given where depression results in pronounced cognitive impairment. However, this term may not be entirely accurate as symptoms do not resemble those of dementia to any great extent, nor is the condition necessarily reversible (Bhalla et al., 2006; Poon, 1992).

Frontostriatal dysfunction is implicated heavily here. It is associated in particular with executive dysfunction as well as with general indifference to one's environment and psychomotor retardation. Vascular disease may also affect the amygdala's mediating role in emotional responding, as does the presence of a pre-existing chronic medical condition. Hippocampal volume appears to be reduced in both depression and dementia (Baldwin et al., 2005).

A much-used framework to explain why some people develop conditions such as depression is the diathesis-stress model (Monroe & Simons, 1991). The diathesis component refers to an individual's particular propensity to develop the condition. This may include genetic predisposition or psychological vulnerability. The stress element refers to the eliciting external event or stimulus. Common examples include loss of a spouse or job.

When looking at potential risk factors, gender plays a major role, with higher rates of depression occurring among women. However, when sexes are compared in the over-eighties, the number of depression symptoms reported is higher among men than women (La Rue, Dessonville, & Jarvik, 1985).

Rates of secondary depression are higher in older adults as a result of increased ill health and use of medication (Cohen, 1990). Physical illness may account for the relatively high prevalence of depression among older adults. Conditions associated with depression include infection, diabetes, cardiovascular disease (especially patients who have had a myocardial infarction), and also dementia. It may also be the case that depression accentuates symptom severity (Krishnan, 2002). There is also evidence that medical conditions may heighten depression. In terms of the latter, this is particularly the case for vascular disease (Ames et al., 2010). There does indeed appear to be a strong link between instances of depression in late adulthood and presence of vascular disease.

There is evidence to suggest that cerebrovascular disease plays an important role in depression. The symptoms here differ from non-vascular forms of depression such that there is a greater level of cognitive impairment, especially in terms of verbal fluency and naming, as well as apathy, psychomotor retardation (but no agitation), and a lack of insight (Camus et al., 2004).

The vascular depression hypothesis reflects late-onset depression, with level of disability experienced being at odds with the severity of depression. The severity of cognitive impairment is also greater than generally seen in other instances of depressive disorder (Baldwin & O'Brien, 2002). By effective management of cardiovascular risk factors, the likelihood of developing vascular depression is reduced.

A number of changes to one's social environment may act as risk factors for the development of depression. These include having low economic status, being socially isolated, experiencing a disability that affects one's level of independence, and also bereavement (Boyce, Walker, & Rodda, 2008). Being the carer for a spouse brings with it an increased risk of developing depression (Hinrichsen & Dick-Siskin, 2000). Increasing physical and emotional burden often ensues, as does growing social isolation. The issue of carer well-being is something that will be picked up later in the chapter when looking at dementia.

As seen in an earlier chapter (see Chapter 10), some individuals respond to a bereavement in a way that does not fit the typical pattern. In such cases of abnormal grief symptoms often resemble those of major depression.

Aside from such clear social risk factors, physical risk factors also occur. Decreased blood flow to the subcortical structures within the brain due to minor vascular lesions may lead to slowing down and apathy (Parmelee, 2007).

Depression is difficult to diagnose in older adults and, as a result, may remain unidentified for some time, and in some cases never (Blazer, 2006). Symptoms of depression are very similar to those of cancer and heart disease, as well as being comparable to some of the negative effects experienced as the result of certain medication (Schneider, 1995). The concept of 'masked depression' among older adults is a real issue (Waxman et al., 1985). Age may mean that depression is experienced differently by both younger and older adults, with more emphasis on somatic complaints occurring among older adults. Increased fatigue and poor sleep are often seen as inevitable as we grow older when, in fact, they may be symptoms of depression (La Rue, Dessonville, & Jarvik, 1985).

As well as being under-diagnosed in older adults, depression may sometimes be over-diagnosed. This is because many measures of depression include items concerned with bodily complaints, such as problems with sleep and bowel disturbances. This may be taken to indicate depression when, in fact, these are merely part of the normal ageing process.

Cognitive difficulties prove a particularly difficult case for diagnosis. To a certain extent cognitive decline is a natural part of the ageing process. Complaints concerning such problems may be seen as symptomatic of depression. On the other hand, they may be seen as indicative of something more insidious, such as Alzheimer's disease (Knight, 2004). This may mean that appropriate treatment is not provided. Under such conditions, differential diagnosis is problematic.

The presence of depression in some instances acts as a warning for dementia to come, either as the initial stages of the disease itself or as a risk factor that may predispose a person to develop dementia at a later stage. This is especially the case in instances where the individual has experienced periods of depression throughout their life. Both Alzheimer's disease and vascular dementia appear to be most connected to depression.

Suicidal ideation often accompanies severe depression (Duberstein & Conwell, 2000). Intentional acts to commit suicide among older adults are more likely to be successful when compared to younger adults (Kastenbaum, 2006). Incidence of suicide among older adults is greater for men than women (Duberstein & Conwell, 2000). This gender effect may, in part, be the result of depression going undiagnosed in men more often than in women. This may be because men frequently fail to report the symptoms needed to make a positive diagnosis of depression (Duberstein & Conwell, 2000). Women, on the other hand, often find it easier to elicit the support they need, drawing upon their social network as well as making appropriate use of healthcare services (Bengston, Rosenthal, & Burton, 1996). In many cases suicide is a response to a severe physical illness, although psychiatric issues generally mediate this effect (O'Connell et al., 2004). Although seen by their physician prior to the suicide, evidence of depressive symptoms may have been overshadowed by comorbid medical complaints.

As is usual, it is essential that any form of physical illness is treated appropriately prior to tackling the depression. A review of medication is essential, as is a gauge of how much alcohol the patient regularly consumes.

A number of successful treatment strategies for depression exist. Antidepressant medication works well in older adults. Selective serotonin reuptake inhibitors offer the least harmful side effects and so may be the preferred first choice. If medication proves ineffective after six weeks, other drug choices should be considered. A six-to-eight-week period is warranted as observable effects of the medication are not observed until much later in older adults compared with younger age groups. Although effectiveness of the drug is undiminished once it takes effect, there are higher rates of relapse in this age group necessitating a longer, and in some cases a continual period of prescription in order to effect long-term change in functioning (Roose & Schatzberg, 2005).

Continued non-response to antidepressant medication may necessitate augmentation strategies that comprise adding a second drug to an existing treatment regime in an attempt to improve clinical response. This usually involves prescribing lithium. Close monitoring is needed in such cases due to the serious side effects associated with this medication (Boyce, Walker, & Rodda, 2008).

Electroconvulsive therapy (ECT) is particular effective in older adults, especially in cases where psychotic symptoms feature. ECT involves applying electrodes to the head in order to provoke seizures. Modern practice requires that muscle relaxants be given prior to treatment to prevent the patient harming themselves during the session by dislocating bones or causing fractures. ECT is considered when the patient's life is at risk as the result of refusing to eat or ingest fluids, or where there is a real danger of suicide. It may also be justified in occurrences where standard antidepressant therapies have failed to yield positive results (Boyce, Walker, & Rodda, 2008).

Response to ECT is faster than to antidepressant medication which, in some instances, can take up to eight weeks for an effect to become noticeable. In contrast to this, a positive effect of ECT can be seen after just a few treatments. A typical course of treatment would consist of six to twelve sessions spaced over a number of weeks (Bentall, 2006b).

There are of course side effects associated with ECT. There is a loss of memory prior to and also following the treatment. These periods of retrograde and anterograde amnesia are usually limited in duration to around 30 minutes. Patients may experience a reasonable level of disorientation and also headache immediately following the procedure.

Cognitive behavioural therapy is effective at improving and maintaining functioning in this patient group (Dick et al., 1999). This approach focuses not only on patient behaviour but on their beliefs and thought processes as well. By challenging habitual behaviour and restructuring thought processes, this approach aims to break the downward spiral into depression (Moulin, 2006). The most effective strategy for treating depression in older adults is a combination of cognitive behavioural therapy and antidepressant medication.

The often needed social support for older adults with depression can be provided through day centres or day hospitals. An alternative would be for the patient to move somewhere that offers more in terms of local support structures. Regular exercise is an important component of any package in treating a patient recovering from depression (Boyce, Walker, & Rodda, 2008).

When looking at the treatment of depression in older adults there does seem to be some discrepancy between predicted rates of recovery based on controlled trials and the actual real-world recovery rate. In other words, there is an inconsistency between treatment efficacy and treatment effectiveness (Mulsant et al., 2003). The likely explanation for this is the presence of co-morbid conditions that are an artefact of everyday life and so interacts with the effectiveness of any treatment. Such comorbidities can be controlled for in clinical trials and so the results are cleaner. Recommending a treatment plan for older adults requires clinicians to take into consideration potential interactions with other medications, both prescribed and over-the-counter, thus taking into consideration the problem of polypharmacy.

Bipolar disorder

The majority of patients with bipolar affective disorder were diagnosed with the condition before older adulthood. In the cases where a manic episode is first experienced at such a late stage, patients had generally been diagnosed with depression earlier in their life. This condition is twice as likely to occur in males than females. Late-onset bipolar disorder occurs around the age of 50. In many cases there are comorbid neurological disease processes also occurring; often in such instances this is referred to as disinhibition syndrome. Manic episodes may be brought on as a result of drug interactions. This is especially a problem among older adults where there is a general increase in the number of medicines prescribed to each person.

When a patient experiences mania their overall mood is raised. This has an effect on a person's self-esteem, as well as inflating levels of optimism. Patients generally become more active and the rate at which they speak increases accordingly. Despite increased levels of activity, sleep length is greatly reduced. Concomitant is an increase in risk-taking behaviours. Other cognitive impairments occur, including distractibility. Psychotic features may also occur, such as grandiose delusions and hallucinations that reinforce their heightened optimism.

Lithium is often used as the drug of choice for treating bipolar disorder in older adults. However, there are a number of important points to consider before prescribing this drug. One is that lithium has a narrow therapeutic window. Therapeutic window refers to the range of doses at which a drug can be safely prescribed in order to achieve the intended outcome. A narrow window indicates that there is a small range of doses available before drug toxicity becomes a major concern. Because of this patients receiving this drug need to be closely monitored even though doses for older adults are lower than for younger age groups. This is because renal clearance – a standard test of kidney function relating to the elimination of a given substance – is not as efficient with age, so it is important to ensure patients do not build up toxic levels of the drug in their body (Boyce, Walker, & Rodda, 2008). More information about how drugs work will be provided later in the chapter as it is both a fascinating field and one that is highly apposite to the treatment of older adults.

An alternative to lithium is sodium valproate. This is an anticonvulsant and seems to work well. There is the added benefit here that patients often report fewer side effects with this drug. Sodium valproate may be used to augment lithium treatment such that doses of lithium are reduced without nullifying the therapeutic effect. Neuroleptics (antipsychotic drugs) may be used in some cases, although a number of side effects are greatly increased in older adults, including among other things diabetes, hypotension, and sedation (Boyce, Walker, & Rodda, 2008).

Benzodiazepines may be used to manage behavioural disturbances associated with manic phases. However, there are potential serious implications prescribing this class of drug for older adults as there is an increased risk of serious injury as a result of falls due to heightened sedation and cognitive confusion (Boyce, Walker, & Rodda, 2008).

Anxiety disorders

Much like depression, anxiety often results in a number of cognitive deficits in memory and attention (Christopher & MacDonald, 2005; Schneider,

1995). Despite this, anxiety in older adults has not received as much attention as depression in the same age group. Anxiety disorders cover a broad range of conditions, including generalized anxiety disorder, phobic disorders, obsessive-compulsive disorder, and post-traumatic stress disorder. Anxiety disorders rarely develop later in life. Instead, such conditions manifest when we are much younger (Gatz, Kasl-Godley, & Karel, 1996).

As with depression, making a positive diagnosis for anxiety in older adults is fraught with problems. It is rare for either depression or anxiety to exist on its own. Comorbidity is, therefore, common. At a certain level both conditions share symptoms. Both lead to symptoms that, on the surface, resemble cardiovascular and endocrine problems (Schneider, 1995) resulting in anxiety being falsely diagnosed as physical in origin. Symptoms such as rapid heart rate and abdominal pain can occur as side effects of medication.

In some instances clinicians may diagnose an anxiety disorder when in fact the patient is experiencing depression. This is largely because older adults find it comparably difficult to express feelings relating to depressed thoughts, referring instead to their nerves as the source of the problem. As seen with depression, the types of cognitive problems faced by individuals with anxiety may mimic symptoms of dementia (Knight, 2004).

When a patient presents with symptoms associated with anxiety, it is important to examine what over-the-counter medications they are currently taking. In addition, a full review of dietary intake is required, especially levels of caffeine and alcohol imbibed on a regular basis.

The most common form of anxiety disorder among older adults is generalized anxiety disorder. The condition is more common in women compared to men. The patient reports feeling anxious most of the time, experiencing tension, heightened physiological arousal, and trepidation. Worry cognitions – the stream of negative thought associated with anxiety disorders – are indiscriminate and so not related to a specific condition or situation.

It is relatively rare for panic disorder to develop in older adulthood. In most cases panic episodes have been experienced at an earlier stage in one's life. It is a chronic condition with relapses occurring sporadically. Panic disorder is characterized by patients experiencing panic attacks at different points in their life. A panic attack is a state of extreme anxiety that seems to occur for no apparent reason. The onset is rapid and the attack may continue for a number of minutes.

Phobic disorders are reasonably common in older adults, with rates being higher in women. Phobic disorders refer to patients experiencing extreme anxiety when presented with a specific object or event. In some cases the mere anticipation of the event is enough to trigger an anxiety response. Phobic disorders can take many forms. Agoraphobia is a condition where patients fear situations where escape would be difficult, such as public transport, and so avoid being exposed to such situations. Agoraphobia may develop as a result of increasing infirmity. Social phobia usually develops relatively early on but is then present across the lifespan. The anxiety in this case is triggered by social situations, once again encouraging the person to avoid potentially threatening encounters.

Post-traumatic stress disorder develops as the result of a specific traumatic event, usually one that is life-threatening. Symptoms do not usually manifest immediately but can instead take up to six months to appear. The main symptom of this condition is intrusive flashbacks to the event itself and recurring dreams. Patients may exhibit episodes of extreme anger and show poor concentration across a number of activities. In many cases patients may also experience depression, anxiety, as well as show an increased likelihood of alcohol or drug use. There is some evidence to suggest that symptoms linked to post-traumatic distress disorder become more apparent once again in older adulthood (Averill & Beck, 2000). Extreme distress may be experienced as a result of a specific stressful event, such as the onset of a physical illness. Likewise, moving into residential care may also elicit extreme emotional disturbance. Such adjustment disorders are particular common in older adults.

As with a number of conditions, obsessive-compulsive disorder usually develops in early adulthood, although it is likely to be a lifelong problem. This condition is associated with obsessions that consist of intrusive thoughts and images that the patient finds disagreeable and so attempts are made to resist these incursions. Compulsive behaviours develop as a result. Patients are unable to prevent compulsive acts from occurring even though they are aware the acts themselves have no purpose other than as a means to relieve the distress they feel. For a positive diagnosis of obsessive-compulsive disorder, symptoms should be severe enough to obstruct with everyday functioning.

Most anxiety disorders are treated using antidepressants, often because of the comorbidity between anxiety and depression. Selective serotonin reuptake inhibitors may be used to treat agoraphobia and social phobia, although specific phobias are generally treated using non-pharmacological methods (see subsequent section). There is little in terms of evidence how best to treat post-traumatic stress disorder in older adults. However, use of selective serotonin reuptake inhibitors and tricyclic antidepressants show some effectiveness. Benzodiazepines are useful for treating anxiety symptoms, although there are concerns with this drug as it may lead to cognitive confusion and increased sedation, thus increasing the likelihood of falls. Beta-blockers may be used to deal with the physiological symptoms of anxiety, although there are considerable side effects when used with older adults (Flint, 2005).

Non-pharmacological treatments include cognitive behavioural therapy. Very few older adults seek treatment for phobic conditions, but when help is sought, behavioural approaches work best. Techniques include gradual exposure to the feared situation in combination with relaxation training such that states of relaxation eventually replace fear. Adjustment disorder is usually conducted through counselling and social support, although medication may be prescribed to deal with specific symptoms of anxiety or depression. As in a number of other cases, there is little specific information on how to manage obsessive-compulsive disorder in older adults. Behavioural therapy is likely to be beneficial as are some antidepressant medication.

Neurotic disorders

'Neurotic disorders' is a term often used to group anxiety disorders, obsessive-compulsive disorders, and phobias. Because of that the symptoms associated with neurotic disorders largely reflect those of depression and anxiety. Somatic symptoms connected to anxiety include muscle tension, headaches, and restlessness. Symptoms such as panic attacks may be misappropriated to physical ailments and so patients are often referred to cardiologists or gastroenterologists. However, given the likelihood of comorbid medical conditions, such caution is often warranted. This is especially the case in instances of somatization, where anxiety or depression manifests as somatic complaints. Ensuing behavioural problems are the result of maladaptive strategies aimed at controlling symptoms. These include avoidant strategies, abuse of alcohol or other substances, and also eating disorders. Genetics is likely to play a role as a consequence of the degree of reactivity people experience during emotive experiences. The impact of physical deterioration or incapacity is particularly salient for older adults.

There is reasonable evidence showing effectiveness of cognitive behavioural therapy for older adults with a range of neurotic disorders. These approaches utilize an array of techniques to combat maladaptive thinking styles associated with these conditions. This process includes challenging negative thoughts as they arise because they are often the result of cognitive distortion, as well as using conditioning and reinforcement strategies to help modify behaviour. When conceiving a treatment plan for older adults, it is important always to consider their level of physical functioning and assess the degree of cognitive impairment as both will impose restrictions on what is possible in terms of a realistic treatment plan (Ames et al., 2010).

On the whole, drug therapies are frequently the treatment of choice for anxiety among older adults. As seen in a previous chapter, historically there has been a shared consensus among psychotherapists that the therapies they offer are not appropriate for older adults (see Chapter 9). However, this does seem to be changing.

Hypochondriasis

Hypochondriasis is classified as a somatoform disorder. This is because the symptoms associated with this condition are suggestive of a physical problem despite evidence to the contrary. Patients deny a psychological explanation for their condition. Individuals with this condition make numerous visits to their GP (Butler, Lewis, & Sunderland, 1998).

Explanations to why this condition occurs in older adults include an over-whelming sense of anxiety concerning a loss of income and prestige, leading to a preoccupation with bodily symptoms. It may also be the case that some individuals may develop this condition in order to offset decline in function-ing as physical infirmity provides a socially acceptable justification for poor performance (Cohen, 1990).

Insomnia

Sleep may be characterized as something that occurs within the confines of a 24-hour endogenous cycle. Although this cycle runs autonomously, it is influ-enced by environmental stimuli such as the presence or absence of sunlight and daily routines (such as meal times) which help to enforce the 24-hour cycle (Czeisler et al., 1989). Given free reign the sleep–wake cycle runs on average between 24.2 and 25.1 hours (Czeisler et al., 1999).

Sleep is characterized by a number of discrete stages that can be detected using electroencephalogram (EEG) measurements. We alternate between non-rapid eye movement sleep (non-REM) and rapid eye movement (REM) phases. An average adult will experience this cycle up to six times each night ('Sleep cycle', 2004).

Poor sleep is an issue for many older adults. This is because age alters the patterns of sleep such that overall time asleep is less than during earlier period in their adult life. Part of this reduction in sleep time is due to a longer delay before sleep actually occurs, and this is compounded by the fact that older adults generally wake earlier. There are also more incidences of awak-ing during the night. The amount of time spend in slow wave sleep is greatly reduced as is REM sleep. These and other factors result in poorer sleep qual-ity overall (Boyce, Walker, & Rodda, 2008).

Insomnia results when quantity and quality of sleep is insufficient for normal healthy functioning. A number of problems are associated with this condition, including everyday cognitive failures in memory and attention, as well as an increased risk of falls. Insomnia may be brought on as the result of an external stressor or disturbance in one's pattern of behaviour. Insomnia may be short-lived (transient or acute insomnia) or it can be chronic (Kamel & Gammack,

2006). Chronic insomnia is the result of disorders of sleep such as sleep apnoea, discomfort from physical illness, and also psychiatric disorders. Dementia severely disrupts sleep patterns. Other factors include side effects of medication, overuse of stimulants such as caffeine and nicotine, alcohol, and also taking naps during the day (Boyce, Walker, & Rodda, 2008).

When assessing the patient it is important to obtain a clear account of their sleep pattern. This is best achieved with a sleep diary. When treating cases of insomnia the first step is to improve a patient's sleep hygiene. This consists of isolating and correcting behaviours that have a negative impact on one's sleep in addition to identifying ways to improve a person's sleep environment. One way of doing this is to request that patients limit the time spent in bed so that bed is viewed as a place for sleep rather than as somewhere to rest in comfort, only retiring when one feels the need to sleep. Use of relaxation techniques and exercise can be useful here, in part as a way to reduce any anxiety experienced by the patient (Boyce, Walker, & Rodda, 2008).

Drugs may also be used although there is concern associated with their use in terms of potential dependency and increased risk of physical injury. Drugs used include benzodiazepines such as zopiclone, zolpidem, and zaleplon.

Schizophrenia

Given the gradual trend towards de-institutionalization over the past several decades, there are increasing numbers of older adults diagnosed with schizophrenia that need to be supported within the community.

The symptoms associated with schizophrenia may be conceived as being either *positive* in the sense that there is the presence of bizarre behaviours and thoughts or *negative* to reflect an absence of behaviour or affect that would normally be present (Bentall, 2006c). The positive symptoms of schizophrenia – delusion, hallucination, thought disorder, and the like – may diminish both in regularity and strength with age. With late-onset schizophrenia patients are more likely to experience hallucinations that relate to already existing impairments in sensory processing. Persecutory delusions seem to prevail more among older adults.

Negative symptoms – avolition (apathy), alogia (impoverished speech), anhedonia, blunted affect, and poor executive function – on the other hand, may worsen. This could largely be due to enforced social isolation as a result of cumulative struggles since the onset of the condition, as well as ineffective support networks and sporadic episodes of hospitalization. Age-related decline in cognitive functioning only intensifies the situation.

Although the majority develop schizophrenia in early adulthood, there are instances of late-onset or very late-onset schizophrenia. There are higher rates of late-onset schizophrenia among females. Two major aspects linked to schizophrenia in late life are impairment in sensory functions and social isolation. There also seems to be an apparent link with patients who showed poor social functioning as well as either schizoid or paranoid personality traits in their adult life.

The coexistence of a physical disorder often goes undetected in patients with schizophrenia. Possible explanations for this include the fact that this patient group is less likely to report symptoms and, even when care is obtained, to adhere to a particular treatment plan. There is also evidence of an increased tolerance to pain in patients with psychosis (Boyce, Walker, & Rodda, 2008).

As is generally the case, it is important to treat comorbid medical conditions as this will be favourable in terms of the patient's general well-being. This is especially the case where the patient developed the condition in early adulthood and so may have ignored their general health as a result (Ames et al., 2010). Given symptoms often result from existing deficits in sensory processing, treating conditions that are reversible, such as improving eyesight or removing wax deposits in the ears, can help relieve some problems (Boyce, Walker, & Rodda, 2008).

Prescribed doses of medication are a fraction of those given to young adults. Even so, there is a very high risk of extrapyramidal side effects. These are acute neurological sequelae due to the effect of the medication on basal ganglia functioning. Such symptoms include dystonias (abrupt muscle contractions), akathesia (hyperactivity), and also pseudo-Parkinsonism (tremor, decreased voluntary activity, flattened affect). The augmented use of antidepressants has been shown to improve cognitive functioning. Cognitive behavioural therapy appears effective here also. The factor that best predicts improved functioning is improved social support. Residential care increasingly becomes the preferred option in instances where severity of symptoms erodes functional capacity (Ames et al., 2010).

Delusional disorder

Patients with delusional disorder develop delusions that often persist throughout the course of their life. Delusions are predominantly persecutory in nature, although they can be somatic and grandiose as well. Onset of the condition usually occurs in a person's forties and is more common in women than men. Factors thought to increase risk of developing this condition include social isolation, financial concerns, sensory impairment, and head injury. There is no overall pattern to the onset of delusional disorder, so in some cases it is gradual, in others acute. Functioning is unaffected in areas that are not part of the delusion. An atypical neuroleptic is the preferred choice here due to a reduced likelihood of the patient developing extra-pyramidal side effects (Bentall, 2006a). Cognitive behavioural therapy is also useful in tackling issues surrounding delusional beliefs the patient holds.

Personality disorders

There is still reasonable debate of the validity of personality disorders as a diagnostic category given that in all cases specific diagnoses refer merely to a clustering of symptoms. This is even more pertinent when attempts are made to diagnose this condition in older adults. This is because, as we enter late adulthood, opportunities for impulsive behaviour diminish making detection of maladaptive behaviour more difficult. On the other hand, actual debility may be falsely construed as merely an artefact of a patient's struggle for dependency (Abrams & Bromberg, 2006).

Personality disorders are characterized by persistent and extreme patterns of behaviour that are fixed and therefore do not offer the flexibility demanded by many of the situations we are faced with on a daily basis. Whereas antisocial, borderline, and passive-aggressive personality disorders are more prevalent among younger adults, older adults tend to be diagnosed with paranoid, schizoid, or anankastic personality disorders (Ames et al., 2010).

There has been little research in the area of personality disorders and older adulthood. As a result, there are no assessments validated for this population. Although it is generally the case that personality remains relatively static as we age, the types of benefits certain traits offer, as well as the susceptibilities incurred, may become increasingly apparent, especially in relation to the types of coping strategies employed. These factors are important determinants of how resilient a person is to changing situations and how successfully they adapt (Ames et al., 2010).

Although in reality an individual may have exhibited symptoms of a personality disorder throughout their adult life, it often happens that a clinical diagnosis is not made until the person has entered late adulthood. There are a number of potential explanations why this may be the case. One is that older adulthood brings with it changes to a person's way of life that are so distinct that no amount of behaviour management can hide evidence that the person is indeed exhibiting symptoms of a personality disorder. In other cases, symptoms of a personality disorder may go unnoticed due to the relative prominence of another condition, such as an eating disorder (Segal, Coolidge, & Rosowsky, 2006).

There is a general consensus that what mental health services can at best offer patients diagnosed with a personality disorder is management of the condition through environmental control.

Paranoid disorders

Paranoid disorders are a DSM-V Axis II disorder under the category of personality disorders. Paranoia may develop in older adulthood (Butler, Lewis, & Sunderland, 1998). Such individuals are suspicious and do not trust others even when there is no clear explanation for such feelings. The development of paranoid thinking in older adults is often the result of a visual or auditory impairment (Knight, 2004). Sensory deficits can lead individuals to misinterpret situations. Such disordered thought may also develop out of cognitive impairment. An accusation of theft may accompany the loss of a wallet when, in fact, the wallet may have been misplaced.

Substance abuse

As we age our ability to metabolize alcohol changes, as does the overall composition of our bodies (see section on pharmacodynamics later in the chapter). The resultant effect is that we are no longer able to cope with the levels of alcohol that we did when we were younger.

Alcohol dependence is diagnosed when the individual exhibits a strong desire to drink alcohol, and that when started there is little evidence that they have control over how much they are drinking. Severe withdrawal symptoms occur if alcohol is not consumed. This behaviour continues even though the patient is aware that it is having a harmful effect on their health.

Consumption of alcohol often decreases as we age such that around half of all older adults are abstinent. In other cases consumption of alcohol actually increases as a result of major life events or because time is no longer structured following retirement. Although a significant problem, substance abuse among older adults is frequently overlooked. Most common is alcohol abuse (Whelan, 2003). Due to a changing demographic, it has been noted that the actual number of older adults with alcohol dependence is rising, culminating in a 'silent epidemic' (O'Connell et al., 2003).

It is difficult to detect extreme alcohol consumption among older adults because circumstances that make misuse of alcohol evident for younger adults are not present for older generations. There is also a general belief that behaviour of this nature is not expected among older adults (Boyce, Walker, & Rodda, 2008). In many cases alcohol-related problems may be misdiagnosed as depression (Dar, 2006).

Alcohol also exerts an effect by intensifying any current physical or psychological disorders the patient may have. There will also be a negative compound effect on cognitive capability as well as on sensory inputs and psychomotor function. There are important implications here in terms of falls in this age group (Ganguli et al., 2005). Chronic excess of alcohol increases vulnerability to cognitive deficits later in life, in addition to increased risk of depression and other psychiatric disorders. There is a reasonable number of individuals whose abuse of alcohol began relatively late in life. This change in behaviour is often the result of a major negative life event, such as a bereavement, change in physical functioning, or retirement.

There is much contention over whether there are any positive effects of moderate alcohol consumption, with some studies suggesting that there may be positive effects for cardiovascular functioning and also in terms of lowering risk of dementia (Grønbæk, 2009). For a number of reasons older adults are more prone to deficiency in nutrients as a result of heavy alcohol use. There is also a greater risk that death will occur due to cirrhosis of the liver. In addition to this, there is a real concern of unintended interactions with medications that patients may be receiving, especially in terms of psychiatric medication and also treatments such as warfarin (an anticoagulant) (Boyce, Walker, & Rodda, 2008).

The neurotoxic effects of alcohol can in some cases lead to alcoholic dementia. This condition is reversible to some extent once alcohol consumption ceases. Thiamine deficiency occurs through chronic misuse of alcohol as alcohol reduces the absorption of the vitamin in the stomach. Symptoms of this deficiency include confusion, opthalmoplegia (paralysis of eye muscles), nystagmus (involuntary eye movements), and ataxia (loss of coordination).

If untreated, death may occur. However, the majority instead go on to develop Korsakoff's psychosis. This is an amnestic condition caused directly by the thiamine deficiency. In these cases patients are unable to form new memories as well as showing evidence of retrograde amnesia, but as with many other cases of amnesia, both working memory and procedural memory are unaffected. Prognosis here is poor (Thomson & Marshall, 2006).

Not only are there severe consequences in terms of one's own health, there are major disruptions in relationships with both family and friends, and there is an increase in the likelihood of being involved in a road traffic accident.

Group therapy appears to be particularly effective for older adults, especially when the group comprises peers. Psychosocial interventions may be complemented by prescribing drugs such as naltrexone that oppose the action of opiates (an opiate antagonist) and so help lessen withdrawal symptoms and minimize the rewarding effects of alcohol consumption. Other drugs may be used to reduce craving for alcohol (Boyce, Walker, & Rodda, 2008).

Withdrawal from alcohol results in intense feelings of anxiety, agitation, tachycardia (rapid heartbeat), and tremor among other symptoms, and in some cases seizures are experienced. Benzodiazepines are used to manage the symptoms. A course of vitamin replacement is prescribed in an attempt to deal with the imbalance (Boyce, Walker, & Rodda, 2008). Delirium tremens develops during the period of withdrawal with the risk of death in some cases if intensive medical care is not available quickly enough (see the next section for more details).

It is likely that from now onwards we will see increasing numbers of those entering older adulthood who will abuse substances that they had taken either in their youth or adulthood, be it alcohol or recreational drugs (Patterson & Jeste, 1999). The 'baby boomer' generation will pose fresh challenges for the type of care offered to older adults of current and future generations.

The long-term prescription of benzodiazepines may pose a problem in terms of dependency for the current generation entering older adulthood. One of the main issues is the likelihood of increased injury, often through falls. In addition, the sedative effect of these drugs likely lead to prolonged immobility, the result of which may be to exacerbate current medical conditions or create new ones.

Delirium

Delirium is reasonably common among older adults. It occurs most frequently following admission to hospital. It is a difficult condition to diagnose accurately as its symptoms resemble those of a number of other disorders. It has been seen that dementia may predispose a person to experience delirium, as does mania and schizophrenia. This can occur as a result of the medication used to treat such conditions. Alternatively the delirium may develop as a result of the person failing to take adequate care of themselves. Whatever the cause, the fact that a person is experiencing delirium is indicative that something is wrong (Ames et al., 2010).

A strong indicator that someone is experiencing delirium is severe cognitive impairment of acute onset. However, onset may be less dramatic in instances where delirium is caused by drugs, although still more rapid than the changes that occur with dementia. It is often the case that the condition resolves itself before it develops beyond the prodromal phase during which the symptoms are less severe.

Delirium may be hyperactive, such as that experienced following the withdrawal of alcohol, a state known as delirium tremens. It is characterized by high levels of aggression, tremor, and myoclonus (muscle spasms), with the patient experiencing hallucinations. In contrast to this, hypoactive delirium is associated with low levels of alertness often communicating a sense of ennui. Although hypoactive delirium is more prevalent among older adults, the symptoms are much harder to detect, increasing the likelihood that it will go undetected by clinicians in many cases (Ames et al., 2010).

Delirium begins with the patient experiencing difficulties maintaining concentration and a sense of feeling slightly confused. Temporal distortions as well as visual–spatial disturbances occur making it increasingly difficult for the individual to maintain an accurate representation of reality. Patients may appear active at night and drowsy during the day. As the condition develops, the severity of the cognitive impairments increase with patients experiencing hallucinations as their hold on reality begins to slip away. Level of awareness is such that patients often exhibit agitation and anger in response to the distress they feel.

To effectively manage this condition it is important to first isolate the cause of the delirium, such as possible drug interactions, infection, or dehydration. Distress is often accompanied by disruptive behaviour. However, it is imperative that before the behaviour is nullified the clinician obtains a true understanding why the person is behaving as they are. The presence of family members can often help reduce the level of distress experienced by the patient, especially if they are being treated in an unfamiliar environment (Meagher, 2001). Recovery from delirium requires emphasis on providing a safe environment, with a great deal of emphasis on orienting the patient to their current time and location.

Dementia

The prevalence of dementia rises exponentially around the age of 64, with almost one third of adults over 85 being positively diagnosed (Ferri et al., 2005). In the UK alone there are 820,000 people living with the condition. One in every three individuals will die with one form of dementia (Alzheimer's Research Trust, 2010). Rather than being discreet, easily diagnosable entities, the dementias are best conceptualized as a syndrome, thereby consisting of a range of symptoms that are of varying origins (Ames et al., 2010). Dementia refers to global cognitive decline (Corey-Bloom, 2000). Problems include major impairments in memory, language, problem solving, and decision making. Such deficits severely impact both work and social life. As seen previously, delirium shares many symptoms with dementia, but it is a temporary condition. Also, consciousness is relatively spared until later stages of dementia, unlike delirium where altered consciousness is a defining feature.

Dementia is a varied condition. Patients rarely present with the same symptoms. Some are more aggressive, others more depressed and withdrawn. The severity of brain damage, individual personality, and a person's living environment results in such huge individual differences. The two most common dementias are Alzheimer's disease and vascular dementia. It is often the case that patients suffer from both conditions (Skoog, Blennow, & Marcusson, 1996).

Fundamental to a diagnosis of dementia is an acquired impairment of cognitive functioning that encompasses all processing domains. The advancement of the disease is in most cases progressive and irremediable. Although memory failures are one of the first symptoms detected, patients show evidence of apraxia (loss of ability to perform voluntary action), dysphasia (difficulty understanding language), as well as marked changes in how they behave (Boyce, Walker, & Rodda, 2008).

In terms of pathology dementias are often divided into those where the primary damage occurs cortically and those where it occurs subcortically. Alzheimer's disease and frontotemporal dementia are examples of cortical dementia; Huntington's disease and progressive supranuclear palsy are subcortical dementias; whereas vascular dementia and dementia with Lewy bodies are examples of mixed dementia.

The main clinical characteristics of cortical dementia are impairments in memory, language, mathematical ability, and visual–spatial processing. For subcortical dementia the main symptoms are changes in personality and mood disturbances, memory impairment, and cognitive slowing. There is a general absence of aphasias and apraxias (Albert, Feldman, & Willis, 1974). Additional features of dementia include extreme agitation, aggression, fluctuating mood, wandering, loss of inhibition, hallucinations, and a disrupted sleep pattern.

It is generally the case that the majority of dementias manifest in late adulthood. However, this is not always so, with some dementias developing much earlier on. Around 50 per cent of early-onset cases occur as a result of a genetic mutation. The apolipoprotein E (ApoE) gene, in particular the ApoE ε4 allele, increases threefold the risk of developing dementia (Ames et al., 2010). ApoE is a cholesterol transporter and is involved in repairing injury to the central nervous system (Reynolds, 2003). The ApoE ε4 allele causes more beta-amyloid (Aβ) to be deposited. Aβ forms the core of the amyloid plaques that form between neurons and so interfere with neuronal transmission (see later for more information).

It is usually a relative or friend who first raises concern that a person has dementia. In some instances, loss of a spouse uncovers cognitive impairment in the survivor that previously went unnoticed, maybe as a consequence of the deceased controlling areas of their shared life that would have made evident early signs of disease progression were that not the case. Because of this, informants are a vital component of the history taking process in addition to accounts from the patient themselves (Ames et al., 2010).

Clinical diagnosis necessitates a full medical history, including medical complaints experienced by the patient's family. This is usually followed by a physical examination. A profile of current medication is essential, although immediate attention is directed towards medications that interfere with central nervous system functioning. As seen previously, depression needs to be screened out, as does anxiety (Ames et al., 2010). An assessment of cognitive functioning forms a vital component of this process (see Chapter 8 for more detail).

Having defined dementia in general, the following sections will examine the more common diagnoses of dementia. We shall start with the most prevalent, Alzheimer's disease.

Alzheimer's disease

Early stages of Alzheimer's disease may go undetected, being seen as normal age-related impairment by many people, including the individual experiencing the problems themselves (Whitehouse, 2007). Some individuals with this disease continue to function effectively both in the workplace and socially during early stages of the condition, thereby making it more difficult to recognize the onset of something far more invidious. However, marked changes do become apparent sooner rather than later. More often than not, the first indication that there is something wrong is when the patient becomes lost in a familiar environment.

Some of the behavioural changes associated with the onset of dementia overlap with symptoms of depression, making a differential diagnosis incredibly difficult. Denial of any appreciable problem by the sufferer often indicates something more progressive. Eventually, cognitive impairments become all too obvious, and the true nature of the condition is brought to light. Aside from profound cognitive impairment, a patient may experience delusions, hallucinations, and paranoia. Physical functioning is greatly affected, with the patient requiring assistance in issues of hygiene and personal care.

Patients diagnosed with Alzheimer's disease often live up to ten years post-onset. Cause of death in most cases is the result of infection, mainly pneumonia, due to greatly reduced mobility (Whitehouse, 2007). Alzheimer's disease rates will increase as a result of our ageing population unless effective treatment is discovered.

Alzheimer's disease is difficult to distinguish from other types of dementia in living patients even with recent advancements in imaging technology. Tests can be run to rule out secondary causes of dementia, such as thyroid problems or vitamin deficiency. Structural abnormalities, as in the case of a tumour, can be identified through imaging. However, a positive diagnosis of Alzheimer's disease can only be made when examining the brain *post-mortem* (Whitehouse, 2007).

Post-mortem inspection allows one to explore the extent of damage triggered by the presence of amyloid plaques and neurofibrillary tangles that characterize Alzheimer's disease. Although such structures are often present in the brain of normally ageing adults, a positive diagnosis of Alzheimer's disease requires that a certain density of plaques and tangles must appear in the brain of the deceased. Cell death and loss of neuronal connections produce the profound cognitive impairment associated with this disease. Vacuoles appear in the brain tissue where once healthy neurons resided.

Alzheimer's disease is the most common form of dementia and accounts for 60 per cent of dementia diagnoses worldwide. It is more prevalent among women than men. The onset of Alzheimer's disease is gradual and the disease follows a trajectory of steady decline. Specific symptoms include poor retention of new information and impaired recall of previously stored knowledge. In addition there may be evidence of aphasia (word-finding difficulties), apraxia (motor coordination problems), agnosia (problems with object recognition), and impairment of executive function (coordination of complex behaviour). Behavioural changes include wandering, irritability, aggression, and loss of inhibition (Blennow, de Leon, & Zetterberg, 2006).

In terms of brain pathology, Alzheimer's disease is associated with the presence of both amyloid (or neuritic) plaques and neurofibrillary tangles. Amyloid plaques consist of an accumulation of damaged neuronal tissue and extracellular deposits of Aβ. These plaques impair the way neurons communicate and also cause cell death. An inflammatory response is provoked as a result of their presence in neural tissue, with the concomitant activation of astrocytes, microglia, and cytokines, leading to neural damage (Martin, 2002). Neurofibrillary tangles are structures that occur within neurons (intracellular) and consist of tau protein that are abnormally hyperphosphorylated, thus making it insoluble and thereby leading to the formation of tangles. These largely occur in the medial temporal lobe and the cerebral cortex. Neurofibrils (microscopic cytoplasmic strands) are used to transport chemicals that will later be converted into neurotransmitters. As a result of this entanglement, this process can no longer occur, directly impacting on synthesis of neurotransmitters (Kensinger & Corkin, 2005). Other changes include a pervasive loss of acetylcholine in the cortex due to pathology of the basal forebrain nuclei.

In addition to this neuropathology, shrinkage or atrophy occurs within the medial temporal lobe, resulting in a loss of around 50 per cent of neuronal tissue. One of the first regions to be affected is the hippocampus, a region of the brain that is intrinsic to the formation of new memories. Considerable loss occurs in the nucleus basalis, a part of the ventral forebrain that houses a large proportion of the brain's cholinergic neurons. This has a dramatic effect on functions that are dependent on the neurotransmitter, acetylcholine, which plays a major role in the maintenance of alertness and awareness (Smythies, 2009). Indeed, many drugs used to treat this condition do so by counteracting this deficit by inhibiting the action of acetylcholine esterase, the enzyme that breaks down acetylcholine.

With time more widespread deterioration occurs, resulting in widening of the ventricles, as well as broadening of the sulci across the surface of the brain. Both the temporal and parietal cortex become affected next, interfering with the processing and integration of sensory information from all modalities, before the disease progresses globally.

In attempting to isolate potential risk factors, complication quickly ensues. One major risk factor, however, is gender, with higher incidence occurring among women, although this finding seems to reflect mainly those of a European ancestry (Reynolds, 2003). Physical exercise has shown beneficial effects, as does a healthy, balanced diet. It may be the case that both active exercise and a nutritious diet reduce the risk of Alzheimer's disease by lowering blood pressure and diabetes. The collective findings are by no means conclusive at this stage. A great deal of research has examined how keeping mentally active affects the development of Alzheimer's disease. This will be explored in greater depth in Chapter 14.

A small proportion of Alzheimer's disease is inherited (familial Alzheimer's disease) and affects adults earlier than the more prevalent form of the disease, sporadic Alzheimer's disease (Kilpatrick, Burns, & Blumbergs, 1983). Sporadic, or late-onset, Alzheimer's disease is the result of a number of possible genetic and environmental factors occurring in combination to instigate the disease process (Kensinger & Corkin, 2005). Although everyone carries the gene that encodes ApoE, a plasma protein vital for the transportation of cholesterol, those with the ε4 allele are at particular risk of developing Alzheimer's disease (Saunders et al., 1993). Other variants of the gene are associated with a reduced likelihood of developing the condition.

Other risk factors include smoking, obesity, diabetes, and vascular disease. In addition, head injury is also implicated as increasing risk of developing the condition, as is a history of depression. The role of depression has been explored already earlier in the chapter. As to why head injury is a risk factor, there is evidence to show that Aβ deposits occur at the site of damage in individuals who carry the ApoE ε4 allele. Individuals with Down's syndrome are more likely to develop Alzheimer's disease largely due to an extra copy of the gene which codes for amyloid precursor protein (APP) from which derives Aβ, a principal component of amyloid plaques.

A number of potential protective factors have been identified. Cognitive reserve has been linked with a high level of educational attainment and activity, both mental and physical, throughout one's life. The issue of cognitive reserve is often heralded as something that may help the patient cope with the initial symptoms of Alzheimer's disease. However, decline in function soon exceeds the respite offered by compensatory strategies. The disease, as a result, only becomes apparent to others at a relatively more advanced stage (Boyce, Walker, & Rodda, 2008).

Women who undergo hormone replacement therapy following menopause have shown a reduced risk of developing the condition, although often results are conflicting (LeBlanc et al., 2001). Oestrogen levels drop at menopause and bring with it a host of memory problems. Indeed, there is some evidence to suggest that this patient group exhibits a better response to cholinesterase inhibiting drugs, but only in cases where they do not carry the ApoE ε4 allele (Reynolds, 2003).

The use of non-steroidal anti-inflammatory drugs, NSAIDs, may act to protect a person from developing Alzheimer's disease. Activation of microglia (phagocytes that accumulate cellular waste) and the presence of cytokines (part of the body's immunologic response to infection) produce inflammation in the brains of patients with Alzheimer's disease. The anti-inflammatory properties of this class of drug may help to counteract this process (Reynolds, 2003).

Activity levels of antioxidants in the brain appear reduced in Alzheimer's disease patients making neurons more vulnerable to oxidative damage. Because of this, additional quantities of Vitamin E to one's diet may prove fruitful.

Current understanding of how the disease develops suggests that, for Alzheimer's disease to progress a number of events need to occur within the brain to first trigger the disease process. Research is focusing currently on the identification of biomarkers that may be used to identify those at risk of developing this condition, as well as diagnosing it earlier than is currently possible. At present one of the best candidates include low levels of Aβ in the cerebrospinal fluid in combination with high levels of tau protein. Together these measures are reasonably sensitive and can be used to differentiate different forms of dementia (Schipper, 2007).

Media interest in Alzheimer's disease has been instrumental in raising the amount of research money allocated to this condition. However, it has also raised awareness and, as a result, anxiety in the general public (Gatz, 2007). There is a tendency now to conclude that cognitive failures in older adults are due to the onset of Alzheimer's disease rather than seeing them as a benign symptom of age (Knight, 2004).

Vascular dementia

Vascular dementia reflects a rise in cognitive impairment as the result of multiple infarct (interrupted blood supply causing tissue damage) or lesions (tissue damage as the result of injury) occurring in the brain (Heindel & Salmon, 2004). Onset is abrupt. Deterioration of functioning is stepwise (Skoog, Blennow, & Marcusson, 1996). Deterioration occurs following the infarct, although this is followed by a period of recovery. Recovery is not complete, however, so that given additional infarcts, there is an overall decline in functioning. Severity of symptoms depends on where damage occurs and how extensive the damage is. Patients usually survive less than three years following diagnosis (Rockwood, 2006). In around half the cases patients die from ischaemic heart disease.

Although there are clear differences here between vascular dementia and Alzheimer's disease, there are noticeable overlaps in symptoms, making it very difficult to differentiate the two conditions. Personality of the patient is preserved until quite late on depending on the severity of damage. Mood does fluctuate and patients may also experience psychotic episodes. An early sign that this condition is developing is the presence of hypochondriasis. Memory functioning is impaired and there is evidence of psychomotor retardation. Parkinsonian symptoms appear as the disease progresses (Trimble & George, 2010).

To make matters worse, individuals aged 85 and above often develop both conditions. The main risk factors associated with this condition are hypertension, smoking, diabetes mellitus, hypercholesterolaemia (high levels of cholesterol in the blood), and a family history of the condition.

Dementia with Lewy bodies

Lewy bodies are spherical inclusion bodies consisting of protein deposits that are located in the cytoplasm of neurons. Their presence in the midbrain and brain stem of patients disrupt neurotransmitter functioning, including that of acetylcholine and dopamine, and are therefore implicated in conditions such as Parkinson's disease and Dementia with Lewy bodies (McKeith, 2010).

The main characteristics of Dementia with Lewy bodies include disruptions in levels of alertness and attention, and also the presence of visual hallucinations and delusions. Patients frequently show evidence of Parkinsonian symptoms, such as bradykinesia (slowed movement). Present also is REM-sleep behaviour disorder such that patients no longer experience muscle atonia (lack of muscle tone) that is normally associated with REM sleep, the effect of this being that patients physically act out their dreams, often displaying violent behaviours. Because of this, there is a higher risk of injury. Part of the management in such cases is to provide a safe sleep environment, not only for the patient but for their partner as well (Boyce, Walker, & Rodda, 2008).

Frontotemporal dementia

Frontotemporal dementia is usually associated with an early onset, often between the ages of 45 and 65. Prevalence is equivalent across the two sexes. A number of conditions exist under this diagnostic term, including Pick's disease, semantic dementia, non-fluent progressive dementia, and progressive supranuclear palsy.

Frontotemporal dementia is characterized by the type of insidious onset and gradual progression seen in Alzheimer's disease. Behaviour is indicative of extreme frontal damage. The pathology associated with Alzheimer's disease is not present here. Regulation of behaviour is impaired early on and patients experience blunting of emotional responses. Thinking becomes inflexible. They show classic symptoms of frontal damage through perseveration and utilization behaviour. They are also highly distracted by events occurring around them. Speech lacks spontaneity, and there is also evidence of echolalia (repeating what someone has said) as well as mutism on occasion (Neary, Snowden, & Mann, 2005). There is little evidence of memory impairment until later stages and some higher-level functioning is retained (Mendez & Shapira, 2009). Patients show akinesia (impaired movement of muscles) and reflexes diminish. There is likely to be incontinence also.

Less common causes of dementia

Huntington's disease is a movement disorder that time and again results in dementia. It is transmitted as an autosomal dominant trait. Because of this, the offspring of a person with the condition have 50 per cent chance of developing it themselves. Onset is early, around the age of 40, although there are rare instances of juvenile-onset in this disease. Men and women are equally prone to the disease. The characteristic pathology of this condition results in a gradual withering of the caudate nucleus and putamen of the basal ganglia. This is an area of the brain that initiates and controls movement. The historical title of Huntington's chorea reflects the fact that it is a movement disorder resulting in dance-like movement of both limbs and facial muscles (chorea). In terms of symptoms relating to dementia, pattern of impairment follows that of the subcortical dementias (see above). Memory impairment occurs relatively early on, in particular problems with retrieval (Bloch, 2007). There are also deficits in attention and speed at which information is processed. Anxiety, depression, personality disorder, and also paranoia may feature in some cases. During later stages of the condition, patients often become more aggressive and show high levels of impulsivity.

Creutzfeldt-Jakob disease is a rare condition. The initial stages of the disease consist only of elusive somatic complaints which are soon followed by changes in both mood and personality. Dementia symptoms then appear, including aphasia and apraxia alongside both extrapyramidal symptoms (tremors and muscular rigidity) and pyramidal symptoms (exaggeration of reflexes – hyperreflexia – and jerking movements). The disease progresses quickly with patients often dying only six months after diagnosis. Muscles wither and the patient experiences convulsions as the disease progresses. In terms of brain pathology, status spongiosus occurs resulting in the propagation of neuroglia – non-neuronal supporting tissue – in the brain (gliosis) on top of loss of neurons and disintegration of tissue. Proteinaceous infectious particles (prions) are also detectable in this condition. Prions are abnormal proteins that behave like a virus.

Human Immunodeficiency Virus (HIV) encephalopathy develops as a result of exposure to the HTLV-111 virus. It is a pathogen borne in the blood. HIV is a retrovirus and as such transcribes its own RNA into the DNA of the T-helper lymphocyte cells it invades, thereby destroying them. T-helper cells assist in the body's production of antibodies. Their loss thus results in a greatly compromised immunologic response to the neurotoxins that are subsequently released, resulting in an emergent infection. This infection can affect brain tissue, as in the case of toxoplasmosis (flu-like symptoms) and cryptococcal meningitis (inflammation of the meninges, the membrane encompassing the brain and spinal cord). Alternatively lymphoma may cultivate in the central nervous system. In terms of neuropathology, microglial nodules appear in the central nervous system and multinucleated giant cells containing HIV-infected macrophages are formed as the result of cell-to-cell fusion (Messam et al., 2002). The patient feels lethargic and there is evidence of cognitive impairment. In the final stages of the condition the patient shows sever dementia-like symptoms, mutism, incontinence, and also paraplegia (paralysis of the lower limbs) in some instances. Great success has been made in treating this condition through the use of highly active antiretroviral therapy (HAART) (Trimble & George, 2010).

Mild cognitive impairment

Mild cognitive impairment, previously called benign senescent forgetfulness, is used to describe a condition where the level of cognitive failures experienced are in excess of those expected for someone at a specific age and level of educational attainment. Patients complain of problems with their memory, but general cognitive function is largely unaffected. The deficits are not deemed sufficiently severe to interfere with how someone is able to lead their lives to any great extent (Gauthier et al., 2006). It does appear that mild cognitive impairment is an intermediate stage of decline such that it may on occasion act as a precursor to dementia later on. On these occasions it is likely to be the subtype of amnestic mild cognitive impairment.

To complicate matters, depression often occurs alongside a diagnosis of mild cognitive impairment. On top of this is the fear people express, fuelled by media campaigns, that they may be developing Alzheimer's disease. The concern here is that hypersensitivity to everyday cognitive failures may escalate worry, thereby leading to a hypochondriacal-like spiral of anguish.

Depression in dementia

As we have already seen, depression is prevalent among older adults. On top of that, around 30 per cent of individuals who are diagnosed with dementia also experience high levels of depression (Lyketsos et al., 2002). Differentiating depression from dementia can be problematic as they both share many symptoms. The challenge here is in part to make an accurate differential diagnosis early on in order that appropriate treatment strategies can be put in place in order to maximize benefits for the individual and those caring for them (Enache, Winblad, & Aarsland, 2011).

Parkinson's disease

A number of neurological conditions exist where dementia is a feature. One example is that of Parkinson's disease, a disease primarily affecting basal ganglia function. These subcortical structures are linked to many other areas of the brain, including the substantia nigra. These interconnections are referred to as the extrapyramidal system. As seen already some medications can induce extrapyramidal symptoms – disruption of movement – as a consequence of interfering with basal ganglia functioning. A reduction in the production of dopamine within the substantia nigra is the mechanism responsible for Parkinson's disease. One consequence being significantly reduced levels of this neurotransmitter available in the striatum, an area of the brain that plays a fundamental role in movement, cognition, and emotion. Those with the condition exhibit tremor when resting, slowed movement (bradykinesia), and muscular rigidity. Initiating movement as well as maintaining repetitive action sequences are also greatly affected, a state referred to as akinesia. However, such 'freezing' can often be overcome when external stimulation is provided (Rakitin & Stern, 2005). The age of onset is around 60 although there are instances where this condition develops earlier (Jahanshahi, 2007). Dementia with Lewy bodies is a related condition. Cognitive impairment is commonly experienced, with severity increasing as the disease progresses. Roughly one fifth of individuals diagnosed with Parkinson's disease also develop dementia, called Parkinson's disease dementia (Brown & Marsden, 1984). Being a subcortical dementia, symptoms differ such that there is a slowing in cognition and marked changes in both mood and personality (Jahanshahi, 2007).

Cognitive impairment is also evident in this patient group where dementia is not present. In these cases deficits in executive function are most prominent.

Drug treatments

Having looked at some of the different forms of dementia, these next sections focus on how these conditions are treated and managed. To begin with we shall examine drug treatments. Cholinesterase inhibitors, such as donepezil, rivastigmine, and galantamine, increase levels of acetylcholine and so improve levels of cognitive functioning. As a result of this, the ability to perform every tasks and activities improves. The likelihood of potential positive effects should always be weighed against the risk of side effects. Cholinesterase inhibitor drugs can lead to vomiting and diarrhoea, and may interfere with heart functioning. In many cases the improvements are subtle, and there is evidence to show transient deceleration in the rate of decline (Ames et al., 2010).

Memantine may also be used in instances where patients experience difficulties when taking cholinesterase inhibitors. This drug is an N-methyl-D-aspartate (NMDA) receptor antagonist and works by protecting the brain against glutamate, an excitatory neurotransmitter that cells damaged by Alzheimer's disease release in excessive quantities. Glutamate stimulates production of reactive free radicals that destroy brain cells by converting adjacent molecules into radicals (a group of atoms that engage in various chemical combinations without change owing to possession of an unpaired electron), thereby starting a chain reaction of cellular destruction.

Certain neuroleptics can be recruited to reduce severe agitation, aggression, and also psychosis in patients with dementia (Ballard & Cream, 2005). There is little if any evidence suggesting older antipsychotic medications like haloperidol are effective in this area. Instead such drugs may lead to the development of extra-pyramidal symptoms. There is also an increased risk of cerebrovascular accident (cerebral haemorrhage, embolism, or thrombosis) although the mechanism has not been identified.

Antidepressants are often used to reduce depressive symptoms in this condition. Tricyclic antidepressants are not used as they exert an anticholinergic effect thereby exacerbating impairment in a condition where there is already loss of acetylcholine. However, selective serotonin reuptake inhibitors, such as sertraline, are effective.

Non-pharmacological management

There are three main forms of non-drug management of individuals diagnosed with dementia. The first incorporates techniques of behaviour management in order to minimize frequency of inappropriate or maladaptive actions mainly through the use of positive reinforcement of target behaviours (O'Connor et al., 2009a, 2009b). To complement this it is important to educate family and carers about the condition and in doing so diminish the anxiety and stress they may otherwise feel. There are more targeted approaches to deal with specific behaviours such as the use of music to soothe agitation (Svansdottir & Snaedal, 2006).

Management of these conditions attempt to maximize a patient's sense of independence by enabling them to largely continue performing daily chores and other activities, often through modification of their living environment. Assistance from Occupational Therapy services is also encouraged. Part of this process consists of a risk assessment being carried out to ensure the living conditions are manageable and safe. Imposing predictable routines for the patient to follow and regular reminders also help in maintaining awareness of time and place, thereby minimizing distress (Boyce, Walker, & Rodda, 2008).

NICE recommendations suggest an initial assessment to identify a potential cause of the observed behavioural disturbances (National Institute for Health and Clinical Excellence, 2006). For the treatment of agitation various options may be possible, such as music therapy and aromatherapy. If the symptoms are sufficiently severe then neuroleptic medication may be considered once associated risks have been assessed. Such risks should be discussed with the patient prior to treatment. It is recommended that low doses are prescribed at first, with dosage being increased gradually to ensure maximal effect. Acetylcholinesterase inhibitors may be prescribed if there are high levels of behavioural disturbance not due to cognitive impairment (Boyce, Walker, & Rodda, 2008).

As already mentioned, sometimes home environments can be modified to better suit the needs of the patient, especially during the early stages of the disease (Erber, 1979). The use of different floor coverings to denote specific areas can help orientate the patient. Such environments ensure greater levels of both physical and mental activity – and, as a result, more independence – which may offset some of the decline associated with conditions such as Alzheimer's disease. Activities that improve sensory ability can also be beneficial. However, it is important to constantly monitor the patient to ensure that the environment in which they are living provides the best fit to their capabilities, otherwise it too will add to the level of distress the patient experiences as a result of their condition. Unless in residential care, issues of general care and nutrition need to be arranged for the patient (Boyce, Walker, & Rodda, 2008).

Support will be provided to the carers also. In part this should take the form of psychoeducation to help them better understand the disease and the needs of the patient. In addition, they will be provided with information about the various support mechanisms that are in place to help not only the patient but the carer as well.

In an attempt to present a more holistic picture of dementia, Kitwood and Bredin (1992) emphasized the influence of personality, life history, physical health, and social functioning on top of neuropsychological impairment. They argued that the social environment often acts to dehumanize the person with dementia, and as a result of this, there is an exacerbation of symptoms. Kitwood and Bredin (1992) argue that such an increase in symptom severity may not be explained solely by the neuropathology but additionally by the impact of society.

Well-being of the carer

It has already been suggested that psychoeducation is needed in order to help the carer better understand both the condition itself and subsequently the needs of the patient. In addition to that, because a great deal of care is provided informally – at least six million in the UK – there is a real need to address the well-being of those who find themselves in this position (Alzheimer's Disease International, 1999). We have already seen that depression is common among those diagnosed with dementia (Lyketsos et al., 2002), but just as worryingly there is a high rate of depression among carers as well, with around 20 per cent showing symptoms (Molyneux et al., 2008). The role of carer is highly demanding, both physically and mentally (Wills & Soliman, 2001). It is essential then that carers feel they have the support needed to help them cope with the challenges they face.

Psychopharmacology

Having looked at some of the main psychological and neurodegenerative conditions experienced by older adults, it is clear that drug treatments are used to either help tackle the condition directly or to assist recovery and management indirectly. This final section of the chapter examines in more detail how drugs operate and what issues need to be considered when prescribing for an older person.

The ability to monitor and control the intake of medication is a major issue in older adults. Not only do prescribed medications come with an assortment of dos and don'ts in regard to when to take the medication and what with, an additional level of complexity is apparent when over-the-counter medications are introduced. Medication prescribed to patients is of a dose deemed relevant by the clinician. In the case of over-the-counter medication generic dosages are provided. Careful monitoring here is therefore much needed. Pharmacists play an important role by providing a failsafe to ensure prescribed medication is considered before dispensing over-the-counter drugs.

It is imperative that one be aware that there are a number of important principles that should be upheld when considering prescribing medication to older adults. These include ensuring that the variety of medications prescribed is kept to a minimum and that, wherever possible, medication plans for each day are easy to understand and administer in order to maximize adherence to the regime. It is essential that medication is reviewed on a regular basis to ensure serious side effects do not develop.

The use of medication to treat psychiatric problems in older adults is particularly problematic. This is because, in many instances, older adults are not included in clinical trials. Where they are included, the samples used are usually free from comorbid conditions that may impact on the outcomes of the trials.

Pharmacokinetics

As we have seen, the impact of individual differences among older adults is greater than at any other time. The older we grow, the less alike we become. Age affects the way drugs are processed by the body. Because of the individual differences effect, variances in terms of these pharmacokinetic effects between similarly aged individuals are pronounced (Boyce, Walker, & Rodda, 2008).

Absorption

It is important to appreciate how medication works. There are four main stages to consider: absorption, distribution, metabolism, and excretion (Hacker, Messer, & Bachmann, 2009). Rate of absorption refers to the time taken for the medication to enter into the patient's bloodstream from ingestion. This depends on how the drug is administered. Medication taken orally must first enter the stomach before it is absorbed through the lining of the small intestine. Perceivable effects of medication may be delayed because of a slowing in blood flow in the gut (splanchnic blood flow). If rate of transition from the stomach to the small intestine is slow there will not be enough active ingredients remaining for absorption to elicit the desired effect. This may mean that the intended effect of the drug may not occur at the time when it is needed. This is problematic in the case of pain relieving medication and hypnotics (Cusack, 2004). The converse is, of course, true. If rate of transition is too fast, an excess of the drug will be absorbed and so eventuate in an overdose.

Distribution

On entering the bloodstream, the effectiveness with which the medication is dispersed depends on the efficiency of the patient's cardiovascular system. A proportion of the drug will bind with plasma protein; the remainder will remain free. Effectiveness of the drug is dependent on the proportion that is unbound, and, therefore, available in the bloodstream. If too much of the drug remains free, then there will be a risk that the unbound levels will reach toxicity. Binding to plasma protein is less successful in older adults. This means that there is a greater risk of toxic levels of the drug building up in a person's bloodstream. Some medications are soluble in water or fat. Distribution of a drug is essentially affected by a reduction in the percentage of body water and an increase in body fat that accompanies age. This diminishes volume of distribution for water-soluble drugs (e.g. aspirin) such that there are higher concentrations of the drug in the plasma compared to the rest of the body, whereas there is a higher volume of distribution for fat-soluble drugs (e.g. antidepressants) such that the plasma contains low concentration of the drug compared to the rest of the body (Cusack, 2004). It is important, therefore, to consider levels of hydration and weight in conjunction with age when prescribing medication (Hacker, Messer, & Bachmann, 2009).

Metabolism

Drugs are metabolized in the liver. Metabolism, or the removal of material from the bloodstream, occurs at a slower rate in older adults. Drugs metabolized in this way are affected by reduction in liver structure and diminished blood flow, both of which impedes how much drug is received by hepatocytes (liver cells), significantly reducing the rate at which toxins are removed from the body (Cusack, 2004). This means that drugs remain active for longer (Bond & Lader, 1996). Again, this has implications for how doses are scheduled. Because the drug remains in the blood for longer, there is a greater risk of toxicity.

Excretion

Excretion of drug material occurs largely in urine via the kidneys. Kidney function deteriorates with age, leading to marked reductions in renal elimination. This also has the effect of increasing the chances of toxic levels being reached if adequate measures are not taken (Hacker, Messer, & Bachmann, 2009). In cases where drugs are metabolized in the liver, a decline in renal elimination results in these toxins accumulating if adequate measures are not put in place (Cusack, 2004).

Pharmacodynamics

Changes in the number of receptors available and their ability to function have important implications for the prescription of medication in older adults. In many cases a reduced dose can achieve the intended effect. Side effects become increasingly likely. For example, a reduction in the number of dopamine receptors compounded by reduced transporter levels – the mechanism whereby reuptake of dopamine into the presynaptic terminal occurs – results in a patient being more sensitive to drugs that exert an antagonistic effect on this neurotransmitter system, the consequence being an increase in extrapyramidal side effects (Boyce, Walker, & Rodda, 2008; Routledge, O'Mahony, & Woodhouse, 2004).

Drug effects may become problematic due to a decline in homeostatic function as we age. Changes in physiological response may not be corrected as efficiently as in younger age groups. Because of this older adults may be at an increased risk of falls, hypo- and hyper-thermia, dehydration, and choking (Boyce, Walker, & Rodda, 2008).

Polypharmacy

Changes in pharmacokinesis and pharmacodynamics increase the likelihood of experiencing adverse drug reactions. To further cloud the picture, older adults tend to take more medication, be it prescribed or over-the-counter. This is often because older adults suffer from more than one complaint. Medication for chronic conditions is also more prevalent (Routledge, O'Mahony, & Woodhouse, 2004). This increases the risk of experiencing undesirable effects (Kane et al., 1994).

Concurrent treatment of more than one medical condition through medication is a complex process. Polypharmacy, then, brings with it additional dangers. Drugs for different conditions may interact in such a way that additional problems manifest; sometimes certain drug combinations have a symbiotic effect; in other instances, some drugs cancel out each other's effect. When secondary conditions arise as the result of drug interactions, such additional symptoms also need to be treated. However, because of this, the primary complaint may not be treated as effectively as it could. More worrying for the older adult, some drug combinations may, in fact, produce symptoms that mimic other conditions.

This is particularly problematic for patients who also take medication for depression. The likelihood of adverse drug interactions increases dramatically. A large number of unwanted side effects occur for patients with some form of cognitive impairment. Drugs that reduce activity of the cholinergic neurotransmitter system are often prescribed to older adults for a range of medical complaints. Many of the drugs used to treat psychiatric conditions

exert the same effect, including tricyclic antidepressants. The anticholinergic effects of each drugs summate to produce extreme confusion in a
patient where there is already a significant level of impairment (Routledge,
O'Mahony, & Woodhouse, 2004). In an older adult population, such symptoms would potentially indicate the onset of dementia, such as Alzheimer's
disease (Arnold, 2008). Finding the right drug combination, therefore, is
often a drawn-out process both for patient and physician. As a result, it can
be costly in terms of money and also in terms of psychological health.

It is essential that medication be monitored regularly, especially among
older adults. However, a perfectly balanced drug regimen requires a perfectly
compliant patient. Directions increase in complexity as a function of the
number of medications prescribed. Questions abound throughout the day.
When should the drug be taken? How much or how many should be taken?
What should be avoided before or after ingestion? There is a great deal to
keep track of here. Considered in the context of the ageing body that also
bring with it varying cognitive and physical difficulties, adherence can be a
major issue (Shea, 2006). The most common reason for lack of adherence is
forgetting to take medication at the designated time.

Adherence

Adherence to a particular medication regime among older adults may be poor
for a number of reasons. A number of psychiatric conditions may affect adherence, often as a result of apathy and psychosis. Level of cognitive functioning
plays a major role in how well a patient is able to remember to take the correct
dose at the appropriate time. This of course is particularly pertinent in cases
of dementia. Physical problems such as manual dexterity and problems swallowing affect the taking of medications in certain forms.

Attempts to deal with potential cognitive deficits can be overcome through
the use of dosette boxes and blister pack that clearly designate when a tablet
should be taken. In cases of dementia, patients may require supervision to
ensure medications are taken appropriately. Issues with dexterity can be miti-
gated through the use of containers that have easy-to-remove lids, or indeed
through the use of dosette boxes as noted previously. If there is a problem
swallowing pills, it is often possible to prescribe medication in liquid form.

A patient's attitude both to their condition and the care they receive is
an important determinant of how effectively they stick to a treatment plan.
Linked to this are patient attitudes on the effectiveness of the medication.
If the patient feels that a certain medication is not working, or that they are
experiencing frequent or worrying side effects, then adherence to a treatment
plan may be poor. Through educating the patient so that they understand
why effects may not be immediately apparent, or indeed why it is important

to continue taking the medicine even though symptoms have abated, can improve adherence.

Summary

Whereas Chapter 11 focused on physical health complaints, here we looked at mental health issues. We have seen that a number of conditions continue into old age having first developed in early adulthood. However, it is equally clear that many conditions manifest at a later age. One of the main problems facing clinicians is that there is a great deal of symptom overlap across conditions. On top of that, there are high levels of comorbidity. This has a number of serious consequences. Being unable, in many cases, to reach a clear diagnosis early on means that initiation of an appropriate treatment strategy is delayed, in many cases with serious consequences. The issue of comorbidity means that older adults invariably find themselves prescribed a range of medications, such as specific drugs for specific conditions and additional preparations that treat the side effects of those drugs.

Obviously there is more to offer than just medication. A range of behavioural interventions was covered. The role of the carer was again discussed, although this time in the context of how their well-being impacts on the patient they are caring for. There are important issues to consider here. The role of informal care is one that will grow with each generation. It is essential that support is provided as many adopt the role in response to the declining health of their spouse.

The final section looked at how drugs work within the body. With age the manner in which drugs are absorbed, distributed, metabolized, and excreted changes. There are important implications here in terms of prescribed doses in order to achieve maximal effectiveness with minimal risk of overdose. Linked to this was the concern over adherence to a particular treatment plan. A number of important factors play a role here, including the level of functioning of the individual and also their knowledge about what to expect when taking (or not taking) the medication.

Further reading

Morris, G. & Morris, J. (2010). *The dementia care workbook*. Berkshire: Open University Press. [This is a detailed and practical guide on caring for someone with dementia.]

Solomon, A. (2001). *The noonday demon: An anatomy of depression*. London: Chatto & Windus. [A fascinating account of a debilitating condition.]

Trimble, M. R. & George, M. S. (2010). *Biological psychiatry*. Oxford: Wiley-Blackwell. [This is an excellent text for those wishing to take a more biomedical approach.]

CHAPTER 13

Neurodevelopmental Disorders

Up until quite recently the study of adults with a range of neurodevelopmental disorders has largely been ignored. Research instead focused almost exclusively on these conditions in childhood and adolescence. Given the severity of these conditions, there is a need to redress this balance and focus instead on how these conditions impact across the entire lifespan. This chapter will draw on recent research that has begun to do exactly that. One of the main challenges of this field is to examine how symptoms undergo a developmental change such that the manifestation of symptoms in adulthood may differ from those in childhood and adolescence.

This chapter is split into two main sections, one focusing on specific learning difficulties (SpLDs), and the other on intellectual development disorders (IDDs). Where possible proposed DSM-V terminology will be used, the exception being when reference is made to studies already published where older diagnostic terms need to be retained to ensure an accurate portrayal of the findings. In the case of SpLDs, this group of conditions consists of learning disorders, autism spectrum disorder, motor disorders, communication disorders, and attention deficit hyperactivity disorder. 'Intellectual development disorder' is a term that replaces mental retardation that was used in DMS-IV-TR and includes Down's syndrome, Fragile X syndrome, and cerebral palsy. At the start of each section there will be a brief overview of the main conditions followed then by an exploration of some of the main issues specific to older adults. This is by no means a comprehensive survey but rather an introduction to some of the key themes. Those interested in learning more about this topic should refer to Bigby's (2004) excellent text on the subject.

Adults and older adults with specific learning difficulties

Specific learning difficulties

Learning disorders

Learning disorders refer to conditions where impairment is seen in academic achievement, language ability, speech, or motor functioning. In these cases the problems are not due to poor education or an IDD. Included in this category are dyslexia and dyscalculia. Dyslexia describes a condition where there are problems recognizing words, poor reading comprehension, and problems spelling. Dyscalculia is a condition where the individual has deficits in conceptualizing and processing number. Dyslexia is by far the most studied condition in this group.

Heritability plays a role in the development of dyslexia (Pennington, 1995). There are important gene–environment interactions such that parental education determines to what extent genes are responsible for the condition. For example, where parents have attained a high level of education, risk of the child developing dyslexia is more likely driven by genetic vulnerability (Friend et al., 2009).

The underlying problem relates to language processing, more specifically phonological awareness (Anthony & Lonigan, 2004). Imaging studies with adults show that, when tested, non-impaired readers utilize areas of the brain one would normally associate with reading. On the other hand, in a group whose reading ability was initially poor but improved in later childhood, activation occurred in areas of the brain not normally associated with reading, thus indicating the acquired use of non-traditional areas as a means to compensate for reading difficulties early in life. In the final group consisting of those who were persistently poor readers, although the areas associated with reading were implicated, so too were regions of the brain linked to memory, thus indicating a reliance on memorizing material (Shaywitz et al., 2003).

Genetics seems to play a role in the number processing deficits seen in dyscalculia, especially poor semantic memory (Plomin & Kovas, 2005). In terms of brain functioning, the intraparietal sulcus appears to play a central role (Wilson & Dehaene, 2007). There seems to be little overlap between dyscalculia and dyslexia (Jordan, 2007).

Autism spectrum disorder

Definitions of this disorder have changed dramatically over the years. The next iteration of the DSM offers no exception. It is likely that the previous diagnoses of autistic disorder, Asperger's disorder, pervasive developmental disorder not otherwise specified, and childhood disintegrative disorder will all be replaced by an umbrella term 'autism spectrum disorder' (ASD). As with all such changes, there will be implications across the board, especially given the current diagnosis of Asperger's disorder is seen by many to reflect a higher level of functioning.

The chief characteristic of ASD is severe impairment in social functioning (Dawson et al., 2004). There is a distinct lack of social engagement, be it in terms of eye contact or spontaneous greetings. A lack of social awareness can be partly explained by the finding that those diagnosed with ASD focus their gaze on a person's mouth but not their eyes. As a result, they are poor at recognizing emotions in others.

Theory of mind is also poor. As seen in Chapter 6, theory of mind refers to one's understanding that other people have their own set of thoughts, beliefs, and emotions, and that these differ from one's own. A lack of ability here leads to the types of social problems faced by this group (Gopnik, Capps, & Meltzoff, 2000). In addition, a person with ASD is likely to take the literal meaning of any interchange with others. Changes to familiar routines are usually met with emotional outbursts. Obsessional behaviour may be evident during recreational activity.

Comorbidity is an issue here such that more than a third of those with a diagnosis of ASD also meet the criteria for another learning disorder (Lichtenstein et al., 2010). Incidence of psychopathology will be discussed shortly in a separate section in this chapter.

Early explanations for the cause of ASD focused on blaming parenting styles. However, it is now clear that there are strong genetic and neurophysiological explanations for the condition. There does indeed appear to be a strong genetic component to this disorder (Lichtenstein et al., 2010). In terms of the brain, a rather obvious difference is in terms of its gross structure: quite simply, those with ASD have larger brains than those without (Courchesne et al., 2001). This increase in size occurs between the ages of two and four (Courchesne, 2004). A larger size brain might indicate that the normal process of synaptic pruning is not occurring in this population whereby the number of neural connections is reduced as performance becomes more efficient. The main areas where increased growth occurs are the frontal and temporal lobes, as well as the cerebellum, all of which are linked explicitly with social behaviour.

Motor disorders

Tourette's disorder. This condition is characterized by involuntary movements and vocal utterances. These are referred to as tics. With time tics become increasingly complex in nature. In terms of muscular activity, tics become increasingly convoluted. Verbal tics may consist of repeated mimicking of phrases heard (echolalia), repetition of words (palilalia), and use of obscenities (coprolalia). Genetics again plays a role.

Developmental coordination disorder. Developmental coordination disorder (DCD) is defined by poor motor precision in the absence of a known neurological condition. Not only is manual dexterity lacking, but gross motor movements are also affected. Both balance and posture are impaired as a result. As with many of the conditions discussed in this chapter, studies of how DCD impacts on a person's life throughout adulthood are few. This needs to be rectified as clearly such behaviours will affect a person's quality of life across the lifespan (Smyth & Cousins, 2005).

Communication disorders

Communication disorders refer to a range of conditions including issues with language impairment, an inability to master the pragmatics of social communication, and poor vocalization.

Attention deficit hyperactivity disorder

Attention deficit hyperactivity disorder (ADHD) is a condition where both hyperactive behaviour and poor concentration are the defining characteristics. In cases of ADHD these problems are both persistent and severe in nature. Symptoms are particularly evident in situations where there is a need to remain seated and not to fidget. Symptoms should be evidence in at least two settings for a positive diagnosis to be made – for example, at home and in school. Behaviour is often aggressive and so affects social relationships (Blachman & Hinshaw, 2002). Academic achievements as well as occupational success are disrupted as a result of behavioural disturbances.

Genetics play a major role in this condition (Thapar et al., 2007), with some studies indicating estimates of heritability of up to 80 per cent (Tannock, 1998). There is also evidence that suggests there are quantitative differences in brain structure in those with and without ADHD. For example, studies have shown that less activation occurs within the frontal lobes in ADHD individuals when required to perform specific tasks (Casey & Durston, 2006). Such low level of activation would fit with the lack of ability to inhibit behaviour seen in this group (Barkley, 1997).

A variety of environmental factors have been implicated in this condition, including among other things food additives (Feingold, 1973), although studies have shown much inconsistency in terms of effect sizes. Of such factors, the most consistent in terms of purported effect is the impact of maternal smoking on the developing child. Exposure to nicotine during foetal development has been linked to higher prevalence of ADHD symptoms in the child follow-ing birth (Linnet et al., 2003). The mechanism here is likely to involve the dopaminergic system, thereby implicating itself in a person's ability to inhibit behavioural responses (Vaglenova et al., 2004).

Although awareness of ADHD has grown dramatically over recent years, little research has been conducted to explore the impact of ADHD on older adults. This is surprising considering the likelihood that incidence will rise as a result of increasing life expectancy. One of the main indicators of impact here is quality of life. A number of negative consequences accompany this condition including a reduced likelihood of completing further or higher edu-cation, higher rates of divorce, and increased substance abuse (Biederman et al., 2006; Biederman et al., 1995; Kollins, McClernon, & Fuemmeler, 2005).

There seems to be tendency to shy away from identifying and treating ADHD in adults, partly because of the lack of data on how this condition manifests in this age group (Wilens et al., 2009). One study has shown that half of all cases of ADHD diagnosed in childhood persist into adulthood (Biederman, Mick, & Faraone, 2000). A recent study showed that older adults share the same symptoms of ADHD and associated impairments as younger adults (Brook et al., 2010). As a result of this persistence of symptoms, most older adults with ADHD described an accumulation of negative effects that impacted across all spheres of their lives, such as professional, social, and financial domains (Brod et al., 2012). However, although impact of symp-toms did grow, severity of symptoms did not appear to become worse with age. Often older adults expressed an enhanced ability to cope with ADHD as they grew older (Brod et al., 2012).

A belief that adults merely have to cope with inattention and impulse con-trol has been overturned by a recent study. It has been shown that hyperactiv-ity is present still (Teicher et al., 2012). This finding indicates that a lack of ability to inhibit motor behaviour continues throughout adulthood (Teicher et al., 2012). This would make intuitive sense considering the degree of exec-utive impairment experienced by this group.

Comorbidity with medical conditions

The issue of comorbidity is something we discussed in relation to mental health issues in the previous chapter. Here we shall examine the issue of comorbidity in terms of SpLDs.

ASDs occur alongside various medical conditions, such as fragile X syn-drome (Gillberg & Billstedt, 2000) as well as intellectual disabilities (ID; this will be replaced by IDD in the DSM-V). Intellectual disabilities bring with it an increased likelihood of psychopathology (Bregman, 1991). The link between ASD, ID, and psychopathology is unclear. The ability to accurately diagnose psychopathology in those with ASD depends largely on the level of functioning, with symptom expression being different between individuals who are either high and low functioning (Bradley et al., 2004). As a result, the little research that exists in this area has tended to focus on cases of higher-functioning ASD.

Another major drawback with the current batch of studies is that the focus has been on children with ASD. Few studies have examined the comorbidity issue among adults with this diagnosis. From the evidence that is available for this age group it is clear that various forms of psychopathology are associated with ASD, including depression (Ghaziuddin, Ghaziuddin, & Greden, 2002), anxiety (Bellini, 2004), and obsessive-compulsive disorder (Russell et al., 2005) among others.

Mental health issues

As described in a previous section, ASDs are associated with a variety of problems relating to social behaviour. As with all SpLDs the focus of attention has been on children and adolescents, with adults being largely ignored. From the small number of studies conducted, it is clear that a number of comorbid mental health conditions occur in adults with ASDs. These include ADHD (Rydén & Bejerot, 2008; Stahlberg et al., 2004), chronic tic disorder (Canitano & Vivanti, 2007), and also mood disorders (Howlin, 2000). Obsessive-compulsive disorder occurs more often in this population that it does for the general population (Hofvander et al., 2009). In some cases psychotic features appear in ASD, such as auditory hallucinations, paranoid ideation, and delusional thinking. There is evidence to suggest that ASD may act as a risk factor for developing schizophrenia in some cases (Nylander, Lugnegård, & Hallerbäck, 2008). Substance abuse is more prevalent in those who have received a diagnosis of pervasive developmental disorder not otherwise specified (PDD NOS).

Unemployment levels are high in this group, and as we will see in a later section; employment status has a major role to play in determining well-being. Those on sick leave are abnormally high here also, as is the number receiving a medical pension. Two fifths of adults with ASDs continue to live with their parents or in community-based homes. The proportion of those either married or living with a partner is low as well (Hofvander et al., 2009).

Issues faced by older adults with specific learning difficulties

In this section I will highlight some of the main problems faced by adults with SpLDs. Given that it is very likely that one individual will meet the diagnostic criteria for a number of related SpLDs, I shall discuss issues that need to be addressed for specific conditions, although given the overlap of symptoms and co-occurrence of diagnoses, these difficulties will likely affect all related disorders.

It is important to consider here also how symptoms may manifest differently with age. Aspects of behaviour that were once problematic when a child may no longer be an issue. Instead previous aspects of functioning have been superseded by other difficulties that arise in response to the changing demands of adult life. The implication associated with such a complex web of comorbidity is something that will need to be addressed in order to improve well-being among adults and older adults.

The importance of employment

A number of problems other than those related to motor coordination are experienced by individuals who have received a diagnosis for DCD. They also experience a range of interpersonal difficulties. As with most conditions of this type, the focus of research up to now has been on children. However, DCD, like other SpLDs, is a condition that is present across the lifespan (Losse et al., 1991). The way problems manifest in adulthood results in poor handwriting as well as deficient organization skills (Kirby et al., 2008).

Alongside these functional impairments there exists in many cases psychopathology that contributes to problems experienced by this group. High rates of both anxiety and depression have been reported (Hill & Brown, 2013). Across the course of one's life, such difficulties are likely to have a negative impact on a person's overall quality of life (Cousins & Smyth, 2003). Evidence shows that ratings of life satisfaction are lower among those who are unemployed, reflecting the important role employment plays in a person's life (Kirby et al., 2013). However, a recent study has shown that levels of anxiety and reported health problems remain high independent of employment status (Kirby et al., 2013).

Diagnosing memory problems

When presenting at clinic complaining of memory problems, premorbid characteristics of ADHD can pose problems for medical practitioners when attempting to identify whether the issue is one of developing dementia, especially when considering the constraints placed upon staff working in clinics (Fischer et al., 2012). ADHD is characterized by an inability to attend to specific information. One effect of this is that information is rarely encoded adequately, and such poor encoding will exert a number of knock-on effects when examining performance at a later stage, especially when related to memory.

Underlying this are deficits in executive functioning (Roth & Saykin, 2004). Indeed there is some evidence to suggest a potential link between Lewy body dementia and ADHD, such that patients with this particular form of dementia exhibited greater levels of impulsivity and hyperactivity as children. This may implicate a link between the existence of both conditions and the associated low levels of dopamine and noradrenaline in these groups (Golimstok et al., 2011).

The implications here are clear with regards to health and psychological well-being of individuals with ADHD (Cohen, 2004). There is likely to be a lack of clarity concerning changes in cognitive functioning such that the ability to distinguish ADHD-related cognitive problems from age-related changes in functioning is relatively poor (Brod et al., 2012), thereby increasing the likelihood that ADHD symptoms may be misattributed to more insidious entities, such as the progression of dementia.

Adults and older adults with intellectual development disorder

Intellectual development disorder

The main criteria for a positive diagnosis consists of a level of intellectual functioning that is significantly below the average expected for a particular age, an inability to adapt to changing situations, and onset prior to the age of 18. The causes for these conditions are generally neurobiological as we will see.

Down's syndrome

Down' syndrome is specifically linked to a person having an extra copy of chromosome 21, a condition referred to as trisomy 21. Those with Down's syndrome may experience IDD. In addition, there are distinct physical correlates associated with the condition, namely a short stature, oval face, and a flat nasal bridge among other things.

Fragile X syndrome

This again is the result of a genetic abnormality linked this time to the X chromosome. Physical signs associated with the condition include large ears and a thin elongated face. Although IDD is present in many, some may instead show learning difficulties. About one third of those with fragile X express symptoms that fall on the autism spectrum (Hagerman, 2006).

Cerebral palsy

Cerebral palsy is a condition where there is marked disturbance of voluntary muscle movement. The underlying cause in this case is brain injury, usually during pregnancy. Intellectual disorders are in evidence in many cases of cerebral palsy. It is not a progressive condition, although there is no treatment available for it.

Healthy ageing

When taking into consideration higher mortality and reduced life expectancy among older adults with IDD, as a whole this group should experience less severe health problems and show more adaptive behaviour (Walker, Walker, & Ryan, 1996). However, this does not appear to be necessarily the case (Cooper, 1998). Instead, this group of older adults tends to experience higher levels of poor health (Evenhuis et al., 2001). This is largely due to pre-existing conditions that increase the risk of certain age-specific diseases (Bigby, 2004). To compound this is a tendency to adopt a less than health-conscious lifestyle, with a larger proportion leading a sedentary existence with poor diet (Janicki et al., 2002). To counteract this, however, rates of smoking and drinking alcohol are often lower.

A clear difference is that there are higher numbers of cases where conditions go untreated (Beange, McElduff, & Baker, 1995) and there is a distinct lack of social infrastructure to assist in such cases (Howells, 1986). Provision of healthcare is a particularly problematic area for this population. Such decisions are often made by those around them, and in most cases their parents. However, in cases of older adults with learning disabilities who have lost their parents, there is no clear substitute for such informal healthcare advice. The concern is even more pertinent when one considers end-of-life issues (Bigby, 2004). Related to this is the increased likelihood of late diagnosis of cancer in this group (Hogg & Tuffrey-Wijne, 2008). The main challenge here is to overcome limitations in the ability to communicate and discuss healthcare with this group of older adults. There is a growing realization that non-verbal means of communication need to be developed to facilitate this process further (Read, 1998).

Psychological well-being

There has been a lack of research examining psychological functioning among older adults with IDD. It is clear that levels of mental health problems are higher in this population (Tor & Chiu, 2002). As in a typically ageing population, the most prevalent conditions are anxiety and depression (Cooper, 1997a). Diagnosis of these conditions poses real challenges for professionals, much like those seen when diagnosing medical conditions. A potential explanation for this could be a combination of both negative life experiences in the past and poor current quality of life (Moss, 1999). This group is less likely to be in employment (Walker, Walker, & Ryan, 1996), have poorer social networks (Bigby, 2000), and more likely to be living in shared accommodation (Emerson, Hatton, & Felce, 2001). All this will exert a major effect on their overall well-being. There are higher rates of Alzheimer's disease in those with Down's syndrome (Cooper, 1997b). Onset of the condition occurs generally at a younger age and the rate of decline may be more abrupt (Wilkinson & Janicki, 2002).

Stereotypes

Given the prevalence of stereotypical and discriminatory attitudes evident in society still, there are real concerns about the quality of life experienced by older adults with IDD. The main upshot of these attitudes include limited available opportunities and lack of access to support networks, both of which are likely linked to low expectations concerning this group (Bigby, 2004). Exposure to such attitudes often results in a self-fulfilling prophesy in terms of how this population lead their lives.

Issues faced by older adults with intellectual development disorder

As we have seen, the impact of increasing life expectancy is being observed across a range of settings. One of the main effects is an increasing number of older adults who are prone to developing age-related diseases. Among these are the dementias. An even more dramatic change is occurring among adults with a lifelong disability. As with typically ageing adults, life expectancy has increased considerably in this group, with an increase in average age expectancy of 50 years since the 1930s (Carter & Jancar, 1983). Life expectancy of those with IDD closely matches that of typically ageing adults in all but a few cases, such as those with Down's syndrome (Janicki et al., 1999). The issues relating to this group are often overlooked in books on ageing. It is clear, however, that in some instances there is a great deal of overlap with previous sections of the book. As seen, there is an increased risk of developing Alzheimer's disease in those with Down's syndrome (Evenhuis et al., 2001). Social issues are particularly pertinent for this group as there is less active participation in the community among those with IDD. The source of support for older adults with IDD is also different, such that input from formal support services is more prominent.

The concept of successful ageing is prominent within the literature. A number of definitions abound. Often such definitions include an emphasis on an absence of any disability and a high level of cognitive functioning (Jorm et al., 1998). This is clearly a problem when considered from the perspective of adults with IDD. As a result there needs to be a reassessment of how one can conceive successful ageing in this group. Successful ageing among this population may be related to being awarded the same rights as other older adults, with inclusion in a range of community activities, instilling a sense of pride, and active encouragement of self-determination (Bigby, 2004). Each of these would help improve overall quality of life.

Cognitive training for adults with intellectual development disorder

Before concluding this chapter, one way of improving quality of life in this group of older adults is to improve cognitive functioning. By doing so, one is making improvements to a person's ability to lead a more independent life. We have seen that life expectancy among adults with IDD is steadily increasing. In fact, the rate of growth of life expectancy among this population is higher than in that of the typically ageing population (Janicki et al., 1999). Even among those with Down syndrome, where life expectancy is reduced, the increases have been significant. Explanations for such improvement rest largely at the hands of improvements in healthcare, both in terms of reducing life-threatening conditions that often accompany Down syndrome, and also in terms of a move towards person-centred models of care.

Concomitant with an increased life expectancy is an increasing likelihood that neurodegenerative diseases of ageing will develop. Although there is an expanding canon of research exploring the effects of dementias such as Alzheimer's disease in typically ageing adults, there is a paucity of research on the impact of such disease processes in individuals with IDD. The following section focuses on a recent review by Perkins and Small (2006) who provide a much needed account of the relevant research in this particular area. This study was pre-DSM-V, so the appropriate diagnostic labels will be used in this account.

When looking at working memory, the interplay between working memory and long-term memory has been largely neglected. It may be argued that differences in performance between adults with ID and a comparison group consisting of children matched on fluid intelligence can be explained to some extent by examining the role played by long-term memory in a particular activity. The adult ID group generally perform at a higher level than the comparison on tasks that rely on accessing long-term memory when compared to measures of working memory capacity (Numminen, Service, & Ruoppila, 2002). This finding has implications in terms of the services offered to this group. Encouraging repetition and integration of material into long-term memory may allow this group to compensate for some of the deficits associated with increasing age. Such studies have demonstrated clear impairment in the functioning of both the phonological loop and visuo-spatial sketch pad components of working memory, reflecting auditory and visual–spatial short-term memory respectively. The phonological loop appears to be particularly affected in the Down syndrome group.

When examining episodic memory, mode of presentation is all important, with better recall being associated with visual presentation compared to verbal (Park, Puglisi, & Sovacool, 1983). When comparing performance across tasks of both explicit and implicit memory, implicit memory remained relatively intact with age, whereas both Down syndrome and Williams syndrome perform at a lower level that the unspecified ID (UID) group on tasks tapping explicit recall (Krinsky-McHale et al., 2005).

When looking at how age affects intelligence, it is generally the case that crystallized intelligence increases as a function of age, whereas fluid intelligence is more likely to show age-related changes as functioning declines (Horn & Donaldson, 1976). When looking at studies comparing age-related effects in ID, age effects are seen for fluid intelligence from around the age of 20, whereas there is less decline for crystallized intelligence from around the age of 30 (Kausler, 1991). There is a need to carry out large-scale longitudinal studies to better understand how age affects intelligence among those with ID.

Risk of developing Alzheimer's disease is much higher among individuals with Down syndrome when compared to the general population. In fact, the majority of those with Down syndrome will manifest the neuropathological characteristics of Alzheimer's disease by the age of 40 (Wisniewski, Wisniewski, & Wen, 1985). This is largely explained by the fact that that the gene controlling the expression of the amyloid precursor protein – the protein responsible for the formation of beta-amyloid plaque – is situated on chromosome 21, the chromosome associated with Down syndrome (Beyreuther et al., 1993). When looking at ID as a group after the removal of Down syndrome, prevalence of Alzheimer's disease is comparable to that of a typically ageing adult population (Organization, 2001). As with the non-ID population, early detection of Alzheimer's disease among those with ID before the clinical characteristics of the disease manifest is vitally important in order to maximize the range of appropriate treatment options available.

There is much research assessing the validity of cognitive training regimes in improving functioning for ID. Often there is a need for much time and effort in order to evidence change, although recent studies have shown significant improvements to occur in the short-term (Lifshitz, Tzuriel, & Weiss, 2005). Improvements have been observed in those with severe ID as well as more moderate levels of ID. Moreno and Saldana (2005) focused on improving metacognitive awareness in a group with severe ID and demonstrated improvements that were still evident at six-month follow-up.

There is a real need to redress the balance of research with more studies examining the impact of ageing in adults with IDD, especially in terms of cognitive deficits. A number of challenges face such research, not least the issue with obtaining samples large enough for appropriate analysis. This will also limit how participants can be subgrouped according to age ranges. It may not be possible to split IDD samples into young-old, old-old, and oldest-old as is standard in the typically ageing literature. In addition, a real problem for researchers in this field is the selection of an appropriate control group. Comparison groups in this area generally have large variations in ratings of general ability. Overall, it is essential that longitudinal studies are conducted in order to better explore age-related changes as a result of IDD.

Summary

It is difficult to believe that awareness of the needs of older adults who have been diagnosed with either SpLD or an IDD is lacking across many sectors of the community and healthcare services. Given that there is much to be done to improve quality of life for these groups, such apparent inattention is inexcusable. We have seen that these conditions do not cease once adolescence is reached – a conclusion one might draw from much of the literature – but instead continue across the lifespan. Those with SpLDs may experience new challenges on account of changing demands imposed on us during our adult lives. A prime example here would be ADHD. The same is true for many of the conditions classified as IDDs.

Comorbidity with a range of physical and mental health problems is prevalent, be it in terms of a poor diet or a lack of social engagement due to imposed constraints. In the case of conditions such as Down's syndrome, life expectancy is increasing, bringing with it a greater likelihood that Alzheimer's disease will develop. Care and discussion of health issues is particularly problematic among the IDDs. However, there is evidence to indicate that well-being in this group can be enhanced through the use of cognitive training strategies. Here, as in many other cases, more research is needed in order to obtain a better understanding of what can be achieved with such techniques. The issue of cognitive training is something that we shall explore further in the next and final chapter.

Further reading

Baron-Cohen, S. (1995). *Mindblindness: An essay on autism and theory of mind.* London: MIT Press. [This is a classic text from one of the leading experts in the field.]

Bigby, C. (2004). *Ageing with a lifelong disability: A guide to practice, program, and policy issues for human services professionals.* London; New York: Jessica Kingsley. [This is an authoritative text on the issue of living with an intellectual development disorder.]

Dryden-Edwards, R. C. & Combrinck-Graham, L. (2010). *Developmental disabilities from childhood to adulthood: What works for psychiatrists in community and institutional settings.* Baltimore, MD: The John Hopkins University Press. [This is an informative text on how clinicians can help individuals with developmental disorders across the lifespan.]

CHAPTER 14

Looking Forward

This being the final chapter, the topics covered will largely be future oriented and speculative in nature. We shall look at structural changes within the brain and examine to what extent physical and mental training can impede typical age-related decline. There will be a look at how gaming technology is being incorporated into treatment plans for individuals with a range of conditions. In a similar vein, the growing assimilation of smart technologies in homes will be surveyed and the implications of its use considered. Before moving on to medical aspects, this section will end with a look at how technological products are designed specifically for use by older adults.

Medicine has much to offer the individual whose aim is to halt time's arrow. Various medicines that purport an anti-ageing effect will be looked at, as will surgical interventions that are increasingly seen as being a panacea for the growing numbers who are disaffected with their ageing bodies. This chapter, and indeed the book, will end with a contemplation of the future of humanity.

Neural plasticity and the ageing brain

In Chapter 2, there was a discussion focusing on age-related changes in brain functioning. It appears that, unlike during our youth, as we age there is a move away from lateralization. It has been suggested that this is evidence of compensatory strategies at the neural level to counteract the decline in functioning associated with age. This is indicative, therefore, of brain plasticity. Although largely associated with instances of brain trauma, where adaptive changes occur within the brain allowing the individuals to resume normal functioning, plasticity refers to changes in brain structure and functioning as a response to environmental demands.

When looking specifically at cognitive performance, there is evidence to show that, given training in the use of appropriate strategies, scores attained by older adults outstrip those of younger controls (Baltes & Kliegl, 1992). As seen in a number of other related studies, however, such gains in performance are task-specific and do not, as a result, generalize to other types of activities. Contrary to this, there is evidence to suggest that, as long as there is a reasonable degree of comparability across tasks in terms of the cognitive processes employed, performance enhancement can transcend tasks (Dahlin et al., 2008a).

Neurogenesis

It is generally held that the growth of new cells within the brain – a process called neurogenesis – ceases as we emerge from childhood into adulthood. More recent research using animal models provides evidence to the contrary, showing instead the presence of neural stem cells within the adult brain. These stem cells provide the substrate for the development of new neurons (Jessberger & Gage, 2009). By comparing the effects of an enriched environment (ever-changing arrangement of objects and toys) against that of a deprived environment (no change), performance on spatial memory tasks was improved in the group exposed to the enriched environment (Kempermann, Gast, & Gage, 2002). Comparable effects were observed at the cellular level. The enriched environment resulted in neurogenesis within the hippocampal region in the mature mice (Jessberger & Gage, 2009).

There is some evidence to suggest that comparable events occur within the human brain. With regard to older adults, following a five-week training course in the use of mnemonic strategy use, a variety of biochemical changes within the medial temporal lobe (a region of the brain containing the hippocampus) were measured related to, among other things, an increase in metabolic processes within cells to produce energy (Valenzuela et al., 2003). When comparing the changes occurring within the brains of younger and older participant, it was shown that, although there was evidence for neural plasticity in some of the older adults studies, age does in fact limit the growth potential, thereby restricting improvement in cognitive functioning (Nyberg et al., 2003).

Improving cognitive functioning

The concept of individual differences is evident throughout all realms of functioning; however, variability is greatest among older adults. A number of possible explanations present themselves. It is inevitable that one's level of general health will exert a major effect on how well one is able to function. Linked to this is a corpus of lifestyle choices, such as the diet your body has been exposed to, the degree of exercise it has endured, the level of mental stimulation offered it, and so on. A healthy diet, regular aerobic activity, and a high level of mental activity have all been linked to greater resistance to the effects of ageing. However, it is important to consider to what extent such activity does guard against the onslaught of time.

Cognitive training can be assessed in a number of ways. To begin with one can assess the size or magnitude of the improvement. It is also important to assess the degree to which such improvement can be generalized or transferred to other activities. Finally, it is necessary to gauge the stability of the effect (Hertzog et al., 2008). Most studies of this type have demonstrated improvements in working memory on the tasks specific to, or in some instances closely related to, the tasks used in the training programme (Borella et al., 2010; Richmond et al., 2011). There is more evidence for a transferal of effect for younger adults compared to older adults (Dahlin et al., 2008b; Jaeggi et al., 2008). Evidence is also suggestive that the effect is relatively stable for older adults over a period of a number of months (Richmond et al., 2011).

When conducting such studies it is important to select an appropriate control group. The control group used with most frequency is one where participants are tested pre- and post-intervention, with no additional contact in between (Li et al., 2008). Such a passive control group does not control for many of the situations experienced by the treatment group, such as having repeated contact with the experimenter and expectation of improvement as the result of training among other things. To some extent, this can be seen as being analogous to the therapist effect, a factor that poses many a problem when attempting to assess treatment efficacy for mental health conditions. An alternative control group would be where participants carry out activities that are unrelated to the cognitive training programme, but which nonetheless involve some element of participation, such as completion of questionnaires concerning memory and well-being (Richmond et al., 2011).

A recent study by Brehmer and colleagues (Brehmer, Westerberg, & Backman, 2012) presented both intervention and control groups with the same computer programs used in the training regime. The only difference here was that the control group received the tasks at a constant level of difficulty, whereas the intervention group received tasks that changed difficulty level in response to their performance (Hertzog et al., 2008). The findings from this study provided evidence of positive gains from such adaptive training regardless of age. There was also evidence of various transfer effects. The performance improvements remained on retesting five weeks post-intervention for both young and old adult groups for both subjective ratings of cognitive failures and objective measures of sustained attention. Both training and transfer effects were also evident after being reassessed at three months. Such improvements cannot be explained away as being merely the effect of a practice effect as both control and intervention groups performed the same tasks throughout the study, albeit at different levels of difficulty. Taking such effects into consideration, there was still evidence for improvement as a result of adaptive training. As seen previously, larger gains were observed in the younger adult group.

The literature on cognitive training protocols is indeed varied. The main issue seems to be that, when an effect has been demonstrated, improvements do not seem to generalize to other tasks or activities. It could be argued that the tasks used in training do not map particularly well onto everyday activities. However, training regimes that focused on computer games have shown such effects to some extent (Green, Li, & Bavelier, 2010). It may be argued that computer gaming involves complex and variable processing. In such cases, a number of cognitive processes are being honed and so more evidence of generalized improvement is seen due to relative proxy of such complex activity to the cognitive demands of everyday life (McDougall & House, 2012).

One such study utilized a range of verbal training activities. Across all activities a variety of core cognitive skills were targeted. The training schedule was intense, with training taking place for one hour, five days a week for up to ten weeks (Mahncke, Bronstone, & Merzenich, 2006). However, the measures used to assess the transferability of training were very similar to the training tasks themselves, making it difficult to adequately assess any evidence of generalizability (McDougall & House, 2012).

Little research has been conducted examining the effectiveness of off-the-shelf brain training packages, such as those available for the Nintendo DS (Owen et al., 2010). A recent study has looked specifically at utilizing the Nintendo DS found a positive effect of training for older adults, but one that is limited to a very small area of improvement, albeit one reflecting improvements in speed of processing and executive function, and so of fundamental importance for improving independence (McDougall & House, 2012).

In addition to assessing the effect of brain training, this study also examined the impact of underlying beliefs about one's own ability on outcome following the training regime. One argument is that those who believe themselves to be more competent in terms of cognitive functioning will likely benefit to a greater extent from training when compared to someone who does not feel competent. As predicted evidence showed that the ratings individuals made in relation to both cognitive functioning and quality of life appeared to mediate how effective the training was (McDougall & House, 2012).

Physical exercise in relation to improving cognitive function

Although the literature on brain training is plagued by inconsistent findings, there is one form of exercise that does show consistent improvement in cognitive functioning, and that is cardiovascular exercise (Colcombe &

Kramer, 2003). Among older adults who showed high levels of aerobic fitness, the decline in brain volume within the hippocampal regions was less when compared to a less active group (Erickson et al., 2009). As seen previously, the hippocampus is central to learning and memory.

To some extent, the improvements in cognitive functioning are higher for older adults. Imaging studies have provided evidence that aerobic exercise seems to work by increasing activation levels in the specific areas of the brain – the frontal and parietal cortices – involved in controlling working memory activity (Colcombe et al., 2004). The mechanism underlying such improvement is unclear. One possibility is that such activity stimulates the release of neurotrophin – growth factors that prevent apoptosis and encourage cell growth – which then increases neuronal connections. Being correlational in nature, studies such as these are unable to shed light on the potential therapeutic effects of aerobic exercise in terms of reversing cellular loss within essential brain regions.

Studies have also shown that older adults who exercise regularly react more quickly compared to older adults who are not physically active. In fact, some older exercisers have reaction times as fast as many young adults (Clarkson-Smith & Hartley, 1989). However, the findings for short-term exercise are mixed. Hawkins, Kramer, and Capaldi (1992) found older adults improved their speed of performance after participating in a ten-week aerobic exercise programme. However, others (Blumenthal & Madden, 1988) do not find that short-term exercise results in faster responding. Extended periods of training, long-term habits of physical activity, and general physical fitness seem to be the most effective means of increasing older adults' speed of processing.

Use of technology

We are facing the situation where there is an ageing population. With time, an increasing proportion of older adults live alone (Nations, 2006). On top of this there is an increasing likelihood of disability the older we get. Family sizes are smaller nowadays, so there is a depleted pool of potential support for those in need. An area that offers much potential is that of technology. The scope of scientific advancement is constantly expanding. Increasingly, the potential to convert such breakthrough into practical use is also growing. Nowhere is it more needed than in areas aimed at improving quality of life of older adults – a state increasingly referred to as gerontechnology. Such advancements may take the form of adaptations to a particular environment, portable aids, and also electronic gadgetry.

An important question to consider here is to what extent older adults are amenable to hi-tech wizardry. One potential gauge of this is engagement with online resources. A study conducted in 2006 in the United Kingdom showed that only 20 per cent of those aged 65 or more accessed the Internet in the preceding three-month period, compared to 63 per cent across other age groups. More encouraging findings were seen in 2000 from the findings of a large-scale study conducted in the European Union (Ekberg, 2002). As one would expect, there was a great deal of variation in technological expertise among the older adults. However, it was heartening to note that over half of the over-seventies interviewed were eager to develop more expertise in this area.

It is interesting to note that, love it or loathe it, technology is becoming ingrained into our lives, and older adults are no exception. Just take GP surgeries as an example. Instead of presenting yourself to the receptionist, most surgeries have a touchscreen device which demands that you enter your details so that your presence is logged in to the system, indicating to the doctor that you are in fact in the waiting room. Indeed, the speed at which the current generation of older adults have embraced advancements in technology is nothing short of amazing. It is unlikely that any future generation will experience such massive changes in one lifetime. As a result of this acceptance of information and communication technology, there are a number of knock-on effects. One possibility is that capacity may be enhanced, thus enabling this age group to continue working for much longer (Charness & Czaja, 2005).

There are a number of ways in which gerontechnology could enrich the lives of older adults. These include ways that help the individual to maintain contact with the outside world, be it in terms of access to sources of information or social networking sites; technology can assist with domestic and mobility issues, such as improving hygiene; finally, it can provide medical assistance and be implemented as part of a treatment plan (Tinker et al., 1999). These target areas can be expanded to include more psychological issues, such as issues with balance, vision and hearing, motor functioning, memory, as well as the ability to select or divide attention (Bouma et al., 2007).

The expansion of telemedicine and telecare has enabled support and healthcare provision to be provided to those who live in more remote areas of the country. Among other things, this approach allows healthcare professionals to monitor ongoing conditions remotely, promoting in many cases a more efficient and effective service. Use of telecare technology can include the use of various sensors that enable clinicians to assess a person in their own environment, and more specifically, to detect deviations from the norm, or in the extreme, to detect an emergency should it arise (Hanson et al., 2007). Such monitoring may eventually occur via an intelligent system without the need for human involvement.

One particular area of expansion is in the use of technology to assist with the care of those with dementia. The use of cameras and sensors allow such individuals to be monitored day and night. A series of failsafe measures can be taken to reduce risks normally associated with dementia. For example, auditory prompts may prevent a person from inadvertently leaving their house unaccompanied, or automatically turning off taps to prevent a bath from being overfilled. A more extreme option is the use of tagging in order to accurately pinpoint the location of an individual at any time. In the past behaviour of dementia patients has usually taken the form of either physical restraint or pharmacological intervention, both of which are highly restrictive (Tondu & Bardou, 2008). The use of in-home technology is in-line with the current trend for older adults to remain in their own accommodation rather than entering into institutional care (Office for National Statistics, 2001).

Advances in technology may also provide support to those who care for older adults. As seen in previous chapters, there is a rise in informal care, so it is important to better meet the needs of family and friends when they are called on to support a loved one. Access to online services is just one mechanism that can contribute to this carer support structure.

An important consideration relating to housing design is that of future-proofing so that the design will allow adaptations to be installed easily should the need arise at some future date. Smart housing is becoming more prominent. This is where many devices and facilities are controlled electronically, often through a computer-controlled hub. Such systems enable the resident to control a number of operations easily, such as lights, central heating, alarm systems, and so on. The installation of motion sensitive lighting can be used to decrease the likelihood of falls during the night (Tinker & Hanson, 2007).

The most likely focus for such advancements is the mobile phone. No longer is it confined to being a telecommunication device. Modern smartphones harbour more computing power than the average desktop computer at the turn of the millennium (Bronswijk, Kearns, & Normie, 2007) when it would often take a week to download a page of text from the Internet, longer if there were images (a slight exaggeration, but that is what it felt like at the time). They are also more user-friendly (unless you want to make a call). The use of mobile phones to monitor health behaviour is fast becoming an efficient and effective tool. Such devices enable the collection of a range of medical data, including blood sugar levels and blood pressure. This information is sent to a central processing system which is able to identify potential problems and activate appropriate alerts. Reminders about when to take medication or when to visit one's doctor can be automated using this technology. Video conferencing facilities are likely also to offer both patient and doctor many benefits in the future.

Alongside such advancement are burgeoning concerns over ethics, especially as such surveillance could be directed towards less benevolent outcomes. There is a need to achieve a successful and appropriate balance between privacy and healthcare needs (Taipale, 2008). Data protection is a major issue, especially in instances where devices form part of a computer network (Hoof et al., 2007). These are issues that will need addressing as the rate at which technology is adopted and adapted rises each day.

Use of gaming technology

In the previous section we explored how mobile phones could be utilized and how there is a growing market for smart technology around the home. Here we shall focus on the use of gaming technology to supplement care provided to older adults. Most homes have some form of games console, many of which now utilize motion sensitive devices that track movement so that there is no longer a reliance on hand-held keypads. Increasing numbers of older adults have experienced their use, in many cases actively taking part in the games. This latest breed of gaming hardware has introduced a virtual reality-like environment into our homes.

Virtual reality operates through a combination of visual and auditory feedback. Its adaptability means that it lends itself to a range of activities that under normal circumstances would be too risky or too costly. Virtual reality is increasingly being used as a tool for rehabilitation from a number of conditions. It is becoming increasingly available and, as a result, cheaper. A great deal of games consoles for the home now include elements of virtual reality, and as a result offer a community-based version of virtual reality therapy that is affordable and available.

Such devices offer therapy without the need of a therapist being physically present during the session because feedback is provided in the virtual reality environment. A recent study looking at the effectiveness of unsupervised rehabilitation using games console virtual reality systems found significant improvements in both hip muscle strength and balance in a group of older adults. Improvements of this type would be most helpful in facilitating a reduced likelihood of falls occurring within this vulnerable age group (Kim et al., 2013).

Postural control plays an important role in susceptibility to falls and decrease in physical function (Butler, Lord, & Fitzpatrick, 2011; Kloos et al., 2010). Use of force platforms and three-dimensional camera systems have led to advancements in assessing this aspect of functioning. Recent studies have utilized computer gaming technology such as Microsoft's Kinect™ as a means of providing clinicians with a more cost-effective and less unwieldy tool for clinical assessment. This system utilizes a camera and infra-red light to produce a three-dimensional representation of the gamer (Menna et al., 2011). The ability of this device to accurately map movement, especially at joints, is well supported (Dutta, 2012). A recent study has shown that the

Kinect™ system can be effective as a clinical screening tool for patients to assess postural control (Clark et al., 2012).

Designing products for older consumers

When considering any form of human–technology interaction, it is important to reflect on the capabilities inherent in the individual. These capabilities are the result of each person's unique interaction with the environment in which they have lived (Charness, Champion, & Yordon, 2010). Any form of technology, be it a refrigerator or a laptop computer, makes demands on these capacities. If there is a good fit between product demands and user abilities, the outcomes are positive, often enhancing performance in a particular realm of functioning. When there is a mismatch between demand and ability, systems become unusable, thereby impacting on attitudes towards and acceptance in using a particular product. This harks back to Norman's work on the subversive effect of poor design whereby we are falsely led to perform actions against our intention (Norman, 1998).

A good example here would be mobile phones. To some extent mobile phone is increasingly a misnomer. Current smartphone technology offers the user much in terms of functionality. The fact these devices are mobile telephones frequently goes unnoticed in the global marketing arena. Often it is easier, more intuitive even, to perform some whizzy function on one's smartphone – finding out details of a track played during an advert by holding the 'phone' in front of the television speakers, for example – than it is to actually make a call. I am sure I am not the only person to fall foul here. When examining interaction with technology on the basis of demand–capability fit, it is easy to see how such interfacing will have an influential effect on a person's belief in their own competency to perform certain behaviours and functions – on their self-efficacy, in other words (Czaja et al., 2006).

It is important to remember that demands imposed on the user also refer to how easy the product is to control, as in the case of touchscreen devices, or how easy it is to understand the instruction manual. These may be very real barriers preventing older adults from making that initial purchase (Charness et al., 2010).

The issue of individual differences is pertinent here. The fact that the variability among older adults increases with age is a very real issue for both the design and marketing of a product. To overcome some of the changes wrought by advancing age, product designers have identified some of the key concerns. Because there are often changes in vision there is a need to increase the level of illumination a device provides whilst at the same time reducing the amount of glare. Font size, or even better, user-defined variable font size is a real bonus here (Charness et al., 2010).

The fact that hearing wanes with age can be offset to some extent by ensuring auditory prompts are of a sufficient intensity and occur within an appropriate range of pitch. Detection of sound is particularly problematic for older adults when there is a reasonable level of background noise. Increasing volume is not sufficient to cancel out this issue with signal-to-noise ratio (Charness et al., 2010).

Reduction in fine motor control also occurs necessitating the need for on-screen target zones for selecting tasks to be widened to reflect this change, for example. This is a very real issue when one considers that technological advancements are often translated as increased miniaturization (Charness et al., 2010).

There is the need to also consider changes in cognitive functioning. As we have seen, the speed at which information is processed may slow, as may our ability to manipulate and integrate information. In this sense, it is important that technology provides means for accommodating change in this domain, such as avoiding being timed out when in the middle of performing a particular operation (Charness et al., 2010). In the case of mobile phones, the use of menu trees rather than individual screens that change with each choice reduce the number of errors made (Ziefle & Bay, 2006).

Anti-ageing medicine

Having explored some of the methods whereby we can enhance our functioning through the use of various forms of cognitive and physical training, this next section examines what medicine has to offer to combat the ageing process. Over the years a number of treatments have been proposed to counteract the effects of ageing. These have included various hormonal treatments whose sole aim was to boost levels of key hormones to that found in young adults. This included the use of growth hormone, although this has been shown to have the opposite effect in rats (Olshansky, Hayflick, & Carnes, 2002). Other approaches have been based on mechanistic accounts of ageing. Among other things is the proposal that antioxidants reverse the effects of reactive oxygen species (ROS), the by-products of cellular metabolism, thereby minimizing oxidative damage. Telomerase activators have also been offered, although there is no evidence to suggest this would be beneficial.

Caloric restriction is a potential mechanism whereby food intake is reduced by around 40 per cent. In particular, the use of caloric restriction mimetics offer a more plausible alternative for the majority due to the potential effects of such dietary restraints. These mimetics exert similar effects but without the need to necessarily reduce calories. One example is resveratrol, a constituent of red wine. This particular drug has been shown to increase the survival of mice fed a high-calorific diet, thereby implying potential as a treatment for obesity-related disorders. Rapamycin, an immunosuppressant, increased the lifespan of mice, again showing potential as a possible treatment (Harrison et al., 2009).

Regardless of continued attempts to offset age, no treatments as yet offer hope of delaying the ageing process. The vision of a future where ageing is halted through the deactivation of a specific gene as foretold in *The End Specialist* is still very much science fiction (Magary, 2011). In such a future the 'cure' for ageing brings with it a promise that, although you will never age, all that is guaranteed, 'is that you will never die a natural, peaceful death'. The types of questions raised by science fiction novelists provide much food for thought. However, the search for such elixirs continues unabated. However, for some, extending life is not the challenge. As Groucho Marx quipped, 'Getting older is no problem. You just have to live long enough.'

The ageing body

We are all too aware of the effects of age on our body. Be it in terms of agility, sensations, controllability, or physical appearance, time rarely deals a generous hand. Often there is a need to make use of technology in order to help people through their daily lives (Tiggemann, 2004). Research on body image among older adults is relatively scarce when given the level of change that occurs. There is evidence to suggest quite predictably that higher levels of body dissatisfaction occur in this population (Montepare, 1996), whereas yet other evidence indicates a more gung-ho approach where age transcends such concerns (Harris & Carr, 2001). It is plausible that the focus for concern rests of function rather than appearance (Rumsey & Harcourt, 2005).

There may be a mismatch between how a person appears to the world at large – their mirror-self – and how that person actually feels about themselves. Older adults often do not think of themselves are being old. In such cases our interactions with these same individuals would be doing them an injustice as we would be behaving with the wrong image in mind and all the various assumptions that go with it (Knight, 2012). This is because we would be operating under the assumed principle that our bodies are a reflection of a person's inner self. Satisfaction, or indeed dissatisfaction, with our body image has major implications in terms of one's self-esteem, affecting our mood, and also mediating the fear we may have about growing old (Knight, 2012).

The issue of appearance for older adults is likely to become more of a debated topic as time progresses. Current cosmetic procedures provide means to the wealthy few whereby a more youthful appearance is sculpted, at least for a limited time. It is reasonable to assume that more advanced techniques will become available and that progress in technology will drive down the cost so that such procedures would be a realistic option for a larger proportion of older adults. Clearly, if that is not the case, there will be wider sociological implications in terms of 'us' and 'them', those who can afford and those who can't.

The options provided by these techniques are likely to be supplemented by innovations in medical interventions that offer more than mere aesthetic alterations, instead manipulating how our bodies' internal processes response to age. Nutritional neuroscience is a growing field of study. Findings here would have major practical implications in terms of how diet may be modified in order to better cope with age-related changes, or indeed offset some of these changes.

Even if various successful options do become available, might there not be a point beyond which all treatments fail? Cosmetic practices may enhance someone's appearance, but repeated procedures applied to a relentlessly ageing body may have unintended effects in terms of how one looks. The surgeon has, after all, a limited palette with which to work.

The same may be true in the case of dietary supplements and physiological enhancements. At some point, decline will supersede what technology can offer in terms of restoration. Take, for example, changes in cognitive functioning in a typically ageing adult. Decline to some extent in inevitable: processing becomes slower, memory lapses occur. Drugs may offer some level of cognitive enhancement. However, one could argue that a fundamental aspect of being human is our ability to adapt. People across the world display much creativity in how they modify their behaviour to better deal with age-related changes in functioning. It is also important not to forget that forgetting is important. Our minds have evolved in such a way that a number of mechanisms are in place whereby rarely-used or redundant information is purged from our memories automatically in much the same way as Windows occasionally requests whether it should delete unused desktop icons (Schacter, 2001).

What are the implications in cases where there are more insidious forces at work, such as those diagnosed with Alzheimer's disease? It is important to remember here that as more and more people reach older adulthood, the prevalence of disease will rise in tandem. It is also highly likely that older adults may fall foul of more than one medical condition. Treating one successfully may mean only that the person dies of another complaint that cannot be treated with the same degree of success. In the case of dementia, improvements in nootropic medication may allow patients to experience a greater degree of independence for a longer period of time, but is seems very unlikely that we will reach a point where the effects of such disease processes can be reversed entirely. At some stage the disease process will erode functioning to such an extent that no level of intervention will be able to counteract the level of deterioration. At this point, patients will be faced with a situation that they may be ill prepared to receive. Rather than having to face the challenge presented by the disease from the offset, medicine merely offered an extended sojourn.

There is the issue of carers to consider here also. What would be the likely impact of a sudden deterioration in the loved one following this period of respite? How would they be able to cope, both physically and mentally, to the change? The quality of life issue is surely something to consider here.

What of the future?

Our understanding of genetics is continually growing, as are technologies that enable us to utilize this information. Personal genomics will improve diagnosis and allow us to potentially identify predispositions to a range of medical conditions early on as well as facilitating the selection of personalized treatment plans to better remedy the condition (Stevenson, 2012).

As we have seen, advancement in technology has led to a society that is increasingly dependent on its many applications. We are already comfortable with the concept of integrating machines into our bodies to improve functioning. The concept of transhumanism was originally coined by Julian Huxley during the first quarter of the twentieth century to refer to the transcendence of the human race beyond its biological givens (Huxley, 1979). Our current conception of ageing no longer applies here. The transhumanist philosophy is that scientific advancement not only increasingly allows us to live longer, it allows us to also enhance our capabilities beyond that which nature has bestowed on us. Medical science has long since offered prostheses in cases where individuals have lost limbs: 'Modern medicine is also full of cyborgs, of couplings between organism and machine' (Haraway, 1985). Future breakthroughs are likely to enable healthy individuals to lead physically and psychologically augmented lives (Stevenson, 2012). The potential for extended life with enhancements may swiftly move from the pages of science fiction writers into reality. The often fine divide between intervention-as-therapy and intervention-as-enhancement will be blurred further by such developments. The prospect of utilizing biointerfaces to boost human cognitive functioning is both appealing and worrying. Aside from the therapeutic use, such advancements would likely interest increasing numbers of healthy adults were it available. We are already embracing devices that augment reality in order to facilitate the way we operate (Brooks, 2002).

If this does indeed happen a number of serious philosophical questions will need to be addressed. Clearly this is beyond the remit of this book. However, novelists such as Peter F. Hamilton have explored the issue of future post-human societies where a glimpse of immortality is seen as every person's right (Hamilton, 2010). In this novel of the future, inhabitants grow up with the expectation that once a certain age is reached, or something befalls us, a person's store of memories will be downloaded into an artificially engineered, genetically identical body that will allow that person to live out their lives *ad infinitum*. Science fiction, yes. At the moment. The questions it raises are pertinent now with our current level of technological know-how regardless of whether re-life procedures become reality. For example, how will societies adapt to people living longer? What about overpopulation? Aside from SG-1, as far as I am aware there is no technology in existence that will allow us to utilize wormholes for the purpose of colonizing other planets in order to relieve the population pressure on Earth. Will the need for retirement become moot? What will the impact be on interpersonal relationships? What impact will there be in terms of our sense of self? Will we be sufficiently resilient to the adaptations demanded by such change?

Philosophers who wrestle with the issue of human–machine interaction prophesy a point in time when growth in knowledge that is the direct result of a combination of human creativity and machine-driven computational power expands at a rate hitherto unheard of. At this stage, they argue, there would be no option but to finalize our merger with the machines. We would have reached 'The Singularity' (Kurzweil, 2005).

Summary

The aim with this book was not to offer a tome that merely set out how and to what extent our bodies and mind will deteriorate with age. Hopefully that has not been the case, although to some extent there is a sense of inevitability about it all. That is unavoidable, perhaps. However, it was the intention that, with this final chapter, the mood could be rather more speculative and positive in its overall outlook. Much has been said about how various functions become less efficient and effective. To counteract that, it is clear that many of us show resilience and optimism during times of change. Here we examined how exercise, both physical and mental, can be used to help maintain healthy cognitive functioning into older adulthood. We also looked at various interventions and treatments that have shown varying degrees of success at combating age. What is clear is that, aside from physical changes, there are real psychological implications to many of these techniques that will have a tangible impact on a person's quality of life.

The quest to prolong and enhance life will, no doubt, prove to be an ever-expanding field of research. A caveat here is that the scientific worth of many a claim professing to enhance a person's brain power or prolong life need to be assessed independently as there is a huge market for such products, and potentially huge profits. So one must be especially wary and avoid at all costs pseudoscientific claims. Still, there is a sense of vigour and determination among researchers that great advancements will be made that will enable future generations of older adults to lead independent and fruitful lives for many a year.

> Hope springs eternal in the human breast:
> Man never is, but always to be blest
> (Pope, 1767, *An Essay on Man*)

Further reading

Begley, S. (2009). *The plastic mind*. London: Constable. [For those wanting to learn more about neuroplasticity, this is a very readable account.]

Stevenson, M. (2012). *An optimist's tour of the future*. London: Profile Books. [A wonderful book that examines what the future may offer us.]

Wenk, G. L. (2010). *Your brain on food: How chemicals control your thoughts and feelings*. New York: Oxford University Press. [If you are interested in nutritional neuroscience, then this is an excellent introduction.]

References

Aartsen, M. J., Smits, C. H., van Tilburg, T., Knipscheer, K. C., & Deeg, D. J. (2002). Activity in older adults: Cause or consequence of cognitive functioning? A longitudinal study on everyday activities and cognitive performance in older adults. [Research Support, Non-U.S. Gov't]. *Journals of Gerontology B: Psychological Sciences and Social Sciences, 57*(2), P153–162.

Abayomi, O. K. (2002). Pathogenesis of cognitive decline following therapeutic irradiation for head and neck tumors. [Review]. *Acta Oncologica, 41*(4), 346–351.

Abraham, K. & Jones, E. (1979). *Selected papers of Karl Abraham, M.D.* New York: Brunner/Mazel.

Abrams, R. C. & Bromberg, C. E. (2006). Personality disorders in the elderly: A flagging field of inquiry. [Editorial; Review]. *International Journal of Geriatric Psychiatry, 21*(11), 1013–1017. doi: 10.1002/gps.1614.

Abrams, L., Farrell, M. T., & Margolin, S. J. (2010). Older adults' detection of misspellings during reading. *Journals of Gerontology B: Psychological Sciences and Social Sciences, 65*(6), 680–3.

Abramson, L. Y., Seligman, M. E., & Teasdale, J. D. (1978). Learned helplessness in humans: Critique and reformulation. *Journal of Abnormal Psychology, 87*(1), 49–74.

ACEmobile (2013). Dementia assessment made easy and free. Retrieved from http://www.acemobile.org/index.html.

Adams, R. G. & Ueno, K. (2006). Middle-aged and older adult men's friendships. In V. H. Bedford & B. F. Turner (Eds), *Men in relationships: A new look from a life course perspective* (pp. 103–124). New York: Springer; [Edinburgh: Churchill Livingstone].

Adolphs, R. (1999). The human amygdala and emotion. *The Neuroscientist, 5*(2), 125–137. doi: 10.1177/107385849900500216.

Adrover-Roig, D., Sese, A., Barcelo, F., & Palmer, A. (2012). A latent variable approach to executive control in healthy ageing. [Research Support, Non-U.S. Gov't]. *Brain and Cognition, 78*(3), 284–299. doi: 10.1016/j.bandc.2012.01.005.

Aggleton, J. P. & Brown, M. W. (1999). Episodic memory, amnesia, and the hippocampal-anterior thalamic axis. *Behavioral and Brain Sciences, 22*(3), 425–444.

Aiken, L. R. (1989). *Later life* (3rd edn). Hillsdale, NJ: L. Erlbaum Associates.

Ainsworth, M. D. S. (1978). *Patterns of attachment: A psychological study of the strange situation.* New Jersey; New York; London: [Wiley].

Albert, M. L., Feldman, R. G., & Willis, A. L. (1974). The 'subcortical dementia' of progressive supranuclear palsy. *Journal of Neurology, Neurosurgery, and Psychiatry, 37*(2), 121–130.

Albert, M. S., Moss, M. B., Tanzi, R., & Jones, K. (2001). Preclinical prediction of AD using neuropsychological tests. [Research Support, U.S. Gov't, P.H.S.]. *Journal of the International Neuropsychological Society, 7*(5), 631–639.

Aldwin, C. M. & Gilmer, D. F. (2004). *Health, illness, and optimal aging: Biological and psychosocial perspectives.* Thousand Oaks, CA; London: Sage Publications.

Aldwin, C. M. & Levenson, M. R. (1994). Aging and personality assessment. In M. P. Lawton & J. Teresi (Eds), *Annual review of gerontology/geriatrics* (pp. 182–209). New York: Springer.

Alexopoulos, G. S. (2005). Depression in the elderly. [Research Support, N.I.H., Extramural; Research Support, Non-U.S. Gov't; Research Support, U.S. Gov't, P.H.S.; Review]. *Lancet*, *365*(9475), 1961–1970. doi: 10.1016/S0140-6736(05)66665-2.

Allen, H. A., Hutchinson, C. V., Ledgeway, T., & Gayle, P. (2010). The role of contrast sensitivity in global motion processing deficits in the elderly. [Comparative Study; Research Support, Non-U.S. Gov't]. *Journal of Vision*, *10*(10), 15. doi: 10.1167/10.10.15.

Allen, P. A., Madden, D. J., Weber, T. A., & Groth, K. E. (1993). Influence of age and processing stage on visual word recognition. [Research Support, Non-U.S. Gov't; Research Support, U.S. Gov't, P.H.S.]. *Psychology and Aging*, *8*(2), 274–282.

Allport, A. (1989). Visual attention. In M. I. Posner (Ed.), *Foundations of cognitive science* (pp. 631–682). Cambridge, MA: The MIT Press.

Almada, S. J., Zonderman, A. B., Shekelle, R. B., Dyer, A. R., Daviglus, M. L., Costa, P. T., Jr, & Stamler, J. (1991). Neuroticism and cynicism and risk of death in middle-aged men: The Western Electric Study. [Research Support, Non-U.S. Gov't; Research Support, U.S. Gov't, P.H.S.]. *Psychosomatic Medicine*, *53*(2), 165–175.

Almeida, O. P. & Flicker, L. (2001). The mind of a failing heart: A systematic review of the association between congestive heart failure and cognitive functioning. [Review]. *Internal Medicine Journal*, *31*(5), 290–295.

Alzheimer's Disease International (1999). The prevalence of dementia (Vol. Fact Sheet 3). Alzheimer's Disease International.

Alzheimer's Research Trust (2010). Dementia 2010: Alzheimer's Research Trust.

American Psychiatric Association. (2000). *Diagnostic and statistical manual of mental disorders: DSM-IV-TR* (4th edn, text revision). Washington, DC: American Psychiatric Association.

Ames, D., Chiu, E., Lindesay, J., & Shulman, K. I. (2010). Guide to the psychiatry of old age. Retrieved from Dawson Era database, http://www.dawsonera.com/depp/reader/protected/external/AbstractView/S9780511772863.

Ancoli-Israel, S. & Cooke, J. R. (2005). Prevalence and comorbidity of insomnia and effect on functioning in elderly populations. [Research Support, N.I.H., Extramural; Research Support, Non-U.S. Gov't; Research Support, U.S. Gov't, Non-P.H.S.; Research Support, U.S. Gov't, P.H.S.; Review]. *Journal of the American Geriatrics Society*, *53*(Suppl. 7), S264–271. doi: 10.1111/j.1532-5415.2005.53392.x.

Andel, R., Crowe, M., Pedersen, N. L., Fratiglioni, L., Johansson, B., & Gatz, M. (2008). Physical exercise at midlife and risk of dementia three decades later: A population-based study of Swedish twins. [Research Support, N.I.H., Extramural; Research Support, Non-U.S. Gov't; Twin Study]. *Journals of Gerontology Series A: Biological Sciences and Medical Sciences*, *63*(1), 62–66.

Anderson, N. D., Craik, F. I., & Naveh-Benjamin, M. (1998). The attentional demands of encoding and retrieval in younger and older adults: 1. Evidence from divided attention costs. *Psychology and Aging*, *13*(3), 405–423.

Angelucci, L. (2000). The glucocorticoid hormone: From pedestal to dust and back. [Review]. *European Journal of Pharmacology*, *405*(1–3), 139–147.

Anstey, K. J., Dear, K., Christensen, H., & Jorm, A. F. (2005). Biomarkers, health, lifestyle, and demographic variables as correlates of reaction time performance in early, middle, and late adulthood. [Research Support, Non-U.S. Gov't]. *Quarterly Journal of Experimental Psychology A*, *58*(1), 5–21. doi: 10.1080/02724980443000232.

Anstey, K. J., Luszcz, M. A., & Sanchez, L. (2001). A reevaluation of the common factor theory of shared variance among age, sensory function, and cognitive function in older adults. [Research Support, Non-U.S. Gov't]. *J Gerontol B Psychol Sci Soc Sci*, 56(1), P3-11.

Anthony, J. L. & Lonigan, C. J. (2004). The nature of phonological awareness: Converging evidence from four studies of preschool and early grade school children. *Journal of Educational Psychology*, 96(1), 43–55.

Antonovsky, A. (1979). *Health, stress and coping*. San Francisco; London: Jossey-Bass.

Aoi, W. (2009). Exercise and food factors. [Review]. *Forum of Nutrition*, 61, 147–155. doi: 10.1159/000212747.

'Apoptosis' (2003) *The Macmillan encyclopedia*. Basingstoke: Macmillan. Retrieved from http://www.credoreference.com/entry/move/apoptosis.

Arbuckle, T. Y. & Gold, D. P. (1993). Aging, inhibition, and verbosity. [Research Support, Non-U.S. Gov't]. *Journal of Gerontology*, 48(5), P225–232.

Arbuckle, T. Y., Nohara-LeClair, M., & Pushkar, D. (2000). Effect of off-target verbosity on communication efficiency in a referential communication task. [Research Support, Non-U.S. Gov't]. *Psychology and Aging*, 15(1), 65–77.

Ardelt, M. (2000). Antecedents and effects of wisdom in old age – A longitudinal perspective on aging well. *Research on Aging*, 22(4), 360–394.

Argyle, M. (1999). *Causes and correlates of happiness*. New York: Russell Sage Foundation.

Arnett, J. J. (2006). Socialization in emerging adulthood: From the family to the wider world, from socialization to self-socialization. In J. E. Grusec & P. D. Hastings (Eds), *Handbook of socialization: Theory and research* (pp. 208–231). New York; London: Guilford.

Arnold, M. (2008). Polypharmacy and older adults: A role for psychology and psychologists. *Professional Psychology: Research and Practice*, 38, 283–289.

Ashton, M. C., Lee, K., Vernon, P. A., & Jang, K. L. (2000). Fluid intelligence, crystallized intelligence, and the openness/intellect factor. *Journal of Research in Personality*, 34(2), 198–207.

Aspinwall, L. G. & Taylor, S. E. (1992). Modeling cognitive adaptation: A longitudinal investigation of the impact of individual differences and coping on college adjustment and performance. [Research Support, U.S. Gov't, Non-P.H.S.; Research Support, U.S. Gov't, P.H.S.]. *Journal of Personality and Social Psychology*, 63(6), 989–1003.

Aspinwall, L. G. & Taylor, S. E. (1997). A stitch in time: Self-regulation and proactive coping. [Research Support, Non-U.S. Gov't; Research Support, U.S. Gov't, Non-P.H.S.; Research Support, U.S. Gov't, P.H.S.; Review]. *Psychological Bulletin*, 121(3), 417–436.

Atkinson, R. C. & Shiffrin, R. M. (1968). Human memory: A proposed system and its control processes. In K. W. Spence & J. T. Spence (Eds), *The psychology of learning and motivation: Advances in research and theory* (Vol. 2, pp. 89–105). New York: Academic Press.

Attig, T. (1996). *How we grieve: Relearning the world*. New York; Oxford: Oxford University Press.

'Autobiographical memory' (2006) *Encyclopaedic dictionary of psychology*. London: Hodder Education.

Averill, P. M. & Beck, J. G. (2000). Posttraumatic stress disorder in older adults: A conceptual review. [Research Support, U.S. Gov't, P.H.S.; Review]. *Journal of Anxiety Disorders*, 14(2), 133–156.

Backman, L. & Molander, B. (1986). Adult age differences in the ability to cope with situations of high arousal in a precision sport. [Research Support, Non-U.S. Gov't]. *Psychology and Aging*, 1(2), 133–139.

Backman, L. & Nilsson, L-G. (1984). Aging effect in free recall: An exception to the rule. *Human Learning*, 3, 53–69.

Backman, L., Ginovart, N., Dixon, R. A., Wahlin, T. B., Wahlin, A., Halldin, C., & Farde, L. (2000). Age-related cognitive deficits mediated by changes in the striatal dopamine system. [Research Support, Non-U.S. Gov't]. *American Journal of Psychiatry, 157*(4), 635–637.

Backman, L., Nyberg, L., Lindenberger, U., Li, S. C., & Farde, L. (2006). The correlative triad among aging, dopamine, and cognition: Current status and future prospects. [Research Support, Non-U.S. Gov't; Review]. *Neuroscience and Biobehavioral Reviews, 30*(6), 791–807. doi: 10.1016/j.neubiorev.2006.06.005.

Baddeley, A. D. (1992). Working memory. [Research Support, Non-U.S. Gov't; Review]. *Science, 255*(5044), 556–559.

Baddeley, A. D. (2000). Short-term and working memory. In E. Tulving & F. I. M. Craik (Eds), *The Oxford handbook of memory* (pp. 77–92): Oxford University Press.

Baddeley, A. D. (2001). Is working memory still working? [Addresses; Research Support, Non-U.S. Gov't]. *American Psychologist, 56*(11), 851–864.

Baddeley, A. D. (2006). Working memory: An overview. In S. J. Pickering (Ed.), *Working memory and education*. Amsterdam; London: Elsevier/Academic Press.

Baddeley, A. D. (2009). Memory and aging. In A. D. Baddeley, M. W. Eysenck, & M. C. Anderson (Eds), *Memory* (pp. 293–316). Hove: Psychology Press.

Baddeley, A. D., Emslie, H., & Nimmo-Smith, I. (1994). *Doors and people: A test of visual and verbal recall and recognition*. Bury St Edmunds: Thames Valley Test Company.

Baddeley, A. D., Eysenck, M. W., & Anderson, M. C. (2009). *Memory*. Hove: Psychology Press.

Baddeley, A. D. & Hitch, G. J. (1974). Working memory. In G. A. Bower (Ed.), *Recent advances in learning and motivation* (Vol. 8, pp. 47–90). New York: Academic Press.

Bailey, P. E. & Henry, J. D. (2008). Growing less empathic with age: Disinhibition of the self-perspective. [Research Support, Non-U.S. Gov't]. *Journals of Gerontology B: Psychological Sciences and Social Sciences, 63*(4), P219–P226.

Baldwin, R., Jeffries, S., Jackson, A., Sutcliffe, C., Thacker, N., Scott, M., & Burns, A. (2005). Neurological findings in late-onset depressive disorder: Comparison of individuals with and without depression. [Comparative Study; Research Support, Non-U.S. Gov't]. *British Journal of Psychiatry, 186*, 308–313. doi: 10.1192/bjp.186.4.308.

Baldwin, R. C. & O'Brien, J. (2002). Vascular basis of late-onset depressive disorder. [Review]. *British Journal of Psychiatry, 180*, 157–160.

Ball, K. & Sekuler, R. (1986). Improving visual perception in older observers. [Research Support, U.S. Gov't, P.H.S.]. *Journal of Gerontology, 41*(2), 176–182.

Ball, K., Edwards, J. D., & Ross, L. A. (2007). The impact of speed of processing training on cognitive and everyday functions. [Meta-Analysis; Research Support, N.I.H., Extramural; Review]. *Journals of Gerontology B: Psychological Sciences and Social Sciences, 62*(Spec. No. 1), 19–31.

Ballard, C. & Cream, J. (2005). Drugs used to relieve behavioral symptoms in people with dementia or an unacceptable chemical cosh? *International Psychogeriatrics, 17*(1), 4–12. doi: 10.1017/s1041610205221026.

Baltes, M. M. (1996). *The many faces of dependency in old age*. Cambridge: Cambridge University Press.

Baltes, M. M. & Carstensen, L. L. (1996). The process of successful aging. *Aging and Society, 16*, 397–422.

Baltes, P. B. (1997). On the incomplete architecture of human ontogeny. Selection, optimization, and compensation as foundation of developmental theory. [Research Support, Non-U.S. Gov't; Review]. *American Psychologist, 52*(4), 366–380.

Baltes, P. B. & Baltes, B. B. (1990). Psychological perspectives on successful aging: The model of selective optimization with compensation. In P. B. Baltes & M. M. Baltes (Eds), *Successful aging: Perspectives from the behavioral sciences*. Cambridge: Cambridge University Press.

Baltes, P. B. & Kliegl, R. (1992). Further testing of limits of cognitive plasticity: Negative age differences in a mnemonic skill are robust. *Developmental Psychology, 28*(1), 121–125.

Baltes, P. B. & Smith, J. (1990). Toward a psychology of wisdom and its ontogenesis. In R. J. Sternberg (Ed.), *Wisdom: Its nature, origins and development* (pp. 87–120). Cambridge: Cambridge University Press.

Baltes, P. B. & Staudinger, U. M. (2000). Wisdom. A metaheuristic (pragmatic) to orchestrate mind and virtue toward excellence. *American Psychologist, 55*(1), 122–136.

Baltes, P. B. (1983). Life-span developmental psychology: Observations on history and theory revisited. In R. M. Lerner (Ed.), *Developmental psychology: Historical and philosophical perspectives* (pp. 79–111). Hillsdale, NJ: L. Erlbaum Association.

Baltes, P. B., Freund, A. M., & Li, S-C. (2005). The psychological science of human ageing. In M. L. Johnson (Ed.), *The Cambridge handbook of age and ageing* (pp. 47–71). Cambridge: Cambridge University Press.

Baltes, P. B. & Lindenberger, U. (1997). Emergence of a powerful connection between sensory and cognitive functions across the adult life span: A new window to the study of cognitive aging? *Psychology and Aging, 12*(1), 12–21.

Baltes, P. B. & Nesselroade, J. R. (1979). History and rationale of longitudinal research. In J. R. Nesselroade & P. B. Baltes (Eds), *Longitudinal research in the study of behaviour and development* (pp. 1–39). New York; London: Academic Press.

Baltes, P. B., Reese, H. W., & Lipsitt, L. P. (1980). Life-span developmental psychology. [Research Support, U.S. Gov't, P.H.S.]. *Annual Review of Psychology, 31*, 65–110. doi: 10.1146/annurev.ps.31.020180.000433.

Baltes, P. B. & Singer, T. (2001). Plasticity and the aging mind: An exemplar of the biocultural orchestration of brain and behaviour. *European Review: Interdisciplinary Journal of the Academia Europaea, 9*, 59–76.

Baltes, P. B. & Smith, J. (2008). The fascination of wisdom: Its nature, ontogeny, and function. *Perspectives on Psychological Science, 3*(1), 56–64.

Baltes, P. B., Smith, J., & Staudinger, U. M. (1992). *Wisdom and successful aging* (Vol. 39). Lincoln, Nebraska: University of Nebraska Press.

Baltes, P. B., Staudinger, U. M., Maercker, A., & Smith, J. (1995). People nominated as wise: A comparative study of wisdom-related knowledge. *Psychology and Aging, 10*(2), 155–166.

Bandura, A. (1997). *Self-efficacy: The exercise of control*. New York: W. H. Freeman.

Bandura, A. (2004). Self-efficacy. In W. E. Craighead & C. B. Nemeroff (Eds), *The concise Corsini encyclopedia of psychology and behavioral science* (3rd edn, pp. 1534–1536). New York; Chichester: Wiley.

Barkley, R. A. (1997). Behavioral inhibition, sustained attention, and executive functions: Constructing a unifying theory of ADHD. [Research Support, U.S. Gov't, P.H.S.; Review]. *Psychological Bulletin, 121*(1), 65–94.

Baron-Cohen, S. (1988). Social and pragmatic deficits in autism: Cognitive or affective?. *Journal of Autism and Developmental Disorders, 18*(3), 379-402

Baron-Cohen, S. (1995). *Mindblindness: An essay on autism and theory of mind*. Cambridge, MA; London: MIT Press.

Baron-Cohen, S., Ring, H. A., Wheelwright, S., Bullmore, E. T., Brammer, M. J., Simmons, A., & Williams, S. C. (1999). Social intelligence in the normal and autistic brain: An fMRI study. [Research Support, Non-U.S. Gov't]. *European Journal of Neuroscience*, *11*(6), 1891–1898.

Baron-Cohen, S., Wheelwright, S., Hill, J., Raste, Y., & Plumb, I. (2001). The 'Reading the Mind in the Eyes' Test revised version: A study with normal adults, and adults with Asperger syndrome or high-functioning autism. [Research Support, Non-U.S. Gov't; Validation Studies]. *Journal of Child Psychology and Psychiatry, and Allied Disciplines*, *42*(2), 241–251.

Baron-Cohen, S., Wheelwright, S., & Jolliffe, T. (1997). Is there a 'language of the eyes'? Evidence from normal adults and adults with autism or Asperger syndrome. *Visual Cognition*, *4*, 311–332.

Barrett, L. F. (2004). Feelings or words? Understanding the content in self-report ratings of experienced emotion. [Research Support, U.S. Gov't, Non-P.H.S.; Research Support, U.S. Gov't, P.H.S.]. *Journal of Personality and Social Psychology*, *87*(2), 266–281. doi: 10.1037/0022-3514.87.2.266.

Baumeister, R. F. (1996). *Self-regulation and ego threat: Motivated cognition, self deception, and destructive goal setting*. New York; London: Guilford Press.

Baumeister, R. F., Bratslavsky, E., Finkenauer, C., & Vohs, K. D. (2001). Bad is stronger than good. *Review of General Psychology*, *5*(4), 323–370.

Beange, H., McElduff, A., & Baker, W. (1995). Medical disorders of adults with mental retardation: A population study. [Clinical Trial; Comparative Study; Randomized Controlled Trial; Research Support, Non-U.S. Gov't]. *American Journal of Mental Retardation*, *99*(6), 595–604.

Beck, A. T. & Steer, R. A. (1993). *Beck anxiety inventory*. San Antonio: Psychological Corporation.

Beck, A. T., Steer, R. A., & Brown, G. K. (1996). *Beck Depression Inventory-II (BDI-II)*. San Antonio: Psychological Corporation.

Beer, J. S. & Ochsner, K. N. (2006). Social cognition: A multi level analysis. [Review]. *Brain Research*, *1079*(1), 98–105. doi: 10.1016/j.brainres.2006.01.002.

Bell, D. (1976). *The coming of post-industrial society: A venture in social forecasting*. Harmondsworth: Penguin.

Bellini, S. (2004). Social skill deficits and anxiety in high-functioning adolescents with autism spectrum disorders. *Focus on Autism and Other Developmental Disabilities*, *19*(2), 78–86.

Bengston, V., Rosenthal, C., & Burton, L. (1996). Paradoxes of families and aging. In R. H. Binstock & L. K. George (Eds), *Handbook of aging and the social sciences* (4th edn, pp. 253–282). San Diego; London: Academic.

Benloucif, S., Orbeta, L., Ortiz, R., Janssen, I., Finkel, S. I., Bleiberg, J., & Zee, P. C. (2004). Morning or evening activity improves neuropsychological performance and subjective sleep quality in older adults. [Research Support, Non-U.S. Gov't; Research Support, U.S. Gov't, P.H.S.]. *Sleep*, *27*(8), 1542–1551.

Bentall, R. P. (2006a). Antypical antipsychotic drugs. In G. Davey (Ed.), *The encyclopaedic dictionary of psychology*. London: Hodder Arnold. Retrieved from http://www.credoreference.com/entry/hodderdpsyc/atypical_antipsychotic_drugs.

Bentall, R. P. (2006b). Electroconvulsive therapy. In G. Davey (Ed.), *The encyclopaedic dictionary of psychology*. London: Hodder Arnold. Retrieved from http://www.credoreference.com/entry/hodderdpsyc/electroconvulsive_therapy_ect.

Bentall, R. P. (2006c). Negative symptoms of schizophrenia. In G. Davey (Ed.), *The encyclopaedic dictionary of psychology*. London: Hodder Arnold. Retrieved from http://www.credoreference.com/entry/hodderdpsyc/negative_symptoms_of_schizophrenia.

Berry, J. M. (1999). Memory self-efficacy in its social cognitive context. In T. M. Hess & F. Blanchard-Fields (Eds), *Social cognition and aging* (pp. 69–96). San Diego; London: AP Professional.

Betik, A. C. & Hepple, R. T. (2008). Determinants of VO2 max decline with aging: An integrated perspective. [Review]. *Applied Physiology, Nutrition and Metabolism, 33*(1), 130–140. doi: 10.1139/H07-174.

Beyreuther, K., Pollwein, P., Multhaup, G., Monning, U., Konig, G., Dyrks, T., Schubert, W., & Masters, C. L. (1993). Regulation and expression of the Alzheimer's beta/A4 amyloid protein precursor in health, disease, and Down's syndrome. [Research Support, Non-U.S. Gov't; Review]. *Annals of the New York Academy of Sciences, 695*, 91–102.

Bhalla, R. K., Butters, M. A., Mulsant, B. H., Begley, A. E., Zmuda, M. D., Schoderbek, B., Pollock, B. G., Reynolds, C. F., 3rd, & Becker, J. T. (2006). Persistence of neuropsychologic deficits in the remitted state of late-life depression. [Comparative Study; Research Support, N.I.H., Extramural]. *American Journal of Geriatric Psychiatry, 14*(5), 419–427. doi: 10.1097/01.JGP.0000203130.45421.69.

Biederman, J., Faraone, S. V., Spencer, T. J., Mick, E., Monuteaux, M. C., & Aleardi, M. (2006). Functional impairments in adults with self-reports of diagnosed ADHD: A controlled study of 1001 adults in the community. [Comparative Study; Research Support, N.I.H., Extramural; Research Support, Non-U.S. Gov't]. *Journal of Clinical Psychiatry, 67*(4), 524–540.

Biederman, J., Mick, E., & Faraone, S. V. (2000). Age-dependent decline of symptoms of attention deficit hyperactivity disorder: Impact of remission definition and symptom type. [Research Support, U.S. Gov't, P.H.S.]. *American Journal of Psychiatry, 157*(5), 816–818.

Biederman, J., Wilens, T., Mick, E., Milberger, S., Spencer, T. J., & Faraone, S. V. (1995). Psychoactive substance use disorders in adults with attention deficit hyperactivity disorder (ADHD): Effects of ADHD and psychiatric comorbidity. [Research Support, U.S. Gov't, P.H.S.]. *American Journal of Psychiatry, 152*(11), 1652–1658.

Bigby, C. (2000). *Moving on without parents: Planning, transitions, and sources of support for middle-aged and older adults with intellectual disability*. Baltimore, MD: Paul H. Brookes.

Bigby, C. (2004). *Ageing with a lifelong disability: A guide to practice, program, and policy issues for human services professionals*. London; New York: Jessica Kingsley.

Biggs, S. (2005). Psychodynamic approaches to the lifecourse and ageing. *The Cambridge Handbook of Age and Ageing*. Cambridge: Cambridge University Press.

Birditt, K. S., Fingerman, K. L., & Almeida, D. M. (2005). Age differences in exposure and reactions to interpersonal tensions: A daily diary study. [Research Support, Non-U.S. Gov't]. *Psychology and Aging, 20*(2), 330–340. doi: 10.1037/0882-7974.20.2.330.

Birren, J. E. (1974). Translations in gerontology – From lab to life. Psychophysiology and speed of response. [Research Support, U.S. Gov't, Non-P.H.S.]. *American Psychologist, 29*(11), 808–815.

Birren, J. E. & Fisher, L. M. (1990). The elements of wisdom: Overview and integration. In R. J. Sternberg (Ed.), *Wisdom: Its nature, origins and development* (pp. 317–332). Cambridge: Cambridge University Press.

Blachman, D. R. & Hinshaw, S. P. (2002). Patterns of friendship among girls with and without attention-deficit/hyperactivity disorder. [Research Support, U.S. Gov't, Non-P.H.S.; Research Support, U.S. Gov't, P.H.S.]. *Journal of Abnormal Child Psychology, 30*(6), 625–640.

Blanchard-Fields, F. (1994). Age differences in causal attributions from an adult developmental perspective. [Research Support, U.S. Gov't, P.H.S.]. *Journal of Gerontology, 49*(2), P43–51.

Blanchard-Fields, F. (1999). Social schemacity and causal attributions. In T. M. Hess & F. Blanchard-Fields (Eds), *Social cognition and aging* (pp. 219–236). San Diego; London: AP Professional.

Blanchard-Fields, F. (2007). Everyday problem solving and emotion: An adult developmental perspective. *Current Directions in Psychological Science, 16*(1), 26–31. doi: 10.1111/j.1467-8721.2007.00469.x.

Blanchard-Fields, F., Baldi, R., & Stein, R. (1999). Age relevance and context effects on attributions across the adult lifespan. *International Journal of Behavioral Development, 23*(3), 665–683.

Blanchard-Fields, F., Jahnke, H. C., & Camp, C. (1995). Age differences in problem-solving style: The role of emotional salience. *Psychology and Aging, 10*(2), 173–180.

Blanchard-Fields, F., Mienaltowski, A., & Seay, R. B. (2007). Age differences in everyday problem-solving effectiveness: Older adults select more effective strategies for interpersonal problems. [Research Support, N.I.H., Extramural]. *Journals of Gerontology B: Psychological Sciences and Social Sciences, 62*(1), P61–64.

Blazer, D. G. (2006). Depression. In R. Schulz (Ed.) with L. S. Noelker, K. Rockwood, & R. L. Sprott (Assoc. eds), *Encyclopedia of aging: A comprehensive resource in gerontology and geriatrics* (4th edn, pp. 303–306). New York: Springer.

Blennow, K., de Leon, M. J., & Zetterberg, H. (2006). Alzheimer's disease. [Review]. *Lancet, 368*(9533), 387–403. doi: 10.1016/S0140-6736(06)69113-7.

Bloch, M. (2007). Huntington's disease. In S. Ayers (Ed.), *Cambridge handbook of psychology, health and medicine* (2nd edn). Cambridge: Cambridge University Press. Retrieved from http://www.credoreference.com/entry/cupphm/huntington_s_disease.

Blumenthal, J. A. & Madden, D. J. (1988). Effects of aerobic exercise training, age, and physical fitness on memory-search performance. [Research Support, Non-U.S. Gov't'; Research Support, U.S. Gov't, P.H.S.]. *Psychology and Aging, 3*(3), 280–285.

Boden, D. & Bielby, D. D. (1983). The past as resource. A conversational analysis of elderly talk. *Human Development, 26*(6), 308–319.

Boelen, P. A., Van den Hout, M. A., & Van den Bout, J. (2006). A cognitive-behavioral conceptualization of complicated grief. *Clinical Psychology, 13*, 109–128.

Boerner, K. & Jopp, D. (2007). Improvement/maintenance and reorientation as central features of coping with major life change and loss: Contributions of three life-span theories. *Human Development, 50*(4), 171–195.

Bolger, N. & Schilling, E. A. (1991). Personality and the problems of everyday life: The role of neuroticism in exposure and reactivity to daily stressors. [Research Support, U.S. Gov't, P.H.S.]. *Journal of Personality, 59*(3), 355–386.

Bond, A. J. & Lader, M. H. (1996). *Understanding drug treatment in mental health care.* Chichester: Wiley.

Bonini, M.V., & Mansur, L. L. (2009). Comprehension and storage of sequentially presented radio news items by healthy elderly. *Dement. neuropsychol, 3*(2), 118–123.

Bopp, K. L. & Verhaeghen, P. (2005). Aging and verbal memory span: A meta-analysis. [Comparative Study; Meta-Analysis; Research Support, N.I.H., Extramural; Research Support, U.S. Gov't, P.H.S.]. *Journals of Gerontology B: Psychological Sciences and Social Sciences, 60*(5), P223–233.

Borella, E., Carretti, B., Riboldi, F., & De Beni, R. (2010). Working memory training in older adults: Evidence of transfer and maintenance effects. [Randomized Controlled Trial]. *Psychology and Aging, 25*(4), 767–778. doi: 10.1037/a0020683.

Bosse, R., Aldwin, C. M., Levenson, M. R., Spiro, A., 3rd, & Mroczek, D. K. (1993). Change in social support after retirement: Longitudinal findings from the Normative

Aging Study. [Research Support, U.S. Gov't, Non-P.H.S.; Research Support, U.S. Gov't, P.H.S.]. *Journal of Gerontology, 48*(4), P210–217.

Bosse, R. & Ekerdt, D. J. (1981). Change in self-perception of leisure activities with retirement. [Comparative Study; Research Support, U.S. Gov't, Non-P.H.S.; Research Support, U.S. Gov't, P.H.S.]. *Gerontologist, 21*(6), 650–654.

Botwinick, J. (1984). *Aging and behavior: A comprehensive integration of research findings* (3rd edn, updated and expanded). New York: Springer.

Bouma, H., Fozard, J. L., Bouwhuis, D. G., & Taipale, V. (2007). Gerontechnology in perspective. *Gerontechnology, 6*(4), 190–216.

Bowlby, J. (1969). *Attachment and loss.* London: Hogarth.

Bowlby, J. (1973). *Attachment and loss.* London: Hogarth; Institute of Psycho-analysis.

Bowling, A. (2005). *Ageing well: Quality of life in old age.* Maidenhead: Open University Press.

Bowling, A. & Browne, P. D. (1991). Social networks, health, and emotional well-being among the oldest old in London. [Research Support, Non-U.S. Gov't; Review]. *Journal of Gerontology, 46*(1), S20–32.

Boyce, N., Walker, Z., & Rodda, J. (2008). *The old age psychiatry handbook: A practical guide.* Chichester: John Wiley & Sons Ltd.

Boyle, P. A., Barnes, L. L., Buchman, A. S., & Bennett, D. A. (2009). Purpose in life is associated with mortality among community-dwelling older persons. [Comparative Study; Research Support, N.I.H., Extramural]. *Psychosomatic Medicine, 71*(5), 574–579. doi: 10.1097/PSY.0b013e3181a5a7c0.

Boyle, S. H., Jackson, W. G., & Suarez, E. C. (2007). Hostility, anger, and depression predict increases in C3 over a 10-year period. [Research Support, N.I.H., Extramural]. *Brain, Behavior, and Immunity, 21*(6), 816–823. doi: 10.1016/j.bbi.2007.01.008.

Bradley, E. A., Summers, J. A., Wood, H. L., & Bryson, S. E. (2004). Comparing rates of psychiatric and behavior disorders in adolescents and young adults with severe intellectual disability with and without autism. [Comparative Study; Research Support, Non-U.S. Gov't]. *Journal of Autism and Developmental Disorders, 34*(2), 151–161.

Brandtstadter, J. (1999). Sources of resilience in the aging self. In T. M. Hess & F. Blanchard-Fields (Eds), *Social cognition and aging* (pp. 123–141). San Diego; London: AP Professional.

Brandtstadter, J. & Renner, G. (1990). Tenacious goal pursuit and flexible goal adjustment: Explication and age-related analysis of assimilative and accommodative strategies of coping. [Research Support, Non-U.S. Gov't]. *Psychology and Aging, 5*(1), 58–67.

Brandstadter, J. & Wentura, D. (1995). Adjusting to shifting possibility frontiers in later life: Complementary adaptive models. In R. A. Dixon & L. Backman (Eds), *Compensating for psychological deficits and declines: Managing losses and promoting gains* (pp. 83–105). Mahwah, NJ: Lawrence Erlbaum Associates.

Bregman, J. D. (1991). Current developments in the understanding of mental retardation. Part II: Psychopathology. [Research Support, Non-U.S. Gov't; Research Support, U.S. Gov't, P.H.S.; Review]. *Journal of the American Academy of Child and Adolescent Psychiatry, 30*(6), 861–872. doi: 10.1097/00004583-199111000-00001.

Brehmer, Y., Westerberg, H., & Backman, L. (2012). Working-memory training in younger and older adults: Training gains, transfer, and maintenance. *Frontiers in Human Neuroscience, 6*, 63. doi: 10.3389/fnhum.2012.00063.

Brinley, J. F. (1965). Cognitive sets, speed and accuracy of performance in the elderly. In A. T. Welford & J. E. Birren (Eds), *Behavior, aging and the nervous system* (pp. 114–149). Springfield, IL: Thomas.

Brissette, I., Scheier, M. F., & Carver, C. S. (2002). The role of optimism in social network development, coping, and psychological adjustment during a life transition. [Research

Support, U.S. Gov't, P.H.S.]. *Journal of Personality and Social Psychology, 82*(1), 102–111.

Broadbent, D. E., Broadbent, M. H., & Jones, J. L. (1986). Performance correlates of self-reported cognitive failure and of obsessionality. [Research Support, Non-U.S. Gov't]. *British Journal of Clinical Psychology, 25*(Pt 4), 285–299.

Broadbent, D. E., Cooper, P. F., FitzGerald, P., & Parkes, K. R. (1982). The Cognitive Failures Questionnaire (CFQ) and its correlates. [Research Support, Non-U.S. Gov't]. *Br J Clin Psychol, 21 (Pt 1)*, 1-16.

Broadbent, D. E. & Gregory, M. (1965). Some confirmatory results on age differences in memory for simultaneous stimulation. *British Journal of Psychology, 56*, 77–80.

Brockmole, J. R., Parra, M. A., Della Sala, S., & Logie, R. H. (2008). Do binding deficits account for age-related decline in visual working memory? [Research Support, Non-U.S. Gov't]. *Psychonomic Bulletin and Review, 15*(3), 543–547.

Brod, M., Schmitt, E., Goodwin, M., Hodgkins, P., & Niebler, G. (2012). ADHD burden of illness in older adults: A life course perspective. *Quality of Life Research, 21*(5), 795–799. doi: 10.1007/s11136-011-9981-9.

Broese van Groenou, M. I., & Deeg, D. J. H. (2010). Formal and informal social participation of the 'young-old' in The Netherlands in 1992 and 2002. *Ageing and Society, 30*, 445–465.

Bronswijk, J. v., Kearns, W. D., & Normie, L. R. (2007). ICT infrastructures in the aging society. *Gerontechnology, 6*(3), 129–134.

Brook, D. W., Brook, J. S., Zhang, C., & Koppel, J. (2010). Association between attention-deficit/hyperactivity disorder in adolescence and substance use disorders in adulthood. [Research Support, N.I.H., Extramural]. *Archives of Pediatrics and Adolescent Medicine, 164*(10), 930–934. doi: 10.1001/archpediatrics.2010.180.

Brooks, R. A. (2002). *Flesh and machines: How robots will change us*. New York: Pantheon Books.

Brothers, L. & Ring, B. (1992). A neuroethological framework for the representation of minds. *Journal of Cognitive Neuroscience, 4*, 107–118.

Brown, J. I., Fishco, V. V., & Hanna, G. (1993). *Nelson-Denny Reading Test*. Itasca, IL: Riverside Publishing Company.

Brown, L. A. & Brockmole, J. R. (2010). The role of attention in binding visual features in working memory: Evidence from cognitive ageing. [Research Support, Non-U.S. Gov't]. *Quarterly Journal of Experimental Psychology (Hove), 63*(10), 2067–2079. doi: 10.1080/17470211003721675.

Brown, R. & McNeill, D. (1966). The 'tip of the tongue' phenomenon. *Journal of Verbal Learning and Verbal Behavior, 5*(4), 325–337.

Brown, R. G. & Marsden, C. D. (1984). How common is dementia in Parkinson's disease? *Lancet, 2*(8414), 1262–1265.

Bruce, D. (1985). The how and why of ecological memory. *Journal of Experimental Psychology: General, 114*(1), 78–90. doi: 10.1037/0096-3445.114.1.78.

Brummett, B. H., Babyak, M. A., Williams, R. B., Barefoot, J. C., Costa, P. T., & Siegler, I. C. (2006). NEO personality domains and gender predict levels and trends in body mass index over 14 years during midlife. *Journal of Research in Personality, 40*(3), 222–236.

Buchner, D. M. & Larson, E. B. (1987). Falls and fractures in patients with Alzheimer-type dementia. [Research Support, Non-U.S. Gov't; Research Support, U.S. Gov't, P.H.S.]. *JAMA, 257*(11), 1492–1495.

Buckner, R. L. (2004). Memory and executive function in aging and AD: Multiple factors that cause decline and reserve factors that compensate. [Research Support, Non-U.S. Gov't; Research Support, U.S. Gov't, P.H.S.; Review]. *Neuron, 44*(1), 195–208. doi: 10.1016/j.neuron.2004.09.006.

Bucks, R. S. & Radford, S. A. (2004). Emotion processing in Alzheimer's disease. *Aging and Mental Health*, *8*(3), 222–232. doi: 10.1080/13607860410001669750.

Buhler, C. (1933). *Der menschliche Lebenslauf als psychologisches Problem*. Leipzig: S. Hirzel.

Buhr, G. T., Kuchibhatla, M., & Clipp, E. C. (2006). Caregivers' reasons for nursing home placement: Clues for improving discussions with families prior to the transition. [Research Support, N.I.H., Extramural; Research Support, U.S. Gov't, Non-P.H.S.]. *Gerontologist*, *46*(1), 52–61.

Bull, R., Phillips, L. H., & Conway, C. A. (2008). The role of control functions in mentalizing: Dual-task studies of theory of mind and executive function. [Comparative Study; Randomized Controlled Trial]. *Cognition*, *107*(2), 663–672. doi: 10.1016/j.cognition.2007.07.015.

Bunce, D. J., Anstey, K. J., Christensen, H., Dear, K., Wen, W., & Sachdev, P. (2007). White matter hyperintensities and within-person variability in community-dwelling adults aged 60–64 years. [Research Support, Non-U.S. Gov't]. *Neuropsychologia*, *45*(9), 2009–2015. doi: 10.1016/j.neuropsychologia.2007.02.006.

Bunce, D. J., Warr, P. B., & Cochrane, T. (1993). Blocks in choice responding as a function of age and physical fitness. *Psychology and Aging*, *8*(1), 26–33.

Burke, D. M., MacKay, D. G., Worthley, J. S., & Wade, E. (1991). On the tip of the tongue: What causes word finding failures in young and older adults? *Journal of Memory and Language*, *30*(5), 542–579. doi: 10.1016/0749-596x(91)90026-g.

Butcher, J. N., Dahlstrom, W. G., Graham, J. R., Tellegen, A., & Kaemmer, B. (1989). *Manual for the restandardized Minnesota multiphasic personality inventory: MMPI-2. An administrative and interpretative guide*. Minneapolis, MN: University of Minnesota Press.

Butler, A. A., Lord, S. R., & Fitzpatrick, R. C. (2011). Reach distance but not judgment error is associated with falls in older people. [Research Support, Non-U.S. Gov't]. *Journals of Gerontology A: Biological Sciences and Medical Sciences*, *66*(8), 896–903. doi: 10.1093/gerona/glr071.

Butler, R. N. (1969). Age-ism: Another form of bigotry. *The Gerontologist*, *9*(4 Pt 1), 243–246.

Butler, R. N., Lewis, M. I., & Sunderland, T. (1998). *Aging and mental health: Positive psychosocial and biomedical approaches* (5th edn). Boston: Allyn & Bacon.

Byrd, M. (1985). Age differences in the ability to recall and summarize textual information. *Experimental Aging Research*, *11*(2), 87–91.

Cabeza, R. (2002). Hemispheric asymmetry reduction in older adults: The HAROLD model. [Research Support, Non-U.S. Gov't; Review]. *Psychology and Aging*, *17*(1), 85–100.

Cabeza, R. (2004). Neuroscience frontiers in cognitive aging. In R. A. Dixon, L. Backman, & L. G. Nilsson (Eds), *New frontiers in cognitive aging* (pp. 179–196). New York: Oxford University Press.

Cacace, A. T. (2003). Expanding the biological basis of tinnitus: Crossmodal origins and the role of neuroplasticity. [Review]. *Hearing research*, *175*(1–2), 112–132.

Campisi, J. (1997). Aging and cancer: The double-edged sword of replicative senescence. [Research Support, U.S. Gov't, Non-P.H.S.; Research Support, U.S. Gov't, P.H.S.; Review]. *Journal of the American Geriatrics Society*, *45*(4), 482–488.

Campbell-Sills, L., Cohan, S. L., & Stein, M. B. (2006). Relationship of resilience to personality, coping, and psychiatric symptoms in young adults. [Research Support, N.I.H., Extramural]. *Behaviour Research and Therapy*, *44*(4), 585–599. doi: 10.1016/j.brat.2005.05.001.

Camus, V., Kraehenbuhl, H., Preisig, M., Bula, C. J., & Waeber, G. (2004). Geriatric depression and vascular diseases: What are the links? [Review]. *Journal of Affective Disorders, 81*(1), 1–16. doi: 10.1016/j.jad.2003.08.003.

Canitano, R. & Vivanti, G. (2007). Tics and Tourette syndrome in autism spectrum disorders. *Autism, 11*(1), 19–28. doi: 10.1177/1362361307070992.

Cantor, M. H. (1991). Family and community: Changing roles in an aging society. [Research Support, Non-U.S. Gov't]. *Gerontologist, 31*(3), 337–346.

Cappell, K. A., Gmeindl, L., & Reuter-Lorenz, P. A. (2010). Age differences in prefontal recruitment during verbal working memory maintenance depend on memory load. [Research Support, N.I.H., Extramural]. *Cortex, 46*(4), 462–473. doi: 10.1016/j. cortex.2009.11.009.

Carr, D. S., Nesse, R. M., & Wortman, C. B. (2006). *Spousal bereavement in late life.* New York, NY: Springer.

Carroll, C. C., Dickinson, J. M., Haus, J. M., Lee, G. A., Hollon, C. J., Aagaard, P., Magnusson, S. P., & Trappe, T. A. (2008). Influence of aging on the in vivo properties of human patellar tendon. [Comparative Study; Research Support, N.I.H., Extramural; Research Support, Non-U.S. Gov't]. *Journal of Applied Physiology, 105*(6), 1907–1915. doi: 10.1152/japplphysiol.00059.2008.

Carstensen, L. L. (1995). Evidence for a life-span theory of socioemotional selectivity. *Current Directions in Psychological Science, 4*(5), 151–156.

Carstensen, L. L., Fung, H. H., & Charles, S. T. (2003). Socioemotional selectivity theory and the regulation of emotion in the second half of life. *Motivation and Emotion, 27,* 103–123.

Carstensen, L. L., Isaacowitz, D. M., & Charles, S. T. (1999). Taking time seriously. A theory of socioemotional selectivity. [Research Support, U.S. Gov't, P.H.S.; Review]. *American Psychologist, 54*(3), 165–181.

Carstensen, L. L., Pasupathi, M., Mayr, U., & Nesselroade, J. R. (2000). Emotional experience in everyday life across the adult life span. [Research Support, U.S. Gov't, P.H.S.]. *Journal of Personality and Social Psychology, 79*(4), 644–655.

Carter, G. & Jancar, J. (1983). Mortality in the mentally handicapped: A 50-year survey at the Stoke Park group of hospitals (1930–1980). *Journal of Mental Deficiency Research, 27*(Pt 2), 143–156.

Cartwright-Hatton, S. & Wells, A. (1997). Beliefs about worry and intrusions: The Meta-Cognitions Questionnaire and its correlates. [Research Support, Non-U.S. Gov't]. *Journal of Anxiety Disorders, 11*(3), 279–296.

Carver, C. S., Kus, L. A., & Scheier, M. F. (1994). Effects of good versus bad mood and optimistic versus pessimistic outlook on social acceptance versus rejection. *Journal of Social and Clinical Psychology, 13*(2), 138–151.

Carver, C. S. & Scheier, M. F. (1999). Stress, coping, and self-regulatory processes. In L. A. Pervin & O. P. John (Eds), *Handbook of personality: Theory and research* (2nd edn, pp. 553–573). New York; London: Guilford Press.

Casey, B. J. & Durston, S. (2006). From behavior to cognition to the brain and back: What have we learned from functional imaging studies of attention deficit hyperactivity disorder? [Comment; Editorial]. *Journal of Mental Deficiency Research, 163*(6), 957–960. doi: 10.1176/appi.ajp.163.6.957.

Casey, B. J., Tottenham, N., Liston, C., & Durston, S. (2005). Imaging the developing brain: What have we learned about cognitive development? [Research Support, N.I.H., Extramural; Research Support, U.S. Gov't, P.H.S.; Review]. *Trends in Cognitive Sciences, 9*(3), 104–110. doi: 10.1016/j.tics.2005.01.011.

Caspi, A., McClay, J., Moffitt, T. E., Mill, J., Martin, J., Craig, I. W., Taylor, A., & Poulton, R. (2002). Role of genotype in the cycle of violence in maltreated children. [Research Support, Non-U.S. Gov't; Research Support, U.S. Gov't, P.H.S.]. *Science, 297*(5582), 851–854. doi: 10.1126/science.1072290.

Casten, R. J., Rovner, B. W., Edmonds, S. E., DeAngelis, D., & Basford, C. (1999). *Personality traits as predictors of vision-specific function among older people experiencing vision loss.* Paper presented at the American Psychological Association, Boston.

Cattell, R. B. (1963). Theory of fluid and crystallized intelligence: A critical experiment. *Journal of Educational Psychology, 54*(1), 1–22.

Cavanaugh, J. C., Grady, J. G., & Perlmutter, M. (1983). Forgetting and use of memory aids in 20 to 70 year olds everyday life. [Research Support, U.S. Gov't, Non-P.H.S.; Research Support, U.S. Gov't, P.H.S.]. *International Journal of Aging and Human Development, 17*(2), 113–122.

Cerella, J. (1994). Generalized slowing in Brinley plots. [Research Support, U.S. Gov't, Non-P.H.S.]. *Journal of Gerontology, 49*(2), P65–71.

Chap, J. B. (1985). Moral judgment in middle and late adulthood: The effects of age-appropriate moral dilemmas and spontaneous role taking. *International Journal of Aging and Human Development, 22*(3), 161–172.

Charles, S. T. & Carstensen, L. L. (2010). Social and emotional aging. [Research Support, N.I.H., Extramural; Review]. *Annual Review of Psychology, 61,* 383–409. doi: 10.1146/annurev.psych.093008.100448.

Charlton, R. A., Barrick, T. R., Markus, H. S., & Morris, R. G. (2009). Theory of mind associations with other cognitive functions and brain imaging in normal aging. [Comparative Study; Research Support, Non-U.S. Gov't]. *Psychology and Aging, 24*(2), 338–348. doi: 10.1037/a0015225.

Charman, W. N. (2008). The eye in focus: Accommodation and presbyopia. [Review]. *Clinical and Experimental Optometry, 91*(3), 207–225. doi: 10.1111/j.1444-0938.2008.00256.x.

Charness, N. (1985). Ageing and problem-solving performance. In N. Charness (Ed.), *Ageing and human performance* (pp. 225–260). Chichester: John Wiley.

Charness, N., Champion, M., & Yordon, R. (2010). Designing products for older consumers: A human factors perspective. In A. L. Drolet, N. D. p. Schwarz, & C. Yoon (Eds), *The aging consumer* (pp. 249–268). London: Routledge.

Charness, N. & Czaja, S. J. (2005). Adaptations to new technologies. In M. L. Johnson (Ed.), *The Cambridge handbook of age and ageing* (pp. 662–996). Cambridge: Cambridge University Press.

Chen, J. C., Brunner, R. L., Ren, H., Wassertheil-Smoller, S., Larson, J. C., Levine, D. W., Allison, M., Naughton, M. J., & Stefanick, M. L. (2008). Sleep duration and risk of ischemic stroke in postmenopausal women. [Research Support, N.I.H., Extramural]. *Stroke, 39*(12), 3185–3192. doi: 10.1161/STROKEAHA.108.521773.

Cheng, S. T., Fung, H. H., & Chan, A. C. (2009). Self-perception and psychological well-being: The benefits of foreseeing a worse future. [Research Support, Non-U.S. Gov't]. *Psychology and Aging, 24*(3), 623–633. doi: 10.1037/a0016410.

Chida, Y. & Steptoe, A. (2008). Positive psychological well-being and mortality: A quantitative review of prospective observational studies. [Research Support, Non-U.S. Gov't; Review]. *Psychosomatic Medicine, 70*(7), 741–756. doi: 10.1097/PSY.0b013e31818105ba.

Christensen, H., Dear, K. B., Anstey, K. J., Parslow, R. A., Sachdev, P., & Jorm, A. F. (2005). Within-occasion intraindividual variability and preclinical diagnostic status: Is intraindividual variability an indicator of mild cognitive impairment? [Comparative Study; Research Support, Non-U.S. Gov't]. *Neuropsychology, 19*(3), 309–317. doi: 10.1037/0894-4105.19.3.309.

Christopher, G. & MacDonald, J. (2005). The impact of clinical depression on working memory. *Cognitive Neuropsychiatry, 10*(5), 379–399. doi: 10.1080/13546800444000128.

Christopher, G., Sutherland, D., & Smith, A. (2005). Effects of caffeine in non-withdrawn volunteers. [Clinical Trial; Comparative Study; Controlled Clinical Trial; Research Support, Non-U.S. Gov't]. *Human Psychopharmacology, 20*(1), 47–53. doi: 10.1002/hup.658.

Clark, R. A., Pua, Y. H., Fortin, K., Ritchie, C., Webster, K. E., Denehy, L., & Bryant, A. L. (2012). Validity of the Microsoft Kinect for assessment of postural control. [Comparative Study; Research Support, Non-U.S. Gov't; Validation Studies]. *Gait and Posture, 36*(3), 372–377. doi: 10.1016/j.gaitpost.2012.03.033.

Clarke, I. H. & Griffin, M. (2008). Visible and invisible ageing: Beauty work as a response to ageism. *Ageing and Society, 28*, 653–674.

Clarke, R., Emberson, J., Fletcher, A., Breeze, E., Marmot, M., & Shipley, M. J. (2009). Life expectancy in relation to cardiovascular risk factors: 38 year follow-up of 19,000 men in the Whitehall study. [Research Support, Non-U.S. Gov't]. *BMJ, 339*, b3513. doi: 10.1136/bmj.b3513.

Clarkson-Smith, L. & Hartley, A. A. (1989). Relationships between physical exercise and cognitive abilities in older adults. *Psychology and Aging, 4*(2), 183–189.

Cohen, G. D. (1990). Psychology and mental health in the mature and elderly adult. In J. E. Birren & K. W. Schaie (Eds) with M. Gatz, T. Salthouse & C. Schooler (Assoc. eds), *Handbook of the psychology of aging* (3rd edn, pp. 359–371). San Diego; London: Academic Press.

Cohen, J. D. & Servan-Schreiber, D. (1992). Context, cortex, and dopamine: A connectionist approach to behavior and biology in schizophrenia. [Research Support, Non-U.S. Gov't; Research Support, U.S. Gov't, P.H.S.; Review]. *Psychological Review, 99*(1), 45–77.

Cohen, S. (2004). Social relationships and health. [Addresses; Research Support, U.S. Gov't, P.H.S.]. *American Psychologist, 59*(8), 676–684. doi: 10.1037/0003-066X.59.8.676.

Cohn, L. D. & Westenberg, P. M. (2004). Intelligence and maturity: Meta-analytic evidence for the incremental and discriminant validity of Loevinger's measure of ego development. [Meta-Analysis; Research Support, Non-U.S. Gov't]. *Journal of Personality and Social Psychology, 86*(5), 760–772. doi: 10.1037/0022-3514.86.5.760.

Colcombe, S. J., Erickson, K. I., Raz, N., Webb, A. G., Cohen, N. J., McAuley, E., & Kramer, A. F. (2003). Aerobic fitness reduces brain tissue loss in aging humans. [Comparative Study; Research Support, U.S. Gov't, P.H.S.]. *Journals of Gerontology Series A: Biological Sciences and Medical Sciences, 58*(2), 176–180.

Colcombe, S. J. & Kramer, A. F. (2003). Fitness effects on the cognitive function of older adults: A meta-analytic study. [Meta-Analysis; Research Support, Non-U.S. Gov't; Research Support, U.S. Gov't, P.H.S.]. *Psychological Science: A journal of the American Psychological Society/APS, 14*(2), 125–130.

Colcombe, S. J., Kramer, A. F., Erickson, K. I., Scalf, P., McAuley, E., Cohen, N. J., Webb, A., Jerome, G. J., Marquez, D. X., & Elavsky, S. (2004). Cardiovascular fitness, cortical plasticity, and aging. [Clinical Trial; Comparative Study; Randomized Controlled Trial; Research Support, Non-U.S. Gov't; Research Support, U.S. Gov't, P.H.S.]. *Proceedings of the National Academy of Sciences of the United States of America, 101*(9), 3316–3321. doi: 10.1073/pnas.0400266101.

Comijs, H. C., Gerritsen, L., Penninx, B. W., Bremmer, M. A., Deeg, D. J., & Geerlings, M. I. (2010). The association between serum cortisol and cognitive decline in older persons. [Research Support, Non-U.S. Gov't]. *American Journal of Geriatric Psychiatry, 18*(1), 42–50. doi: 10.1097/JGP.0b013e3181b970ae.

'Congestive heart failure' (2008) *The Columbia encyclopedia*. New York: Columbia University Press. Retrieved from http://www.credoreference.com/entry/columency/congestive_heart_failure.

Connell, C. (1994). Impact of spouse caregiving on health behaviors and physical and mental health status. *American Journal of Alzheimer's Disease and Other Dementias, 9*, 26–36.

Connidis, I. A. (2001). *Family ties & aging*. Thousand Oaks, CA; London: Sage.

Connor, L. T., Spiro, A., 3rd, Obler, L. K., & Albert, M. L. (2004). Change in object naming ability during adulthood. [Research Support, U.S. Gov't, Non-P.H.S.; Research Support, U.S. Gov't, P.H.S.]. *Journals of Gerontology B: Psychological Sciences and Social Sciences, 59*(5), P203–209.

Consedine, N. S. & Magai, C. (2003). Attachment and emotion experience in later life: The view from emotions theory. [Research Support, U.S. Gov't, P.H.S.]. *Attachment and Human Development, 5*(2), 165–187. doi: 10.1080/1461673031000108496.

Cook, I. A., Leuchter, A. F., Morgan, M. L., Dunkin, J. J., Witte, E., David, S., Mickes, L., O'Hara, R., Simon, S., Lufkin, R., Abrams, M., & Rosenberg, S. (2004). Longitudinal progression of subclinical structural brain disease in normal aging. [Research Support, U.S. Gov't, P.H.S.]. *American Journal of Geriatric Psychiatry, 12*(2), 190–200.

Cooney, M. T., Dudina, A., De Bacquer, D., Wilhelmsen, L., Sans, S., Menotti, A., De Backer, G., Jousilahti, P., Keil, U., Thomsen, T., Whincup, P., & Graham, I. M. (2009). HDL cholesterol protects against cardiovascular disease in both genders, at all ages and at all levels of risk. [Multicenter Study]. *Atherosclerosis, 206*(2), 611–616. doi: 10.1016/j.atherosclerosis.2009.02.041.

Cooper, S. A. (1997a). Epidemiology of psychiatric disorders in elderly compared with younger adults with learning disabilities. [Comparative Study]. *American Psychologist, 170*, 375–380.

Cooper, S. A. (1997b). Psychiatry of elderly compared to younger adults with intellectual disabilities. *Journal of Applied Research in Intellectual Disabilities, 10*(4), 303–311.

Cooper, S. A. (1998). Clinical study of the effects of age on the physical health of adults with mental retardation. *American Journal of Mental Retardation, 102*(6), 582–589.

Cordingley, L. & Webb, C. (1997). Independence and aging. *Reviews in Clinical Gerontology, 7*(2), 137–146.

Corey-Bloom, J. (2000). Dementia. In S. K. Whitbourne (Ed.), *Psychopathology in later adulthood* (pp. 217–243). New York; Chichester: Wiley.

Coricelli, G. (2005). Two-levels of mental states attribution: From automaticity to voluntariness. [Research Support, Non-U.S. Gov't]. *Neuropsychologia, 43*(2), 294–300. doi: 10.1016/j.neuropsychologia.2004.11.015.

Cornoldi, C. & Vecchi, T. (2002). *Visuo-spatial working memory and individual differences*. Hove: Psychology Press.

Corr, C. A., Nabe, C., & Corr, D. M. (2004). *Death and dying, life and living* (4th edn). Belmont, CA; London: Thomson Wadsworth.

Costa, P. T. & McCrae, R. R. (1992). *Professional manual: Revised NEO personality inventory (NEO-PI-R) and the NEO Five-Factor Inventory (NEO-FFI)*. Odessa, FL: Psychological Assessment Resources.

Courchesne, E. (2004). Brain development in autism: Early overgrowth followed by premature arrest of growth. [Research Support, U.S. Gov't, P.H.S.; Review]. *Mental Retardation and Developmental Disabilities Research Reviews, 10*(2), 106–111. doi: 10.1002/mrdd.20020.

Courchesne, E., Karns, C. M., Davis, H. R., Ziccardi, R., Carper, R. A., Tigue, Z. D., Chisum, H. J., Moses, P., Pierce, K., Lord, C., Lincoln, A. J., Pizzo, S., Schreibman, L.,

Haas, R. H., Akshoomoff, N. A., & Courchesne, R. Y. (2001). Unusual brain growth patterns in early life in patients with autistic disorder: An MRI study. [Research Support, U.S. Gov't, P.H.S.]. *Neurology, 57*(2), 245–254.

Cousins, M. & Smyth, M. M. (2003). Developmental coordination impairments in adulthood. *Human Movement Science, 22*(4–5), 433–459.

Covinsky, K. E., Lindquist, K., Dunlop, D. D., & Yelin, E. (2009). Pain, functional limitations, and aging. [Research Support, N.I.H., Extramural]. *Journal of the American Geriatrics Society, 57*(9), 1556–1561. doi: 10.1111/j.1532-5415.2009.02388.x.

Cowan, N. (1995). *Attention and memory: An integrated framework.* New York; Oxford: Oxford University Press; Clarendon Press.

Cowan, N., Naveh-Benjamin, M., Kilb, A., & Saults, J. S. (2006). Life-span development of visual working memory: When is feature binding difficult? [Comparative Study; Research Support, N.I.H., Extramural; Research Support, Non-U.S. Gov't]. *Developmental Psychology, 42*(6), 1089–1102. doi: 10.1037/0012-1649.42.6.1089.

Cramer, P. (2003). Personality change in later adulthood is predicted by defense mechanism use in early adulthood. *Journal of Research in Personality, 37*(1), 76–104.

Cramer, P. & Jones, C. J. (2007). Defense mechanisms predict differential lifespan change in self-control and self-acceptance. *Journal of Research in Personality, 41*(4), 841–855.

Cramer, P. & Jones, C. J. (2008). Narcissism, identification, and longitudinal change in psychological health: Dynamic predictions. *Journal of Research in Personality, 42*(5), 1148–1159.

Craik, F. I. M. (1986). A functional account of age difference in memory. In F. Klix & H. Hagendorf (Eds), *Human memory and cognitive capabilities: Mechanisms and performances* (pp. 409–422). New York: Elsevier Science.

Craik, F. I. M. (2005). On reducing age-related declines in memory. In J. D. Duncan, P. McLeod, & L. Phillips (Eds), *Measuring the mind: Speed, control, and age* (pp. 275–292). Oxford: Oxford University Press.

Craik, F. I. M. & Bialystok, E. (2006). Cognition through the lifespan: Mechanisms of change. [Review]. *Trends in Cognitive Sciences, 10*(3), 131–138. doi: 10.1016/j.tics.2006.01.007.

Craik, F. I. M., Byrd, M., & Swanson, J. M. (1987). Patterns of memory loss in three elderly samples. [Research Support, Non-U.S. Gov't]. *Psychology and Aging, 2*(1), 79–86.

Crocker, J. & Wolfe, C. T. (2001). Contingencies of self-worth. [Research Support, U.S. Gov't, Non-P.H.S.; Research Support, U.S. Gov't, P.H.S.; Review]. *Psychological Review, 108*(3), 593–623.

Cristofalo, V. J., Tresini, M., Francis, M. K., & Volker, C. (1999). Biological theories of senescence. In V. L. Bengtson & K. W. Schaie (Eds), *Handbook of theories of aging* (pp. 98–112). New York: Springer.

Cuddy, A. J. C. & Fiske, S. T. (2002). Doddering but dear: Process, content, and function of stereotyping older persons. In T. D. Nelson (Ed.), *Ageism: Stereotyping and prejudice against older persons* (pp. 3–26). Cambridge, MA; London: MIT Press.

Cuerva, A. G., Sabe, L., Kuzis, G., Tiberti, C., Dorrego, F., & Starkstein, S. E. (2001). Theory of mind and pragmatic abilities in dementia. [Research Support, Non-U.S. Gov't]. *Neuropsychiatry, Neuropsychology, and Behavioral Neurology, 14*(3), 153–158.

Culbertson, W. C. & Zilmer, E. A. (2000). *Tower of London-Drexel University* (2nd edn). North Tonawanda, NY: Multi-Health Systems.

Cumming, E. & Henry, W. E. (1961). *Growing old: The process of disengagement.* New York: Basic Books.

Cummins, R. A. (1997). *Comprehensive Quality of Life Scale: Adult (ComQol-A5): Manual,* Centre for Australia-Asia Studies, Deaking University.

Cusack, B. J. (2004). Pharmacokinetics in older persons. [Review]. *American Journal of Geriatric Pharmacotherapy*, 2(4), 274–302.

Cutler, S. J. & Hodgson, L. G. (1996). Anticipatory dementia: A link between memory appraisals and concerns about developing Alzheimer's disease. [Research Support, Non-U.S. Gov't]. *The Gerontologist*, 36(5), 657–664.

Czaja, S. J., Charness, N., Fisk, A. D., Hertzog, C., Nair, S. N., Rogers, W. A., & Sharit, J. (2006). Factors predicting the use of technology: Findings from the Center for Research and Education on Aging and Technology Enhancement (CREATE). [Research Support, N.I.H., Extramural]. *Psychology and Aging*, 21(2), 333–352. doi: 10.1037/0882-7974.21.2.333.

Czeisler, C. A., Duffy, J. F., Shanahan, T. L., Brown, E. N., Mitchell, J. F., Rimmer, D. W., Ronda, J. M., Silva, E. J., Allan, J. S., Emens, J. S., Dijk, D. J., & Kronauer, R. E. (1999). Stability, precision, and near-24-hour period of the human circadian pacemaker. [Comparative Study; Research Support, U.S. Gov't, Non-P.H.S.; Research Support, U.S. Gov't, P.H.S.]. *Science*, 284(5423), 2177–2181.

Czeisler, C. A., Kronauer, R. E., Allan, J. S., Duffy, J. F., Jewett, M. E., Brown, E. N., & Ronda, J. M. (1989). Bright light induction of strong (type 0) resetting of the human circadian pacemaker. [Research Support, Non-U.S. Gov't; Research Support, U.S. Gov't, P.H.S.]. *Science*, 244(4910), 1328–1333.

Dahlin, E., Neely, A. S., Larsson, A., Backman, L., & Nyberg, L. (2008a). Transfer of learning after updating training mediated by the striatum. [Randomized Controlled Trial; Research Support, Non-U.S. Gov't]. *Science*, 320(5882), 1510–1512. doi: 10.1126/science.1155466.

Dahlin, E., Nyberg, L., Backman, L., & Neely, A. S. (2008b). Plasticity of executive functioning in young and older adults: Immediate training gains, transfer, and long-term maintenance. [Research Support, Non-U.S. Gov't]. *Psychology and Aging*, 23(4), 720–730. doi: 10.1037/a0014296.

Dalton, D. S., Cruickshanks, K. J., Klein, B. E., Klein, R., Wiley, T. L., & Nondahl, D. M. (2003). The impact of hearing loss on quality of life in older adults. [Research Support, U.S. Gov't, P.H.S.]. *The Gerontologist*, 43(5), 661–668.

Dannefer, D. (1987). Aging as intracohort differentiation: Accentuation, the Matthew effect, and the life course. *Sociological Forum*, 2, 211–236.

Dar, K. (2006). Alcohol use disorders in elderly people: Fact or fiction? *Advances in Psychiatric Treatment*, 12(3), 173–181.

Davies, E. & Cartwright, S. (2011). Psychological and psychosocial predictors of attitudes to working past normal retirement age. *Employee Relations*, 33(3), 249–268.

Davis, C. G., Nolen-Hoeksema, S., & Larson, J. (1998). Making sense of loss and benefiting from the experience: Two construals of meaning. [Research Support, Non-U.S. Gov't; Research Support, U.S. Gov't, P.H.S.]. *Journal of Personality and Social Psychology*, 75(2), 561–574.

Davis, S. W., Dennis, N. A., Daselaar, S. M., Fleck, M. S., & Cabeza, R. (2008). Que PASA? The posterior–anterior shift in aging. [Research Support, N.I.H., Extramural]. *Cerebral Cortex*, 18(5), 1201–1209. doi: 10.1093/cercor/bhm155.

Davison, B. J., Kirk, P., Degner, L. F., & Hassard, T. H. (1999). Information and patient participation in screening for prostate cancer. [Clinical Trial; Randomized Controlled Trial; Research Support, Non-U.S. Gov't]. *Patient Education and Counseling*, 37(3), 255–263.

Dawson, G., Toth, K., Abbott, R., Osterling, J., Munson, J., Estes, A., & Liaw, J. (2004). Early social attention impairments in autism: Social orienting, joint attention, and attention to distress. [Research Support, U.S. Gov't, P.H.S.]. *Developmental Psychology*, 40(2), 271–283. doi: 10.1037/0012-1649.40.2.271.

Deal, C. (2004). Osteoarthritis. *Encyclopedia of women's health*. New York: Springer Science+Business Media.

Deeg, D. J. & Huisman, M. (2010). Cohort differences in 3-year adaptation to health problems among Dutch middle-aged, 1992–1995 and 2002–2005. *European Journal of Ageing, 7*(3), 157–165. doi: 10.1007/s10433-010-0157-1.

Degroot, D. W. & Kenney, W. L. (2007). Impaired defense of core temperature in aged humans during mild cold stress. [Comparative Study; Research Support, N.I.H., Extramural]. *American Journal of Physiology: Regulatory, Integrative and Comparative Physiology, 292*(1), R103–108. doi: 10.1152/ajpregu.00074.2006.

de Groot, C. P., Perdigao, A. L., & Deurenberg, P. (1996). Longitudinal changes in anthropometric characteristics of elderly Europeans. SENECA Investigators. *European Journal of Clinical Nutrition, 50* (Suppl. 2), S9–15.

De Groot, J. C., De Leeuw, F. E., Oudkerk, M., Van Gijn, J., Hofman, A., Jolles, J., & Breteler, M. M. (2002). Periventricular cerebral white matter lesions predict rate of cognitive decline. [Research Support, Non-U.S. Gov't]. *Annals of Neurology, 52*(3), 335–341. doi: 10.1002/ana.10294.

Dehon, H. & Bredart, S. (2004). False memories: Young and older adults think of semantic associates at the same rate, but young adults are more successful at source monitoring. [Research Support, Non-U.S. Gov't]. *Psychology and Aging, 19*(1), 191–197. doi: 10.1037/0882-7974.19.1.191.

Dellenbach, M. & Zimprich, D. (2008). Typical intellectual engagement and cognition in old age. [Research Support, Non-U.S. Gov't]. *Neuropsychology, Development, and Cognition. Section B, Aging, Neuropsychology and Cognition, 15*(2), 208–231. doi: 10.1080/13825580701338094.

de Magalhaes, J. P., Costa, J., & Church, G. M. (2007). An analysis of the relationship between metabolism, developmental schedules, and longevity using phylogenetic independent contrasts. [Research Support, N.I.H., Extramural]. *Journals of Gerontology Series A: Biological Sciences and Medical Sciences, 62*(2), 149–160.

Dennis, W. (1966). Creative productivity between the ages of 20 and 80 years. *Journal of Gerontology, 21*(1), 1–8.

DePaulo, B. M. (2007). *Singled out: How singles are stereotyped, stigmatized, and ignored, and still live happily ever after*. New York: St Martin's Griffin.

De Pisapia, N., Repovš, G., & Braver, T. S. (2008). Computational models of attention and cognitive control. *The Cambridge handbook of computational psychology*. Cambridge: Cambridge University Press. Retrieved from http://www.credoreference.com/entry/cupcomppsyc/computational_models_of_attention_and_cognitive_control.

De Rosa, E. & Baxter, M. G. (2005). Basal forebrain. *Encyclopedia of cognitive science*. Chichester, West Sussex: Wiley. Retrieved from http://www.credoreference.com/entry/wileycs/basal_forebrain.

De Vaus, D., Wells, Y., Kendig, H., & Quine, S. (2007). Does gradual retirement have better outcomes than abrupt retirement? Results from an Australian panel study. *Ageing and Society, 27*, 667–682.

de Vries, B. (1996). The understanding of friendship: An adult lifecourse perspective. In C. Magai & S. H. McFadden (Eds), *Handbook of emotion, adult development, and aging*. San Diego, CA; London: Academic Press.

Devolder, P. A. & Pressley, M. (1992). Causal attributions and strategy use in relation to memory performance differences in younger and older adults. *Applied Cognitive Psychology, 6*, 629–642.

Diamond, J. M. (1991). *The rise and fall of the third chimpanzee*. London: Radius.

Dick, L. P., Gallagher-Thompson, D., & Thompson, L. W. (1999). Cognitive-behavioral therapy. In R. T. Woods (Ed.), *Psychological problems of ageing: Assessment, treatment and care* (pp. 253–291). Chichester: Wiley.

Dickin, D. C., Brown, L. A., & Doan, J. B. (2006). Age-dependent differences in the time course of postural control during sensory perturbations. [Comparative Study]. *Aging Clinical and Experimental Research, 18*(2), 94–99.

Diehl, M., Coyle, N., & Labouvie-Vief, G. (1996). Age and sex differences in strategies of coping and defense across the life span. [Research Support, U.S. Gov't, P.H.S.]. *Psychology and Aging, 11*(1), 127–139.

Diehl, M. & Hay, E. L. (2007). Contextualized self-representations in adulthood. [Review]. *Journal of Personality, 75*(6), 1255–1283. doi: 10.1111/j.1467-6494.2007.00475.x.

Diener, E. & Lucas, R. E. (2000). Subjective emotional well-being. In J. M. Haviland-Jones & M. J. Lewis (Eds), *Handbook of emotions* (2nd edn, pp. 325–337). New York; London: Guilford Press.

Dixon, R. A. & Hultsch, D. F. (1999). Intellectual and cognitive potential in late life. In J. C. Cavanaugh & S. K. Whitbourne (Eds), *Gerontology: An interdisciplinary perspective* (pp. 213–237). New York: Oxford University Press.

Dixon, R. A., Backman, L., & Nilsson, L-G. (2004). *New frontiers in cognitive aging.* Oxford: Oxford University Press.

Dodson, C. S., Bawa, S., & Slotnick, S. D. (2007). Aging, source memory, and misrecollections. [Research Support, Non-U.S. Gov't]. *Journal of Experimental Psychology Learning Memory and Cognition, 33*(1), 169–181. doi: 10.1037/0278-7393.33.1.169.

Donahue, E. M., Robins, R. W., Roberts, B. W., & John, O. P. (1993). The divided self: Concurrent and longitudinal effects of psychological adjustment and social roles on self-concept differentiation. [Research Support, U.S. Gov't, Non-P.H.S.; Research Support, U.S. Gov't, P.H.S.]. *Journal of Personality and Social Psychology, 64*(5), 834–846.

Dorshkind, K., Montecino-Rodriguez, E., & Signer, R. A. (2009). The ageing immune system: Is it ever too old to become young again? [Review]. *Nature Reviews Immunology, 9*(1), 57–62. doi: 10.1038/nri2471.

Drexler, A. J. & Robertson, C. (2001). Type 2 diabetes. How new insights, new drugs are changing clinical practice. [Review]. *Geriatrics, 56*(6), 20–24, 32–33.

Duberstein, P. R. & Conwell, Y. (2000). Suicide. In S. K. Whitbourne (Ed.), *Psychopathology in later adulthood* (pp. 245–275). New York; Chichester: Wiley.

Duchesne, D. (2004). More seniors at work. *Perspective on Labour and Income, 16,* 55–67.

Duke, J., Leventhal, H., Brownlee, S., & Leventhal, E. A. (2002). Giving up and replacing activities in response to illness. [Research Support, U.S. Gov't, P.H.S.]. *Journals of Gerontology B: Psychological Sciences and Social Sciences, 57*(4), P367–376.

Dunabeitia, J. A., Marin, A., Aviles, A., Perea, M., & Carreiras, M. (2009). Constituent priming effects: Evidence for preserved morphological processing in healthy old readers. *European Journal of Cognitive Psychology, 21*(2–3), 283–302.

Dunlosky, J. & Nelson, T. O. (1992). Importance of the kind of cue for judgments of learning (JOL) and the delayed-JOL effect. [Research Support, U.S. Gov't, P.H.S.]. *Memory & Cognition, 20*(4), 374–380.

Dutta, T. (2012). Evaluation of the Kinect sensor for 3-D kinematic measurement in the workplace. [Research Support, Non-U.S. Gov't]. *Applied Ergonomics, 43*(4), 645–649. doi: 10.1016/j.apergo.2011.09.011.

Duval, C., Piolino, P., Bejanin, A., Eustache, F., & Desgranges, B. (2011). Age effects on different components of theory of mind. *Consciousness and Cognition, 20*(3), 627–642. doi: 10.1016/j.concog.2010.10.025.

d'Ydewalle, G., Luwel, K., & Brunfaut, E. (1999). The importance of on-going concurrent activities as a function of age in time- and event-based prospective memory. *European Journal of Cognitive Psychology, 11*(2), 219–237. doi: 10.1080/713752309.

Dywan, J. & Jacoby, L. (1990). Effects of aging on source monitoring: Differences in susceptibility to false fame. [Research Support, Non-U.S. Gov't]. *Psychology and Aging, 5*(3), 379–387.

Edginton, T. & Rusted, J. M. (2003). Separate and combined effects of scopolamine and nicotine on retrieval-induced forgetting. [Clinical Trial; Controlled Clinical Trial; Research Support, Non-U.S. Gov't]. *Psychopharmacology, 170*(4), 351–357. doi: 10.1007/s00213-003-1563-2.

Eichenbaum, H. (2003). How does the hippocampus contribute to memory? *Trends in Cognitive Sciences, 7*(10), 427–429.

Ekberg, J. (2002). *European Seniors Watch Survey*. Helsinki: Stakes.

Ekman, P. (1997). Should we call it expression or communication? *Innovations in Social Science Research, 10*, 333–344.

Elias, M. F., Elias, P. K., & Elias, J. W. (1977). *Basic processes in adult developmental psychology*. Saint Louis: Mosby and London: Kimpton.

Eliott, J. & Olver, I. (2008). Choosing between life and death: Patient and family perceptions of the decision not to resuscitate the terminally ill cancer patient. [Research Support, Non-U.S. Gov't]. *Bioethics, 22*(3), 179–189. doi: 10.1111/j.1467-8519.2007.00620.x.

Elliott, E. & Lachman, M. E. (1989). Enhancing memory by modifying control beliefs, attributions, and performance goals in the elderly. In P. S. Fry (Ed.), *Psychological perspectives of helplessness and control in the elderly* (pp. 339–367). Amsterdam; Oxford: North-Holland.

Elovainio, M., Kivimaki, M., Ferrie, J. E., Gimeno, D., De Vogli, R., Virtanen, M., Vahtera, J., Brunner, E. J., Marmot, M. G., & Singh-Manoux, A. (2009). Physical and cognitive function in midlife: Reciprocal effects? A 5-year follow-up of the Whitehall II study. [Research Support, Non-U.S. Gov't]. *Journal of Epidemiology and Community Health, 63*(6), 468–473. doi: 10.1136/jech.2008.081505.

Emerson, E., Hatton, C., & Felce, D. (2001). *Learning disabilities: The fundamental facts*. London: Mental Health Foundation.

Enache, D., Winblad, B., & Aarsland, D. (2011). Depression in dementia: Epidemiology, mechanisms, and treatment. *Current Opinion in Psychiatry, 24*(6), 461–472. doi: 10.1097/YCO.0b013e32834bb9d4.

'Endocrine system' (2008) *Philip's encyclopedia 2008*. Philip's. Retrieved from http://www.credoreference.com/entry/philipency/endocrine_system.

Erber, J. T. (1979). The institutionalized geriatric patient considered in a framework of developmental deprivation. [Research Support, U.S. Gov't, P.H.S.]. *Human Development, 22*(3), 165–179.

Erber, J. T., Szuchman, L. T., & Prager, I. G. (1997). Forgetful but forgiven: How age and life style affect perceptions of memory failure. [Comparative Study; Research Support, U.S. Gov't, P.H.S.]. *Journals of Gerontology B: Psychological Sciences and Social Sciences, 52*(6), P303–307.

Erickson, K. I., Colcombe, S. J., Wadhwa, R., Bherer, L., Peterson, M. S., Scalf, P. E., Kim, J. S., Alvarado, M., & Kramer, A. F. (2007). Training-induced functional activation changes in dual-task processing: An fMRI study. [Randomized Controlled Trial; Research Support, N.I.H., Extramural; Research Support, Non-U.S. Gov't; Research Support, U.S. Gov't, Non-P.H.S.]. *Cerebral Cortex, 17*(1), 192–204. doi: 10.1093/cercor/bhj137.

Erickson, K. I., Prakash, R. S., Voss, M. W., Chaddock, L., Hu, L., Morris, K. S., White, S. M., Wójcicki, T. R., McAuley, E., & Kramer, A. F. (2009). Aerobic fitness is associated with hippocampal volume in elderly humans. *Hippocampus, 19*(10), 1030–1039.

Erikson, E. H. (1982). *The life cycle completed: A review.* New York; London: Norton.

Erikson, E. H., Erikson, J. M., & Kivnick, H. Q. (1986). *Vital involvement in old age* (1st edn). New York: Norton.

Erixon-Lindroth, N., Farde, L., Wahlin, T. B., Sovago, J., Halldin, C., & Backman, L. (2005). The role of the striatal dopamine transporter in cognitive aging. [Research Support, Non-U.S. Gov't]. *Psychiatry Research, 138*(1), 1–12. doi: 10.1016/j.pscychresns.2004.09.005.

Evenhuis, H., Henderson, C. M., Beange, H., Lennox, N., & Chicoine, B. (2001). Healthy ageing – Adults with intellectual disabilities: Physical health issues. *Journal of Applied Research in Intellectual Disabilities, 14*(3), 175–194.

Everard, K. M., Lach, H. W., Fisher, E. B., & Baum, M. C. (2000). Relationship of activity and social support to the functional health of older adults. *Journals of Gerontology B: Psychological Sciences and Social Sciences, 55*(4), S208–S212.

Fahle, M. (2005). Perceptual learning. *Encyclopedia of cognitive science.* Chichester, West Sussex: Wiley. Retrieved from http://www.credoreference.com/entry/wileycs/perceptual_learning.

Feingold, B. F. (1973). *Introduction to clinical allergy, by Ben F. Feingold.* Springfield, Illinois: Thomas.

Fernandes, M. A. & Moscovitch, M. (2000). Divided attention and memory: Evidence of substantial interference effects at retrieval and encoding. *Journal of Experimental Psychology. General, 129*(2), 155–176.

Fernandez-Duque, D., Baird, J. A., & Black, S. E. (2009). False-belief understanding in frontotemporal dementia and Alzheimer's disease. [Research Support, Non-U.S. Gov't]. *Journal of Clinical and Experimental Neuropsychology, 31*(4), 489–497. doi: 10.1080/13803390802282688.

Fernandez-Duque, D., Hodges, S. D., Baird, J. A., & Black, S. E. (2010). Empathy in frontotemporal dementia and Alzheimer's disease. [Research Support, Non-U.S. Gov't]. *Journal of Clinical and Experimental Neuropsychology, 32*(3), 289–298. doi: 10.1080/13803390903002191.

Ferraro, K. F. & Su, Y. (1999). Financial strain, social relations, and psychological distress among older people: A cross-cultural analysis. [Comparative Study; Research Support, U.S. Gov't, P.H.S.]. *Journals of Gerontology B: Psychological Sciences and Social Sciences, 54*(1), S3–15.

Ferrell, B. A., Ferrell, B. R., & Rivera, L. (1995). Pain in cognitively impaired nursing home patients. [Research Support, Non-U.S. Gov't]. *Journal of Pain and Symptom Management, 10*(8), 591–598.

Ferri, C. P., Prince, M., Brayne, C., Brodaty, H., Fratiglioni, L., Ganguli, M., Hall, K., Hasegawa, K., Hendrie, H., Huang, Y., Jorm, A., Mathers, C., Menezes, P. R., Rimmer, E., & Scazufca, M. (2005). Global prevalence of dementia: A Delphi consensus study. [Research Support, Non-U.S. Gov't]. *Lancet, 366*(9503), 2112–2117. doi: 10.1016/S0140-6736(05)67889-0.

Filley, C. M. (2002). Neuroanatomy. In V. S. Ramachandran (Ed.), *Encyclopedia of the human brain.* Elsevier Science. Retrieved from http://www.credoreference.com/entry/esthumanbrain/neuroanatomy.

Fioravanti, M., Nacca, D., Amati, S., Buckley, A. E., & Bisetti, A. (1995). Chronic obstructive pulmonary disease and associated patterns of memory decline. *Dementia, 6*(1), 39–48.

Fiori, K., Consedine, N., & Magai, C. (2008). The adaptive and maladaptive faces of dependency in later life: Links to physical and psychological health outcomes. *Aging and Mental Health, 12*(6), 700–712. doi: 10.1080/13607860802148863.

Fischer, B. L., Gunter-Hunt, G., Steinhafel, C. H., & Howell, T. (2012). The identification and assessment of late-life ADHD in memory clinics. [Research Support, Non-U.S. Gov't]. *Journal of Attention Disorders, 16*(4), 333–338. doi: 10.1177/1087054711398886.

Flavell, J. H. (1971). First discussant's comment: What is memory the development of? *Human Development, 14,* 272–278.

Flavell, J. H. & Wellman, H. M. (1977). Metamemory. In R. Kail & J. W. Hagen (Eds), *Perspectives on the Development of Memory and Cognition.* London: Wiley.

Flint, A. J. (2005). Generalised anxiety disorder in elderly patients: Epidemiology, diagnosis and treatment options. [Review]. *Drugs and Aging, 22*(2), 101–114.

Folkman, S. (1997). Positive psychological states and coping with severe stress. [Research Support, U.S. Gov't, P.H.S.]. *Social Science and Medicine, 45*(8), 1207–1221.

Folkman, S., Chesney, M., Collette, L., Boccellari, A., & Cooke, M. (1996). Postbereavement depressive mood and its prebereavement predictors in HIV+ and HIV– gay men. [Research Support, U.S. Gov't, P.H.S.]. *Journal of Personality and Social Psychology, 70*(2), 336–348.

Folkman, S., Lazarus, R. S., Gruen, R. J., & DeLongis, A. (1986). Appraisal, coping, health status, and psychological symptoms. [Research Support, Non-U.S. Gov't]. *Journal of Personality and Social Psychology, 50*(3), 571–579.

Folstein, M. F., Folstein, S. E., & McHugh, P. R. (1975). 'Mini-mental state'. A practical method for grading the cognitive state of patients for the clinician. *Journal of Psychiatric Research, 12*(3), 189–198.

Fook, L. & Morgan, R. (2000). Hearing impairment in older people: A review. [Review]. *Postgraduate Medical Journal, 76*(899), 537–541.

Fredrickson, B. L. (1998). What good are positive emotions? *Review of General Psychology, 2*(3), 300–319. doi: 10.1037/1089-2680.2.3.300.

Frerichs, F. & Naegele, G. (1997). Discrimination of older workers in Germany: Obstacles and options for the integration into employment. *Journal of Aging and Social Policy, 9*(1), 89–101. doi: 10.1300/J031v09n01_08.

Freud, S. (1957). *The standard edition of the complete psychological works of Sigmund Freud.* London: Hogarth.

Freud, S., Freud, A., Strachey, A., Strachey, J., & Tyson, A. W. (1961). *The ego and the id, and other works; translated under the general editorship of James Strachey in collaboration with Anna Freud, assisted by Alix Strachey and Alan Tyson. [With plates.].* London: Hogarth.

Freund, A. M. & Baltes, P. B. (2002). Life-management strategies of selection, optimization, and compensation: Measurement by self-report and construct validity. *Journal of Personality and Social Psychology, 82*(4), 642–662.

Freund, A. M. & Ebner, N. C. (2005). The aging self: Shifting from promoting gains to balancing losses. In W. Greve, K. Rothermund & D. Wentura (Eds), *The adaptive self: Personal continuity and intentional self-development* (pp. 185–202). Ashland, Ohio: Hogrefe & Huber.

Friedman, M. & Rosenman, R. H. (1974). *Type A behaviour and your heart.* [S.l.]: Knopf.

Friedman, N. P. & Miyake, A. (2004). The relations among inhibition and interference control functions: A latent-variable analysis. [Clinical Trial; Randomized Controlled Trial]. *Journal of Experimental Psychology. General, 133*(1), 101–135. doi: 10.1037/0096-3445.133.1.101.

Friend, A., DeFries, J. C., Olson, R. K., Pennington, B., Harlaar, N., Byrne, B., Samuelsson, S., Willcutt, E. G., Wadsworth, S. J., Corley, R., & Keenan, J. M. (2009). Heritability of high reading ability and its interaction with parental education. [Comparative Study; Research Support, N.I.H., Extramural; Research Support, Non-U.S. Gov't; Twin Study]. *Behavior Genetics, 39*(4), 427–436. doi: 10.1007/s10519-009-9263-2.

Fries, J. F. (2003). Measuring and monitoring success in compressing morbidity. [Research Support, U.S. Gov't, P.H.S.; Review]. *Annals of Internal Medicine*, *139*(5 Pt 2), 455–459.

Frisina, D. R. & Frisina, R. D. (1997). Speech recognition in noise and presbycusis: Relations to possible neural mechanisms. [Clinical Trial; Comparative Study; Controlled Clinical Trial; Research Support, U.S. Gov't, P.H.S.]. *Hearing Research*, *106*(1–2), 95–104.

Froland, C. (1980). Formal and informal care: Discontinuities in a continuum. *Social Service Review*, *54*(4), 572–587.

Fromm, D., Holland, A. L., Nebes, R. D., & Oakley, M. A. (1991). A longitudinal study of word-reading ability in Alzheimer's disease: Evidence from the National Adult Reading Test. [Research Support, U.S. Gov't, P.H.S.]. *Cortex*, *27*(3), 367–376.

Gall, T. L., Evans, D. R., & Howard, J. (1997). The retirement adjustment process: Changes in the well-being of male retirees across time. [Research Support, Non-U.S. Gov't]. *Journals of Gerontology B: Psychological Sciences and Social Sciences*, *52*(3), P110–117.

Galletti, P., Ingrosso, D., Manna, C., Clemente, G., & Zappia, V. (1995). Protein damage and methylation-mediated repair in the erythrocyte. *Biochemical Journal*, *306*(2), 313–326.

Gallo, W. T., Bradley, E. H., Siegel, M., & Kasl, S. V. (2000). Health effects of involuntary job loss among older workers findings from the health and retirement survey. *Journals of Gerontology B: Psychological Sciences and Social Sciences*, *55*(3), S131–S140.

Ganguli, M., Vander Bilt, J., Saxton, J. A., Shen, C., & Dodge, H. H. (2005). Alcohol consumption and cognitive function in late life: A longitudinal community study. [Research Support, N.I.H., Extramural; Research Support, U.S. Gov't, P.H.S.]. *Neurology*, *65*(8), 1210–1217. doi: 10.1212/01.wnl.0000180520.35181.24.

Gardner, H. (1983). *Frames of mind: The theory of multiple intelligences*. London: Heinemann, 1983

Gathercole, S. E., Lamont, E., & Alloway, T. P. (2006). Working memory in the classroom. In S. J. Pickering (Ed.), *Working memory and education* (pp. 220–241). Amsterdam; London: Elsevier/Academic Press.

Gatz, M. (2007). Genetics, dementia, and the elderly. *Current Directions in Psychological Science*, *16*, 123–127.

Gatz, M., Kasl-Godley, J. E., & Karel, J. J. (1996). Aging and mental disorders. In K. W. Schaie & J. E. Birren (Eds) with R. P. Abeles, M. Gatz, & T. A. Salthouse (Vol. assoc. eds), *Handbook of the psychology of aging* (4th edn, pp. 365–382): San Diego, CA; London: Academic, 1996 (1996 [printing]).

Gatz, M. & Smyer, M. A. (2001). Mental health and aging at the outset of the twenty-first century. In J. E. Birren & K. W. Schaie (Eds), *Handbook of the psychology of aging* (5th edn, pp. 523–544). San Diego, CA; London: Academic.

Gauthier, S., Reisberg, B., Zaudig, M., Petersen, R. C., Ritchie, K., Broich, K., Belleville, S., Brodaty, H., Bennett, D., Chertkow, H., Cummings, J. L., de Leon, M., Feldman, H., Ganguli, M., Hampel, H., Scheltens, P., Tierney, M. C., Whitehouse, P., & Winblad, B. (2006). Mild cognitive impairment. [Research Support, Non-U.S. Gov't; Review]. *Lancet*, *367*(9518), 1262–1270. doi: 10.1016/S0140-6736(06)68542-5.

German, T. P. & Hehman, J. A. (2006). Representational and executive selection resources in 'theory of mind': Evidence from compromised belief–desire reasoning in old age. *Cognition*, *101*(1), 129–152. doi: 10.1016/j.cognition.2005.05.007.

Ghaziuddin, M., Ghaziuddin, N., & Greden, J. (2002). Depression in persons with autism: Implications for research and clinical care. [Review]. *Journal of Autism and Developmental Disorders*, *32*(4), 299–306.

Giambra, L. M. (1989). Task-unrelated-thought frequency as a function of age: A laboratory study. *Psychology and Aging*, *4*(2), 136–143.

Giambra, L. M., Arenberg, D., Kawas, C., Zonderman, A. B., & Costa, P. T., Jr (1995). Adult life span changes in immediate visual memory and verbal intelligence. *Psychology and Aging, 10*(1), 123–139.

Gibson, E. J. (1969). *Principles of perceptual learning and development.* New York: Appleton-Century-Crofts.

Giddens, A. (1991). *Modernity and self-identity.* Cambridge: Polity.

Giedd, J. N., Blumenthal, J., Jeffries, N. O., Castellanos, F. X., Liu, H., Zijdenbos, A., Paus, T., Evans, A. C., & Rapoport, J. L. (1999). Brain development during childhood and adolescence: a longitudinal MRI study. [Clinical Trial; Letter]. *Nature Neuroscience, 2*(10), 861–863. doi: 10.1038/13158.

Gignac, M. A., Cott, C., & Badley, E. M. (2000). Adaptation to chronic illness and disability and its relationship to perceptions of independence and dependence. [Research Support, Non-U.S. Gov't]. *Journals of Gerontology B: Psychological Sciences and Social Sciences, 55*(6), P362–372.

Gignac, M. A., Cott, C., & Badley, E. M. (2002). Adaptation to disability: Applying selective optimization with compensation to the behaviors of older adults with osteoarthritis. [Research Support, Non-U.S. Gov't]. *Psychology and Aging, 17*(3), 520–524.

Gilbert, D. T. & Malone, P. S. (1995). The correspondence bias. [Research Support, Non-U.S. Gov't; Research Support, U.S. Gov't, P.H.S.; Review]. *Psychological Bulletin, 117*(1), 21–38.

Gilhooly, M. L., Gilhooly, K. J., Phillips, L. H., Harvey, D., Brady, A., & Hanlon, P. (2007). Real-world problem solving and quality of life in older people. [Research Support, Non-U.S. Gov't]. *British Journal of Health Psychology, 12*(Pt 4), 587–600. doi: 10.1348/135910706X154477.

Gillberg, C. & Billstedt, E. (2000). Autism and Asperger syndrome: Coexistence with other clinical disorders. [Review]. *Acta Psychiatrica Scandinavica, 102*(5), 321–330.

Gilmore, G. C., Wenk, H. E., Naylor, L. A., & Stuve, T. A. (1992). Motion perception and aging. [Research Support, U.S. Gov't, P.H.S.]. *Psychology and Aging, 7*(4), 654–660.

Gluck, J. & Bluck, S. (2007). Looking back across the life span: A life story account of the reminiscence bump. [Research Support, Non-U.S. Gov't]. *Memory & Cognition, 35*(8), 1928–1939.

Gogtay, N., Giedd, J. N., Lusk, L., Hayashi, K. M., Greenstein, D., Vaituzis, A. C., Nugent, T. F., 3rd, Herman, D. H., Clasen, L. S., Toga, A. W., Rapoport, J. L., & Thompson, P. M. (2004). Dynamic mapping of human cortical development during childhood through early adulthood. [Research Support, U.S. Gov't, P.H.S.]. *Proceedings of the National Academy of Sciences of the United States of America, 101*(21), 8174–8179. doi: 10.1073/pnas.0402680101.

Goh, J. O. & Park, D. C. (2009). Neuroplasticity and cognitive aging: The scaffolding theory of aging and cognition. [Research Support, N.I.H., Extramural; Review]. *Restorative Neurology and Neuroscience, 27*(5), 391–403. doi: 10.3233/RNN-2009-0493.

Gold, D., Andres, D., Arbuckle, T., & Schwartzman, A. (1988). Measurement and correlates of verbosity in elderly people. [Comparative Study; Research Support, Non-U.S. Gov't]. *Journal of Gerontology, 43*(2), P27–33.

Golden, C. J. (1978). *Stroop Color and Word Test: Cat. No. 30150M; A manual for clinical and experimental uses.* Chicago, IL: Stoelting.

Goldman-Rakic, P. S., Cools, A., & Srivastava, K. (1996). The prefrontal landscape: Implications of functional architecture for understanding human mentation and the central executive [and discussion]. *Philosophical Transactions of the Royal Society of London. Series B: Biological Sciences, 351*(1346), 1445–1453.

Goldsmith, R. E. & Heiens, R. A. (1992). Subjective age: A test of five hypotheses. [Research Support, Non-U.S. Gov't]. *The Gerontologist, 32*(3), 312–317.

Golimstok, A., Rojas, J. I., Romano, M., Zurru, M. C., Doctorovich, D., & Cristiano, E. (2011). Previous adult attention-deficit and hyperactivity disorder symptoms and risk of dementia with Lewy bodies: A case-control study. *European Journal of Neurology, 18*(1), 78–84. doi: 10.1111/j.1468-1331.2010.03064.x.

Gopnik, A. & Astington, J. W. (1988). Children's understanding of representational change and its relation to the understanding of false belief and the appearance–reality distinction. [Research Support, Non-U.S. Gov't]. *Child Development, 59*(1), 26–37.

Gopnik, A., Capps, L., & Meltzoff, A. N. (2000). Early theories of mind: What the theory can tell us about autism. In S. Baron-Cohen, H. Tager-Flusberg, & D. J. Cohen (Eds), *Understanding other minds: Perspectives from developmental cognitive neuroscience* (2nd edn, pp. 50–72). Oxford: Oxford University Press.

Gottman, J. M. & Levenson, R. W. (2000). The timing of divorce: Predicting when a couple will divorce over a 14-year period. *Journal of Marriage and Family, 62*(3), 737–745.

Gouin, J. P., Hantsoo, L., & Kiecolt-Glaser, J. K. (2008). Immune dysregulation and chronic stress among older adults: A review. [Research Support, N.I.H., Extramural; Research Support, Non-U.S. Gov't; Review]. *Neuroimmunomodulation, 15*(4–6), 251–259. doi: 10.1159/000156468.

Grady, C. L., McIntosh, A. R., Horwitz, B., Maisog, J. M., Ungerleider, L. G., Mentis, M. J., Pietrini, P., Schapiro, M. B., & Haxby, J. V. (1995). Age-related reductions in human recognition memory due to impaired encoding. [Comparative Study]. *Science, 269*(5221), 218–221.

Grady, C. L., Springer, M. V., Hongwanishkul, D., McIntosh, A. R., & Winocur, G. (2006). Age-related changes in brain activity across the adult lifespan. [Comparative Study; Research Support, Non-U.S. Gov't]. *Journal of Cognitive Neuroscience, 18*(2), 227–241. doi: 10.1162/089892906775783705.

Grant, D. A. & Berg, E. A. (1948). A behavioral analysis of degree of reinforcement and ease of shifting to new responses in a Weigl-type card-sorting problem. *Journal of Experimental Psychology, 38*(4), 404–411.

Grant, D. A. & Berg, E. A. (1993). *Wisconsin Card Sorting Test (WCST)*. Odessa, FL: Psychological Assessment Resources.

Green, C. S., Li, R., & Bavelier, D. (2010). Perceptual learning during action video game playing. *Topics in Cognitive Science, 2*(2), 202–216.

Green, D. M. & Swets, J. A. (1966). *Signal detection theory and psychophysics*. New York: John Wiley & Sons.

Gregory, C., Lough, S., Stone, V., Erzinclioglu, S., Martin, L., Baron-Cohen, S., & Hodges, J. R. (2002). Theory of mind in patients with frontal variant frontotemporal dementia and Alzheimer's disease: Theoretical and practical implications. *Brain, 125*(Pt 4), 752–764.

Grimm, L. C. & Thompson, S. K. (2007). Moral reasoning. In C. R. Reynolds & E. Fletcher-Janzen (Eds), *Encyclopedia of special education: A reference for the education of children, adolescents, and adults with disabilities and other exceptional individuals*. New Jersey: Wiley. Retrieved from http://www.credoreference.com/entry/wileyse/moral_reasoning.

Grønbæk, M. (2009). The positive and negative health effects of alcohol and the public health implications. *Journal of Internal Medicine, 265*(4), 407–420.

Gronwall, D. M. (1977). Paced auditory serial-addition task: A measure of recovery from concussion. *Perceptual and Motor Skills, 44*(2), 367–373.

Gross, J. J. (1998). Antecedent- and response-focused emotion regulation: Divergent consequences for experience, expression, and physiology. [Research Support, U.S. Gov't, P.H.S.]. *Journal of Personality and Social Psychology, 74*(1), 224–237.

Gross, J. J. (2001). Emotion regulation in adulthood: Timing is everything. *Current Directions in Psychological Science, 10*, 214–219.

Gross, J. J., Carstensen, L. L., Pasupathi, M., Tsai, J., Skorpen, C. G., & Hsu, A. Y. (1997). Emotion and aging: Experience, expression, and control. [Research Support, Non-U.S. Gov't; Research Support, U.S. Gov't, P.H.S.]. *Psychology and Aging, 12*(4), 590–599.

Grubeck-Loebenstein, B. (2010). Fading immune protection in old age: Vaccination in the elderly. [Review]. *Journal of Comparative Pathology, 142* (Suppl. 1), S116–119. doi: 10.1016/j.jcpa.2009.10.002.

Gruhn, D., Lumley, M. A., Diehl, M., & Labouvie-Vief, G. (2013). Time-based indicators of emotional complexity: Interrelations and correlates. *Emotion, 13*(2), 226–237. doi: 10.1037/a0030363.

Grundy, E. M. (1996). Population review: (5). The population aged 60 and over. [Research Support, Non-U.S. Gov't]. *Population Trends*, (84), 14–20.

Guadalupe-Grau, A., Fuentes, T., Guerra, B., & Calbet, J. A. (2009). Exercise and bone mass in adults. [Research Support, Non-U.S. Gov't; Review]. *Sports Medicine, 39*(6), 439–468. doi: 10.2165/00007256-200939060-00002.

Guaita, A., Malnati, M., Vaccaro, R., Pezzati, R., Marcionetti, J., Vitali, S. F., & Colombo, M. (2009). Impaired facial emotion recognition and preserved reactivity to facial expressions in people with severe dementia. [Comparative Study]. *Archives of Gerontology and Geriatrics, 49*(Suppl. 1), 135–146. doi: 10.1016/j.archger.2009.09.023.

Gubin, D. G., Gubin, G. D., Waterhouse, J., & Weinert, D. (2006). The circadian body temperature rhythm in the elderly: Effect of single daily melatonin dosing. [Controlled Clinical Trial]. *Chronobiol Int, 23*(3), 639–658. doi: 10.1080/07420520600650612.

Hacker, M. P., Messer, W. S., & Bachmann, K. A. (2009). *Pharmacology: Principles and practice*. Amsterdam: Academic.

Hagerman, R. J. (2006). Lessons from fragile X regarding neurobiology, autism, and neurodegeneration. [Research Support, N.I.H., Extramural; Research Support, Non-U.S. Gov't; Review]. *Journal of Developmental and Behavioral Pediatrics, 27*(1), 63–74.

Happe, F. G., Winner, E., & Brownell, H. (1998). The getting of wisdom: Theory of mind in old age. [Comparative Study]. *Developmental Psychology, 34*(2), 358–362.

Hall, G. S. (1922). *Senescence: The last Half of Life*. Appleton.

Hamilton, P. F. (2010). *Pandora's star*. London: Pan.

Hanson, J., Osipovič, D., Hinew, N., Amaral, T., Curry, R., & Barlow, J. (2007). Lifestyle monitoring as a predictive tool in telecare. *Journal of Telemedicine and Telecare, 13*(Suppl. 1), 26–28.

Hansson, R. O., DeKoekkoek, P. D., Neece, W. M., & Patterson, D. W. (1997). Successful aging at work: Annual review, 1992–1996: The older worker and transitions to retirement. *Journal of Vocational Behavior, 51*(2), 202–233.

Haraway, Donna (1985) Manifesto for cyborgs: science, technology and socialist feminism in the 1980s, *Socialist Review* 15(2): 65–107.

Hargrave, R., Maddock, R. J., & Stone, V. (2002). Impaired recognition of facial expressions of emotion in Alzheimer's disease. [Clinical Trial]. *Journal of Neuropsychiatry and Clinical Neurosciences, 14*(1), 64–71.

Harkins, S. W. & Scott, R. B. (1996). Pain and presbyalgos. In J. E. Birren (Ed.), *Encyclopedia of gerontology: Age, aging, and the aged* (Vol. 2, pp. 247–260). San Diego: Academic Press.

Harnishfeger, K. K. & Bjorklund, D. F. (1993). The ontogeny of inhibition mechanisms: A renewed approach to cognitive development. In M. L. Howe & R. Pasnak (Eds), *Emerging themes in cognitive development* (pp. 28–49). New York: Springer-Verlag.

Harris, D. L. & Carr, A. T. (2001). Prevalence of concern about physical appearance in the general population. *British Journal of Plastic Surgery, 54*(3), 223–226. doi: 10.1054/bjps.2001.3550.

Harris, P. B. (2008). Another wrinkle in the debate about successful aging: The undervalued concept of resilience and the lived experience of dementia. *The International Journal of Aging and Human Development, 67*(1), 43–61.

Harrison, D. E., Strong, R., Sharp, Z. D., Nelson, J. F., Astle, C. M., Flurkey, K., Nadon, N. L., Wilkinson, J. E., Frenkel, K., Carter, C. S., Pahor, M., Javors, M. A., Fernandez, E., & Miller, R. A. (2009). Rapamycin fed late in life extends lifespan in genetically heterogeneous mice. [Research Support, N.I.H., Extramural; Research Support, U.S. Gov't, Non-P.H.S.]. *Nature, 460*(7253), 392–395. doi: 10.1038/nature08221.

Hart, J. T. (1965). Memory and the feeling-of-knowing experience. *Journal of Educational Psychology, 56*(4), 208–216.

Hartley, A. A., & Little, D. M. (1999). Age-related differences and similarities in dual-task interference. *Journal of Experimental Psychology: General, 128*(4), 416.

Hartley, J. T. (1986). Reader and text variables as determinants of discourse memory in adulthood. [Research Support, U.S. Gov't, P.H.S.]. *Psychology and Aging, 1*(2), 150–158.

Harwood, R. H. (2001). Visual problems and falls. [Review]. *Age Ageing, 30*(Suppl. 4), 13–18.

Hasher, L., Goldstein, F., & May, C. (2005). It's about time: Circadian rhythms, memory and aging. In C. Izawa & N. Ohta (Eds), *Human learning and memory: Advances in theory and application* (Vol. 18, pp. 179–186). Mahwah, NJ: Lawrence Erlbaum.

Hasher, L. & Zacks, R. T. (1988). Working memory, comprehension and aging: A review and a new view. In G. H. Bower (Ed.), *The psychology of learning and motivation* (Vol. 22, pp. 193–225). New York: Academic Press.

Havighurst, R. J. (1982). The world of work. In B. B. Wolman, G. Stricker, S. J. Ellman, P. Keith-Spiegel, & D. S. Palermo (Eds), *Handbook of developmental psychology* (pp. 771–787). Englewood Cliffs; London: Prentice-Hall.

Hawkins, H. L., Kramer, A. F., & Capaldi, D. (1992). Aging, exercise, and attention. [Research Support, U.S. Gov't, P.H.S.]. *Psychology and Aging, 7*(4), 643–653.

Hay, E. L. & Diehl, M. (2011). Emotion complexity and emotion regulation across adulthood. *European Journal of Ageing, 8*(3), 157–168. doi: 10.1007/s10433-011-0191-7.

Hayflick, L. (1996). *How and why we age* (2nd edn). New York: Ballantine.

Hebben, N. & Milberg, W. (2010). *Essentials of neuropsychological assessment* (2nd edn; editors N. Hebben, W. Milberg, A. S. Kaufman). Hoboken, NJ: Wiley; Chichester: John Wiley.

Heckhausen, J. & Schulz, R. (1995). A life-span theory of control. [Research Support, Non-U.S. Gov't; Research Support, U.S. Gov't, P.H.S.; Review]. *Psychological Review, 102*(2), 284–304.

Hedden, T. & Gabrieli, J. D. (2004). Insights into the ageing mind: A view from cognitive neuroscience. [Research Support, U.S. Gov't, P.H.S.; Review]. *Nature Reviews Neuroscience, 5*(2), 87–96. doi: 10.1038/nrn1323.

Hedden, T. & Yoon, C. (2006). Individual differences in executive processing predict susceptibility to interference in verbal working memory. [Clinical Trial; Research Support, N.I.H., Extramural; Research Support, Non-U.S. Gov't]. *Neuropsychology, 20*(5), 511–528. doi: 10.1037/0894-4105.20.5.511.

Heider, F. (1958). *The psychology of interpersonal relations*. New York: John Wiley & Sons.

Heidrich, S. M. & Ryff, C. D. (1993). Physical and mental health in later life: The self-system as mediator. [Comparative Study; Research Support, Non-U.S. Gov't; Research Support, U.S. Gov't, P.H.S.]. *Psychology and Aging, 8*(3), 327–338.

Heindel, W. C. & Salmon, D. P. (2004). Cognitive approaches to the memory disorders of demented patients. In H. E. Adams & P. B. Sutker (Eds), *Comprehensive handbook of psychopathology*. New York: Springer Science+Business Media. Retrieved from http://www.credoreference.com/entry/sprhp/cognitive_approaches_to_the_memory_ disorders_of_demented_patients.

Henkens, K. (1999). Retirement intentions and spousal support: A multi-actor approach. *Journals of Gerontology B: Psychological Sciences and Social Sciences*, *54*(2), S63–73.

Henretta, J. C. (1997). Changing perspective on retirement. [Editorial]. *Journals of Gerontology B: Psychological Sciences and Social Sciences*, *52*(1), S1–3.

Henry, J. D., MacLeod, M. S., Phillips, L. H., & Crawford, J. R. (2004). A meta-analytic review of prospective memory and aging. [Meta-Analysis; Review]. *Psychology and Aging*, *19*(1), 27–39. doi: 10.1037/0882-7974.19.1.27.

Henry, N. J., Berg, C. A., Smith, T. W., & Florsheim, P. (2007). Positive and negative characteristics of marital interaction and their association with marital satisfaction in middle-aged and older couples. [Research Support, N.I.H., Extramural]. *Psychology and Aging*, *22*(3), 428–441. doi: 10.1037/0882-7974.22.3.428.

Hertzog, C. & Hultsch, D. F. (2000). Metacognition in adulthood and aging. In F. I. M. Craik & T. Salthouse (Eds), *The handbook of aging and cognition* (2nd edn, pp. 417–466). Mahwah, NJ; London: Lawrence Erlbaum Associates.

Hertzog, C., Kramer, A. F., Wilson, R. S., & Lindenberger, U. (2008). Enrichment effects on adult cognitive development: Can the functional capacity of older adults be preserved and enhanced? *Psychological Science in the Public Interest*, *9*(1), 1–65.

Hertzog, C., McGuire, C. L., & Lineweaver, T. T. (1999). Beliefs about memory and aging. In T. M. Hess & F. Blanchard-Fields (Eds), *Social cognition and aging* (pp. 43–68). San Diego; London: AP Professional.

Hertzog, C., Park, D. C., Morrell, R. W., & Martin, M. (2000). Ask and ye shall receive: Behavioural specificity in the accuracy of subjective memory complaints. *Applied Cognitive Psychology*, *14*(3), 257–275. doi: 10.1002/(sici)1099-0720(200005/06)14:3<257::aid-acp651>3.0.co;2-o.

Hess, T. M. (1999). Cognitive and knowledge-based influences on social representations. In T. M. Hess & F. Blanchard-Fields (Eds), *Social cognition and aging* (pp. 239–263). San Diego; London: AP Professional.

Higgs, P., Hyde, M., Wiggins, R., & Blane, D. (2003). Researching quality of life in early old age: The importance of the sociological dimension. *Social Policy & Administration*, *37*(3), 239–252.

Hildon, Z., Smith, G., Netuveli, G., & Blane, D. (2008). Understanding adversity and resilience at older ages. *Sociology of Health & Illness*, *30*(5), 726–740.

Hill, E. L. & Brown, D. (2013). Mood impairments in adults previously diagnosed with developmental coordination disorder. *Journal of Mental Health*. doi: 10.3109/09638237.2012.745187.

Hinrichsen, G. A., & Dick-Siskin, L. P. (2000). General principles of therapy. In S. K. Whitbourne (Ed.), *Psychopathology in later adulthood* (pp. 323–350). New York; Chichester: Wiley.

Hobfoll, S. E. (1989). Conservation of resources. A new attempt at conceptualizing stress. [Review]. *American Psychologist*, *44*(3), 513–524.

Hobfoll, S. E., Johnson, R. J., Ennis, N., & Jackson, A. P. (2003). Resource loss, resource gain, and emotional outcomes among inner city women. *Journal of Personality and Social Psychology*, *84*(3), 632–643.

Hofer, S. M. & Sliwinski, M. J. (2006). Design and analysis of longitudinal studies of aging. In J. E. Birren, K. W. Schaie, R. P. Abeles, M. Gatz, & T. A. Salthouse (Eds), *Handbook of the psychology of aging* (6th edn) (pp. 15–37). New York: Oxford: Academic.

Hofvander, B., Delorme, R., Chaste, P., Nyden, A., Wentz, E., Stahlberg, O., Herbrecht, E., Stopin, A., Anckarsater, H., Gillberg, C., Rastam, M., & Leboyer, M. (2009). Psychiatric and psychosocial problems in adults with normal-intelligence autism spectrum disorders. [Research Support, Non-U.S. Gov't]. *BMC Psychiatry, 9*, 35. doi: 10.1186/1471-244X-9-35.

Hogervorst, E., Huppert, F., Matthews, F. E., & Brayne, C. (2008). Thyroid function and cognitive decline in the MRC cognitive function and ageing study. [Multicenter Study; Research Support, Non-U.S. Gov't]. *Psychoneuroendocrinology, 33*(7), 1013–1022. doi: 10.1016/j.psyneuen.2008.05.008.

Hogg, J. & Tuffrey-Wijne, I. (2008). Cancer and intellectual disability: A review of some key contextual Issues. *Journal of Applied Research in Intellectual Disabilities, 21*(6), 509–518.

Holahan, C. J. & Moos, R. H. (1991). Life stressors, personal and social resources, and depression: A 4-year structural model. [Research Support, U.S. Gov't, Non-P.H.S.; Research Support, U.S. Gov't, P.H.S.]. *Journal of Abnormal Psychology, 100*(1), 31–38.

Holtzman, R. E., Rebok, G. W., Saczynski, J. S., Kouzis, A. C., Wilcox Doyle, K., & Eaton, W. W. (2004). Social network characteristics and cognition in middle-aged and older adults. [Research Support, U.S. Gov't, P.H.S.]. *Journals of Gerontology B: Psychological Sciences and Social Sciences, 59*(6), P278–284.

Holzhausen, M., Kuhlmey, A., & Martus, P. (2010). Individualized measurement of quality of life in older adults: Development and pilot testing of a new tool. *European Journal of Ageing, 7*(3), 201–211.

Hoof, J. v., Kort, H. d., Markopoulos, P., & Soede, M. (2007). Ambient intelligence, ethics and privacy. *Gerontechnology, 6*(3), 155–163.

Hooker, K. & McAdams, D. P. (2003). Personality reconsidered: A new agenda for aging research. [Research Support, Non-U.S. Gov't]. *Journals of Gerontology B: Psychological Sciences and Social Sciences, 58*(6), P296–304.

Horn, J. L. & Donaldson, G. (1976). On the myth of intellectual decline in adulthood. [Research Support, U.S. Gov't, Non-P.H.S.]. *American Psychologist, 31*(10), 701–719.

Howells, G. (1986). Are the medical needs of mentally handicapped adults being met? *Journal of the Royal College of General Practitioners, 36*(291), 449–453.

Howlin, P. (2000). Outcome in adult life for more able individuals with autism or Asperger syndrome. *Autism, 4*(1), 63–83.

Hultsch, D. F. & MacDonald, S. W. S. (2004). Intraindividual variability in performance as a theoretical window onto cognitive aging. In R. A. Dixon, L. Backman & L-G. Nilsson (Eds), *New frontiers in cognitive aging* (pp. 65–88). Oxford: Oxford University Press.

Hultsch, D. F., MacDonald, S. W., & Dixon, R. A. (2002). Variability in reaction time performance of younger and older adults. [Comparative Study; Research Support, Non-U.S. Gov't; Research Support, U.S. Gov't, P.H.S.]. *Journals of Gerontology B: Psychological Sciences and Social Sciences, 57*(2), P101–115.

Humes, L. E. (1996). Speech understanding in the elderly. *Journal of the American Academy of Audiology, 7*(3), 161–167.

Huppert, F. & So, T. (2009). What percentage of people in Europe are flourishing and what characterizes them? Retrieved from www.isqols2009.istitutodeglinnocenti.it/Content_en/Huppert.pdf.

'Hypotension' (2010) *Black's medical dictionary* (42nd edn). London: A & C Black. Retrieved from http://www.credoreference.com/entry/blackmed/hypotension.

Hutchinson, C.V., Arena, A., Allen, H. A., & Ledgeway, T. (2012). Psychophysical correlates of global motion processing in the aging visual system: A critical review. [Review]. *Neuroscience Biobehavioral Reviews, 36*(4), 1266–1272. doi: 10.1016/j.neubiorev.2012.02.009.

Huxley, J. (1979). *Religion without revelation.* Westport, CT: Greenwood Press.

Ingersoll-Dayton, B. & Saengtienchai, C. (1999). Respect for the elderly in Asia: Stability and change. [Research Support, Non-U.S. Gov't; Research Support, U.S. Gov't, P.H.S.]. *International Journal of Aging and Human Development, 48*(2), 113–130.

Ino, T., Asada, T., Ito, J., Kimura, T., & Fukuyama, H. (2003). Parieto-frontal networks for clock drawing revealed with fMRI. *Neuroscience Research, 45*(1), 71–77.

Intons-Peterson, M. J. & Fournier, J. (1986). External and internal memory aids: When and how often do we use them? *Journal of Experimental Psychology: General, 115*(3), 267–280. doi: 10.1037/0096-3445.115.3.267.

Jacoby, L. L. (1999). Ironic effects of repetition: Measuring age-related differences in memory. [Clinical Trial; Randomized Controlled Trial; Research Support, U.S. Gov't, Non-P.H.S.; Research Support, U.S. Gov't, P.H.S.]. *Journal of Experimental Psychology Learning Memory and Cognition, 25*(1), 3–22.

Jackson-Guilford, J., Leander, J. D., & Nisenbaum, L. K. (2000). The effect of streptozotocin-induced diabetes on cell proliferation in the rat dentate gyrus. *Neuroscience Letters, 293*(2), 91–94.

Jaeggi, S. M., Buschkuehl, M., Jonides, J., & Perrig, W. J. (2008). Improving fluid intelligence with training on working memory. [Research Support, N.I.H., Extramural; Research Support, Non-U.S. Gov't; Research Support, U.S. Gov't, Non-P.H.S.]. *Proceedings of the National Academy of Sciences of the United States of America, 105*(19), 6829–6833. doi: 10.1073/pnas.0801268105.

Jahanshahi, M. (2007). Parkinson's disease. In S. Ayers & K. A. Wallston (Eds), *Cambridge handbook of psychology, health and medicine* (pp. 809–810). Cambridge University Press.

James, L., Burke, D., & Austin, A. H. (1999). Production and perception of 'verbosity' in younger and older adults. *Psychology and Aging, 13*, 355–367.

James, W. (1907). *The principles of psychology,* Vol. 1. [S.l.]: Macmillan.

Janicki, M. P., Dalton, A. J., Henderson, C. M., & Davidson, P. W. (1999). Mortality and morbidity among older adults with intellectual disability: Health services considerations. *Disability and Rehabilitation, 21*(5–6), 284–294.

Janicki, M. P., Davidson, P. W., Henderson, C. M., McCallion, P., Taets, J. D., Force, L. T., Sulkes, S. B., Frangenberg, E., & Ladrigan, P. M. (2002). Health characteristics and health services utilization in older adults with intellectual disability living in community residences. [Research Support, U.S. Gov't, P.H.S.]. *Journal of Intellectual Disability Research, 46*(Pt 4), 287–298.

Jaques, E. (1965). Death and the mid-life crisis. *International Journal of Psycho-analysis, 46*(4), 502–514.

Jensen, A. R. (1992). The importance of intraindividual variation in reaction time. *Personality and Individual Differences, 13*(8), 869–881. doi: 10.1016/0191-8869(92)90004-9.

Jessberger, S. & Gage, F. H. (2009). Fate plasticity of adult hippocampal progenitors: Biological relevance and therapeutic use. [Research Support, N.I.H., Extramural; Research Support, Non-U.S. Gov't]. *Trends in Pharmacological Sciences, 30*(2), 61–65. doi: 10.1016/j.tips.2008.11.003.

Jonassaint, C. R., Boyle, S. H., Williams, R. B., Mark, D. B., Siegler, I. C., & Barefoot, J. C. (2007). Facets of openness predict mortality in patients with cardiac disease. [Research Support, N.I.H., Extramural; Research Support, Non-U.S. Gov't]. *Psychosomatic Medicine, 69*(4), 319–322. doi: 10.1097/PSY.0b013e318052e27d.

Jones, C. J., Nesselroade, J. R., & Birkel, R. C. (1991). Examination of staffing level effects in the family household: An application of P-technique factor analysis. *Journal of Environmental Psychology, 11*, 59–73.

Jonides, J., Marshuetz, C., Smith, E. E., Reuter-Lorenz, P. A., Koeppe, R. A., & Hartley, A. (2000). Age differences in behavior and PET activation reveal differences in interference resolution in verbal working memory. [Research Support, U.S. Gov't, Non-P.H.S.; Research Support, U.S. Gov't, P.H.S.]. *Journal of Cognitive Neuroscience, 12*(1), 188–196.

Jopp, D. & Smith, J. (2006). Resources and life-management strategies as determinants of successful aging: On the protective effect of selection, optimization, and compensation. [Research Support, Non-U.S. Gov't]. *Psychology and Aging, 21*(2), 253–265. doi: 10.1037/0882-7974.21.2.253.

Jopp, D. S. & Schmitt, M. (2010). Dealing with negative life events: Differential effects of personal resources, coping strategies, and control beliefs. *European Journal of Ageing, 7*(3), 167–180.

Jordan, N. C. (2007). Do words count? Connections between mathematics and reading difficulties. In D. B. Berch & M. M. M. Mazzocco (Eds), *Why is math so hard for some children? The nature and origins of mathematical learning difficulties and disabilities* (pp. 107–120). Baltimore, MD; London: Paul H. Brookes.

Jorgensen, R. S., Frankowski, I. I., & Carey, M. P. (1999). Sense of coherence, negative life events, and appraisal of physical health. *Personality and Individual Differences, 27*, 1079–1089.

Jorm, A. F. (2000). Is depression a risk factor for dementia or cognitive decline? A review. [Research Support, Non-U.S. Gov't; Review]. *Gerontology, 46*(4), 219–227. doi: 22163.

Jorm, A. F., Christensen, H., Henderson, A. S., Jacomb, P. A., Korten, A. E., & Mackinnon, A. (1998). Factors associated with successful ageing. *Australasian Journal on Ageing, 17*(1), 33–37.

Jung, C. G. (1967, 1930). *The collected works of C G Jung Vol. 13: Alchemical studies*: London: Routledge & Kegan Paul, 1967.

Kamel, N. S. & Gammack, J. K. (2006). Insomnia in the elderly: Cause, approach, and treatment. [Research Support, U.S. Gov't, P.H.S.; Review]. *American Journal of Medicine, 119*(6), 463–469. doi: 10.1016/j.amjmed.2005.10.051.

Kane, M. J., Hasher, L., Stoltzfus, E. R., Zacks, R. T., & Connelly, S. L. (1994). Inhibitory attentional mechanisms and aging. [Research Support, U.S. Gov't, P.H.S.]. *Psychology and Aging, 9*(1), 103–112.

Kaplan, E., Goodglass, H., & Weintraub, S. (2001). *The Boston naming test* (2nd edn). Philadelphia: Lippincott Williams & Wilkins.

Karney, B. R. & Bradbury, T. N. (1995). The longitudinal course of marital quality and stability: A review of theory, method, and research. [Research Support, U.S. Gov't, Non-P.H.S.; Research Support, U.S. Gov't, P.H.S.; Review]. *Psychological Bulletin, 118*(1), 3–34.

Kastenbaum, R. (2006). Suicide. In R. Schulz (Ed.) with L. S. Noelker, K. Rockwood, & R. L. Sprott (Assoc. eds), *Encyclopedia of aging: A comprehensive resource in gerontology and geriatrics* (4th edn, pp. 1155–1156). New York: Springer.

Katz, S. & Peters, K. R. (2008). Enhancing the mind? Memory medicine, dementia, and the aging brain. *Journal of Aging Studies, 22*(4), 348–355. doi: 10.1016/j.jaging.2008.05.007.

Kaufman, A. S., McLean, J. E., Kaufman-Packer, J. L., & Reynolds, C. R. (1991). Is the pattern of intellectual growth and decline across the adult life span different for men and women? *Journal of Clinical Psychology, 47*(6), 801–812.

Kausler, D. H. (1991). *Experimental psychology, cognition, and human aging* (2nd edn). New York: Springer-Verlag.

Kausler, D. H. (1994). *Learning and memory in normal aging*. San Diego, CA; London: Academic Press.

Kawachi, I. & Berkman, L. F. (2000). Social cohesion, social capital and health. In L. F. Berkman & I. Kawachi (Eds), *Social epidemiology* (pp. 174–190). Oxford: Oxford University Press.

Kemenoff, L. A., Miller, B. L., & Kramer, J. H. (2002). Frontal lobe. *Encyclopedia of the human brain*. London: Elsevier Science & Technology. Retrieved from http://www. credoreference.com/entry/esthumanbrain/frontal_lobe.

Kemper, S. & Harden, T. (1999). Experimentally disentangling what's beneficial about elderspeak from what's not. [Comparative Study; Research Support, U.S. Gov't, P.H.S.]. *Psychology and Aging, 14*(4), 656–670.

Kempermann, G., Gast, D., & Gage, F. H. (2002). Neuroplasticity in old age: Sustained fivefold induction of hippocampal neurogenesis by long-term environmental enrichment. [Research Support, Non-U.S. Gov't; Research Support, U.S. Gov't, P.H.S.]. *Annals of Neurology, 52*(2), 135–143. doi: 10.1002/ana.10262.

Kendler, K. S., Thornton, L. M., & Gardner, C. O. (2001). Genetic risk, number of previous depressive episodes, and stressful life events in predicting onset of major depression. [Research Support, Non-U.S. Gov't; Research Support, U.S. Gov't, P.H.S.; Twin Study]. *American Journal of Psychiatry, 158*(4), 582–586.

Kennedy, Q. & Mather, M. (2007). Aging, affect, and decision making. In K. D. Vohs, R. F. Baumeister & G. Loewenstein (Eds), *Do emotions help or hurt decision making? A hedgefoxian perspective* (pp. 245–267). New York: Russell Sage Foundation.

Kenney, W. L. & Munce, T. A. (2003). Invited review: Aging and human temperature regulation. [Review]. *Journal of Applied Physiology, 95*(6), 2598–2603. doi: 10.1152/ japplphysiol.00202.2003.

Kensinger, E. A. & Corkin, S. (2004). Two routes to emotional memory: Distinct neural processes for valence and arousal. [Research Support, Non-U.S. Gov't; Research Support, U.S. Gov't, Non-P.H.S.; Research Support, U.S. Gov't, P.H.S.]. *Proceedings of the National Academy of Sciences of the United States of America, 101*(9), 3310–3315. doi: 10.1073/pnas.0306408101.

Kensinger E. A. & Corkin, S. (2005). Alzheimer Disease. In L. Nadel (Ed.), *Encyclopedia of cognitive science*. Chichester, West Sussex: Wiley. Retrieved from http://www. credoreference.com/entry/wileycs/alzheimer_disease.

Kiecolt-Glaser, J. K. & Glaser, R. (1986). Psychological influences on immunity. [Research Support, U.S. Gov't, P.H.S.]. *Psychosomatics, 27*(9), 621–624. doi: 10.1016/S0033-3182(86)72630-3.

Kilpatrick, C., Burns, R., & Blumbergs, P. C. (1983). Identical twins with Alzheimer's disease. [Case Reports]. *Journal of Neurology, Neurosurgery, and Psychiatry, 46*(5), 421–425.

Kim, J., Son, J., Ko, N., & Yoon, B. (2013). Unsupervised virtual reality-based exercise program improves hip muscle strength and balance control in older adults: A pilot study. *Archives of Physical Medicine and Rehabilitation, 94*(5), 937–943. doi: 10.1016/j. apmr.2012.12.010.

King, V. & Scott, M. E. (2005). A comparison of cohabiting relationships among older and younger adults. *Journal of Marriage and Family, 67*(2), 271–285.

Kipps, C. M. & Hodges, J. R. (2005). Cognitive assessment for clinicians. [Research Support, Non-U.S. Gov't; Review]. *Journal of Neurology, Neurosurgery, and Psychiatry, 76*(Suppl. 1), i22–30. doi: 10.1136/jnnp.2004.059758.

Kirby, A., Sugden, D., Beveridge, S., Edwards, L., & Edwards, R. (2008). Dyslexia and developmental co-ordination disorder in further and higher education – Similarities and differences. Does the 'label' influence the support given? *Dyslexia*, *14*(3), 197–213. doi: 10.1002/dys.367.

Kirby, A., Williams, N., Thomas, M., & Hill, E. L. (2013). Self-reported mood, general health, wellbeing and employment status in adults with suspected DCD. [Research Support, Non-U.S. Gov't]. *Research in Developmental Disabilities*, *34*(4), 1357–1364. doi: 10.1016/j.ridd.2013.01.003.

Kirkwood, T. B. L. (2005). Mechanisms of cellular damage. In M. L. Johnson (Ed.), *The Cambridge handbook of age and ageing*. Cambridge: Cambridge University Press. Retrieved from http://www.credoreference.com/entry/cupage/mechanisms_of_cellular_damage.

Kitwood, T. M. (1997). *Dementia reconsidered: The person comes first*. Buckingham: Open University Press.

Kitwood, T. & Bredin, K. (1992). Towards a theory of dementia care: Personhood and well-being. *Ageing and Society*, *12*, 269–287.

Kivipelto, M., Soininen, H., & Tuomilehto, J. (2002). Hypertension and white matter lesions of the brain. [Comment; Editorial; Review]. *Journal of Hypertension*, *20*(3), 387–389.

Klass, M., Baudry, S., & Duchateau, J. (2007). Voluntary activation during maximal contraction with advancing age: A brief review. [Research Support, Non-U.S. Gov't; Review]. *European Journal of Applied Physiology*, *100*(5), 543–551. doi: 10.1007/s00421-006-0205-x.

Kline, D. W. & Scialfa, C. T. (1997). Sensory and perceptual functioning: Basic research and human factors implications. In A. D. Fisk & W. A. Rogers (Eds), *Handbook of human factors and the older adult* (pp. 27–54). San Diego: Academic Press.

Kloos, A. D., Kegelmeyer, D. A., Young, G. S., & Kostyk, S. K. (2010). Fall risk assessment using the Tinetti mobility test in individuals with Huntington's disease. [Research Support, Non-U.S. Gov't]. *Movement Disorders*, *25*(16), 2838–2844. doi: 10.1002/mds.23421.

Knight, B. (2004). *Psychotherapy with older adults* (3rd edn). Thousand Oaks, CA; London: Sage.

Knight, T. (2012). Body image among older adults. In T. Cash (Ed.), *Encyclopedia of body image and human appearance* (pp. 114–119). San Francisco: Academic Press. Retrieved from https://www.dawsonera.com/abstract/9780123849267.

Knol, M. J., Twisk, J. W., Beekman, A. T., Heine, R. J., Snoek, F. J., & Pouwer, F. (2006). Depression as a risk factor for the onset of type 2 diabetes mellitus. A meta-analysis. [Meta-Analysis; Research Support, Non-U.S. Gov't]. *Diabetologia*, *49*(5), 837–845. doi: 10.1007/s00125-006-0159-x.

Kobasa, S. C. & Maddi, S. R. (1977). Existential personality theory. In R. J. e. Coesini (Ed.), *Current personality theories* (pp. 243–276). [S.l.]: Peacock Pubs.

Kohlberg, L. (1969). Stage and sequence: The cognitive-developmental approach to socialization. In D. A. Goslin (Ed.), *Handbook of socialization theory and research* (pp. 347–480). Chicago: Rand McNally.

Kohlberg, L. (1976). Moral stages and moralization. In T. Lickona (Ed.), *Moral development and behavior: Theory, research, and social issues*. New York; London: Holt, Rinehart and Winston.

Kollins, S. H., McClernon, F. J., & Fuemmeler, B. F. (2005). Association between smoking and attention-deficit/hyperactivity disorder symptoms in a population-based sample of young adults. [Comparative Study; Research Support, N.I.H., Extramural; Research Support, U.S. Gov't, Non-P.H.S.; Research Support, U.S. Gov't, P.H.S.]. *Archives of General Psychiatry*, *62*(10), 1142–1147. doi: 10.1001/archpsyc.62.10.1142.

Koriat, A. & Ackerman, R. (2010). Metacognition and mindreading: Judgments of learning for Self and Other during self-paced study. [Research Support, Non-U.S. Gov't]. *Consciousness and Cognition, 19*(1), 251–264. doi: 10.1016/j.concog.2009.12.010.

Kosberg, J. I., Cairl, R. E., & Keller, D. M. (1990). Components of burden: Interventive implications. [Research Support, Non-U.S. Gov't]. *Gerontologist, 30*(2), 236–242.

Kostka, T. (2005). Quadriceps maximal power and optimal shortening velocity in 335 men aged 23–88 years. [Research Support, Non-U.S. Gov't]. *European Journal of Applied Physiology, 95*(2–3), 140–145. doi: 10.1007/s00421-005-1390-8.

Kramer, A. F., Humphrey, D. G., Larish, J. F., Logan, G. D., & Strayer, D. L. (1994). Aging and inhibition: Beyond a unitary view of inhibitory processing in attention. [Research Support, U.S. Gov't, P.H.S.]. *Psychology and Aging, 9*(4), 491–512.

Kramer, D. (1990). Conceptualizing wisdom: The primacy of affect-cognition relations. In R. J. Sternberg (Ed.), *Wisdom: Its nature, origins and development* (pp. 279–316). Cambridge: Cambridge University Press.

Krause, N. & Shaw, B. A. (2000). Role-specific feelings of control and mortality. [Research Support, U.S. Gov't, P.H.S.]. *Psychology and Aging, 15*(4), 617–626.

Krinsky-McHale, S. J., Kittler, P., Brown, W. T., Jenkins, E. C., & Devenny, D. A. (2005). Repetition priming in adults with Williams syndrome: Age-related dissociation between implicit and explicit memory. [Comparative Study; Research Support, N.I.H., Extramural; Research Support, Non-U.S. Gov't]. *American Journal of Mental Retardation, 110*(6), 482–496. doi: 10.1352/0895-8017(2005)110[482:RPIAWW]2.0.CO;2.

Krishnan, K. R. (2002). Biological risk factors in late life depression. [Review]. *Biological Psychiatry, 52*(3), 185–192.

Kubler-Ross, E. (1969). *On death and dying.* [S.l.]: Macmillan.

Kubzansky, L. D., Cole, S. R., Kawachi, I., Vokonas, P., & Sparrow, D. (2006). Shared and unique contributions of anger, anxiety, and depression to coronary heart disease: A prospective study in the normative aging study. [Research Support, N.I.H., Extramural; Research Support, Non-U.S. Gov't; Research Support, U.S. Gov't, Non-P.H.S.]. *Annals of behavioral medicine: A publication of the Society of Behavioral Medicine, 31*(1), 21–29. doi: 10.1207/s15324796abm3101_5.

Kujala, U. M. (2009). Evidence on the effects of exercise therapy in the treatment of chronic disease. [Review]. *British Journal of Sports Medicine, 43*(8), 550–555. doi: 10.1136/bjsm.2009.059808.

Kunzmann, U. & Grun, D. (2003). *Emotional reactions to sad film clips: Evidence for greater reactivity in old age.* Paper presented at the Annual Meeting of the American Psychological Association, Toronto.

Kurzweil, R. (2005). *The singularity is near: When humans transcend biology.* New York: Viking.

Kynette, D., & Kemper, S. (1986). Aging and the loss of grammatical forms: A cross-sectional study of language performance. *Language & Communication, 6*(1), 65–72.

Labouvie-Vief, G. (1997). Cognitive-emotional integration in adulthood. *Annual Review of Gerontology and Geriatrics, 17*(1), 206–237.

Labouvie-Vief, G. (2003). Dynamic integration: Affect, cognition, and the self in adulthood. *Current Directions in Psychological Science, 12*(6), 201–206. doi: 10.1046/j.0963-7214.2003.01262.x.

Labouvie-Vief, G. (2005). The psychology of emotions and ageing. *The Cambridge handbook of age and ageing.* Cambridge: Cambridge University Press.

Labouvie-Vief, G. & Marquez, M. (2004). Dynamic integration: Affect optimization and differentiation in development. In D. Y. Dai & R. J. Sternberg (Eds), *Motivation, emotion, and cognition: Integrative perspectives on intellectual functioning and development* (pp. 237–272). Mahwah, NJ; London: Lawrence Erlbaum.

Lachman, M. E. (2004). Development in midlife. [Research Support, U.S. Gov't, P.H.S.; Review]. *Annual Review of Psychology, 55*, 305–331. doi: 10.1146/annurev. psych.55.090902.141521.

Lachman, M. E. & Andreoletti, C. (2006). Strategy use mediates the relationship between control beliefs and memory performance for middle-aged and older adults. [Research Support, N.I.H., Extramural]. *Journals of Gerontology B: Psychological Sciences and Social Sciences, 61*(2), P88–94.

Lang, F. R. & Carstensen, L. L. (2002). Time counts: Future time perspective, goals, and social relationships. [Research Support, Non-U.S. Gov't]. *Psychology and Aging, 17*(1), 125–139.

Lang, T., Streeper, T., Cawthon, P., Baldwin, K., Taaffe, D. R., & Harris, T. B. (2010). Sarcopenia: Etiology, clinical consequences, intervention, and assessment. [Review]. *Osteoporosis International, 21*(4), 543–559. doi: 10.1007/s00198-009-1059-y.

Langer, E. J. (1989). *Mindfulness*. Reading, MA: Addison Wesley.

La Rue, A., Dessonville, C., & Jarvik, L. F. (1985). Aging and mental disorders. In J. E. Birren & K. W. Schaie (Eds) with V. Bengtson, L. Jarvik, & T. Salthouse (Assoc. eds), *Handbook of the psychology of aging* (2nd edn, pp. 664–702). New York; Workingham [i.e. Wokingham]: Van Nostrand Reinhold.

Larsen, R. J. & Cutler, S. E. (1996). The complexity of individual emotional lives: A within-subject analysis of affect structure. *Journal of Social and Clinical Psychology, 15*, 206–230.

Lau, A. L., Cummins, R. A., & McPherson, W. (2005). An investigation into the cross-cultural equivalence of the personal wellbeing index. *Social Indicators Research, 72*(3), 403–430.

Lavender, A. P. & Nosaka, K. (2007). Fluctuations of isometric force after eccentric exercise of the elbow flexors of young, middle-aged, and old men. [Clinical Trial]. *European Journal of Applied Physiology, 100*(2), 161–167. doi: 10.1007/s00421-007-0418-7.

Lawton, M. P. (1999). Environmental design features and the well-being of older persons. In M. Duffy (Ed.), *Handbook of counseling and psychotherapy with older adults* (pp. 350–363). New York; Chichester: John Wiley.

Lawton, M. P., Moss, M., & Fulcomer, M. (1986). Objective and subjective uses of time by older people. [Research Support, U.S. Gov't, P.H.S.]. *International Journal of Aging and Human Development, 24*(3), 171–188.

Lawton, M. P., Moss, M. S., Winter, L., & Hoffman, C. (2002). Motivation in later life: Personal projects and well-being. [Research Support, U.S. Gov't, P.H.S.]. *Psychology and Aging, 17*(4), 539–547.

Lawton, M. P. & Nahemow, L. (1973). Ecology and the aging process. In C. Eisdorfer & M. P. Lawton (Eds), *The psychology of adult development and ageing* (pp. 619–674). Washington, DC: American Psychological Association.

Lazarus, R. S. (1976). *Psychological stress and the coping process*. Ann Arbor, MI: [s.n.].

Lazarus, R. S. & Folkman, S. (1984). *Stress, appraisal, and coping*. New York: Springer.

LeBlanc, E., Janowsky, J., Chan, B., & Nelson, H. (2001). Hormone replacement therapy and cognition. *JAMA, 285*, 1489–1499.

Lee, G. R., DeMaris, A., Bavin, S., & Sullivan, R. (2001). Gender differences in the depressive effect of widowhood in later life. *Journals of Gerontology B: Psychological Sciences and Social Sciences, 56*(1), S56–S61.

Lehman, H. C. (1953). *Age and achievement*. Princeton: Princeton University Press.

Lennartsson, C. & Silverstein, M. (2001). Does engagement with life enhance survival of elderly people in Sweden? The role of social and leisure activities. [Research Support, Non-U.S. Gov't]. *Journals of Gerontology B: Psychological Sciences and Social Sciences, 56*(6), S335–342.

Leonardelli, G. J., Hermann, A. D., Lynch, M. E., & Arkin, R. M. (2003). The shape of self-evaluation: Implicit theories of intelligence and judgments of intellectual ability. *Journal of Research in Personality, 37*(3), 141–168.

Leslie, A. M. (1987). Pretense and representation in infancy: The origins of 'theory of mind'. *Psychological Review, 94*, 412–426.

Leveroni, C. L., Seidenberg, M., Mayer, A. R., Mead, L. A., Binder, J. R., & Rao, S. M. (2000). Neural systems underlying the recognition of familiar and newly learned faces. [Research Support, U.S. Gov't, P.H.S.]. *The Journal of Neuroscience: The Official Journal of the Society for Neuroscience, 20*(2), 878–886.

Levinger, G. (1980). Toward the analysis of close relationships. *Journal of Experimental Social Psychology, 16*(6), 510–544.

Levinson, D. J. (1978). *The seasons of a man's life.* New York: Ballantine.

Levy, B. (1996). Improving memory in old age through implicit self-stereotyping. [Clinical Trial; Comparative Study; Randomized Controlled Trial; Research Support, Non-U.S. Gov't; Research Support, U.S. Gov't, Non-P.H.S.]. *Journal of Personality and Social Psychology, 71*(6), 1092–1107.

Levy, B. R., Slade, M. D., Kunkel, S. R., & Kasl, S. V. (2002). Longevity increased by positive self-perceptions of aging. [Research Support, Non-U.S. Gov't; Research Support, U.S. Gov't, P.H.S.]. *Journal of Personality and Social Psychology, 83*(2), 261–270.

Levy, B. R., Slade, M. D., & Kasl, S. V. (2002). Longitudinal benefit of positive self-perceptions of aging on functional health. [Research Support, Non-U.S. Gov't; Research Support, U.S. Gov't, P.H.S.]. *Journals of Gerontology B: Psychological Sciences and Social Sciences, 57*(5), P409–417.

Levy, R. & Goldman-Rakic, P. S. (2000). Segregation of working memory functions within the dorsolateral prefrontal cortex. *Experimental Brain Research, 133*, 23–32.

Lewis, K. G. & Moon, S. (1997). Always single and single again women: A qualitative study. *Journal of Marital and Family Therapy, 23*(2), 115–134.

Lewis, M. D. (2000). Emotional self-organization at three time scales. In M. D. Lewis & I. Granic (Eds), *Emotion, development, and self-organization: Dynamic systems approaches to emotional development.* Cambridge; New York: Cambridge University Press.

Lewis, R. (1995). *Professional user's guide for the digit vigilance test.* Odessa, FL: Psychological Assessment Resources.

Lezak, M. D. (2012). *Neuropsychological assessment* (5th edn). Oxford; New York: Oxford University Press.

Li, K. Z., Krampe, R. T., & Bondar, A. (2005). An ecological approach to studying aging and dual-task performance. In R. W. Engle (Ed.), *Cognitive limitations in aging and psychopathology* (pp. 190–218). Cambridge: Cambridge University Press.

Li, S., Aggen, S. H., Nesselroade, J. R., & Baltes, P. B. (2001). Short-term fluctuations in elderly people's sensorimotor functioning predict text and spatial memory performance: The Macarthur Successful Aging Studies. [Research Support, Non-U.S. Gov't]. *Gerontology, 47*(2), 100–116.

Li, S. C., Schmiedek, F., Huxhold, O., Rocke, C., Smith, J., & Lindenberger, U. (2008). Working memory plasticity in old age: Practice gain, transfer, and maintenance. [Controlled Clinical Trial]. *Psychology and Aging, 23*(4), 731–742. doi: 10.1037/a0014343.

Lichtenstein, P., Carlstrom, E., Rastam, M., Gillberg, C., & Anckarsater, H. (2010). The genetics of autism spectrum disorders and related neuropsychiatric disorders in childhood. [Research Support, Non-U.S. Gov't; Twin Study]. *American Journal of Psychiatry, 167*(11), 1357–1363. doi: 10.1176/appi.ajp.2010.10020223.

Lieberman, M. D., Gaunt, R., Gilbert, D. T., & Trope, Y. (2002). Reflexion and reflection: A social cognitive neuroscience approach to attributional inference. In M. P. Zanna (Ed.), *Advances in experimental social psychology* (Vol. 34, pp. 199–249). San Diego, CA: Academic Press

Lifshitz, H., Tzuriel, D., & Weiss, I. (2005). Effects of training in conceptual versus perceptual analogies among adolescents and adults with intellectual disability. *Journal of Cognitive Education and Psychology, 5,* 144–167.

Light, L. L. (1991). Memory and aging: Four hypotheses in search of data. [Research Support, U.S. Gov't, P.H.S.; Review]. *Annual Review of Psychology, 42,* 333–376. doi: 10.1146/annurev.ps.42.020191.002001.

Light, L. L., Prull, M. W., La Voie, D., & Heal, M. R. (2000). Dual process theories of memory in older age. In T. J. Perfect & E. Maylor (Eds), *Theoretical Debate in Cognitive Aging* (pp. 238–300). Oxford: Oxford University Press.

Lindenberger, U., Scherer, H., & Baltes, P. B. (2001). The strong connection between sensory and cognitive performance in old age: Not due to sensory acuity reductions operating during cognitive assessment. [Clinical Trial; Randomized Controlled Trial]. *Psychology and Aging, 16*(2), 196–205.

Lineweaver, T. T. & Hertzog, C. (1998). Adults' efficacy and control beliefs regarding memory and aging: Separating general from personal beliefs. *Aging, Neuropsychology, and Cognition, 5*(4), 264–296. doi: 10.1076/anec.5.4.264.771.

Linnet, K. M., Dalsgaard, S., Obel, C., Wisborg, K., Henriksen, T. B., Rodriguez, A., Kotimaa, A., Moilanen, I., Thomsen, P. H., Olsen, J., & Jarvelin, M. R. (2003). Maternal lifestyle factors in pregnancy risk of attention deficit hyperactivity disorder and associated behaviors: Review of the current evidence. [Comparative Study; Research Support, Non-U.S. Gov't; Review]. *American Journal of Psychiatry, 160*(6), 1028–1040.

Litwak, E. (1985). *Helping the elderly: The complementary roles of informal networks and formal systems.* New York: Guilford Press.

Lockenhoff, C. E. & Carstensen, L. L. (2007). Aging, emotion, and health-related decision strategies: Motivational manipulations can reduce age differences. [Research Support, N.I.H., Extramural; Research Support, N.I.H., Intramural; Research Support, Non-U.S. Gov't]. *Psychology and Aging, 22*(1), 134–146. doi: 10.1037/0882-7974.22.1.134.

Loevinger, J. & Blasi, A. (1976). *Ego development.* San Francisco; London: Jossey-Bass.

Logan, J. M., Sanders, A. L., Snyder, A. Z., Morris, J. C., & Buckner, R. L. (2002). Underrecruitment and nonselective recruitment: Dissociable neural mechanisms associated with aging. [Research Support, Non-U.S. Gov't; Research Support, U.S. Gov't, Non-P.H.S.; Research Support, U.S. Gov't, P.H.S.]. *Neuron, 33*(5), 827–840.

Logie, R. H. & Della Sala, S. (2005). Disorders of visuospatial working memory. In P. Shah & A. Miyake (Eds), *The Cambridge handbook of visuospatial thinking* (pp. 81–120). Cambridge: Cambridge University Press.

Logie, R. H. & Maylor, E. A. (2009). An Internet study of prospective memory across adulthood. *Psychology and Aging, 24*(3), 767–774. doi: 10.1037/a0015479.

Lombardi, G., Tauchmanova, L., Di Somma, C., Musella, T., Rota, F., Savanelli, M. C., & Colao, A. (2005). Somatopause: Dismetabolic and bone effects. [Review]. *Journal of Endocrinological Investigation, 28*(Suppl. 10), 36–42.

Losse, A., Henderson, S. E., Elliman, D., Hall, D., Knight, E., & Jongmans, M. (1991). Clumsiness in children – Do they grow out of it? A 10-year follow-up study. [Research Support, Non-U.S. Gov't]. *Developmental Medicine and Child Neurology, 33*(1), 55–68.

Lovasi, G. S., Lemaitre, R. N., Siscovick, D. S., Dublin, S., Bis, J. C., Lumley, T., .Psaty, B. M. (2007). Amount of leisure-time physical activity and risk of nonfatal myocardial infarction. [Research Support, N.I.H., Extramural Research Support, U.S. Gov't, Non-P.H.S.]. *Ann Epidemiol, 17*(6), 410-416. doi: 10.1016/j.annepidem.2006.10.012

Lu, T. & Finkel, T. (2008). Free radicals and senescence. [Review]. *Experimental Cell Research, 314*(9), 1918–1922. doi: 10.1016/j.yexcr.2008.01.011.

Lupien, S. J., McEwen, B. S., Gunnar, M. R., & Heim, C. (2009). Effects of stress throughout the lifespan on the brain, behaviour and cognition. [Review]. *Nature Reviews Neuroscience, 10*(6), 434–445. doi: 10.1038/nrn2639.

Lyketsos, C. G., Lopez, O., Jones, B., Fitzpatrick, A. L., Breitner, J., & DeKosky, S. (2002). Prevalence of neuropsychiatric symptoms in dementia and mild cognitive impairment: Results from the cardiovascular health study. [Research Support, U.S. Gov't, P.H.S.]. *JAMA, 288*(12), 1475–1483.

Lysaker, P. H., Olesek, K. L., Warman, D. M., Martin, J. M., Salzman, A. K., Nicolo, G., Salvatore, G., & Dimaggio, G. (2011). Metacognition in schizophrenia: Correlates and stability of deficits in theory of mind and self-reflectivity. *Psychiatry Research, 190*(1), 18–22. doi: 10.1016/j.psychres.2010.07.016.

MacKay, D. G. & Abrams, L. (1998). Age-linked declines in retrieving orthographic knowledge: Empirical, practical, and theoretical implications. [Comparative Study; Research Support, U.S. Gov't, Non-P.H.S.; Research Support, U.S. Gov't, P.H.S.]. *Psychology and Aging, 13*(4), 647–662.

MacKay, D. G., Abrams, L., & Pedroza, M. J. (1999). Aging on the input versus output side: Theoretical implications of age-linked asymmetries between detecting versus retrieving orthographic information. [Research Support, U.S. Gov't, Non-P.H.S.; Research Support, U.S. Gov't, P.H.S.]. *Psychology and Aging, 14*(1), 3–17.

MacKay, D. G. & Miller, M. D. (1996). Can cognitive aging contribute to fundamental psychological theory? Repetition deafness as a test case. *Aging, Neuropsychology, and Cognition, 3*(3), 169–186.

Magai, C., Cohen, C., Milburn, N., Thorpe, B., McPherson, R., & Peralta, D. (2001). Attachment styles in older European American and African American adults. [Research Support, U.S. Gov't, P.H.S.]. *Journals of Gerontology B: Psychological Sciences and Social Sciences, 56*(1), S28–35.

Magai, C., Consedine, N. S., Gillespie, M., O'Neal, C., & Vilker, R. (2004). The differential roles of early emotion socialization and adult attachment in adult emotional experience: Testing a mediator hypothesis. [Research Support, U.S. Gov't, P.H.S.]. *Attachment and Human Development, 6*(4), 389–417. doi: 10.1080/1461673042000303118.

Magai, C. & Passman, V. (1997). The interpersonal basis of emotional behavior and emotion regulation in adulthood. *Annual Review of Gerontology and Geriatrics, 17*(1), 104–137.

Magary, D. (2011). *The end specialist.* London: Harper Voyager.

Mahlberg, R., Tilmann, A., Salewski, L., & Kunz, D. (2006). Normative data on the daily profile of urinary 6-sulfatoxymelatonin in healthy subjects between the ages of 20 and 84. [Research Support, Non-U.S. Gov't]. *Psychoneuroendocrinology, 31*(5), 634–641. doi: 10.1016/j.psyneuen.2006.01.009.

Mahncke, H. W., Bronstone, A., & Merzenich, M. M. (2006). Brain plasticity and functional losses in the aged: Scientific bases for a novel intervention. [Review]. *Progress in Brain Research, 157*, 81–109. doi: 10.1016/S0079-6123(06)57006-2.

Main, M. & Solomon, J. (1986). Discovery of an insecure–disorganized/disoriented attachment pattern. In T.B. Brazelton & M.W. Yogman (Eds), *Affective development in infancy* (pp. 95–124). Norwood, NJ: Ablex

Major, B., Richards, C., Cooper, M. L., Cozzarelli, C., & Zubek, J. (1998). Personal resilience, cognitive appraisals, and coping: an integrative model of adjustment to abortion. [Research Support, U.S. Gov't, P.H.S.]. *Journal of Personality and Social Psychology, 74*(3), 735–752.

Mäkikangas, A., Kinnunen, U., & Feldt, T. (2004). Self-esteem, dispositional optimism, and health: Evidence from cross-lagged data on employees. *Journal of Research in Personality, 38*(6), 556–575.

Malouff, J. M., Thorsteinsson, E. B., Schutte, N. S., Bhullar, N., & Rooke, S. E. (2010). The five-factor model of personality and relationship satisfaction of intimate partners: A meta-analysis. *Journal of Research in Personality, 44*(1), 124–127.

Margrain, T. H. & Boulton, M. (2005). Sensory impairment. In M. L. Johnson (Ed.), *The Cambridge handbook of age and ageing*. Cambridge: Cambridge University Press. Retrieved from http://www.credoreference.com/entry.do?id=9272856.

Markesbery, W. R. (2010). Neuropathologic alterations in mild cognitive impairment: A review. [Research Support, N.I.H., Extramural; Research Support, Non-U.S. Gov't; Review]. *Journal of Alzheimer's Disease, 19*(1), 221–228. doi: 10.3233/JAD-2010-1220.

Markus, H. & Nurius, P. (1986). Possible selves. *American Psychologist, 41*(9), 954–969.

Marshall, L. A. (2004). Hormone replacement therapy. *Encyclopedia of women's health*. New York: Springer Science+Business Media. Retrieved from http://www.credoreference.com/entry/sprwh/hormone_replacement_therapy.

Marsiske, M., Klumb, P., & Baltes, M. M. (1997). Everyday activity patterns and sensory functioning in old age. [Research Support, Non-U.S. Gov't]. *Psychology and Aging, 12*(3), 444–457.

Martin, L. J. (2002). Neurodegenerative disorders. In V. S. Ramachandran (Ed.), *Encyclopedia of the human brain*. Oxford: Elsevier Science & Technology. Retrieved from http://www.credoreference.com/entry/esthumanbrain/neurodegenerative_disorders.

Martin, M. & Zimprich, D. (2005). Cognitive development in midlife. In M. Martin & S. L. Willis (Eds), *Middle adulthood: A lifespan perspective* (pp. 179–206). Thousand Oaks: Sage.

Martin-Matthews, A. (1999). Widowhood: Dominant renditions, changing demographics, and variable meaning. In S. M. Neysmith (Ed.), *Critical issues for future social work practice with aging persons* (pp. 27–46). New York; Chichester: Columbia University Press.

Masuda, M. & Holmes, T. H. (1967). The Social Readjustment Rating Scale: A cross-cultural study of Japanese and Americans. *Journal of Psychosomatic Research, 11*(2), 227–237.

Matus, A. (2005). Growth of dendritic spines: A continuing story. [Review]. *Current Opinion in Neurobiology, 15*(1), 67–72. doi: 10.1016/j.conb.2005.01.015.

Maurer, T. J., Weiss, E. M., & Barbeite, F. G. (2003). A model of involvement in work-related learning and development activity: The effects of individual, situational, motivational, and age variables. [Research Support, U.S. Gov't, P.H.S.]. *Journal of Applied Psychology, 88*(4), 707–724.

May, C. P., Hasher, L., & Kane, M. J. (1999). The role of interference in memory span. [Research Support, U.S. Gov't, P.H.S.]. *Memory & Cognition, 27*(5), 759–767.

Maylor, E. A. (1996). *Does prospective memory decline with age?* Mahwah, NJ: Lawrence Erlbaum Associates.

Maylor, E. A. & Wing, A. M. (1996). Age differences in postural stability are increased by additional cognitive demands. [Comparative Study]. *Journals of Gerontology B: Psychological Sciences and Social Sciences, 51*(3), P143–154.

Maylor, E. A., Moulson, J. M., Muncer, A. M., & Taylor, L. A. (2002). Does performance on theory of mind tasks decline in old age? *British Journal of Psychology, 93*(Pt 4), 465–485.

McAdams, D. P. (1992). The five-factor model in personality: A critical appraisal. [Review]. *Journal of Personality, 60*(2), 329–361.

McArdle, J. J. & Hamagami, F. (2006). Longitudinal tests of dynamic hypotheses on intellectual abilities measured over sixty years. In C. S. Bergeman & S. M. Boker (Eds), *Methodological issues in aging research* (pp. 43–98). Mahwah, NJ; London: Lawrence Erlbaum Associates.

McCarthy, L. H., Bigal, M. E., Katz, M., Derby, C., & Lipton, R. B. (2009). Chronic pain and obesity in elderly people: Results from the Einstein aging study. [Research Support, N.I.H., Extramural]. *Journal of the American Geriatrics Society, 57*(1), 115–119. doi: 10.1111/j.1532-5415.2008.02089.x.

McCrae, R. R. & Costa, P. T. (2003). *Personality in adulthood: A five-factor theory perspective* (2nd edn). New York; London: Guilford Press.

McCrae, R. R., & Costa, P. T., Jr (1997). Personality trait structure as a human universal. [Comparative Study]. *American Psychologist, 52*(5), 509–516.

McDermott, D. & Snyder, C. R. (2000). *Making hope happen*. Oakland, CA: New Harbinger Publications.

McDonald-Miszczak, L., Hertzog, C., & Hultsch, D. F. (1995). Stability and accuracy of metamemory in adulthood and aging: A longitudinal analysis. [Research Support, U.S. Gov't, P.H.S.]. *Psychology and Aging, 10*(4), 553–564.

McDougall, S. & House, B. (2012). Brain training in older adults: Evidence of transfer to memory span performance and pseudo-Matthew effects. [Comparative Study; Research Support, Non-U.S. Gov't]. *Neuropsychology, Development, and Cognition. Section B, Aging, Neuropsychology and Cognition, 19*(1–2), 195–221. doi: 10.1080/13825585. 2011.640656.

McDowd, J. M. (1986). The effects of age and extended practice on divided attention performance. *Journal of Gerontology, 41*(6), 764–769.

McDowd, J. M. & Craik, F. I. (1988). Effects of aging and task difficulty on divided attention performance. *Journal of Experimental Psychology: Human Perception and Performance, 14*(2), 267–280.

McDowd, J. M., Vercruyssen, M., & Birren, J. E. (1991). Aging, divided attention, and dual task performance. In D. Damos (Ed.), *Multiple task performance* (pp. 387–414). London: Taylor & Francis.

McDowell, C. L., Harrison, D. W., & Demaree, H. A. (1994). Is right hemisphere decline in the perception of emotion a function of aging? [Research Support, U.S. Gov't, P.H.S.]. *International Journal of Neuroscience, 79*(1–2), 1–11.

McFarland, C., Ross, M., & Giltrow, M. (1992). Biased recollections in older adults: The role of implicit theories of aging. [Research Support, Non-U.S. Gov't]. *Journal of Personality and Social Psychology, 62*(5), 837–850.

McGinnis, D. & Zelinski, E. M. (2000). Understanding unfamiliar words: The influence of processing resources, vocabulary knowledge, and age. [Comparative Study; Research Support, U.S. Gov't, P.H.S.]. *Psychology and Aging, 15*(2), 335–350.

McGinnis, D. & Zelinski, E. M. (2003). Understanding unfamiliar words in young, young-old, and old-old adults: Inferential processing and the abstraction-deficit hypothesis. [Comparative Study; Research Support, U.S. Gov't, P.H.S.]. *Psychology and Aging, 18*(3), 497–509. doi: 10.1037/0882-7974.18.3.497.

McKeith, I. (2010). What is dementia with Lewy bodies (DLB)? Retrieved from http:// www.alzheimers.org.uk/site/scripts/documents_info.php?documentID=113.

McLean, J. F. & Hitch, G. J. (1999). Working memory impairments in children with specific arithmetic learning difficulties. *Journal of Experimental Child Psychology*, 74(3), 240–260. doi: 10.1006/jecp.1999.2516.

McLean, K. C. (2008). Stories of the young and the old: Personal continuity and narrative identity. [Comparative Study; Research Support, Non-U.S. Gov't]. *Developmental Psychology*, 44(1), 254–264. doi: 10.1037/0012-1649.44.1.254.

Meacham, J. (1990). The loss of wisdom. In R. J. Sternberg (Ed.), *Wisdom: Its nature, origins and development* (pp. 89–102). Cambridge: Cambridge University Press.

Meagher, D. J. (2001). Delirium: Optimising management. [Review]. *BMJ*, 322(7279), 144–149.

Mecacci, L. & Righi, S. (2006). Cognitive failures, metacognitive beliefs and aging. *Personality and Individual Differences*, 40(7), 1453–1459. doi: 10.1016/j.paid.2005.11.022.

Meisami, E. (1994). Aging of the sensory system. In P. S. Timiras (Ed.), *Physiological basis of aging and geriatrics* (pp. 115–131). Boca Raton, FL: CRC Press Inc.

Meltzoff, A. N. (2010). Social cognition and the origin of imitation, empathy, and theory of mind. In U. Goswami (Ed.), *The Wiley-Blackwell handbook of childhood cognitive development* (pp. 49–75). Chichester, West Sussex: Wiley-Blackwell.

Mendez, M. F. & Shapira, J. S. (2009). Altered emotional morality in frontotemporal dementia. *Cognitive Neuropsychiatry*, 14(3), 165–179.

Menna, F., Remendino, F., Battisti, R., & Nocerino, E. (2011). *Geometric investigation of a gaming active device*. Paper presented at The International Society for Optical Engineering.

'Menopause' (2010) *Black's medical dictionary* (42nd edn). London: A & C Black. Retrieved from http://www.credoreference.com/entry/blackmed/menopause.

Mercier, P. (2009). *Night train to Lisbon* (Updated edn). London: Atlantic.

Messam, C. A., Hou, J., Janabi, N., Monaco, M. C., Gravell, M., & Major, E. O. (2002). IV. Microglial cells. In V. S. Ramachandran (Ed.), *Encyclopedia of the human brain*. Oxford: Elsevier Science & Technology.

Meyer, B. J., Russo, C., & Talbot, A. (1995). Discourse comprehension and problem solving: Decisions about the treatment of breast cancer by women across the life span. *Psychology and Aging*, 10(1), 84–103.

Meyer, B. J., Talbot, A. P., & Ranalli, C. (2007). Why older adults make more immediate treatment decisions about cancer than younger adults. [Research Support, N.I.H., Extramural]. *Psychology and Aging*, 22(3), 505–524. doi: 10.1037/0882-7974.22.3.505.

Mikels, J. A., Reed, A. E., & Simon, K. I. (2009). Older adults place lower value on choice relative to young adults. [Research Support, N.I.H., Extramural; Research Support, Non-U.S. Gov't]. *Journals of Gerontology B: Psychological Sciences and Social Sciences*, 64(4), 443–446. doi: 10.1093/geronb/gbp021.

Miller, G. A. (1956). The magical number seven plus or minus two: Some limits on our capacity for processing information. *Psychological Review*, 63(2), 81–97.

Miller, L. M. S., Stine-Morrow, E. A., Kirkorian, H. L., & Conroy, M. L. (2004). Adult age differences in knowledge-driven reading. *Journal of Educational Psychology*, 96(4), 811–821.

Miller, R. B., Hemesath, K., & Nelson, B. (1997). Marriage in middle and later life. In T. D. Hargrave & S. M. Hanna (Eds), *The aging family: New visions in theory, practice, and reality* (pp. 178–198). New York: Brunner/Mazel.

Miller, S. A. (2009). Children's understanding of second-order mental states. [Review]. *Psychological Bulletin*, 135(5), 749–773. doi: 10.1037/a0016854.

Mioshi, E., Dawson, K., Mitchell, J., Arnold, R., & Hodges, J. R. (2006). The Addenbrooke's Cognitive Examination Revised (ACE-R): A brief cognitive test battery for dementia screening. [Evaluation Studies; Research Support, Non-U.S. Gov't; Validation

Studies]. *International Journal of Geriatric Psychiatry, 21*(11), 1078–1085. doi: 10.1002/gps.1610.

Mireles, D. E. & Charness, N. (2002). Computational explorations of the influence of structured knowledge on age-related cognitive decline. [Research Support, U.S. Gov't, P.H.S.]. *Psychology and Aging, 17*(2), 245–259.

Mitchell, P. & Lewis, C. (1994). Critical issues in children's early understanding of mind. In C. Lewis & P. Mitchell (Eds), *Children's early understanding of mind: Origins and development* (pp. 1–16). Hove: L. Erlbaum Associates.

Mittenberg, W., Seidenberg, M., O'Leary, D. S., & DiGiulio, D. V. (1989). Changes in cerebral functioning associated with normal aging. *Journal of Clinical and Experimental Neuropsychology, 11*(6), 918–932. doi: 10.1080/01688638908400945.

Miyake, A., Friedman, N. P., Emerson, M. J., Witzki, A. H., Howerter, A., & Wager, T. D. (2000). The unity and diversity of executive functions and their contributions to complex 'frontal lobe' tasks: A latent variable analysis. [Research Support, U.S. Gov't, Non-P.H.S.]. *Cognitive Psychology, 41*(1), 49–100. doi: 10.1006/cogp.1999.0734.

Miwa, S., Beckman, K. B., & Muller, F. L. (2008). *Oxidative stress in aging.* New York: Humana Press.

Mocchegiani, E., Malavolta, M., Muti, E., Costarelli, L., Cipriano, C., Piacenza, F., Tesei, S., Giacconi, R., & Lattanzio, F. (2008). Zinc, metallothioneins and longevity: Interrelationships with niacin and selenium. [Research Support, Non-U.S. Gov't; Review]. *Current Pharmaceutical Design, 14*(26), 2719–2732.

Mojon-Azzi, S. M., Sousa-Poza, A., & Mojon, D. S. (2008). Impact of low vision on well-being in 10 European countries. [Comparative Study; Multicenter Study]. *Ophthalmologica, 222*(3), 205–212. doi: 10.1159/000126085.

Molyneux, G. J., McCarthy, G. M., McEniff, S., Cryan, M., & Conroy, R. M. (2008). Prevalence and predictors of carer burden and depression in carers of patients referred to an old age psychiatric service. *International Psychogeriatrics, 20*, 1193–1202.

Monczunski, J. (1991). That incurable disease. *Notre Dame Magazine, 20*, 37.

Montepare, J. (1996). An assessment of adults' perceptions of their psychological, physical, and social ages. *Journal of Clinical Geropsychology, 2*, 117–128.

Montross, L. P., Depp, C., Daly, J., Reichstadt, J., Golshan, S., Moore, D., Sitzer, D., & Jeste, D. V. (2006). Correlates of self-rated successful aging among community-dwelling older adults. [Research Support, N.I.H., Extramural; Research Support, Non-U.S. Gov't; Research Support, U.S. Gov't, Non-P.H.S.]. *American Journal of Geriatric Psychiatry, 14*(1), 43–51. doi: 10.1097/01.JGP.0000192489.43179.31.

Monroe, S. M. & Simons, A. D. (1991). Diathesis-stress theories in the context of life stress research: Implications for the depressive disorders. [Research Support, U.S. Gov't, P.H.S.; Review]. *Psychological Bulletin, 110*(3), 406–425.

Mor, V., Branco, K., Fleishman, J., Hawes, C., Phillips, C., Morris, J., & Fries, B. (1995). The structure of social engagement among nursing home residents. *Journals of Gerontology Series B: Psychological Sciences and Social Sciences, 50*(1), P1–P8.

Moreno, J. & Saldana, D. (2005). Use of a computer-assisted program to improve meta-cognition in persons with severe learning disabilities. *Research in Developmental Disabilities, 26*, 341–357.

Morin, A. (2006). Levels of consciousness and self-awareness: A comparison and integration of various neurocognitive views. [Comparative Study; Review]. *Consciousness and Cognition, 15*(2), 358–371. doi: 10.1016/j.concog.2005.09.006.

Moss, S. (1999). Mental health issues of access and quality of life. In S. S. Herr & G. Weber (Eds), *Aging, rights, and quality of life: Prospects for older people with developmental disabilities* (pp. 55–72). Baltimore, MD: Paul H. Brookes Publishing.

Moulin, C. J. (2006). Cognitive behavioural therapy. In G. Davey (Ed.), *The encyclopaedic dictionary of psychology*. London: Hodder Arnold. Retrieved from http://www.credoreference.com/entry/hodderdpsyc/cognitive_behavioural_therapy_cbt.

Mroczek, D. K. & Almeida, D. M. (2004). The effect of daily stress, personality, and age on daily negative affect. [Research Support, Non-U.S. Gov't; Research Support, U.S. Gov't, P.H.S.]. *Journal of Personality, 72*(2), 355–378.

Mroczek D.K., Almeida DM, Spiro A, Pafford C. 2006. Modeling intraindividual stability and change in personality. In Mroczek D. K. & Little T.D. (Eds). *Handbook of Personality Development* (pp. 163–80). Mahwah, NJ: Erlbaum.

Mroczek, D. K., Spiro, A., & Griffin, P. W. (2006). Personality and aging. In J. E. Birren, K. W. Schaie, R. P. Abeles, M. Gatz, & T. A. Salthouse (Eds), *Handbook of the psychology of aging* (6th edn, pp. 363–375). New York: Oxford: Academic.

Mulkana, S. S. & Hailey, B. J. (2001). The role of optimism in health-enhancing behavior. *American Journal of Health Behavior, 25*(4), 388–395.

Mulsant, B. H., Whyte, E., Lenze, E. J., Lotrich, F., Karp, J. F., Pollock, B. G., & Reynolds, C. F., 3rd (2003). Achieving long-term optimal outcomes in geriatric depression and anxiety. [Research Support, U.S. Gov't, Non-P.H.S.; Research Support, U.S. Gov't, P.H.S.; Review]. *CNS Spectrums, 8*(12 Suppl. 3), 27–34.

Murphy, M. D., Sanders, R. E., Gabriesheski, A. S., & Schmitt, F. A. (1981). Metamemory in the aged. [Comparative Study; Research Support, Non-U.S. Gov't; Research Support, U.S. Gov't, Non-P.H.S.]. *Journal of Gerontology, 36*(2), 185–193.

Murrell, S. A., Meeks, S., & Walker, J. (1991). Protective functions of health and self-esteem against depression in older adults facing illness or bereavement. [Research Support, U.S. Gov't, P.H.S.]. *Psychology and Aging, 6*(3), 352–360.

Nakamura, T., Meguro, K., Yamazaki, H., Okuzumi, H., Tanaka, A., Horikawa, A., Yamaguchi, K., Katsuyama, N., Nakano, M., Arai, H., & Sasaki, H. (1997). Postural and gait disturbance correlated with decreased frontal cerebral blood flow in Alzheimer disease. [Research Support, Non-U.S. Gov't]. *Alzheimer Disease and Associated Disorders, 11*(3), 132–139.

Nasreddine, Z. S., Phillips, N. A., Bedirian, V., Charbonneau, S., Whitehead, V., Collin, I., Cummings, J. L., & Chertkow, H. (2005). The Montreal Cognitive Assessment, MoCA: A brief screening tool for mild cognitive impairment. [Evaluation Studies; Research Support, Non-U.S. Gov't; Research Support, U.S. Gov't, P.H.S.]. *Journal of the American Geriatrics Society, 53*(4), 695–699. doi: 10.1111/j.1532-5415.2005.53221.x.

National Health Service. (2013). End of life care. Retrieved from http://www.nhs.uk/Planners/end-of-life-care/Pages/End-of-life-care.aspx.

National Institute for Health and Clinical Excellence (2006). NICE clinical guidelines 42 – Dementia: Supporting people with dementia and their carers in health and social care: National Institute for Health and Clinical Excellence.

Nations, U. (2006). *Population ageing, 2006*. New York: United Nations.

Naveh-Benjamin, M. (2000). Adult age differences in memory performance: Tests of an associative deficit hypothesis. [Comparative Study; Research Support, Non-U.S. Gov't]. *Journal of Experimental Psychology Learning Memory and Cognition, 26*(5), 1170–1187.

Naveh-Benjamin, M., Guez, J., & Marom, M. (2003). The effects of divided attention at encoding on item and associative memory. [Research Support, Non-U.S. Gov't]. *Memory & Cognition, 31*(7), 1021–1035.

Navon, D. & Gopher, D. (1979). On the economy of the human-processing system. *Psychological Review, 86*(3), 214–255.

Neary, D., Snowden, J., & Mann, D. (2005). Frontotemporal dementia. [Review]. *Lancet Neurology*, *4*(11), 771–780. doi: 10.1016/S1474-4422(05)70223-4.

Neimeyer, R. A. (2001). *Meaning reconstruction & the experience of loss*. Washington, DC; London: American Psychological Association.

Neimeyer, R. A. (2004). Fostering post-traumatic growth: A narrative contribution. *Psychological Inquiry*, *15*, 53–59.

Nelson, E. A. & Dannefer, D. (1992). Aged heterogeneity: Fact or fiction? The fate of diversity in gerontological research. *The Gerontologist*, *32*(1), 17–23. doi: 10.1093/geront/32.1.17.

Nelson, H. E. (1982). *National Adult Reading Test (NART): For the assessment of premorbid intelligence in patients with dementia: Test manual*. Windsor: NFER-Nelson.

Nelson, T. O. & Narens, L. (1990). Metamemory: A theoretical framework and new findings. In G. H. Bower (Ed.), *The psychology of learning and motivation: Advances in research and theory* (pp. 125–173). New York; London: Academic Press.

Neyer, F. J. & Asendorpf, J. B. (2001). Personality–relationship transaction in young adulthood. [Research Support, Non-U.S. Gov't]. *Journal of Personality and Social Psychology*, *81*(6), 1190–1204.

Ngan, R. (2011). Social care and older people. In I. Stuart-Hamilton (Ed.), *An introduction to gerontology* (pp. 126–158). Cambridge: Cambridge University Press.

Niedenthal, P. M. (2005). Emotion. *Encyclopedia of cognitive science*. Chichester, West Sussex: Wiley.

Niederehe, G. & Yoder, C. (1989). Metamemory perceptions in depressions of young and older adults. [Research Support, U.S. Gov't, P.H.S.]. *Journal of Nervous and Mental Disease*, *177*(1), 4–14.

Nikitin, N. P., Loh, P. H., de Silva, R., Witte, K. K., Lukaschuk, E. I., Parker, A., Farnsworth, T. A., Alamgir, F. M., Clark, A. L., & Cleland, J. G. (2006). Left ventricular morphology, global and longitudinal function in normal older individuals: A cardiac magnetic resonance study. [Comparative Study]. *International Journal of Cardiology*, *108*(1), 76–83. doi: 10.1016/j.ijcard.2005.04.009.

Nolen-Hoeksema, S. (2001). Ruminative coping and adjustment to bereavement. In M. S. Stroebe (Ed.), *Handbook of bereavement research: Consequences, coping & care* (pp. 545–562). Washington, DC: American Psychological Association.

Nordahl, C. W., Ranganath, C., Yonelinas, A. P., Decarli, C., Fletcher, E., & Jagust, W. J. (2006). White matter changes compromise prefrontal cortex function in healthy elderly individuals. [Research Support, N.I.H., Extramural]. *Journal of Cognitive Neuroscience*, *18*(3), 418–429. doi: 10.1162/089892906775990552.

Nordberg, A. (2008). Amyloid imaging in Alzheimer's disease. [Research Support, Non-U.S. Gov't; Review]. *Neuropsychologia*, *46*(6), 1636–1641. doi: 10.1016/j.neuropsychologia.2008.03.020.

Norman, D. A. (1998). *The design of everyday things*. London: MIT.

Numminen, H., Service, E., & Ruoppila, I. (2002). Working memory, intelligence and knowledge base in adult persons with intellectual disability. [Research Support, Non-U.S. Gov't]. *Research in Developmental Disabilities*, *23*(2), 105–118.

Nyberg, L., Maitland, S. B., Ronnlund, M., Backman, L., Dixon, R. A., Wahlin, A., & Nilsson, L. G. (2003). Selective adult age differences in an age-invariant multifactor model of declarative memory. [Research Support, Non-U.S. Gov't; Research Support, U.S. Gov't, P.H.S.]. *Psychology and Aging*, *18*(1), 149–160.

Nylander, L., Lugnegård, T., & Hallerbäck, M. U. (2008). Autism spectrum disorders and schizophrenia spectrum disorders in adults – Is there a connection? A literature review and some suggestions for future clinical research. *Clinical Neuropsychiatry*, *5*(1), 43–54.

O'Connor, D. W., Ames, D., Gardner, B., & King, M. (2009a). Psychosocial treatments of behavior symptoms in dementia: A systematic review of reports meeting quality standards. [Research Support, Non-U.S. Gov't; Review]. *International Psychogeriatrics*, *21*(2), 225–240. doi: 10.1017/S1041610208007588.

O'Connor, D. W., Ames, D., Gardner, B., & King, M. (2009b). Psychosocial treatments of psychological symptoms in dementia: a systematic review of reports meeting quality standards. [Research Support, Non-U.S. Gov't; Review]. *International Psychogeriatrics*, *21*(2), 241–251. doi: 10.1017/S1041610208008223.

O'Connell, H., Chin, A-V., Cunningham, C., & Lawlor, B. (2003). Alcohol use disorders in elderly people – Redefining an age old problem in old age. *BMJ*, *327*(7416), 664–667.

O'Connell, H., Chin, A-V., Cunningham, C., & Lawlor, B. A. (2004). Recent developments: Suicide in older people. [Review]. *BMJ*, *329*(7471), 895–899. doi: 10.1136/bmj.329.7471.895.

O'Donovan, D., Hausken, T., Lei, Y., Russo, A., Keogh, J., Horowitz, M., & Jones, K. L. (2005). Effect of aging on transpyloric flow, gastric emptying, and intragastric distribution in healthy humans – Impact on glycemia. [Research Support, Non-U.S. Gov't]. *Digestive Diseases and Sciences*, *50*(4), 671–676.

Office for National Statistics (2001). 2001 Census: Office for National Statistics.

Office for National Statistics (2010). Marital Status Population Projections for England & Wales, 2008-based marital status projections. Retrieved 25 May 2013 from http://www.ons.gov.uk/ons/rel/npp/marital-status-population-projections-for-england---wales/2008-based-marital-status-projections/index.html.

Office for National Statistics (2012). Ageing in the UK. Retrieved 25 May 2013 from http://www.statistics.gov.uk/hub/population/ageing/older-people/index.html.

Olshansky, S. J., Hayflick, L., & Carnes, B. A. (2002). No truth to the fountain of youth. *Scientific American*, *286*(6), 92–95.

Ong, A. D. & Bergeman, C. S. (2004). The complexity of emotions in later life. *Journals of Gerontology B: Psychological Sciences and Social Sciences*, *59*(3), P117–122.

Ong, A. D., Bergeman, C. S., Bisconti, T. L., & Wallace, K. A. (2006). Psychological resilience, positive emotions, and successful adaptation to stress in later life. [Research Support, N.I.H., Extramural; Research Support, Non-U.S. Gov't]. *Journal of Personality and Social Psychology*, *91*(4), 730–749. doi: 10.1037/0022-3514.91.4.730.

ONS (1998). *Living in Britain: Results from the 1996 General Household Survey*. London: Office of National Statistics.

Organization, W. H. (2001). *Mental health: New understanding, new hope*. Geneva: WHO.

Orrell, M., Howard, R., Payne, A., Bergmann, K., Woods, R., Everitt, B. S., & Levy, R. (1992). Differentiation between organic and functional psychiatric illness in the elderly: An evaluation of four cognitive tests. *International Journal of Geriatric Psychiatry*, *7*, 263–275.

O'Rourke, N. & Cappeliez, P. (2005). Marital satisfaction and self-deception: Reconstruction of relationship histories among older adults. *Social Behavior and Personality*, *33*, 273–282.

Orwoll, L. & Perlmutter, M. (1990). The study of wise persons: Integrating a personality perspective. In R. J. Sternberg (Ed.), *Wisdom: Its nature, origins and development* (pp. 160–177). Cambridge: Cambridge University Press.

Osterweis, M., Solomon, F., & Green, M. (1984). *Bereavement: Reactions, consequences and care*. Washington, DC: Institute of Medicine. Committee for the Study of Health Consequences of the Stress of Bereavement.

Ouelette, S. C. & Diplacido, J. (2001). Personality's role in the protection and enhancement of health: Where the research has been, where it is stuck, how it might move. In T. A. Revenson, J. E. Singer, & A. Baum (Eds), *Handbook of health psychology* (pp. 175–193). Mahwah, NJ; [London]: Lawrence Erlbaum Associates.

Owen, A. M., Hampshire, A., Grahn, J. A., Stenton, R., Dajani, S., Burns, A. S., Howard, R. J., & Ballard, C. G. (2010). Putting brain training to the test. [Randomized Controlled Trial; Research Support, Non-U.S. Gov't]. *Nature, 465*(7299), 775–778. doi: 10.1038/nature09042.

Owsley, C., Ball, K., McGwin, G., Jr, Sloane, M. E., Roenker, D. L., White, M. F., & Overley, E. T. (1998). Visual processing impairment and risk of motor vehicle crash among older adults. [Research Support, Non-U.S. Gov't; Research Support, U.S. Gov't, P.H.S.]. *JAMA, 279*(14), 1083–1088.

Pankow, L. J. & Solotoroff, J. M. (2007). Biological aspects and theories of aging. In J. A. Blackburn & C. N. Dulmus (Eds), *Handbook of gerontology: Evidence-based approaches to theory, practice, and policy* (pp. 19–56). Hoboken, NJ: John Wiley.

Park, D. C., Hertzog, C., Kidder, D. P., Morrell, R. W., & Mayhorn, C. B. (1997). Effect of age on event-based and time-based prospective memory. [Comparative Study]. *Psychology and Aging, 12*(2), 314–327.

Park, D. C., Lautenschlager, G., Hedden, T., Davidson, N. S., Smith, A. D., & Smith, P. K. (2002). Models of visuospatial and verbal memory across the adult life span. [Research Support, U.S. Gov't, P.H.S.]. *Psychology and Aging, 17*(2), 299–320.

Park, D. C., Puglisi, J. T., & Sovacool, M. (1983). Memory for pictures, words, and spatial location in older adults: Evidence for pictorial superiority. [Research Support, U.S. Gov't, P.H.S.]. *Journal of Gerontology, 38*(5), 582–588.

Park, D. C. & Reuter-Lorenz, P. (2009). The adaptive brain: Aging and neurocognitive scaffolding. [Research Support, N.I.H., Extramural; Review]. *Annual Review of Psychology, 60*, 173–196. doi: 10.1146/annurev.psych.59.103006.093656.

Parker, S. (2009a). Bone disorders. *The human body book: An illustrated guide to its structure, function and disorders.* New York: Dorling Kindersley Publishing, Inc.

Parker, S. (2009b). Male reproductive system. *The human body book: An illustrated guide to its structure, function and disorders.* New York: Dorling Kindersley Publishing, Inc.

Parkes, C. M. (1996). *Bereavement: Studies of grief in adult life* (3rd edn). London: Routledge.

Parkes, C. M. (2007). Coping with death and dying. In S. Ayers, A. Baum, C. McManus, S. Newman, K. A. Wallston, J. Weinman, & R. Wesley (Eds), *Cambridge handbook of psychology, health and medicine* (pp. 55–58). Cambridge: Cambridge University Press. Retrieved from http://www.credoreference.com/entry/cupphm/coping_with_death_and_dying.

Parkin, A. J. (1997). *Memory and amnesia: An introduction* (2nd edn). Oxford: Blackwell.

Parkin, A. J. & Walter, B. M. (1992). Recollective experience, normal aging, and frontal dysfunction. [Research Support, Non-U.S. Gov't]. *Psychology and Aging, 7*(2), 290–298.

Parkinson, S. R., Inman, V. W., & Dannenbaum, S. E. (1985). Adult age differences in short-term forgetting. *Acta Psychologica, 60*(1), 83–101.

Parmelee, P. A. (2007). Depression. In J. E. Birren (Ed.), *Encyclopedia of gerontology* (2nd edn, pp. 400–409). Amsterdam; London: Elsevier.

Parmelee, P. A., Smith, B., & Katz, I. R. (1993). Pain complaints and cognitive status among elderly institution residents. [Research Support, U.S. Gov't, P.H.S.]. *Journal of the American Geriatrics Society, 41*(5), 517–522.

Pasupathi, M. & Staudinger, U. M. (2000). A 'talent' for knowledge and judgment about life: The lifespan development of wisdom. *International Handbook of Giftedness and Talent.* Oxford: Elsevier Science & Technology.

Patterson, T. L. & Jeste, D. V. (1999). The potential impact of the baby-boom generation on substance abuse among elderly persons. [Research Support, U.S. Gov't, Non-P.H.S.; Research Support, U.S. Gov't, P.H.S.; Review]. *Psychiatric Services, 50*(9), 1184–1188.

Paulson, Q. X., Hong, J., Holcomb, V. B., & Nunez, N. P. (2010). Effects of body weight and alcohol consumption on insulin sensitivity. [Research Support, N.I.H., Extramural;

Research Support, Non-U.S. Gov't]. *Nutrition Journal, 9,* 1–14. doi: 10.1186/1475-2891-9-14.

Paus, T. (2005). Mapping brain maturation and cognitive development during adolescence. [Research Support, Non-U.S. Gov't; Review]. *Trends in cognitive sciences, 9*(2), 60–68. doi: 10.1016/j.tics.2004.12.008.

Pautex, S., Michon, A., Guedira, M., Emond, H., Le Lous, P., Samaras, D., Michel, J. P., Herrmann, F., Giannakopoulos, P., & Gold, G. (2006). Pain in severe dementia: Self-assessment or observational scales? [Comparative Study; Randomized Controlled Trial; Research Support, Non-U.S. Gov't]. *Journal of the American Geriatrics Society, 54*(7), 1040–1045. doi: 10.1111/j.1532-5415.2006.00766.x.

Pearlin, L. I. & Schooler, C. (1978). The structure of coping. *Journal of Health and Social Behavior, 19*(1), 2–21.

Pearson, J. C. (1996). Forty-forever years? Primary relationships and senior citizens. In N. Vanzetti & S. Duck (Eds), *A lifetime of relationships* (pp. 383–405). Pacific Grove, CA; London: Brooks/Cole.

Pellicano, E. (2007). Links between theory of mind and executive function in young children with autism: Clues to developmental primacy. *Developmental Psychology, 43*(4), 974–990. doi: 10.1037/0012-1649.43.4.974.

Peng, K. & Nisbett, R. E. (1999). Culture, dialectics, and reasoning about contradiction. *American Psychologist, 54*(9), 741–755.

Pennington, B. F. (1995). Genetics of learning disabilities. [Research Support, Non-U.S. Gov't; Research Support, U.S. Gov't, P.H.S.; Review]. *Journal of Child Neurology, 10*(Suppl. 1), S69–77.

Pepper, S. C. (1942). *World hypotheses: A study in evidence.* Berkeley; Los Angeles: University of California Press.

'Perception' (2008) *The Columbia encyclopedia.* New York: Columbia University Press. Retrieved from http://www.credoreference.com/entry/columency/perception.

Percy, W. (1975). *The message in the bottle: How queer man is, how queer language is, and what one has to do with the other.* New York: Farrar, Straus and Giroux.

Perkins, E. A. & Small, B. J. (2006). Aspects of cognitive functioning in adults with intellectual disabilities. *Journal of Policy and Practice in Intellectual Disabilities, 3*(3), 181–194.

Perlow, E. (2010). Accessibility: Global gateway to health literacy. *Health Promotion Practice, 11*(1), 123–131. doi: 10.1177/1524839908321942.

Perna, L., Mielck, A., Lacruz, M. E., Emeny, R. T., Holle, R., Breitfelder, A., & Ladwig, K. H. (2012). Socioeconomic position, resilience, and health behaviour among elderly people. [Research Support, Non-U.S. Gov't]. *International Journal of Public Health, 57*(2), 341–349. doi: 10.1007/s00038-011-0294-0.

Perner, J. & Davies, G. (1991). Understanding the mind as an active information processor: Do young children have a 'copy theory of mind'? [Research Support, Non-U.S. Gov't]. *Cognition, 39*(1), 51–69.

Perner, J. & Wimmer, H. (1985). John thinks that Mary thinks that attribution of second-order false beliefs by 5- to 10-year-old children. *Journal of Experimental Child Psychology, 39,* 437–447.

Persson, J., Nyberg, L., Lind, J., Larsson, A., Nilsson, L. G., Ingvar, M., & Buckner, R. L. (2006). Structure-function correlates of cognitive decline in aging. [Controlled Clinical Trial; Research Support, Non-U.S. Gov't]. *Cerebral Cortex, 16*(7), 907–915. doi: 10.1093/cercor/bhj036.

Peterson, C. (2000). The future of optimism. [Research Support, U.S. Gov't, P.H.S.]. *American Psychologist, 55*(1), 44–55.

Phillips, L. H., Scott, C., Henry, J. D., Mowat, D., & Bell, J. S. (2010). Emotion perception in Alzheimer's disease and mood disorder in old age. [Research Support, Non-U.S. Gov't]. *Psychology and Aging*, *25*(1), 38–47. doi: 10.1037/a0017369.

Phillips, P. A., Bretherton, M., Johnston, C. I., & Gray, L. (1991). Reduced osmotic thirst in healthy elderly men. [Clinical Trial; Randomized Controlled Trial; Research Support, Non-U.S. Gov't]. *American Journal of Physiology*, *261*(1 Pt 2), R166–171.

Piaget, J. (1952). *The origins of intelligence in children; translated by Margaret Cook*. New York: International Universities Press.

Piaget, J. & Gabian, M. (1977). *The moral judgement of the child*. Harmondsworth: Penguin.

Pichora-Fuller, M. K. (2003). Processing speed and timing in aging adults: Psychoacoustics, speech perception, and comprehension. *International Journal of Audiology*, *42*, S59–S67.

Pichora-Fuller, M. K., Schneider, B. A., & Daneman, M. (1995). How young and old adults listen to and remember speech in noise. [Comparative Study; Research Support, Non-U.S. Gov't]. *The Journal of the Acoustical Society of America*, *97*(1), 593–608.

Pietschmann, P., Rauner, M., Sipos, W., & Kerschan-Schindl, K. (2009). Osteoporosis: An age-related and gender-specific disease – A mini-review. [Research Support, Non-U.S. Gov't; Review]. *Gerontology*, *55*(1), 3–12. doi: 10.1159/000166209.

Piquard, A., Derouesne, C., Lacomblez, L., & Sieroff, E. (2004). [Planning and activities of daily living in Alzheimer's disease and frontotemporal dementia]. [Clinical Trial]. *Psychologie and Neuropsychiatrie du Vieillissement*, *2*(2), 147–156.

Pisoni, D. B. (1993). Long-term memory in speech perception: Some new findings on talker variability, speaking rate and perceptual learning. *Speech Communication*, *13*(1–2), 109–125.

Plato (427–347 BC, 1994). *Symposium*. Oxford: Oxford University Press.

Plomin, R. & Kovas, Y. (2005). Generalist genes and learning disabilities. [Research Support, Non-U.S. Gov't; Review]. *Psychological Bulletin*, *131*(4), 592–617. doi: 10.1037/0033-2909.131.4.592.

Poon, L. W. (1992). Towards an understanding of cognitive functioning in geriatric depression. *International Psychogeriatrics*, *4*, 241–266.

Pope, A. (1767). *An essay on man, in four ethic epistles. By Alexander Pope, Esq*. London: Thomas Reddish.

Porter, C. A. & Suedfeld, P. (1981). Integrative complexity in the corresponding of literary figures: Effects of personal and societal stress. *Journal of Personality and Social Psychology*, *40*, 321–330.

Pratt, M. W., Diessner, R., Pratt, A., Hunsberger, B., & Pancer, S. M. (1996). Moral and social reasoning and perspective taking in later life: A longitudinal study. [Research Support, Non-U.S. Gov't]. *Psychology and Aging*, *11*(1), 66–73.

Preece, P. F. W. (1982). The fan-spread hypothesis and the adjustment for initial differences between groups in uncontrolled studies. *Educational and Psychological Measurement*, *42*(3), 759–762. doi: 10.1177/001316448204200305.

Pride, N. B. (2005). Ageing and changes in lung mechanics. [Comment; Editorial]. *European Respiratory Journal*, *26*(4), 563–565. doi: 10.1183/09031936.05.00079805.

Prigerson, H. G. & Jacobs, S. C. (2001). Diagnostic criteria for traumatic grief. In M. S. Stroebe (Ed.), *Handbook of bereavement research: Consequences, coping & care* (pp. 614–646). Washington, DC: American Psychological Association.

Prigerson, H. G. & Maciejewski, P. K. (2006). A call for sound empirical testing and evaluation of criteria for complicated grief proposed for DSM-V. *Omega*, *52*, 9–19.

Pulkki-Raback, L., Elovainio, M., Kivimaki, M., Raitakari, O. T., & Keltikangas-Jarvinen, L. (2005). Temperament in childhood predicts body mass in adulthood: The cardiovascular risk in young Finns study. [Research Support, Non-U.S. Gov't]. *Health*

Psychology: Official Journal of the Division of Health Psychology, American Psychological Association, 24(3), 307–315. doi: 10.1037/0278-6133.24.3.307.

Pushkar, D., Basevitz, P., Arbuckle, T., Nohara-LeClair, M., Lapidus, S., & Peled, M. (2000). Social behavior and off-target verbosity in elderly people. *Psychology and Aging, 15*(2), 361–374.

Quadagno, J. S. (2008). *Aging and the life course: An introduction to social gerontology* (4th edn). Boston; London: McGraw-Hill.

'Quality of life in older age: Messages from the Growing Older Programme' (2005). In H. t. Aged (Ed.). London: Help the Aged.

Quinn, K. A., Mcrae, C. N., & Bodenhausen, G. V. (2005). Social cognition. *Encyclopedia of cognitive science*. Chichester, West Sussex: Wiley.

Rabbitt, P. & Abson, V. (1990). 'Lost and found': Some logical and methodological limitations of self-report questionnaires as tools to study cognitive ageing. *British Journal of Psychology, 81*(Pt 1), 1–16.

Rabbitt, P., Maylor, E., McInnes, L., Bent, N., & Moore, B. (1995). What goods can self-assessment questionnaires deliver for cognitive gerontology? *Applied Cognitive Psychology, 9*, S127–S152.

Rabbitt, P., Osman, P., Moore, B., & Stollery, B. (2001). There are stable individual differences in performance variability, both from moment to moment and from day to day. *Quarterly Journal of Experimental Psychology A, 54*(4), 981–1003. doi: 10.1080/713756013.

Rahhal, T. A., May, C. P., & Hasher, L. (2002). Truth and character: Sources that older adults can remember. [Research Support, U.S. Gov't, P.H.S.]. *Psychological Science: A Journal of the American Psychological Society/APS, 13*(2), 101–105.

Raj, I. S., Bird, S. R., & Shield, A. J. (2010). Aging and the force-velocity relationship of muscles. [Review]. *Experimental Gerontology, 45*(2), 81–90. doi: 10.1016/j.exger.2009.10.013.

Rakitin, B. C. & Stern, Y. (2005). Parkinson Disease. In L. Nadel (Ed.), *Encyclopedia of cognitive science*. Chichester, West Sussex: Wiley, Retrieved from .http://www.credoreference.com/entry/wileycs/parkinson_disease

Rapp, M. A., Krampe, R. T., & Baltes, P. B. (2006). Adaptive task prioritization in aging: Selective resource allocation to postural control is preserved in Alzheimer's disease. [Research Support, Non-U.S. Gov't]. *American Journal of Geriatric Psychiatry, 14*(1), 52–61. doi: 10.1097/01.JGP.0000192490.43179.e7.

Rasmussen, H. N., Scheier, M. F., & Greenhouse, J. B. (2009). Optimism and physical health: A meta-analytic review. [Meta-Analysis; Research Support, N.I.H., Extramural; Review]. *Annals of Behavioral Medicine: A Publication of the Society of Behavioral Medicine, 37*(3), 239–256. doi: 10.1007/s12160-009-9111-x.

Ratcliff, R., Thapar, A., Gomez, P., & McKoon, G. (2004). A diffusion model analysis of the effects of aging in the lexical-decision task. *Psychology and Aging, 19*(2), 278–289.

Raven, J. (1995). *Manual for the coloured progressive matrices* (Revised). Windsor, UK: NFRE-Nelson.

Raz, N. (2000). Aging of the brain and its impact on cognitive performance: Integration of structural and functional findings. In F. I. Craik & T. A. Salthouse (Eds), *The handbook of aging and cognition* (2nd ed., pp. 1–90). Mahwah, NJ: Erlbaum.

Raz, N., Gunning-Dixon, F., Head, D., Rodrigue, K. M., Williamson, A., & Acker, J. D. (2004). Aging, sexual dimorphism, and hemispheric asymmetry of the cerebral cortex: Replicability of regional differences in volume. [Research Support, U.S. Gov't, P.H.S.]. *Neurobiology of Aging, 25*(3), 377–396. doi: 10.1016/S0197-4580(03)00118-0.

Raz, N. & Rodrigue, K. M. (2006). Differential aging of the brain: Patterns, cognitive correlates and modifiers. [Research Support, N.I.H., Extramural; Research Support, Non-U.S. Gov't; Review]. *Neuroscience and Biobehavioral Reviews, 30*(6), 730–748. doi: 10.1016/j.neubiorev.2006.07.001.

Read, S. (1998). The palliative care needs of people with learning disabilities. *British Journal of Community Nursing, 3*(7), 356–361.

Rendell, P. G. & Thomson, D. M. (1999). Aging and prospective memory: Differences between naturalistic and laboratory tasks. [Clinical Trial; Randomized Controlled Trial; Research Support, Non-U.S. Gov't]. *Journals of Gerontology B: Psychological Sciences and Social Sciences, 54*(4), P256–269.

Reuter-Lorenz, P. A. & Cappell, K. A. (2008). Neurocognitive aging and the compensation hypothesis. *Current Directions in Psychological Science, 17*(3), 177–182. doi: 10.1111/j.1467-8721.2008.00570.x.

Reynolds, C. A. (2003). Alzheimer Disease. In D. N. Cooper (Ed.), *Encyclopedia of the human genome*. Chichester, West Sussex: Wiley, from http://www.credoreference.com/entry/wileyhg/alzheimer_disease.

Reynolds, K., Lewis, B., Nolen, J. D., Kinney, G. L., Sathya, B., & He, J. (2003). Alcohol consumption and risk of stroke: A meta-analysis. [Meta-Analysis; Research Support, U.S. Gov't, P.H.S.]. *JAMA, 289*(5), 579–588.

Rice, G. E. & Okun, M. A. (1994). Older readers' processing of medical information that contradicts their beliefs. [Research Support, U.S. Gov't, P.H.S.]. *Journal of Gerontology, 49*(3), P119–128.

Riby, L. M., Perfect, T. J., & Stollery, B. (2004). The effects of age and task domain on dual task performance: A meta-analysis. *European Journal of Cognitive Psychology, 16*, 863–891.

Richmond, L. L., Morrison, A. B., Chein, J. M., & Olson, I. R. (2011). Working memory training and transfer in older adults. [Randomized Controlled Trial; Research Support, N.I.H., Extramural]. *Psychology and Aging, 26*(4), 813–822. doi: 10.1037/a0023631.

Ring, L. (2007). Quality of life. In S. Ayers (Ed.), *Cambridge handbook of psychology, health and medicine* (pp. 178—181). Cambridge: Cambridge University Press. Retrieved from http://www.credoreference.com/entry/cupphm/quality_of_life.

Roberts, B. W. & DelVecchio, W. F. (2000). The rank-order consistency of personality traits from childhood to old age: A quantitative review of longitudinal studies. [Meta-Analysis]. *Psychological Bulletin, 126*(1), 3–25.

Robertson, I. H., Ward, T., Ridgeway, V., & Nimmo-Smith, I. (1994). *The test of everyday attention: TEA*. Bury St Edmunds: Thames Valley Test Company.

Rockwood, K. (2006). Vascular cognitive impairment. In R. Schulz (Ed.) with L. S. Noelker, K. Rockwood, & R. L. Sprott (Assoc. eds), *Encyclopedia of aging: A comprehensive resource in gerontology and geriatrics* (4th edn, pp. 1208–1210). New York: Springer.

Roediger, H. L. & Geraci, L. (2007). Aging and the misinformation effect: A neuropsychological analysis. [Research Support, N.I.H., Extramural]. *Journal of Experimental Psychology Learning Memory and Cognition, 33*(2), 321–334. doi: 10.1037/0278-7393.33.2.321.

Roediger, H. L. & McDermott, K. B. (1995). Creating false memories: Remembering words not presented in lists. *Journal of Experimental Psychology: Learning, Memory and Cognition, 21*, 803–814.

Roediger, H. L., McDermott, K. B., & Robinson, K. (1998). The role of associative processes in creating false memories. In M. A. Conway, S. E. E. Gathercole, & C. E. Cornoldi (Eds), *Theories of Memory. Vol. 2* (pp. 187–246). Hove: Psychology Press.

Rogers, W. A. & Fisk, A. D. (2001). Understanding the role of attention in cognitive aging research. In J. E. Birren & K. W. Schaie (Eds), *Handbook of the psychology of aging* (5th edn, pp. 267–287). San Diego: Academic Press.

Roose, S. P. & Schatzberg, A. F. (2005). The efficacy of antidepressants in the treatment of late-life depression. *Journal of Clinical Psychopharmacology, 25*(4), S1–S7.

Rosen, A. C., Prull, M. W., Gabrieli, J. D., Stoub, T., O'Hara, R., Friedman, L., Yesavage, J. A., & deToledo-Morrell, L. (2003). Differential associations between entorhinal and hippocampal volumes and memory performance in older adults. [Research Support, Non-U.S. Gov't; Research Support, U.S. Gov't, P.H.S.]. *Behavioral Neuroscience, 117*(6), 1150–1160. doi: 10.1037/0735-7044.117.6.1150.

Roskies, E. & Louis-Guerin, C. (1990). Job insecurity in managers: Antecedents and consequences. *Journal of Organizational Behavior, 11*, 345–359.

Roth, M., Tym, E., Mountjoy, C. Q., Huppert, F. A., Hendrie, H., Verma, S., & Goddard, R. (1986). CAMDEX. A standardised instrument for the diagnosis of mental disorder in the elderly with special reference to the early detection of dementia. [Research Support, Non-U.S. Gov't]. *British Journal of Psychiatry, 149*, 698–709.

Roth, R. M. & Saykin, A. J. (2004). Executive dysfunction in attention-deficit/hyperactivity disorder: Cognitive and neuroimaging findings. [Research Support, Non-U.S. Gov't; Review]. *Psychiatric Clinics of North America, 27*(1), 83–96, ix. doi: 10.1016/S0193-953X(03)00112-6.

Rotter, J. B. (1982). *The development and applications of social learning theory: Selected papers.* New York: Praeger.

Routledge, P. A., O'Mahony, M. S., & Woodhouse, K. W. (2004). Adverse drug reactions in elderly patients. [Review]. *British Journal of Clinical Pharmacology, 57*(2), 121–126.

Rowe, G., Hasher, L., & Turcotte, J. (2009). Age and synchrony effects in visuospatial working memory. [Research Support, N.I.H., Extramural; Research Support, Non-U.S. Gov't]. *Quarterly Journal of Experimental Psychology (Hove), 62*(10), 1873–1880. doi: 10.1080/17470210902834852.

Rowe, J. W. & Kahn, R. L. (1987). Human aging: Usual and successful. [Research Support, Non-U.S. Gov't; Review]. *Science, 237*(4811), 143–149.

Royall, D. R., Cordes, J. A., & Polk, M. (1998). CLOX: An executive clock drawing task. [Comparative Study; Research Support, Non-U.S. Gov't]. *Journal of Neurology, Neurosurgery, and Psychiatry, 64*(5), 588–594.

Rubin, D. C., Rahhal, T. A., & Poon, L. W. (1998). Things learned in early adulthood are remembered best. [Comparative Study; Research Support, Non-U.S. Gov't; Research Support, U.S. Gov't, P.H.S.]. *Memory & Cognition, 26*(1), 3–19.

Rumsey, N. & Harcourt, D. (2005). *The psychology of appearance.* Maidenhead, England; New York: Open University Press.

Ruscher, J. B. & Hurley, M. M. (2000). Off-target verbosity evokes negative stereotypes of older adults. *Journal of Language and Social Psychology, 19*(1), 141–149.

Russell, A. J., Mataix-Cols, D., Anson, M., & Murphy, D. G. (2005). Obsessions and compulsions in Asperger syndrome and high-functioning autism. [Comparative Study]. *British Journal of Psychiatry, 186*, 525–528. doi: 10.1192/bjp.186.6.525.

Ruta, D. A., Garratt, A. M., Leng, M., Russell, I. T., & MacDonald, L. M. (1994). A new approach to the measurement of quality of life. The Patient-Generated Index. [Clinical Trial; Research Support, Non-U.S. Gov't]. *Medical Care, 32*(11), 1109–1126.

Ryan, E. B., Giles, H., Bartolucci, G., & Henwood, K. (1986). Psycholinguistic and social psychological components of communication by and with the elderly. *Language & Communication, 6*(1), 1–24.

Rydén, E. & Bejerot, S. (2008). Autism spectrum disorders in an adult psychiatric population. A naturalistic cross-sectional controlled study. *Clinical Neuropsychiatry, 5*(1), 13-21.

Ryff, C. D. (1989). Happiness is everything, or is it? Explorations on the meaning of psychological well-being. *Journal of Personality and Social Psychology, 57*(6), 1069–1081.

Ryff, C. D. & Singer, B. (1998). The contours of positive human health. *Psychological Inquiry, 9*, 1–28.

Sagi, D. (2011). Perceptual learning in Vision Research. [Research Support, Non-U.S. Gov't; Review]. *Vision Research, 51*(13), 1552–1566. doi: 10.1016/j.visres.2010.10.019.

Saito, M. & Marumo, K. (2010). Collagen cross-links as a determinant of bone quality: A possible explanation for bone fragility in aging, osteoporosis, and diabetes mellitus. [Review]. *Osteoporosis International, 21*(2), 195–214. doi: 10.1007/s00198-009-1066-z.

Salthouse, T. A. (1991). *Theoretical perspectives on cognitive aging.* Hillsdale: Lawrence Erlbaum Associates.

Salthouse, T. A. (1996). The processing-speed theory of adult age differences in cognition. [Research Support, U.S. Gov't, P.H.S.; Review]. *Psychological Review, 103*(3), 403–428.

Salthouse, T. A. (2007). Reaction time. In J. E. Birren (Ed.), *Encyclopedia of gerontology: Age, aging, and the aged* (2nd edn, pp. 407–410). Boston: Elsevier Academic Press.

Salthouse, T. A., Babcock, R. L., & Shaw, R. J. (1991). Effects of adult age on structural and operational capacities in working memory. [Research Support, U.S. Gov't, P.H.S.]. *Psychology and Aging, 6*(1), 118–127.

Salthouse, T. A., Rogan, J. D., & Prill, K. A. (1984). Division of attention: Age differences on a visually presented memory task. [Research Support, Non-U.S. Gov't; Research Support, U.S. Gov't, P.H.S.]. *Memory & Cognition, 12*(6), 613–620.

Saretzki, G. & Von Zglinicki, T. (2002). Replicative aging, telomeres, and oxidative stress. [Review]. *Annals of the New York Academy of Sciences, 959*, 24–29.

Sarter, M., Givens, B., & Bruno, J. P. (2001). The cognitive neuroscience of sustained attention: Where top-down meets bottom-up. [Research Support, U.S. Gov't, P.H.S.; Review]. *Brain Research: Brain Research Reviews, 35*(2), 146–160.

Saunders, A. M., Strittmatter, W. J., Schmechel, D., George-Hyslop, P. H., Pericak-Vance, M. A., Joo, S. H., Rosi, B. L., Gusella, J. F., Crapper-MacLachlan, D. R., Alberts, M. J. et al. (1993). Association of apolipoprotein E allele epsilon 4 with late-onset familial and sporadic Alzheimer's disease. [Research Support, Non-U.S. Gov't; Research Support, U.S. Gov't, P.H.S.]. *Neurology, 43*(8), 1467–1472.

Schacter, D. L. (2001). *The seven sins of memory: How the mind forgets and remembers.* Boston, MA: Houghton, Miffin and Company.

Schaffer, H. R. (2006). *Social cognition.* London: Sage.

Schaie, K. W. (1965). A general model for the study of developmental problems. *Psychological Bulletin, 64*, 92–107.

Schaie, K. W. (1977). Toward a stage theory of adult cognitive development. *The International Journal of Aging and Human Development, 8*(2), 129–138.

Schaie, K. W. (2005). What can we learn from longitudinal studies of adult development? *Research in Human Development, 2*(3), 133–158. doi: 10.1207/s15427617rhd0203_4.

Schaie, K. W., Boron, J. B., & Willis, S. L. (2005). Everyday competence in older adults. *The Cambridge handbook of age and ageing.* Cambridge: Cambridge University Press.

Schaie, K., Nguyen, H., Willis, S., Dutta, R., & Yue, G. (2001). Environmental factors as a conceptual framework for examining cognitive performance in Chinese adults. *International Journal of Behavioral Development, 25*(3), 193–202.

Schaie, K. W., Willis, S. L., & Caskie, G. I. (2004). The Seattle longitudinal study: Relationship between personality and cognition. *Neuropsychology, Development, and*

Cognition. Section B, Aging, Neuropsychology and Cognition, 11(2–3), 304–324. doi: 10.1080/13825580490511134.

Schaie, K. W. & Zanjani, F. A. K. (2006). Intellectual development across adulthood. In C. H. Hoare (Ed.), *Handbook of adult development and learning* (pp. 99–122). New York; Oxford: Oxford University Press.

Scheier, M. F. & Carver, C. S. (1985). Optimism, coping, and health: Assessment and implications of generalized outcome expectancies. [Research Support, U.S. Gov't, Non-P.H.S.]. *Health Psychology: Official Journal of the Division of Health Psychology, American Psychological Association, 4*(3), 219–247.

Scheier, M. F., Carver, C. S., & Bridges, M. W. (1994). Distinguishing optimism from neuroticism (and trait anxiety, self-mastery, and self-esteem): A reevaluation of the Life Orientation Test. [Comparative Study; Research Support, Non-U.S. Gov't; Research Support, U.S. Gov't, Non-P.H.S.; Research Support, U.S. Gov't, P.H.S.]. *Journal of Personality and Social Psychology, 67*(6), 1063–1078.

Scheier, M. F., Carver, C. S., & Bridges, M. W. (2001). Optimism, pessimism, and psychological well-being. In E. C. Chang (Ed.), *Optimism & pessimism: Implications for theory, research, and practice* (pp. 189–216). Washington, DC; London: American Psychological Association.

Schiffman, S. S. (1997). Taste and smell losses in normal aging and disease. [Research Support, U.S. Gov't, P.H.S.; Review]. *JAMA, 278*(16), 1357–1362.

Schipper, H. M. (2007). The role of biologic markers in the diagnosis of Alzheimer's disease. *Alzheimer's and Dementia, 3*(4), 325–332. doi: 10.1016/j.jalz.2007.07.015.

Schneider, B. A. & Pichora-Fuller, M. K. (2000). Implications of perceptual deterioration for cognitive aging research. In F. I. M. Craik & T. Salthouse (Eds), *The handbook of aging and cognition* (2nd edn, pp. 155–219). Mahwah, NJ: Erlbaum.

Schneider, L. S. (1995). Efficacy of clinical treatment for mental disorders among older people. In M. Gatz (Ed.), *Emerging issues in mental health and aging* (pp. 19–71). Washington, DC: American Psychological Association.

Schröder, K. E., Schwarzer, R., & Konertz, W. (1998). Coping as a mediator in recovery from cardiac surgery. *Psychology and Health, 13*(1), 83–97.

Schwarz, N. (1999). *Cognition, aging, and self-reports*. Philadelphia, PA: Psychology Press.

Seale, C. (2005). The transformation of dying in old societies. In M. L. Johnson (Ed.), *The Cambridge handbook of age and ageing* (pp. 378—386). Cambridge: Cambridge University Press. Retrieved from http://www.credoreference.com/entry/cupage/introduction/8.

Seale, C. & Cartwright, A. (1994). *The year before death*. Aldershot: Avebury.

Segal, D. L., Coolidge, F. L., & Rosowsky, E. (2006). *Personality disorders and older adults: Diagnosis, assessment, and treatment*. Hoboken, NJ; [Chichester]: Wiley.

Segal, D. L., Needham, T. N., & Coolidge, F. L. (2009). Age differences in attachment orientations among younger and older adults: Evidence from two self-report measures of attachment. [Comparative Study]. *International Journal of Aging and Human Development, 69*(2), 119–132.

Segerstrom, S. C., Castañeda, J. O., & Spencer, T. E. (2003). Optimism effects on cellular immunity: Testing the affective and persistence models. *Personality and Individual Differences, 35*(7), 1615–1624.

Segerstrom, S. C., Taylor, S. E., Kemeny, M. E., & Fahey, J. L. (1998). Optimism is associated with mood, coping, and immune change in response to stress. [Research Support, Non-U.S. Gov't; Research Support, U.S. Gov't, P.H.S.]. *Journal of Personality and Social Psychology, 74*(6), 1646–1655.

Seidman, S. N. (2003). The aging male: Androgens, erectile dysfunction, and depression. [Comparative Study; Research Support, Non-U.S. Gov't]. *Journal of Clinical Psychiatry, 64*(Suppl. 10), 31–37.

Seligman, M. E. P. (1991). *Learned optimism.* New York: Knopf.

Seligman, M. E. P. (2011). *Flourish: A new understanding of happiness and well-being – and how to achieve them.* London: Nicholas Brealey.

Senchina, D. S. (2009). Effects of regular exercise on the aging immune system: A review. [Comment]. *Clinical Journal of Sport Medicine, 19*(5), 439–440. doi: 10.1097/01. jsm.0000358882.07869.20.

Shafto, M. (2010). Orthographic error monitoring in old age: Lexical and sublexical availability during perception and production. *Psychology and Aging, 25*(4), 991–1001.

Shamay-Tsoory, S. G., Aharon-Peretz, J., & Levkovitz, Y. (2007). The neuroanatomical basis of affective mentalizing in schizophrenia: Comparison of patients with schizophrenia and patients with localized prefrontal lesions. [Comparative Study; Research Support, Non-U.S. Gov't]. *Schizophrenia Research, 90*(1–3), 274–283. doi: 10.1016/j.schres. 2006.09.020.

Shamay-Tsoory, S. G., Tomer, R., Berger, B. D., Goldsher, D., & Aharon-Peretz, J. (2005). Impaired 'affective theory of mind' is associated with right ventromedial prefrontal damage. [Research Support, Non-U.S. Gov't]. *Cognitive and Behavioral Neurology, 18*(1), 55–67.

Shaw, R. M., Helmes, E., & Mitchell, D. (2006). Age-related change in visual, spatial and verbal memory. *Australasian Journal on Ageing, 25*(1), 14–19. doi: 10.1111/j.1741-6612.2006.00134.x.

Shaywitz, S. E., Shaywitz, B. A., Fulbright, R. K., Skudlarski, P., Mencl, W. E., Constable, R. T., Pugh, K. R., Holahan, J. M., Marchione, K. E., Fletcher, J. M., Lyon, G. R., & Gore, J. C. (2003). Neural systems for compensation and persistence: Young adult outcome of childhood reading disability. [Research Support, U.S. Gov't, P.H.S.]. *Biological Psychiatry, 54*(1), 25–33.

Shea, S. C. (2006). *Improving medication adherence: How to talk with patients about their medications.* Philadelphia, PA; London: Lippincott Williams & Wilkins.

Sherman, A. M., de Vries, B., & Lansford, J. E. (2000). Friendship in childhood and adulthood: Lessons across the life span. [Review]. *International Journal of Aging and Human Development, 51*(1), 31–51.

Shipley, B. A., Der, G., Taylor, M. D., & Deary, I. J. (2006). Cognition and all-cause mortality across the entire adult age range: Health and lifestyle survey. *Psychosomatic Medicine, 68*(1), 17–24. doi: 10.1097/01.psy.0000195867.66643.0f.

Shulman, K. I., Herrmann, N., Brodaty, H., Chiu, H., Lawlor, B., Ritchie, K., & Scanlan, J. M. (2006). IPA survey of brief cognitive screening instruments. [Multicenter Study; Research Support, Non-U.S. Gov't]. *International Psychogeriatrics, 18*(2), 281–294. doi: 10.1017/S1041610205002693.

Shulman, K. I. & Silver, I. L. (2006). Assessment of older adults. In D. S. Goldbloom (Ed.), *Psychiatric clinical skills* (pp. 315–325). St. Louis, MO; London: Elsevier Mosby.

Shweder, R. A., Mahapatra, M., & Miller, J. G. (1990). Culture and moral development. In J. W. Stigler, R. A. Shweder, & G. H. Herdt (Eds), *Cultural psychology: Essays on comparative human development* (pp. 130–204). Cambridge: Cambridge University Press.

Siegler, I. C. (1995). Functional age. In G. L. Maddox (Ed.), *The encyclopedia of aging* (2nd edn, p. 385). New York: Springer.

Siegler, I. C. & Botwinick, J. (1979). A long-term longitudinal study of intellectual ability of older adults: The matter of selective subject attrition. [Research Support, U.S. Gov't, P.H.S.]. *Journal of Gerontology, 34*(2), 242–245.

Siegler, I. C., Costa, P. T., Brummett, B. H., Helms, M. J., Barefoot, J. C., Williams, R. B., Dahlstrom, W. G., Kaplan, B. H., Vitaliano, P. P., Nichaman, M. Z., Day, R. S., & Rimer, B. K. (2003). Patterns of change in hostility from college to midlife in the UNC Alumni Heart Study predict high-risk status. [Research Support, U.S. Gov't, P.H.S.]. *Psychosomatic Medicine, 65*(5), 738–745.

Simoneau, G. G. & Leibowitz, H. W. (1996). Posture, gait, and falls. In K. W. Schaie & J. E. Birren (Eds) with R. P. Abeles, M. Gatz, & T. A. Salthouse (Vol. assoc. eds), *Handbook of the psychology of aging* (4th edn, pp. 204–217). London: Academic Press.

Simons, J. S., Dodson, C. S., Bell, D., & Schacter, D. L. (2004). Specific- and partial-source memory: Effects of aging. *Psychology and Aging, 19*(4), 689–694. doi: 10.1037/0882-7974.19.4.689.

Simonton, D. K. (1990). Creativity in the later years: Optimistic prospects for achievement. *The Gerontologist, 30*(5), 626–631.

Sinnott, J. D. (1996). *The developmental approach: Post-formal thought as adaptive intelligence.* New York; London: McGraw-Hill.

Skoog, I., Blennow, K., & Marcusson, J. (1996). Dementia. In J. E. Birren (Ed.), *Encyclopedia of gerontology: Age, aging, and the aged* (pp. 383–403). San Diego; London: Academic.

'Sleep cycle' (2004). In W. E. Craighead & C. B. Nemeroff (Eds), *The concise Corsini encyclopedia of psychology and behavioral science* (3rd edn). New York; Chichester: Wiley. Retrieved from http://www.credoreference.com/entry/wileypsych/sleep_cycle.

Smith, A., Brice, C., Nash, J., Rich, N., & Nutt, D. J. (2003). Caffeine and central noradrenaline: Effects on mood, cognitive performance, eye movements and cardiovascular function. [Clinical Trial; Comparative Study; Controlled Clinical Trial; Research Support, Non-U.S. Gov't]. *Journal of Psychopharmacology, 17*(3), 283–292.

Smith, A. D. (2006). Memory and memory theory. In R. Schulz (Ed.) with L. S. Noelker, K. Rockwood, & R. L. Sprott (Assoc. eds), *Encyclopedia of aging: A comprehensive resource in gerontology and geriatrics* (4th edn, pp. 755–759). New York: Springer.

Smith, C. D., Walton, A., Loveland, A. D., Umberger, G. H., Kryscio, R. J., & Gash, D. M. (2005). Memories that last in old age: Motor skill learning and memory preservation. [Clinical Trial; Research Support, U.S. Gov't, P.H.S.]. *Neurobiology of Aging, 26*(6), 883–890. doi: 10.1016/j.neurobiolaging.2004.08.014.

Smith, E. E. & Jonides, J. (1998). Neuroimaging analyses of human working memory. [Research Support, U.S. Gov't, Non-P.H.S.; Research Support, U.S. Gov't, P.H.S.; Review]. *Proceedings of the National Academy of Sciences of the United States of America, 95*(20), 12061–12068.

Smith, J. & Freund, A. M. (2002). The dynamics of possible selves in old age. *Journals of Gerontology B: Psychological Sciences and Social Sciences, 57*(6), P492–500.

Smith, T. W. & MacKenzie, J. (2006). Personality and risk of physical illness. [Review]. *Annual Review of Clinical Psychology, 2*, 435–467. doi: 10.1146/annurev.clinpsy.2.022305.095257.

Smith, T. W. & Williams, P. G. (1992). Personality and health: Advantages and limitations of the five-factor model. [Review]. *Journal of Personality, 60*(2), 395–423.

Smyth, M. M. & Cousins, M. (2005). Developmental coordination disorder. In B. Hopkins (Ed.), *Cambridge encyclopedia of child development* (pp. 424–428). Cambridge: Cambridge University Press.

Smythies, J. (2009). The neurochemistry of consciousness. In W. P. Banks (Ed.), *Encyclopedia of consciousness.* Oxford: Elsevier Science & Technology. Retrieved from http://www.credoreference.com/entry/estcon/the_neurochemistry_of_consciousness.

Sneed, J. R. & Whitbourne, S. K. (2003). Identity processing and self-consciousness in middle and later adulthood. *Journals of Gerontology B: Psychological Sciences and Social Sciences, 58*(6), P313–319.

Sommers, M. S. (1996). The structural organization of the mental lexicon and its contribution to age-related declines in spoken-word recognition. [Comparative Study; Research Support, Non-U.S. Gov't]. *Psychology and Aging, 11*(2), 333–341.

Snowden, J. S., Gibbons, Z. C., Blackshaw, A., Doubleday, E., Thompson, J., Craufurd, D., Foster, J., Happé, F., & Neary, D. (2003). Social cognition in frontotemporal dementia and Huntington's disease. [Comparative Study]. *Neuropsychologia, 41*(6), 688–701.

Snyder, C. R. (2000). *The psychology of hope.* New York: Simon and Schuster.

Snyder, C. R. (2002). Hope theory: Rainbows in the mind. *Psychological Inquiry, 13*(4), 249–275.

Souri, H. & Hasanirad, T. (2011). Relationship between resilience, optimism and psychological well-being in students of medicine. *Procedia-Social and Behavioral Sciences, 30*, 1541–1544.

Sowell, E. R., Peterson, B. S., Thompson, P. M., Welcome, S. E., Henkenius, A. L., & Toga, A. W. (2003). Mapping cortical change across the human life span. [Research Support, Non-U.S. Gov't; Research Support, U.S. Gov't, Non-P.H.S.; Research Support, U.S. Gov't, P.H.S.]. *Nature Neuroscience, 6*(3), 309–315. doi: 10.1038/nn1008.

Spearman, C. (1904). 'General Intelligence', objectively determined and measured. *American Journal of Psychology, 15*, 201–293.

Spinnler, H., Della Sala, S., Bandera, R., & Baddeley, A. D. (1988). Dementia, ageing and the structure of human memory. *Cognitive Neuropsychology, 5*, 193–211.

Spoletini, I., Marra, C., Di Iulio, F., Gianni, W., Sancesario, G., Giubilei, F., Trequattrini, A., Bria, P., Caltagirone, C., & Spalletta, G. (2008). Facial emotion recognition deficit in amnestic mild cognitive impairment and Alzheimer disease. [Research Support, Non-U.S. Gov't]. *American Journal of Geriatric Psychiatry, 16*(5), 389–398. doi: 10.1097/ JGP.0b013e318165dbce.

Spreen, O. & Benton, A. L. (1977). *Neurosensory center comprehensive examination for aphasia* (Rev. edn). [S.l.]: University of Victoria; Neuropsychology laboratory.

Spreng, R. N., Wojtowicz, M., & Grady, C. L. (2010). Reliable differences in brain activity between young and old adults: A quantitative meta-analysis across multiple cognitive domains. [Research Support, Non-U.S. Gov't; Review]. *Neuroscience Biobehavioral Reviews, 34*(8), 1178–1194. doi: 10.1016/j.neubiorev.2010.01.009.

Stahlberg, O., Soderstrom, H., Rastam, M., & Gillberg, C. (2004). Bipolar disorder, schizophrenia, and other psychotic disorders in adults with childhood onset AD/HD and/or autism spectrum disorders. [Comparative Study]. *Journal of Neural Transmission, 111*(7), 891–902. doi: 10.1007/s00702-004-0115-1.

Stanley, T. O., Mackensen, G. B., Grocott, H. P., White, W. D., Blumenthal, J. A., Laskowitz, D. T., Landolfo, K. P., Reves, J. G., Mathew, J. P., & Newman, M. F. (2002). The impact of postoperative atrial fibrillation on neurocognitive outcome after coronary artery bypass graft surgery. [Research Support, U.S. Gov't, P.H.S.]. *Anesthesia and Analgesia, 94*(2), 290–295.

Staudinger, U. M. (2001). Life reflection: A social–cognitive analysis of life review. *Review of General Psychology, 5*(2), 148–160.

Staudinger, U. M., Lopez, D. F., & Baltes, P. B. (1997). The psychometric location of wisdom-related performance. *Personality and Social Psychology Bulletin, 23*, 1200–1214.

Stelmach, G. E., Zelaznik, H. N., & Lowe, D. (1990). The influence of aging and attentional demands on recovery from postural instability. [Research Support, U.S. Gov't, P.H.S.]. *Aging (Milano), 2*(2), 155–161.

Sternberg, R. J. (1985). *Beyond IQ: A triarchic theory of human intelligence.* Cambridge: Cambridge University Press.

Sternberg, R. J. (1990). *Wisdom: Its nature, origins and development*. Cambridge: Cambridge University Press.

Sternberg, R. J. (1996). *Successful intelligence: How practical and creative intelligence determine success in life*. New York: Plume Books.

Sternberg, R. J. (1998). A balance theory of wisdom. *Review of General Psychology*, 3, 347–365.

Sternberg, R. J. (1999). The theory of successful intelligence. *Review of General Psychology*, 3(4), 292–316.

Sternberg, R. J. (2000). *Practical intelligence in everyday life*. Cambridge: Cambridge University Press.

Sternberg, R. J. (2006). A duplex theory of love. In R. J. Sternberg & K. Weis (Eds), *The new psychology of love* (pp. 184–199). New Haven, CT; London: Yale University Press.

Sternberg, R. J. & Lubart, T. I. (2001). Wisdom and creativity. In K. W. Schaie, J. E. Birren, R. P. Abeles, M. Gatz, & T. Salthouse (Eds) with R. P. Abeles, M. Gatz, & T. A. Salthouse (Assoc. eds), *Handbook of the psychology of aging* (5th edn, pp. 500–522). San Diego, CA; London: Academic Press.

Sternberg, R. J., Wagner, R. K., Williams, W. M., & Horvath, J. A. (1995). Testing common sense. *American Psychologist*, 50, 912–927.

Sterns, H. L. & Gray, J. H. (1999). Work, leisure, and retirement. In J. C. Cavanaugh & S. K. Whitbourne (Eds), *Gerontology: An interdisciplinary perspective* (pp. 355--390). New York: Oxford University Press.

Stevenson, M. (2012). *An optimist's tour of the future* (Updated edn). London: Profile Books.

Stewart, M. (2006). Extroversion. *Encyclopaedic dictionary of psychology*. Routledge. Retrieved from http://www.credoreference.com/entry/hodderdpsyc/extroversion.

Stine, E. A. L., Soederberg, L. M., & Morrow, D. G. (1996). Language and discourse processing through adulthood. In F. Blanchard-Fields & T. M. Hess (Eds), *Perspectives on cognitive change in adulthood and aging* (pp. 255–290). New York; London: McGraw-Hill.

Stine-Morrow, E. A., Noh, S. R., & Shake, M. C. (2010). Age differences in the effects of conceptual integration training on resource allocation in sentence processing. [Research Support, N.I.H., Extramural]. *Quarterly Journal of Experimental Psychology (Hove)*, 63(7), 1430–1455. doi: 10.1080/17470210903330983.

Stine-Morrow, E. A. L., Noh, S. R., & Shake, M. C. (2006). Memory: Discourse. In R. Schulz (Ed.) with L. S. Noelker, K. Rockwood, & R. L. Sprott (Assoc. eds), *Encyclopedia of aging: A comprehensive resource in gerontology and geriatrics* (4th edn, pp. 741–744). New York: Springer.

Straif, K., Benbrahim-Tallaa, L., Baan, R., Grosse, Y., Secretan, B., El Ghissassi, F., Bouvard, V., Guha, N., Freeman, C., Galichet, L., & Cogliano, V. (2009). A review of human carcinogens – Part C: Metals, arsenic, dusts, and fibres. [Congresses; News]. *Lancet Oncology*, 10(5), 453–454.

Strauss, E., MacDonald, S. W., Hunter, M., Moll, A., & Hultsch, D. F. (2002). Intraindividual variability in cognitive performance in three groups of older adults: Cross-domain links to physical status and self-perceived affect and beliefs. [Research Support, Non-U.S. Gov't]. *Journal of the International Neuropsychological Society*, 8(7), 893–906.

Stroebe, M. & Schut, H. (1999). The dual process model of coping with bereavement: Rationale and description. *Death Stud*, 23(3), 197–224. doi: 10.1080/074811899201046.

Stroebe, M. S., Schut, H., & Stroebe, W. (2007). Coping with bereavement. In S. Ayers (Ed.), *Cambridge handbook of psychology, health and medicine* (2nd edn, pp. 41–45). Cambridge: Cambridge University Press. Retrieved from Table of contents only http://www.loc.gov/catdir/toc/ecip0620/2006028358.html; Publisher description http://www.loc.gov/catdir/enhancements/fy0729/2006028358-d.html; Contributor biographical information http://www.loc.gov/catdir/enhancements/fy0729/2006028358-b.html.

Stuss, D. T. (2007). New approaches to prefrontal lobe testing. In B. L. Miller & B. J. Cummings (Eds), *The human frontal lobe: Functions and disorders* (2nd edn, pp. 292–305). New York: Guilford Press.

Stuss, D. T. & Floden, D. (2005). Frontal cortex. *Encyclopedia of cognitive science*. London: Wiley. Retrieved from http://www.credoreference.com/entry/wileycs/frontal_cortex.

Suls, J. & Rittenhouse, J. D. (1990). Models of linkages between personality and disease. In H. S. Friedman (Ed.), *Personality and disease* (pp. 38–64). New York; Chichester: Wiley.

Sun, X., Chen, Y., Chen, X., Wang, J., Xi, C., Lin, S., & Liu, X. (2009). Change of glomerular filtration rate in healthy adults with aging. [Research Support, Non-U.S. Gov't]. *Nephrology (Carlton)*, 14(5), 506–513. doi: 10.1111/j.1440-1797.2009.01098.x.

Sutin, A. R., Terracciano, A., Deiana, B., Naitza, S., Ferrucci, L., Uda, M., Schlessinger, D., & Costa, P. T., Jr. (2010a). High neuroticism and low conscientiousness are associated with interleukin-6. [Multicenter Study; Research Support, N.I.H., Intramural]. *Psychological Medicine*, 40(9), 1485–1493. doi: 10.1017/S0033291709992029.

Sutin, A. R., Terracciano, A., Deiana, B., Uda, M., Schlessinger, D., Lakatta, E. G., & Costa, P. T., Jr. (2010b). Cholesterol, triglycerides, and the Five-Factor Model of personality. [Research Support, N.I.H., Intramural]. *Biological Psychology*, 84(2), 186–191. doi: 10.1016/j.biopsycho.2010.01.012.

Svansdottir, H. B. & Snaedal, J. (2006). Music therapy in moderate and severe dementia of Alzheimer's type: A case-control study. [Randomized Controlled Trial; Research Support, Non-U.S. Gov't]. *International Psychogeriatrics*, 18(4), 613–621. doi: 10.1017/S1041610206003206.

Tabbarah, M., Crimmins, E. M., & Seeman, T. E. (2002). The relationship between cognitive and physical performance: MacArthur Studies of Successful Aging. [Research Support, Non-U.S. Gov't; Research Support, U.S. Gov't, P.H.S.]. *Journals of Gerontology A: Biological Sciences and Medical Sciences*, 57(4), M228–235.

Taipale, V. (2008). User perspective and the development of gerontechnology. *Gerontechnology*, 7(2), 218.

Tales, A. & Porter, G. (2009). Visual attention-related processing in Alzheimer's disease. *Reviews in Clinical Gerontology*, 18(03), 229. doi: 10.1017/s0959259809002792.

Tang, H. Y., Harms, V., Speck, S. M., Vezeau, T., & Jesurum, J. T. (2009). Effects of audio relaxation programs for blood pressure reduction in older adults. [Comparative Study; Randomized Controlled Trial; Research Support, Non-U.S. Gov't]. *European Journal of Cardiovascular Nursing*, 8(5), 329–336. doi: 10.1016/j.ejcnurse.2009.06.001.

Tannock, R. (1998). Attention deficit hyperactivity disorder: Advances in cognitive, neurobiological, and genetic research. [Research Support, U.S. Gov't, P.H.S.; Review]. *Journal of Child Psychology and Psychiatry, and Allied Disciplines*, 39(1), 65–99.

Taylor, M. D., Whiteman, M. C., Fowkes, G. R., Lee, A. J., Allerhand, M., & Deary, I. J. (2009). Five Factor Model personality traits and all-cause mortality in the Edinburgh Artery Study cohort. [Comparative Study; Research Support, Non-U.S. Gov't]. *Psychosomatic Medicine*, 71(6), 631–641. doi: 10.1097/PSY.0b013e3181a65298.

Teasdale, N., Bard, C., LaRue, J., & Fleury, M. (1992). Posture and elderly persons: Evidence for deficits in the central integrative mechanisms. In G. E. Stelmach & J. Requin (Eds), *Tutorials in motor behavior II* (pp. 917–931). Amsterdam; London: North-Holland.

Teicher, M. H., Polcari, A., Fourligas, N., Vitaliano, G., & Navalta, C. P. (2012). Hyperactivity persists in male and female adults with ADHD and remains a highly discriminative feature of the disorder: A case-control study. [Research Support, N.I.H., Extramural; Research Support, Non-U.S. Gov't]. *BMC Psychiatry*, 12, 190. doi: 10.1186/1471-244X-12-190.

'Telomere' (2007) *Dorland's illustrated medical dictionary*. Philadelphia: Elsevier Health Sciences. Retrieved from http://www.credoreference.com/entry/ehsdorland/telomere.

Teng, E., Lu, P. H., & Cummings, J. L. (2007). Deficits in facial emotion processing in mild cognitive impairment. [Research Support, N.I.H., Extramural; Research Support, Non-U.S. Gov't]. *Dementia and Geriatric Cognitive Disorders*, 23(4), 271–279. doi: 10.1159/000100829.

Teri, L., Larson, E. B., & Reifler, B. V. (1988). Behavioral disturbance in dementia of the Alzheimer's type. [Research Support, U.S. Gov't, P.H.S.]. *Journal of the American Geriatrics Society*, 36(1), 1–6.

Terracciano, A. & Costa, P. T., Jr. (2004). Smoking and the Five-Factor Model of personality. *Addiction*, 99(4), 472–481. doi: 10.1111/j.1360-0443.2004.00687.x.

Terracciano, A., McCrae, R. R., Brant, L. J., & Costa, P. T., Jr (2005). Hierarchical linear modeling analyses of the NEO-PI-R scales in the Baltimore Longitudinal Study of Aging. [Comparative Study; Research Support, Non-U.S. Gov't]. *Psychology and Aging*, 20(3), 493–506. doi: 10.1037/0882-7974.20.3.493.

Thapar, A., Langley, K., Owen, M. J., & O'Donovan, M. C. (2007). Advances in genetic findings on attention deficit hyperactivity disorder. [Research Support, Non-U.S. Gov't; Review]. *Psychological Medicine*, 37(12), 1681–1692. doi: 10.1017/S0033291707000773.

The Guardian (2012). More people cohabiting without being married, *The Guardian*, 2 November. Retrieved from http://www.guardian.co.uk/lifeandstyle/2012/nov/02/more-people-cohabiting-without-married.

Thomas, A. K. & Bulevich, J. B. (2006). Effective cue utilization reduces memory errors in older adults. *Psychology and Aging*, 21(2), 379–389. doi: 10.1037/0882-7974.21.2.379.

Thompson, R. F. & Madigan, S. A. (2005). *Memory: The key to consciousness*. Washington, DC: Joseph Henry Press.

Thomson, A. D. & Marshall, E. J. (2006). The natural history and pathophysiology of Wernicke's Encephalopathy and Korsakoff's Psychosis. *Alcohol and Alcoholism*, 41(2), 151–158. doi: 10.1093/alcalc/agh249.

Thorndike, R. L., Hagen, E. P., & Sattler, J. M. (1986). *Stanford-Binet intelligence scale*. Rolling Meadows, IL: Riverside Publishing Company.

Thurstone, L. L. (1938). *Primary mental abilities*. Chicago, Ill.: Univ. of Chicago Press.

Tiggemann, M. (2004). Body image across the adult life span: Stability and change. *Body Image*, 1(1), 29–41. doi: 10.1016/S1740-1445(03)00002-0.

Tindle, H. A., Chang, Y. F., Kuller, L. H., Manson, J. E., Robinson, J. G., Rosal, M. C., Siegle, G. J., & Matthews, K. A. (2009). Optimism, cynical hostility, and incident coronary heart disease and mortality in the Women's Health Initiative. [Research Support, N.I.H., Extramural]. *Circulation*, 120(8), 656–662. doi: 10.1161/CIRCULATIONAHA.108.827642.

Tinetti, M. E., Speechley, M., & Ginter, S. F. (1988). Risk factors for falls among elderly persons living in the community. [Research Support, Non-U.S. Gov't; Research Support, U.S. Gov't, P.H.S.]. *The New England Journal of Medicine*, 319(26), 1701–1707. doi: 10.1056/NEJM198812293192604.

Tinker, A. & Hanson, J. (2007). *Remodelling sheltered housing and residential care homes to extra care housing*. London: King's College London and University College London.

Tinker, A., Wright, F., McCreadie, C., Askham, J., Hancock, R., & Holmans, A. (1999). Alternative models of care for older people. *Report for the Royal Commission on Long Term Care*. London: TSO.

Tondu, B. & Bardou, N. (2008). A systemic approach applied to the design of a strolling corridor for elderly persons with Alzheimer's-type dementia. *Gerontechnology*, 7(2), 223–238.

Tor, J. & Chiu, E. (2002). The elderly with intellectual disability and mental disorder: A challenge for old age psychiatry. *Current Opinion in Psychiatry*, *15*, 383–386.

Torres, J. L. & Ash, M. J. (2007). Cognitive development. In C. R. Reynolds & E. Fletcher-Janzen (Eds), *Encyclopedia of special education: A reference for the education of children, adolescents, and adults with disabilities and other exceptional individuals.* Wiley.

Townsend, J. T. (2005). Reaction time. *Encyclopedia of cognitive science*. Chichester, West Sussex: Wiley. Retrieved from http://www.credoreference.com/entry/wileycs/reaction_time.

Trimble, M. R. & George, M. S. (2010). *Biological psychiatry* (3rd edn). Oxford: Wiley-Blackwell.

Trzesniewski, K. H., Donnellan, M. B., & Robins, R. W. (2003). Stability of self-esteem across the life span. [Research Support, Non-U.S. Gov't; Research Support, U.S. Gov't, P.H.S.]. *Journal of Personality and Social Psychology*, *84*(1), 205–220.

Tucker, K. L. (2009). Osteoporosis prevention and nutrition. [Review]. *Current Osteoporosis Reports*, *7*(4), 111–117.

Tulving, E. (1972). Episodic and semantic memory. In E. Tulving & W. Donaldson (Eds), *Organization of Memory*. New York; London: Academic Press.

Tulving, E. & Thomson, D. M. (1973). Encoding specificity and retrieval processes in episodic memory. *Psychological Review*, *80*, 352–373.

Tun, P. A. & Wingfield, A. (1995). Does dividing attention become harder with age? Findings from the divided attention questionnaire. *Aging, Neuropsychology, and Cognition*, *2*(1), 39–66. doi: 10.1080/13825589508256588.

Turk-Charles, S., Meyerowitz, B. E., & Gatz, M. (1997). Age differences in information-seeking among cancer patients. [Research Support, Non-U.S. Gov't]. *International Journal of Aging and Human Development*, *45*(2), 85–98.

Turner, G. R. & Spreng, R. N. (2012). Executive functions and neurocognitive aging: Dissociable patterns of brain activity. [Review]. *Neurobiology of Aging*, *33*(4), 826 e821–813. doi: 10.1016/j.neurobiolaging.2011.06.005

Van Someren, E. J. (2007). Thermoregulation and aging. [Comment; Editorial]. *American Journal of Physiology: Regulatory, Integrative and Comparative Physiology*, *292*(1), R99–102. doi: 10.1152/ajpregu.00557.2006.

Vecera, S. P. & Luck, S. J. (2002). Attention. *Encyclopedia of the human brain*. London: Academic Press. Retrieved from http://www.credoreference.com/entry/esthumanbrain/attention.

Vaglenova, J., Birru, S., Pandiella, N. M., & Breese, C. R. (2004). An assessment of the long-term developmental and behavioral teratogenicity of prenatal nicotine exposure. [Research Support, Non-U.S. Gov't; Research Support, U.S. Gov't, P.H.S.]. *Behavioural Brain Research*, *150*(1–2), 159–170. doi: 10.1016/j.bbr.2003.07.005.

Valenzuela, M. J., Jones, M., Wen, W., Rae, C., Graham, S., Shnier, R., & Sachdev, P. (2003). Memory training alters hippocampal neurochemistry in healthy elderly. [Comparative Study; Research Support, Non-U.S. Gov't]. *Neuroreport*, *14*(10), 1333–1337. doi: 10.1097/01.wnr.0000077548.91466.05.

Vaillant, G. E. (2000). Adaptive mental mechanisms. Their role in a positive psychology. [Research Support, Non-U.S. Gov't; Research Support, U.S. Gov't, P.H.S.]. *American Psychologist*, *55*(1), 89–98.

Vecchi, T. & Richardson, J. T. E. (2000). Active processing in visuo-spatial working memory. *Cahiers de Psychologie Cognitive*, *19*, 3–32.

Verhaeghen, P. (2006). Reaction time. In R. Schulz (Ed.), *The encyclopedia of aging* (4th edn, pp. 1006–1009). New York: Springer.

Verhaeghen, P. & Cerella, J. (2002). Aging, executive control, and attention: A review of meta-analyses. [Research Support, U.S. Gov't, P.H.S.; Review]. *Neuroscience Biobehavioral Reviews, 26*(7), 849–857.

Verhaeghen, P., Marcoen, A., & Goossens, L. (1993). Facts and fiction about memory aging: A quantitative integration of research findings. [Meta-Analysis; Research Support, Non-U.S. Gov't]. *Journal of Gerontology, 48*(4), P157–171.

Vitevitch, M. S. & Sommers, M. S. (2003). The facilitative influence of phonological similarity and neighborhood frequency in speech production in younger and older adults. [Research Support, Non-U.S. Gov't; Research Support, U.S. Gov't, P.H.S.]. *Memory & Cognition, 31*(4), 491–504.

Wagner, D. L. (1997). *Comparative analysis of caregiver data for caregivers to the elderly 1987 and 1997.* Bethesda, MD: National Alliance for Caregiving.

Walke, L. M., Gallo, W. T., Tinetti, M. E., & Fried, T. R. (2004). The burden of symptoms among community-dwelling older persons with advanced chronic disease. [Research Support, Non-U.S. Gov't; Research Support, U.S. Gov't, Non-P.H.S.; Research Support, U.S. Gov't, P.H.S.]. *Archives of Internal Medicine, 164*(21), 2321–2324. doi: 10.1001/archinte.164.21.2321.

Walker, A. (2005). *Understanding quality of life in old age.* Maidenhead: Open University Press.

Walker, A., Walker, C., & Ryan, T. (1996). Older people with learning difficulties leaving institutional care: A case of double jeopardy. *Ageing and Society, 16*(2), 125–150.

Wanberg, C. R. & Banas, J. T. (2000). Predictors and outcomes of openness to changes in a reorganizing workplace. [Research Support, Non-U.S. Gov't]. *Journal of Applied Psychology, 85*(1), 132–142.

Wanberg, C. R. & Marchese, M. C. (1994). Heterogeneity in the unemployment experience: A cluster analytic investigation. *Journal of Applied Social Psychology, 24*(6), 473–488.

Wang, M. (2007). Profiling retirees in the retirement transition and adjustment process: Examining the longitudinal change patterns of retirees' psychological well-being. *Journal of Applied Psychology, 92*(2), 455–474.

Watkins, M. J. & Gardiner, J. M. (1979). An appreciation of the generate-recognise theory of recall. *Journal of Verbal Learning and Verbal Behaviour, 18*, 687–704.

Waxman, H. M., McCreary, G., Weinrit, R. M., & Carner, E. A. (1985). A comparison of somatic complaints among depressed and non-depressed older persons. [Comparative Study]. *Gerontologist, 25*(5), 501–507.

Wechsler, D. (1955). *Manual for the Wechsler Adult Intelligence Scale.* New York: Psychological Corporation.

Wechsler, D. (1981). *WAIS-R manual: Wechsler adult intelligence scale-revised.* San Antonio, Texas: Psychological Corporation.

Wechsler, D. (1997). *WMS-III: Wechsler memory scale administration and scoring manual.* San Antonio, Texas: Psychological Corporation.

Wechsler, D. (2001). *Wechsler Test of Adult Reading.* San Antonio: Psychological Corporation.

Wechsler, D. (2008). *Wechsler Adult Intelligence Scale* (4th edn). San Antonio: Psychological Corporation.

Wedisinghe, L. & Perera, M. (2009). Diabetes and the menopause. [Review]. *Maturitas, 63*(3), 200–203. doi: 10.1016/j.maturitas.2009.04.005.

Weiner, D. K., Rudy, T. E., Morrow, L., Slaboda, J., & Lieber, S. (2006). The relationship between pain, neuropsychological performance, and physical function in community-dwelling older adults with chronic low back pain. [Research Support, N.I.H., Extramural]. *Pain Medicine, 7*(1), 60–70. doi: 10.1111/j.1526-4637.2006.00091.x.

Weiss, A. & Costa, P. T., Jr. (2005). Domain and facet personality predictors of all-cause mortality among Medicare patients aged 65 to 100. [Comparative Study]. *Psychosomatic Medicine, 67*(5), 724–733. doi: 10.1097/01.psy.0000181272.58103.18.

Wellman, H. M. & Woolley, J. D. (1990). From simple desires to ordinary beliefs: The early development of everyday psychology. [Research Support, U.S. Gov't, P.H.S.]. *Cognition, 35*(3), 245–275.

Wenk, G. L. (2005). Neurotransmitters. *Encyclopedia of cognitive science.* Chichester, West Sussex: Wiley. Retrieved from http://www.credoreference.com/entry/wileycs/ neurotransmitters.

Werth, J. L., Jr, Gordon, J. R., & Johnson, R. R., Jr (2002). Psychosocial issues near the end of life. [Review]. *Aging and Mental Health, 6*(4), 402–412. doi: 10.1080/ 1360786021000007027.

West, R., Murphy, K. J., Armilio, M. L., Craik, F. I. M., & Stuss, D. T. (2002). Lapses of intention and performance variability reveal age-related increases in fluctuations of executive control. [Comparative Study; Research Support, Non-U.S. Gov't; Research Support, U.S. Gov't, P.H.S.]. *Brain and Cognition, 49*(3), 402–419.

West, R. L. (1996). An application of prefrontal cortex function theory to cognitive aging. [Review]. *Psychological Bulletin, 120*(2), 272–292.

Wetherell, J. L., Reynolds, C. A., Gatz, M., & Pedersen, N. L. (2002). Anxiety, cognitive performance, and cognitive decline in normal aging. [Research Support, Non-U.S. Gov't; Research Support, U.S. Gov't, P.H.S.]. *Journals of Gerontology B: Psychological Sciences and Social Sciences, 57*(3), P246–255.

Whelan, G. (2003). Alcohol: A much neglected risk factor in elderly mental disorders. *Current Opinion in Psychiatry, 1*, 609–614.

Whitbourne, S. K. (1996). *The aging individual: Physical and psychological perspectives.* New York: Springer.

Whitbourne, S. K. & Collins, K. C. (1998). Identity and physical changes in later adulthood: Theoretical and clinical implications. *Psychotherapy, 35*, 519–530.

Whitbourne, S. K., Sneed, J. R., & Skultety, K. M. (2002). Identity processes in adulthood: Theoretical and methodological challenges. *Identity Development through Adulthood, 2*(1), 29–45.

Whitehouse, P. J. (2007). Dementia: Alzheimer's. In J. E. Birren (Ed.), *Encyclopedia of gerontology* (2nd edn, pp. 374–397). Amsterdam; London: Elsevier.

Whitlock, G., Lewington, S., Sherliker, P., Clarke, R., Emberson, J., Halsey, J., Qizilbash, N., Collins, R., & Peto, R. (2009). Body-mass index and cause-specific mortality in 900 000 adults: Collaborative analyses of 57 prospective studies. [Research Support, N.I.H., Extramural; Research Support, Non-U.S. Gov't]. *Lancet, 373*(9669), 1083–1096. doi: 10.1016/S0140-6736(09)60318-4.

WHO (2000). WHO issues new healthy life expectancy ranking. Retrieved from www.who. int/inf-pr-2000/en/pr2000-life.html.

Wilens, T. E., Biederman, J., Faraone, S. V., Martelon, M., Westerberg, D., & Spencer, T. J. (2009). Presenting ADHD symptoms, subtypes, and comorbid disorders in clinically referred adults with ADHD. [Comparative Study; Research Support, N.I.H., Extramural]. *Journal of Clinical Psychiatry, 70*(11), 1557–1562. doi: 10.4088/JCP. 08m04785pur.

Wilkinson, G. S. & Robertson, G. J. (2006). *Wide Range Achievement Test 4 (WRAT4) professional manual.* Lutz, FL: Psychological Assessment Resources.

Wilkinson, H. & Janicki, M. P. (2002). The Edinburgh Principles with accompanying guidelines and recommendations. [Guideline; Practice Guideline]. *Journal of Intellectual Disability Research, 46*(Pt 3), 279–284.

Williams, B. R., Hultsch, D. F., Strauss, E. H., Hunter, M. A., & Tannock, R. (2005). Inconsistency in reaction time across the life span. [Comparative Study; Research Support, Non-U.S. Gov't]. *Neuropsychology*, *19*(1), 88–96. doi: 10.1037/0894-4105.19.1.88.

Williams, P. G., Smith, T. W., Guinn, H., & Uchino, B. N. (2011). Personality and stress: Individual differences in exposure, reactivity, recovery, and restoration. In R. J. Contrada & A. Baum (Eds), *The handbook of stress science: Biology, psychology, and health* (pp. 231–246). New York; London: Springer.

Wills, W. & Soliman, A. (2001). Understanding the needs of the family carers of people with dementia. *Mental Health Review*, *6*, 25–28.

Wilson, A. J. & Dehaene, S. (2007). Number sense and developmental dyscalculia. In D. Coch, G. Dawson & K. W. Fischer (Eds), *Human behavior, learning, and the developing brain. Atypical development* (pp. 212–238). New York; London: Guilford.

Wilson, B. A., Alderman, N., Burgess, P. W., Emslie, H., & Evans, J. J. (1996). *Behavioural assessment of the dysexecutive syndrome*. Bury St Edmunds: Thames Valley Test Company.

Wilson, B. A., Cockburn, J., & Baddeley, A. (2008). *The Rivermead behavioural memory test* (3rd edn). London: Pearson.

Wilson, R. S., Mendes de Leon, C. F., Bienias, J. L., Evans, D. A., & Bennett, D. A. (2004). Personality and mortality in old age. [Research Support, U.S. Gov't, P.H.S.]. *Journals of Gerontology B: Psychological Sciences and Social Sciences*, *59*(3), P110–116.

Wilson, R. S., Schneider, J. A., Arnold, S. E., Bienias, J. L., & Bennett, D. A. (2007). Conscientiousness and the incidence of Alzheimer disease and mild cognitive impairment. [Comparative Study; Research Support, N.I.H., Extramural]. *Archives of General Psychiatry*, *64*(10), 1204–1212. doi: 10.1001/archpsyc.64.10.1204.

Wingfield, A., Tun, P. A., & McCoy, S. L. (2005). Hearing loss in older adulthood. *Current Directions in Psychological Science*, *14*(3), 144–148. doi: 10.1111/j.0963-7214.2005.00356.x.

Wise, D. (1993). Firms pension policy and early retirement. In A. B. Atkinson & M. Rein (Eds), *Age, work and social security: Conference: Papers and discussions* (pp. 51–88). New York: St Martin's Press.

Wisniewski, K. E., Wisniewski, H. M., & Wen, G. Y. (1985). Occurrence of neuropathological changes and dementia of Alzheimer's disease in Down's syndrome. *Annals of Neurology*, *17*(3), 278–282. doi: 10.1002/ana.410170310.

Wolkove, N., Elkholy, O., Baltzan, M., & Palayew, M. (2007). Sleep and aging: 1. Sleep disorders commonly found in older people. [Review]. *CMAJ*, *176*(9), 1299–1304. doi: 10.1503/cmaj.060792.

Woodard, J. L. (2010). Geriatric neuropsychological assessment. In P. A. Lichtenberg (Ed.), *Handbook of assessment in clinical gerontology* (2nd edn, pp. 461–502). London: Academic.

Woollacott, M. & Shumway-Cook, A. (2002). Attention and the control of posture and gait: A review of an emerging area of research. [Review]. *Gait Posture*, *16*(1), 1–14.

Worden, J. W. (2009). *Grief counselling and grief therapy: A handbook for the mental health practitioner* (4th edn). London: Routledge.

World Health Organization (1948). Preamble to the Constitution of the World Health Organization as adopted by the International Health Conference, New York, 19–22 June, 1946 (pp. 100). World Health Organization.

Wright, R. E. (1981). Aging, divided attention, and processing capacity. *Journal of Gerontology*, *36*(5), 605–614.

Wulf, H. C. (2006). Skin aging. *The Encyclopedia of Aging*: Springer Publishing Company.

Wyatt, C. M., Kim, M. C., & Winston, J. A. (2006). Therapy insight: How changes in renal function with increasing age affect cardiovascular drug prescribing. [Review]. *Nature Clinical Practice Cardiovascular Medicine*, 3(2), 102–109. doi: 10.1038/ncpcardio0433.

Yang, Z., Bishai, D., & Harman, J. (2008). Convergence of body mass with aging: The longitudinal interrelationship of health, weight, and survival. *Economics and Human Biology*, 6(3), 469–481. doi: 10.1016/j.ehb.2008.06.006.

Yonan, C. A. & Sommers, M. S. (2000). The effects of talker familiarity on spoken word identification in younger and older listeners. [Research Support, Non-U.S. Gov't; Research Support, U.S. Gov't, P.H.S.]. *Psychology and Aging*, 15(1), 88–99.

Yung, L. M., Laher, I., Yao, X., Chen, Z. Y., Huang, Y., & Leung, F. P. (2009). Exercise, vascular wall and cardiovascular diseases: An update (part 2). [Research Support, Non-U.S. Gov't; Review]. *Sports Medicine*, 39(1), 45–63. doi: 10.2165/00007256-200939010-00004.

Zamboni, M., Mazzali, G., Fantin, F., Rossi, A., & Di Francesco, V. (2008). Sarcopenic obesity: A new category of obesity in the elderly. [Research Support, Non-U.S. Gov't; Review]. *Nutrition, Metabolism and Cardiovascular Diseases*, 18(5), 388–395. doi: 10.1016/j.numecd.2007.10.002.

Ziefle, M. & Bay, S. (2006). How to overcome disorientation in mobile phone menus: A comparison of two different types of navigation aids. *Human–Computer Interaction*, 21(4), 393–433.

Author Index

Aartsen, M. J., 138
Abayomi, O. K., 138
Abraham, K., 126
Abrams, R. C., 191
Abrams, L., 104
Abramson, L. Y., 168
Adams, R. G., 149
Adolphs, R., 93
Adrover-Roig, D., 65
Aggleton, J. P., 114
Aiken, L. R., 147
Albert, M. L., 196
Albert, M. S., 123
Aldwin, C. M., 21, 24, 26, 28–9, 134
Alexopoulos, G. S., 179
Allen, H. A., 54
Allen, P. A., 103
Allport, A., 49
Almada, S. J., 167
Almeida, O. P., 137
Ames, D., 178, 180, 187, 190–1, 194–6, 205
Ancoli-Israel, S., 41–2
Andel, R., 25
Anderson, N. D., 63
Angelucci, L., 34
Anstey, K. J., 44, 52
Anthony, J. L., 214
Antonovsky, A., 171
Arbuckle, T. Y., 67, 107
Ardelt, M., 141
Argyle, M., 100
Arnett, J. J., 148
Ashton, M. C., 129
Aspinwall, L. G., 89, 169
Atkinson, R. C., 59
Attig, T., 155
Averill, P. M., 186

Backman, L., 40, 63, 73
Baddeley, A. D., 59–61, 63, 65, 69, 74, 78, 120–1
Bailey, P. E., 92
Baldwin, R., 180
Ball, K., 54–5, 65
Ballard, C., 205
Baltes, M. M., 7–8
Baltes, P. B., 5–9, 44, 51, 63, 101, 140–2, 174–6, 228
Bandura, A., 148, 168
Barkley, R. A., 216
Baron-Cohen, S., 90–1, 93, 226
Barrett, L. F., 89
Baumeister, R. F., 131
Beange, H., 221
Beck, A. T., 115–6, 186
Beer, J. S., 90
Bell, D., 152
Bellini, S., 218
Bengston, V., 182
Benloucif, S., 42
Bentall, R. P., 182, 189, 191
Berry, J. M., 86
Betik, A. C., 29
Beyreuther, K., 224
Bhalla, R. K., 179
Biederman, J., 217
Bigby, C., 213, 221–3, 226
Biggs, S., 126
Birditt, K. S., 100
Birren, J. E., 48, 140
Blanchard-Fields, F., 87, 89, 99–100, 102–3
Blazer, D. G., 181
Blennow, K., 198
Bloch, M., 202
Blumenthal, J. A., 231
Boden, D., 107

Boelen, P. A., 154
Boerner, K., 147
Bolger, N., 167
Bond, A. J., 209
Bonini, M. V., 106
Bopp, K. L., 61, 63
Borella, E., 229
Bosse, R., 146–7
Botwinick, J., 46–8
Bouma, H., 232
Bowlby, J., 128–9
Bowling, A., 152
Boyce, N., 180, 182–4, 188–90,
    192–3, 196, 199, 201, 206, 208,
    210
Boyle, P. A., 174
Boyle, S. H., 166
Bradley, E. A., 218
Brandtstadter, J., 147
Bregman, J. D., 217
Brehmer, Y., 229
Brinley, J. F., 48
Brissette, I., 170
Broadbent, D. E., 63, 84
Brockmole, J. R., 62
Brod, M., 217, 220
Broese van Groenou, M. I., 173
Bronswijk, J. v., 233
Brook, D. W., 217
Brooks, R. A., 239
Brown, J. I., 121
Brown, L. A., 62
Brown, R., 105
Brown, R. G., 204
Bruce, D., 85
Brummett, B. H., 166
Buchner, D. M., 64
Buckner, R. L., 37, 39
Bucks, R. S., 94
Buhler, C., 1
Buhr, G. T., 152
Bull, R., 92
Bunce, D. J., 39, 52
Burke, D. M., 73, 105
Butcher, J. N., 116
Butler, A. A., 234
Butler, R. N., 145, 188, 192, 234
Byrd, M., 105

Cabeza, R., 35–6
Cacace, A. T., 29
Campisi, J., 19
Campbell-Sills, L., 167, 172
Camus, V., 180
Canitano, R., 218
Cantor, M. H., 152
Cappell, K. A., 37, 68
Carr, A., 177
Carr, D. S., 154
Carroll, C. C., 22
Carstensen, L. L., 88–9, 149, 175
Carter, G., 222
Cartwright-Hatton, S., 84
Carver, C. S., 169–70, 172
Casey, B. J., 45, 216
Caspi, A., 133
Casten, R. J., 27
Cattell, R. B., 136
Cavanaugh, J. C., 84
Cerella, J., 47
Chap, J. B., 99
Charles, S. T., 130
Charlton, R. A., 92
Charman, W. N., 26
Charness, N., 63, 232, 235–6
Chen, J. C., 41
Cheng, S. T., 132
Chida, Y., 172
Christensen, H., 53
Christopher, G., 56, 85, 179, 184
Clark, R. A., 235
Clarke, I. H., 24
Clarke, R., 162
Clarkson-Smith, L., 231
Cohen, G. D., 180, 188
Cohen, J. D., 40
Cohen, S., 220
Cohn, L. D., 127
Colcombe, S. J., 34, 230–1
Comijs, H. C., 34
Connell, C., 175
Connidis, I. A., 149–50
Consedine, N. S., 129
Cook, I. A., 39
Cooney, M. T., 162
Cooper, S. A., 221–2
Cordingley, L., 151

Corey-Bloom, J., 195
Coricelli, G., 91, 93
Cornoldi, C., 62
Corr, C. A., 156
Courchesne, E., 215
Cousins, M., 219
Covinsky, K. E., 28
Cowan, N., 49, 62
Cramer, P., 128, 132
Craik, F. I. M., 44–5, 61, 66, 71, 73
Crocker, J., 174–5
Cristofalo, V. J., 18–9
Cuddy, A. J. C., 101
Cuerva, A. G., 94
Culbertson, W. C., 120
Cumming, E., 155
Cummins, R. A., 153
Cusack, B. J., 208–9
Cutler, S. J., 84–5
Czaja, S. J., 235
Czeisler, C. A., 188

Dahlin, E., 228–9
Dalton, D. S., 28
Dannefer, D., 174
Dar, K., 192
Davies, E., 146
Davis, C. G., 142
Davis, S. W., 67
Davison, B. J., 97
Dawson, G., 215
Deal, C., 22
Deeg, D. J., 174
de Groot, C. P., 22
Degroot, D. W., 41
De Groot, J. C., 39
Dehon, H., 76
Dellenbach, M., 108
de Magalhaes, J. P., 18
Dennis, W., 140
DePaulo, B. M., 149
De Pisapia, N., 49
De Rosa, E., 56
De Vaus, D., 146
de Vries, B., 149
Devolder, P. A., 84
Diamond, J. M., 20
Dick, L. P., 183
Dickin, D. C., 29
Diehl, M., 89, 128

Diener, E., 176
Dixon, R. A., 84, 138
Dodson, C. S., 75
Donahue, E. M., 89
Dorshkind, K., 34
Drexler, A. J., 138
Duberstein, P. R., 181–2
Duchesne, D., 144
Duke, J., 147
Dunabeitia, J. A., 103
Dunlosky, J., 81
Dutta, T., 234
Duval, C., 92–3
d'Ydewalle, G., 78
Dywan, J., 75

Edginton, T., 40
Eichenbaum, H., 79
Ekberg, J., 232
Ekman, P., 94
Elias, M. F., 5
Eliott, J., 158
Elliott, E., 83
Elovainio, M., 138
Emerson, E., 222
Erber, J. T., 87, 206
Erickson, K. I., 67, 231
Erikson, E. H., 126–7, 141
Erixon-Lindroth, N., 40
Evenhuis, H., 221
Everard, K. M., 155

Fahle, M., 55
Feingold, B. F., 216
Fernandes, M. A., 63
Fernandez-Duque, D., 94
Ferraro, K. F., 146
Ferrell, B. A., 157
Ferri, C. P., 195
Filley, C. M., 36
Fioravanti, M., 137
Fiori, K., 151
Fischer, B. L., 219
Flavell, J. H., 82
Flint, A. J., 186
Folkman, S., 154, 169
Folstein, M. F., 116
Fook, L., 28
Fredrickson, B. L., 172
Frerichs, F., 145

Freud, S., 125–7
Freund, A. M., 7–8
Friedman, M., 166
Friedman, N. P., 65
Fries, J. F., 146
Frisina, D. R., 106
Froland, C., 152
Fromm, D., 117

Gall, T. L., 146
Gallo, W. T., 146
Ganguli, M., 193
Gardner, H., 138, 143
Gathercole, S. E., 59
Gatz, M., 178–9, 185, 200
Gauthier, S., 203
Ghaziuddin, M., 218
Giambra, L. M., 50, 73
Gibson, E. J., 55
Giddens, A., 157
Giedd, J. N., 45
Gignac, M. A., 8, 25
Gilbert, D. T., 103
Gilhooly, M. L., 101
Gillberg, C., 217
Gilmore, G. C., 54
Gluck, J., 73
Gogtay, N., 39
Goh, J. O., 41
Gold, D., 107
Goldman-Rakic, P. S., 113
Goldsmith, R. E., 3
Golimstok, A., 220
Gopnik, A., 91, 215
Gottman, J. M., 150
Gouin, J. P., 38
Grady, C. L., 37
Grant, D. A., 66, 120
Green, C. S., 230
Green, D. M., 46
Gregory, C., 94
Grimm, L. C., 98
Grønbæk, M., 193
Gronwall, D. M., 119
Gross, J. J., 88–9, 95
Grubeck-Loebenstein, B., 34
Gruhn, D., 89
Grundy, E. M., 158
Guadalupe-Grau, A., 164

Guaita, A., 94
Gubin, D. G., 34

Hacker, M. P., 208–9
Hagerman, R. J., 220
Hall, G. S., 1
Hamilton, P. F., 240
Hanson, J., 232
Hansson, R. O., 146
Haraway, D., 239
Hargrave, R., 94
Harkins, S. W., 27
Harnishfeger, K. K., 65
Harris, D. L., 237
Harris, P. B., 175
Harrison, D. E., 237
Hart, J. T., 81
Hartley, A. A., 63
Hartley, J. T., 76
Harwood, R. H., 54
Hasher, L., 41, 50, 61, 65, 104
Havighurst, R. J., 145
Hawkins, H. L., 231
Hay, E. L., 89
Hayflick, L., 18
Hedden, T., 52, 65
Heider, F., 102
Heidrich, S. M., 175
Heindel, W. C., 200
Henkens, K., 144
Henretta, J. C., 147
Henry, J. D., 78
Henry, N. J., 150
Hertzog, C., 82–3, 85–6, 229
Hess, T. M., 101
Higgs, P., 151
Hildon, Z., 175
Hill, E. L., 219
Hinrichsen, G. A., 180
Hobfoll, S. E., 148
Hofer, S. M., 9
Hofvander, B., 218
Hogervorst, E., 34
Hogg, J., 221
Holahan, C. J., 148
Holtzman, R. E., 155
Holzhausen, M., 176
Hoof, J. v., 234
Horn, J. L., 224
Howlin, P., 218

Hultsch, D. F., 40, 52
Humes, L. E., 103
Huppert, F., 177
Hutchinson, C. V., 54
Huxley, J., 239

Ino, T., 115
Intons-Peterson, M. J., 85

Jacoby, L. L., 76
Jackson-Guilford, J., 137
Jaeggi, S. M., 229
Jahanshahi, M., 204
James, L., 107
James, W., 49
Janicki, M. P., 221–3
Jaques, E., 132
Jensen, A. R., 52
Jessberger, S., 228
Jonassaint, C. R., 172
Jones, C. J., 133
Jonides, J., 67
Jopp, D., 148
Jordan, N. C., 214
Jorgensen, R. S., 171
Jorm, A. F., 179, 223
Jung, C. G., 128

Kane, M. J., 210
Kaplan, E., 121
Kastenbaum, R., 181
Katz, S., 38
Kaufman, A. S., 136, 138
Kausler, D. H., 47, 50, 105, 224
Kawachi, I., 152
Kemenoff, L. A., 66
Kemper, S., 108
Kempermann, G., 228
Kendler, K. S., 167
Kennedy, Q., 96
Kenney, W. L., 41
Kensinger, E. A., 87, 198–9
Kiecolt-Glaser, J. K., 167
Kilpatrick, C., 199
Kim, J., 234
King, V., 149
Kipps, C. M., 110–1, 116
Kirby, A., 219
Kirkwood, T. B. L., 19, 43
Kitwood, T. M., 153, 207

Kivipelto, M., 39
Klass, M., 22
Kline, D. W., 48
Kloos, A. D., 234
Knight, B., 181, 185, 192, 200
Knight, T., 237
Knol, M. J., 165
Kobasa, S. C., 171
Kohlberg, L., 98
Kollins, S. H., 217
Koriat, A., 92
Kosberg, J. I., 152
Kostka, T., 22
Kramer, D., 141
Kramer, A. F., 66
Krause, N., 148
Krinsky-McHale, S. J., 224
Krishnan, K. R., 180
Kubler-Ross, E., 155
Kubzansky, L. D., 166
Kujala, U. M., 164
Kunzmann, U., 88
Kurzweil, R., 240
Kynette, D., 106

Labouvie-Vief, G., 87–88, 99–100, 128
Lachman, M. E., 83, 86, 133, 148
Lang, F. R., 131
Lang, T., 22
Langer, E. J., 83
La Rue, A., 180–1
Larsen, R. J., 89
Lau, A. L., 153
Lavender, A. P., 22
Lawton, M. P., 6, 147
Lazarus, R. S., 147, 169
LeBlanc, E., 200
Lee, G. R., 151
Lehman, H. C., 140
Lennartsson, C., 155
Leonardelli, G. J., 136
Leslie, A. M., 90
Leveroni, C. L., 36
Levinger, G., 149
Levinson, D. J., 132–3
Levy, B., 85, 132, 174
Levy, R., 113
Lewis, K. G., 149
Lewis, M. D., 87
Lewis, R., 119

Lezak, M. D., 110, 124
Li, K. Z., 63–4
Li, S., 52, 229
Lichtenstein, P., 215
Lieberman, M. D., 93
Lifshitz, H., 225
Light, L. L., 72, 75, 77
Lindenberger, U., 44
Lineweaver, T. T., 83
Linnet, K. M., 217
Litwak, E., 152
Lockenhoff, C. E., 97
Loevinger, J., 127
Logan, J. M., 37
Logie, R. H., 60, 78
Lombardi, G., 34
Losse, A., 219
Lovasi, G. S., 161
Lu, T., 19
Lupien, S. J., 38
Lyketsos, C. G., 204, 207
Lysaker, P. H., 92

MacKay, D. G., 104, 106
Magai, C., 100, 129, 155
Magary, D., 237
Mahncke, H. W., 230
Main, M., 129
Major, B., 172
Mäkikangas, A., 170
Malouff, J. M., 173
Margrain, T. H., 26–8
Markesbery, W. R., 94
Markus, H., 131
Marshall, L. A., 33
Marsiske, M., 44
Martin, L. J., 198
Martin, M., 52
Martin-Matthews, A., 151
Masuda, M., 147
Matus, A., 41
Maurer, T. J., 145
May, C. P., 61
Maylor, E. A., 64, 78, 92
McAdams, D. P., 131
McArdle, J. J., 137
McCarthy, L. H., 28
McCrae, R. R., 129, 133
McDermott, D., 171
McDonald-Miszczak, L., 84, 86

McDougall, S., 230
McDowd, J. M., 63
McDowell, C. L., 94
McFarland, C., 83
McGinnis, D., 104
McKeith, I., 201
McLean, J. F., 118
McLean, K. C., 73
Meacham, J., 141
Meagher, D. J., 195
Mecacci, L., 84
Meisami, E., 27
Meltzoff, A. N., 90
Mendez, M. F., 202
Menna, F., 234
Mercier, P., 20, 157
Messam, C. A., 203
Meyer, B. J., 97
Mikels, J. A., 174
Miller, G. A., 58
Miller, L. M. S., 105
Miller, R. B., 150
Miller, S. A., 92
Mioshi, E., 117
Mireles, D. E., 74
Mitchell, P., 90
Mittenberg, W., 64
Miyake, A., 65
Miwa, S., 19
Mocchegiani, E., 38
Mojon-Azzi, S. M., 26–7
Molyneux, G. J., 207
Monczunski, J., 18
Montross, L. P., 173
Monroe, S. M., 180
Mor, V., 155
Moreno, J., 225
Morin, A., 91
Moss, S., 222
Moulin, C. J., 183
Mroczek, D. K., 89, 125, 133
Mulkana, S. S., 170
Mulsant, B. H., 183
Murphy, M. D., 86
Murrell, S. A., 174–5

Nakamura, T., 64
Nasreddine, Z. S., 116, 122
Nations, U., 231
Naveh-Benjamin, M., 72, 77

Navon, D., 60
Neary, D., 202
Neimeyer, R. A., 154
Nelson, E. A., 7
Nelson, H. E., 117
Nelson, T. O., 82
Neyer, F. J., 133
Ngan, R., 152
Niedenthal, P. M., 88
Niederehe, G., 85
Nikitin, N. P., 29
Nolen-Hoeksema, S., 154
Nordahl, C. W., 39
Nordberg, A., 41
Norman, D. A., 235
Nyberg, L., 228
Nylander, L., 218

O'Connor, D. W., 206
O'Connell, H., 182, 192
O'Donovan, D., 32
Olshansky, S. J., 236
Ong, A. D., 89
Orrell, M., 179
O'Rourke, N., 150
Osterweis, M., 153
Ouelette, S. C., 172
Owen, A. M., 230
Owsley, C., 53

Pankow, L. J., 20
Park, D. C., 37, 39–40, 62, 67, 78–80
Parker, S., 23, 33
Parkes, C. M., 153, 156
Parkin, A. J., 70, 77
Parkinson, S. R., 61
Parmelee, P. A., 157, 181
Pasupathi, M., 141
Patterson, T. L., 194
Paulson, Q. X., 165
Paus, T., 40
Pautex, S., 157
Pearlin, L. I., 172
Pearson, J. C., 146
Pellicano, E., 92
Peng, K., 102
Pepper, S. C., 5
Percy, W., 141
Perkins, E. A., 223
Perlow, E., 108

Perna, L., 174
Perner, J., 90–1
Persson, J., 67
Peterson, C., 170
Phillips, L. H., 94
Phillips, P. A., 41
Piaget, J., 98, 135
Pichora-Fuller, M. K., 44, 103, 106
Pietschmann, P., 164
Piquard, A., 94
Pisoni, D. B., 106
Plato, 88
Plomin, R., 214
Poon, L. W., 73, 179
Pope, A., 241
Porter, C. A., 87
Pratt, M. W., 99
Preece, P. F. W., 52
Pride, N. B., 31
Prigerson, H. G., 153
Pulkki-Raback, L., 166
Pushkar, D., 107

Quadagno, J. S., 4
Quinn, K. A., 90

Rabbitt, P., 52, 84–5, 92
Rahhal, T. A., 75
Raj, I. S., 22
Rakitin, B. C., 204
Rapp, M. A., 51
Rasmussen, H. N., 172
Ratcliff, R., 103
Raven, J., 118
Raz, N., 39, 45
Read, S., 221
Rendell, P. G., 78
Reuter-Lorenz, P. A., 37, 65
Reynolds, C. A., 196, 200
Reynolds, K., 161, 199
Rice, G. E., 77
Riby, L. M., 63
Richmond, L. L., 229
Ring, L., 176
Roberts, B. W., 130
Robertson, I. H., 118–9
Rockwood, K., 201
Roediger, H. L., 75–6
Rogers, W. A., 50
Roose, S. P., 182

Roskies, E., 145
Roth, M., 116
Roth, R. M., 220
Rotter, J. B., 168
Routledge, P. A., 210–1
Rowe, J. W., 42, 173
Royall, D. R., 121
Rubin, D. C., 73
Rumsey, N., 237
Ruscher, J. B., 107
Russell, A. J., 218
Ruta, D. A., 176
Ryan, E. B., 107
Ryff, C. D., 134, 174, 176

Sagi, D., 55
Saito, M., 23
Salthouse, T. A., 47, 50, 57, 63, 65, 137
Saretzki, G., 19
Sarter, M., 56
Saunders, A. M., 199
Schacter, D. L., 238
Schaffer, H. R., 90
Schaie, K. W., 10, 96, 134, 137–8
Scheier, M. F., 169–70, 172
Schiffman, S. S., 27
Schipper, H. M., 200
Schneider, B. A., 44
Schneider, L. S., 181, 184–5
Schröder, K. E., 170
Schwarz, N., 84
Seale, C., 156–7
Segal, D. L., 129, 191
Segerstrom, S. C., 170
Seidman, S. N., 33
Seligman, M. E. P., 168–9, 176–7
Senchina, D. S., 38
Shafto, M., 104
Shamay-Tsoory, S. G., 90–1
Shaw, R. M., 62
Shaywitz, S. E., 214
Shea, S. C., 211
Sherman, A. M., 149
Shipley, B. A., 52
Shulman, K. I., 122, 179
Shweder, R. A., 99
Siegler, I. C., 3, 9, 167
Simoneau, G. G., 64
Simons, J. S., 75
Simonton, D. K., 140

Skoog, I., 195, 200
Smith, A., 56
Smith, A. D., 72
Smith, C. D., 74
Smith, E. E., 67
Smith, J., 132
Smith, T. W., 166, 172
Smyth, M. M., 216
Smythies, J., 198
Sneed, J. R., 132
Sommers, M. S., 105
Snowden, J. S., 93
Snyder, C. R., 170–1
Souri, H., 174
Sowell, E. R., 39
Spearman, C., 136
Spinnler, H., 61
Spoletini, I., 94
Spreen, O., 119
Spreng, R. N., 67
Stahlberg, O., 218
Stanley, T. O., 138
Staudinger, U. M., 142
Stelmach, G. E., 64
Sternberg, R. J., 100, 139, 149
Sterns, H. L., 146
Stevenson, M., 239, 241
Stine, E. A. L., 76
Stine-Morrow, E. A., 76, 107
Straif, K., 163
Strauss, E., 52
Stroebe, M., 153–4
Stuss, D. T., 66, 92
Suls, J., 166
Sun, X., 32
Sutin, A. R., 167
Svansdottir, H. B., 206

Tabbarah, M., 137
Taipale, V., 233
Tales, A., 56–7
Tang, H. Y., 162
Tannock, R., 216
Taylor, M. D., 172
Teasdale, N., 64
Teicher, M. H., 217
Teng, E., 94
Teri, L., 153
Terracciano, A., 130, 166
Thapar, A., 216

Thomas, A. K., 75
Thompson, R. F., 59
Thomson, A. D., 193
Thorndike, R. L., 136
Thurstone, L. L., 136
Tiggemann, M., 237
Tindle, H. A., 172
Tinetti, M. E., 64
Tinker, A., 232–3
Tondu, B., 233
Torres, J. L., 135
Townsend, J. T., 47
Trimble, M. R., 201, 203, 212
Trzesniewski, K. H., 174
Tucker, K. L., 164
Tulving, E., 70, 72
Tun, P. A., 63
Turk-Charles, S., 97
Turner, G. R., 68

Van Someren, E. J., 41
Vecera, S. P., 49
Vaglenova, J., 217
Valenzuela, M. J., 228
Vaillant, G. E., 127
Vecchi, T., 62
Verhaeghen, P., 47–8, 50–1, 61
Vitevitch, M. S., 105

Wagner, D. L., 175
Walke, L. M., 157
Walker, A., 151, 221–2
Wanberg, C. R., 145, 170
Wang, M., 146
Watkins, M. J., 72
Waxman, H. M., 181
Wechsler, D., 117–8, 136
Wedisinghe, L., 163

Weiner, D. K., 28
Weiss, A., 166
Wellman, H. M., 90
Wenk, G. L., 56, 241
Werth, J. L., Jr, 158
West, R., 52
West, R. L., 45
Wetherell, J. L., 138
Whelan, G., 192
Whitbourne, S. K., 28, 86, 132, 143
Whitehouse, P. J., 197
Whitlock, G., 162
Wilens, T. E., 217
Wilkinson, G. S., 118
Wilkinson, H., 222
Williams, B. R., 40
Williams, P. G., 173
Wills, W., 207
Wilson, A. J., 167
Wilson, B. A., 119
Wilson, R. S., 125, 167
Wingfield, A., 44
Wise, D., 146
Wisniewski, K. E., 224
Wolkove, N., 41
Woodard, J. L., 123
Woollacott, M., 64
Worden, J. W., 153
Wright, R. E., 63
Wulf, H. C., 21

Yang, Z., 22
Yonan, C. A., 106
Yung, L. M., 161

Zamboni, M., 22
Ziefle, M., 236

Subject Index

acalculia, 114
acetylcholine, *see* neurotransmitters
Addenbrooke's Cognitive Examination
    Revised, 117
    see also assessment, neuropsychological
adaptation, 6–7, 131, 135, 154, 174, 231,
    240
age, definitions of, 2–3
    biological, 2
    chronological, 2
    functional, 3
    psychological, 3
    social, 3
age-complexity hypothesis, 47
ageing population, *see* demographic,
    changing
ageing, theories of
    caloric intake, 18, 236
    contextual perspective, 5, 8, 141
    cross linking, 19
    frontal lobe theory of ageing, 36–7
    implicit theory of ageing, 86
    mechanistic perspective, 5
    metabolic rate, 17–8, 34
    organismic perspective, 5
    oxidative stress, 19
    programmed cell death, 20
    telomeres,
ageism, 3–4, 24
agreeableness, 129–30, 172–3
alcohol, 111, 153, 161, 164–5, 182, 185–7,
    189, 192–4, 221
    see also substance abuse
Alzheimer's disease, *see* dementia
amnesia, 13, 70, 114, 183, 193
    anterograde amnesia, 114, 183
    retrograde amnesia, 114, 183, 193
amygdala, 56, 87, 93, 180
amyloid plaques, 36, 40, 196–9
amyloid precursor protein (APP), 199, 224

andropause, 33
angina pectoris, 30, 161
anti-ageing medicine, 236–7
antidepressant medication, 182–3, 186–7,
    190, 205, 209, 211
    selective serotonin reuptake inhibitors
        (SSRI), 182, 186, 205
    see also medication
antioxidants, 19, 200, 236
anxiety, 15, 84–5, 115–6, 138, 153, 166,
    179, 184–9, 193, 196, 202, 206,
    218–9, 222
anxiety disorders, 179, 184–9
    agoraphobia, 185–6
    generalized anxiety disorder, 185
    obsessive-compulsive disorder, 185–7,
        218
    panic disorder, 185
    phobic disorder, 185
    post-traumatic stress disorder, 185–6
    social phobia, 186
apolipoprotein E (ApoE), 196, 199–200
apoptosis, *see* programmed cell death
appearance, 21, 24–5, 237–8
apraxia, 115, 196, 198
arthritis, 8, 23–5, 85, 137, 164
    osteoarthritis, 8, 24–5, 164
    rheumatoid arthritis, 24–5, 85
assessment, neuropsychological, 11, 110–24
    attention, 112–3, 116–9
    background information, 111–2, 114
    computerised assessment, 116–7, 123–4
    confounding variables, 111–2, 122–3
    executive function, 113, 116, 119–20
    language, 114, 116, 121
    normative data, 111, 122–3
    premorbid ability, 112, 117
    psychopathology, 115–6
    test batteries, 116–7, 124
    working memory, 113, 118

associative deficit hypothesis, 72, 77
atherosclerosis, 30
attachment, 128–9
attention, 2, 40, 44, 46, 48–55–7, 58, 60,
    64–7, 70, 72, 77, 79, 86, 90, 92–3,
    112–3, 116–9, 149, 179, 184, 188,
    201–2, 217, 229, 232
  divided attention, 50–1, 119
  selective attention, 51–2, 57, 119
  sustained attention, 50, 118–9, 229
  task switching, 51
attentional field, 53
attentional resources, 40, 49–50, 60,
    64–5, 77, 92–3
attribution theory, causal, 102
autism, see specific learning difficulties
autobiographical memory, see long-term
    memory

baby boomer, 194
balance, 23, 29, 38, 51, 64, 216, 232,
    234
Behavioural Assessment of the
    Dysexecutive Syndrome, 119
  see also assessment, neuropsychological
benzodiazepines, 184, 186, 189, 193–4
bereavement, 153–4, 180–1, 193
  dual process model of coping with
    bereavement, 154
beta-amyloid (Aβ), 36, 40, 196, 198–200,
    224
beta-blockers, 186
bipolar disorder, 179, 183–4
binding, 62
biocultural co-constructivism, 6
bioethics, 156–8
biomarker, 52, 200
bladder, 32
bones, 23–5, 164, 182
Boston Naming Test, 104, 121
  see also assessment, neuropsychological
bottom-up processing, 49, 97, 101
brain
  shrinkage, 39, 198
  volume, 39–40, 45, 180, 231
brain training, see cognitive training
Brinley plots, 48

caloric intake, see age, definitions of
caloric restriction, 236

Cambridge Cognitive Examination, 116
  see also assessment, neuropsychological
Cambridge Neuropsychological Test
    Automated Battery, 117
  see also assessment, neuropsychological
cancer, 18–20, 24, 33, 97, 138, 146, 153,
    160, 162–3, 181, 221
cardiovascular disease, 18–9, 30–1, 162,
    166, 180
cardiovascular system, 29–31, 161, 209
care, provision of, 15, 24, 97, 111, 128,
    140, 144, 150–3, 156–8, 175–7,
    180–2, 186, 190, 206–8, 211–2, 223,
    232–4, 239
  formal care, 151–2
  informal care, 152, 212, 233
caregiver, see carer
carer, 111, 128, 150, 152, 175, 177, 180–1,
    206–7, 212, 233, 239
cerebral cortex, 36, 198
cerebrovascular accident, 30–1, 205
cholesterol, 29, 162, 167, 196, 199, 201
chronic conditions, 156, 210
chronic bronchitis, 31–2
chronic obstructive pulmonary disease,
    31, 137, 165
circadian rhythm, 34, 41
Clock Drawing Test, 121–2
  see also assessment, neuropsychological
cognitive behavioural therapy, 183, 186–7,
    190–1
cognitive development, stages of, 98,
    134–6
cognitive enhancement, 238
cognitive functioning, 28, 35–6, 42, 44–7,
    52–3, 55, 84–7, 92, 100, 105, 111,
    116–7, 124, 127, 134, 137–8, 174,
    189–90, 195, 197, 205, 211, 220, 223,
    228, 230–1, 236, 238–40
cognitive reserve, 65, 199
cognitive training, 65, 223–5, 229–30
  see also cognitive enhancement
coherence, sense of, 171
comorbidity, 16, 178, 185–6, 212, 215,
    217–9, 225
compensation, 7–8, 36–7, 41–2, 63–5, 68,
    74, 76, 78, 106–7, 143, 154, 175, 199,
    214, 224, 227
competence, 6, 86, 96, 100–1, 107, 137–8
comprehension, see language

conscientiousness, 27, 129–30, 133,
    166–7, 172
congestive heart failure, 30, 161
coping, 89, 131, 147–8, 154, 168–70, 190
    emotion-focused, 147, 169–70
    problem-focused, 100, 169–70
creativity, 14, 125, 139–40, 142–3, 238,
    240
Creutzfeldt-Jakob disease, 202
critical flicker fusion threshold, 48
cross linking, *see* age, definitions of

death,
decision making, 14, 72, 96–7, 99, 103,
    108, 141, 195
    see also treatment options
declarative memory, 70
    see also non-declarative memory
dedifferentiation, 65
Deese-Roediger-McDermott (DRM)
    paradigm, 75
default network, 37–8
delirium, 15, 111, 178–9, 193–5
delusional disorder, 190–1
dementia, 43, 53, 55, 94, 116–7, 123, 153,
    178–81, 185, 189, 193–205, 207, 211,
    219–20, 222–3, 232–3, 238
    Alzheimer's disease, 36, 38, 40, 56–7,
        64, 84–5, 94–5, 114, 123, 167, 181,
        195–202, 204–7, 211, 222–5, 238
    behaviour management, 191
    cortical dementia, 196
    Creutzfeldt-Jakob disease, 202
    dementia with Lewy bodies, 196, 201,
        204
    frontotemporal dementia, 196, 201–2
    Human Immunodeficiency Virus (HIV)
        encephalopathy, 203
    Huntington's disease, 38, 196, 202
    mixed dementia, 196
    Parkinson's disease, 38, 201, 204–5
    subcortical dementia, 116, 196, 202, 204
    vascular dementia, 181, 195–6, 200–1
    see also mild cognitive impairment
demographic, changing, 1, 4–5, 146, 192
dependence, 150–1, 173
depression, 29, 55, 85–6, 115, 148, 151,
    153, 155–7, 167, 169, 171, 178–87,
    192–3, 196–7, 199, 202–4, 207, 210,
    218–9, 222

see also antidepressant medication;
    masked depression; vascular
    depression hypothesis
design, research
    age effects, 8, 53–4, 63, 65, 92–3, 106,
        224
    case studies, 8, 11
    cohort effects, 8
    correlational studies, 11
    cross-sectional design, 9
    experimental studies, 10
    longitudinal design, 8–9
    quasi-experimental studies, 10
    sequential design, 10
    time-lag design, 9–10
    time-of-measurement effects, 10
diabetes, 18, 26, 30, 137–8, 163, 165, 180,
    184, 199, 201
Diagnostic and Statistical Manual of
    Mental Disorders (DSM), 94, 153,
    178, 192, 213–4, 217, 223
diathesis-stress model, 180
Digit Vigilance Test, 119
    see also assessment, neuropsychological
discourse memory, *see* long-term memory
discrimination, age, 4, 145
disengagement theory, 155
disinhibition syndrome, 183
dopamine, *see* neurotransmitters
Doors and People Test, 120
    see also assessment, neuropsychological
drug treatment, *see* medication
dual-task cost, 51
dual-task performance, 50–1, 63–4
dyscalculia, 214
dysgraphia, 114
dyslexia, 214
dyspraxia, 114
dysthymia, 179

ecological model of ageing, 6
elaborative encoding, 71, 75
elderspeak, *see* language
electroconvulsive therapy (ECT), 182–3
emotion, 29, 34, 46, 75, 87–91, 93–5, 99,
    100, 119, 128–31, 138, 140–1, 147,
    149–50, 152, 154–5, 167, 169–70,
    172, 175–7, 180, 186, 202, 204, 215
emotion complexity, 89
emotional disengagement, 175

emotion regulation, 87–9, 130
emotional reactivity, 88
empathy, 91
emphysema, 31–2
encoding specificity hypothesis, 72, 79–80
endocrine system, 33–4, 41–2, 185
end-of-life issues, 156–7, 221
environmental press, 6
episodic memory, *see* long-term memory
euthanasia, 158–9
evolution, 7, 20, 49, 66, 70, 81, 90
executive function, 36, 39, 58, 60, 64–8, 91–2, 95, 113, 116, 119–20, 189, 198, 205, 220, 230
  see also working memory
exercise, 22, 24–5, 38, 111, 161–2, 164–6, 183, 189, 199, 228, 230–1, 240
extrapyramidal side effects, 190, 202, 204, 210
extraversion, 129–30, 133, 167, 172

facial expression, 94
false fame effect, 75
false memories, 75
familiarity, sense of, 72, 75, 77
feeling of knowing, 81
frontal lobes, 36, 39, 58, 60, 66–7, 95, 216
  see also executive function
fundamental attribution error, 103
  see also attribution theory, causal

gaming technology, 227, 230, 234–5
gerontechnology, 231–2
global motion, 54
glucocorticoid cascade hypothesis, 34
grey matter, 39, 45
grief, 153–6, 181

hair, 21, 25
Hayflick limit, 18
health, 22–3, 28, 30, 38, 42–3, 77, 88, 96–7, 99, 108, 124, 125, 128, 132–4, 137–8, 143, 146–8, 150–2, 155, 158, 160–77, 180, 188, 190, 192–3, 207, 212, 219–221, 228–9, 233, 239–40
  definitions, 160–1
  personality, 133–4, 160, 166–8, 171–2, 174

  see also chronic conditions; coping; optimism; resilience
hearing, 28–9, 42, 46, 76, 103, 123, 232, 236
heart disease, 33, 137–8, 153, 160–3, 166, 174, 181, 201
height, 22
hemispheric dominance, 36
hope, 160, 168, 170–1, 176
hormones, 33–4, 164–5, 167, 236
hostility, 167
Human Immunodeficiency Virus (HIV) encephalopathy, 203
Huntington's disease, *see* dementia
hyperalertness, 156
hypertension, 31, 151, 162, 201
hyperthermia, 41
hypochondriasis, 116, 188, 201
hypotension, 31, 184
hypothermia, 41

immune system, 33–4, 38, 43, 170
implicit memory, *see* long-term memory
impulsive behaviour, 100, 191
independence, 23, 25, 28, 44–5, 63, 94, 96, 101, 110, 126, 134, 151–2, 176, 180, 206, 230, 238
information-processing approach, 5, 48
inhibitory control, 40, 52, 68, 92
inhibitory deficit model, 50
insomnia, 188–9
intellectual development disorders (IDDs), 214, 217, 220–225
  Cerebral palsy, 221
  Down's syndrome, 199, 213, 220, 222, 225
  Fragile X syndrome, 213
intelligence, 11, 104, 112, 117–8, 125, 129, 134, 136–9, 139–40, 143, 223–4
  crystallized intelligence, 104, 129, 136–7, 138, 224
  fluid intelligence, 136–9, 223–4
  multiple intelligences, 138–9, 143
  triarchic theory, 139
  see also creativity; wisdom
intra-individual variability, 39–40, 52–3, 133
introspectionism, 81

judgement of learning, 81

knowledge, 45–6, 58, 70–1, 73, 76–7, 79–80, 82, 86, 90, 100–2, 104–5, 106, 108, 112, 130, 134–5, 137–42, 198
  formal knowledge, 139
  tacit knowledge, 139

language, 36, 44, 59, 73, 76, 96, 103, 109, 114, 116, 121, 135, 138, 195–6, 214, 216
  comprehension, story, 105–6
  elderspeak, 107–8
  pronunciation, 104
  reading, 59, 103, 108, 114, 117–8, 121, 214
  speech, production, 31, 106–7, 189, 202, 214
  speech, understanding, 28, 76, 106
  spelling, 103–4, 114, 117, 214
  word meaning, 104–5
  word recognition, 103
lateralization, 227
learned helplessness, 168
leisure, 146–7, 156
lifespan approach, 6–8
lithium, 182, 184
locus of control, 168
longevity, 2, 4, 18, 157, 159
long-term memory, 60–1, 65–6, 70–80, 82, 223–4
  autobiographical memory, 73–4
  discourse memory, 76–7
  episodic memory, 40, 70–3, 75, 79, 113, 224
  implicit memory, 74–5, 121, 224
  procedural memory, 70, 74, 193
  prospective memory, 77–9
  semantic memory, 70, 73, 79, 114, 214
  source memory, 75–6
  see also short-term memory; working memory

macular degeneration, 26
major neurocognitive disorder, 94
maladaptive thinking styles, 187
mania, 184, 194
  see also bipolar disorder
medication, 24, 27, 29, 32, 75, 85–6, 111–2, 158, 162, 164, 179–83, 185, 187, 189–90, 193–4, 196, 204–12, 233, 238

medication adherence, 85, 179, 208, 211–2
memantine, 205
memory, *see* short-term memory; long-term memory; working memory
menopause, 5, 23, 33, 200
mental representation, 49, 104, 135
metabolic rate, *see* age, definitions of
metabolic syndrome, 162
metabolism, 18, 22, 32, 40, 208–9, 236
metacognition, 81–95, 105
  see also emotion regulation; metamemory
metamemory, 82–3, 86
methodology
  behavioural measures, 11, 34
  diary data, 11
  focus groups, 11
  interviews, 11
  observational studies, 12
  self-report measures, 11
middle age, 3, 22, 33–4, 52, 83, 86, 92, 128, 132, 141–2, 148, 173–4
midlife crisis, 132–3
mild cognitive impairment, 53, 94, 116, 203–4
Mini-Mental State Examination, 116
  see also assessment, neuropsychological
mobility, 3, 23–4, 157, 197, 232
Montreal Cognitive Assessment, 116
  see also assessment, neuropsychological
moral reasoning, 96, 98–9
  cognitive-developmental model, 98–9
  perspective taking, moral, 99
movement detection, 27, 54–5
multiple intelligences, *see* intelligence
myelin, 39, 45
muscle, 19, 22–3, 29–30, 33, 153, 161, 163, 187, 190, 193–4, 201–3, 221, 234
myocardial infarction, 30, 161, 180

narcissistic personality, 128
National Adult Reading Test, 104, 117
  see also assessment, neuropsychological
Nelson-Denny Reading Test, 121
  see also assessment, neuropsychological
nervous system, 38–42, 48, 52, 55–6, 196, 203
neural plasticity, 227–8
neural scaffolding, 67

neurodevelopmental disorders, *see* intellectual development disorders; specific learning difficulties
neurofibrillary tangles, 36, 40, 197–8
neurogenesis, 228
neuroimaging, 17, 34–5, 58, 66–8
  activation imaging approach, 35
  correlational approach, 35
  neuropsychological perspective, 35
neuroleptics, 184, 205
  see also medication
neurotic disorders, 187
neuroticism, 129–30, 133, 166–7, 172
neurotransmitters, 38, 55–6, 198
  acetylcholine, 38, 55–6, 198, 201, 205
  dopamine, 38, 40, 55, 201, 204, 210, 217, 220
  noradrenaline, 55–6, 220
  serotonin, 55, 182, 186, 205
non-declarative memory, 70
  see also declarative memory
non-normative life events, 5
nootropic, 238
normative age-graded influence, 5
normative history-graded influence, 5

obesity, 22, 28, 30, 162, 164–5, 199, 237
object permanence, 135
oestrogen, 23–4, 33, 163–4, 200
off-target verbosity, 67, 107
openness, 129, 172
opiate antagonist, 193
optimism, 160, 168–172, 176–7, 184, 240
  dispositional optimism, 169–70
  learned optimism, 168, 170
  situational optimism, 170
  see also coping
osteoarthritis, *see* arthritis
osteoporosis, 23–4, 33, 164
oxidative stress, *see* age, definitions of

Paced Auditory Serial Addition Test, 119
  see also assessment, neuropsychological
pain, 24–5, 27–8, 30, 122, 157, 160–1, 163–4, 185, 190, 208
palliative care, 157–8
paranoia, 116, 192, 197, 202
paranoid disorder, 192
Parkinson's disease, 38, 201, 204–5
pension, 145–6, 218

perception, 26, 46–8, 54, 79–80, 121
perceptual learning, 55
perseveration, 67, 202
personal resources, 148
personality, 27, 101–3, 116, 125–34, 138, 141, 143, 160, 166–8, 171–2, 174, 176, 190–2, 195–6, 201–2, 204, 207
  adult attachment, 128–9
  defence mechanisms, 126–9
  identity process theory, 132
  possible selves theory, 131
  psychosocial perspective, 126
  psychodynamic perspective, 125–7
  socioemotional selectivity theory, 88, 130
  structure-process model, 131
  trait perspective, 129–30
personality disorder, 191–2, 202
plastic surgery, 25
positivity effect, 96
perspective taking, 99
  see also moral reasoning
polypharmacy, 183, 210–11
positivity, 96–7, 142
prefrontal cortex, *see* frontal lobes
prejudice, *see* ageism
presbycusis, 28, 103
problem solving, 96, 99–101, 118, 120, 135, 147–8, 195
procedural memory, *see* long-term memory
productivity, 127, 140
programmed cell death, *see* age, definitions of
progressive supranuclear palsy, 196, 202
  see also dementia
pronunciation, *see* language
prospective memory, *see* long-term memory
pseudodementia, 179
psychopharmacology, 179, 207–12
  absorption, 193, 208
  distribution, 208–9
  excretion, 208–9
  metabolism, 32, 208–9
  pharmacodynamics, 210
  pharmacokinetics, 208
  see also medication adherence; polypharmacy
psychosis, 190, 193, 205, 211

quality of life, 10, 28–9, 54, 83, 94, 100–1, 143, 146, 151–3, 157–8, 160, 175–6, 216–7, 219, 222–3, 225, 230–1, 239–40

rapid eye movement sleep (REM), 41, 188, 201
Raven's Progressive Matrices, 118
  see also assessment, neuropsychological
reaction formation, 128
reaction time, 39, 47, 52, 56–7, 231
reading, *see* language
reasoning, 96, 118, 120, 135–7
recall memory, 37, 40, 58, 61–3, 71–7, 80–2, 104–5, 113, 120–2, 150, 198, 224
recognition memory, 72–3, 75, 104, 113, 120
reduced attentional resources/capacity model, 50
regulation, behavioural, 82
relationships, 102, 127, 129–31, 144, 148–51, 152, 158, 173, 175, 193, 216, 240
  cohabitation, 149
  death, 150, 153, 155–7, 174
  divorce, 150, 217
  friendship, 148–9
  marriage, 133, 149–50
  romantic, 149
  spouse, 5, 150–1, 154, 175, 180, 196, 212
renal clearance, 184
reproductive system, 32–3
resilience, 87, 129, 134, 160, 167–8, 170–77, 240
respiratory system, 17, 29, 31–2
retirement, 2, 15, 134, 144–7, 150–1, 158–9, 192–3, 240
retraining, 145
rheumatoid arthritis, *see* arthritis
Rivermead Behavioural Memory Test, 121
  see also assessment, neuropsychological

scaffolding theory of ageing and cognition (STAC), 37
schema, 88, 90, 101–2, 131
schizophrenia, 189–90, 194, 218
selective optimization with compensation (SOC), 7–8, 63–4

self-concept, 24, 128
self-concept incoherence, 89
self-efficacy, 86, 145, 148, 168, 176, 235
self-esteem, 29, 132, 170–1, 174–5, 177, 184, 237
self narrative, 154
semantic memory, *see* long-term memory
sensorimotor activity, 64
serotonin, *see* neurotransmitters
short-term memory, 58–69, 116
  see also long-term memory; working memory
sight, 3, 25–7, 42, 190
signal detection theory, 46
signal-to-noise ratio, 67, 106, 236
skin, 21
sleep, 33–4, 41–2, 56, 179, 181, 184, 188–9, 196, 201
sleep apnea, 42
sleep hygiene, 189
smart homes, 227, 233–4
smell, 17, 27, 46
smoking, 21, 30–1, 161, 163–5, 199, 201, 216, 221
social cognition, 89–95, 96, 101–3, 109
  see also theory of mind
social problem solving, 99–100
socioemotional selectivity theory, 130
sodium valproate, 184
somatic symptoms, 187
somatoform disorder, 188
somatopause, 33
source memory, *see* long-term memory
specific learning difficulties (SpLDs), 213, 214–220, 225
  Asperger's disorder, 215
  attention deficit hyperactivity disorder, 213, 216–7
  autism spectrum disorder, 213, 214–5, 220
  communication disorders, 213
  developmental coordination disorder, 216, 219
  learning disorders, 213–4
  motor disorders, 213, 215–6
  Tourette's disorder, 215–6
speech, *see* language
spelling, *see* language
stereotypes, 24, 32, 222
stimulus persistence theory, 48

stress, 31, 34, 38, 89, 100, 127–8, 152, 154,
     165, 167, 169–73, 175, 180, 185–6,
     188, 206
     see also coping
Stroop Color and Word Test, 120
     see also assessment, neuropsychological
substance abuse, 156, 179, 192–4, 217–8
     alcohol, 111, 153, 161, 164–5, 182,
          185–7, 189, 192–4, 221
     drugs, 111, 194
     withdrawal, 192–4
suicidal ideation, 181
symbolic representation, 135

taste, 17, 27, 46
technology, 57, 123, 145, 227, 231–40
telecare, 232
telemedicine, 232
telomeres, *see* age, definitions of
temperature, body, 21, 41
Test of Everyday Attention, 119
     see also assessment, neuropsychological
theory of mind, 90–5, 215, 226
     see also social cognition
therapeutic window, 184
thiamine, 193
thyroid, 24, 33–4, 197
tinnitus, 29
tip-of-the-tongue phenomena, 104–5, 109
     see also metacognition
top-down processing, 49, 82, 97, 101
touch, 27–8, 46
Tower of London-Drexel University, 120
     see also assessment, neuropsychological
Trail-making test, 118
     see also assessment, neuropsychological
trait diagnosticity, 101–2
transhumanism, 239
trauma, 111, 153, 185–6, 227
treatment options, 36, 97, 163–4, 178,
     224
     see also decision making

University of the Third Age (U3A), 3
urinary system, 32

vascular depression hypothesis, 180
Verbal Fluency Test, 119–20
     see also assessment, neuropsychological
vigilance, 49–50, 56, 119
visual attention, 53–5
weight, 22, 34, 161, 163, 165–6, 209

Wechsler Adult Intelligence Scale, 117–8,
     136
     see also assessment, neuropsychological
Wechsler Test of Adult Reading, 117–8
     see also assessment, neuropsychological
well-being, 5, 8, 17, 21, 27, 43–4, 64,
     84–5, 87, 96, 103, 108, 130, 137, 143,
     147–8, 152–6, 158, 160–1, 167,
     169–71, 174–77, 190, 207, 212,
     218–22, 225, 229
white matter, 36, 39, 45, 67
white matter hyperintensity, 39
white matter integrity, 45
Wide Range Achievement Test – 4 – Word
     Reading, 118
     see also assessment, neuropsychological
Wisconsin Card Sorting Test, 66, 120
     see also assessment, neuropsychological
wisdom, 125, 139–43
within-person differences, *see*
     intra-individual variability
word meaning, *see* language
word recognition, *see* language
work, 111–2, 134, 144–5, 147, 150, 152,
     158, 195, 197
working memory, 37, 40, 58–69, 70, 74,
     79, 94, 105, 113, 118, 193, 223–4,
     229, 231
     central executive, 60–2
     episodic buffer, 60–1
     phonological loop, 59–61, 224
     visuo-spatial sketch pad, 59–62, 224

Printed and bound in Great Britain by
CPI Group (UK) Ltd, Croydon, CR0 4YY